CRIMINAL JUSTICE AND TAXATION

OXFORD MONOGRAPHS ON CRIMINAL LAW AND JUSTICE

Series Editor: Andrew Ashworth CBE QC, Emeritus Vinerian Professor of English Law, All Souls College, Oxford

This series aims to cover all aspects of criminal law and procedure including criminal evidence. The scope of this series is wide, encompassing both practical and theoretical works.

OTHER TITLES IN THIS SERIES

In Search of Criminal Responsibility
Ideas, Interests, and Institutions
Nicola Lacey

Character in the Criminal Trial
Mike Redmayne

Preventive Justice
Andrew Ashworth and Lucia Zedner

Homicide and the Politics of Law Reform
Jeremy Horder

The Insecurity State
Vulnerable Autonomy and the Right to Security in the Criminal Law
Peter Ramsay

Manifest Madness
Mental Incapacity in the Criminal Law
Arlie Loughnan

The Ethics of Plea Bargaining
Richard L. Lippke

Punishment and Freedom
Alan Brudner

Prosecuting Domestic Violence
A Philosophical Analysis
Michelle Madden Dempsey

Abuse of Process and Judicial Stays of Criminal Proceedings
Andrew L.-T. Choo

A Philosophy of Evidence Law
Justice in the Search for Truth
Hock Lai Ho

The Criminal Justice System and Healthcare
Edited by Charles A. Erin and Suzanne Ost

Rethinking Imprisonment
Richard Lippke

Killing in Self-Defence
Fiona Leverick

Criminal Justice and Taxation

PETER ALLDRIDGE

Drapers' Professor of Law, Queen Mary University of London

OXFORD
UNIVERSITY PRESS

OXFORD
UNIVERSITY PRESS

Great Clarendon Street, Oxford, OX2 6DP,
United Kingdom

Oxford University Press is a department of the University of Oxford. It furthers the University's objective of excellence in research, scholarship, and education by publishing worldwide. Oxford is a registered trade mark of Oxford University Press in the UK and in certain other countries

First Edition published in 2017

Published in the United States of America by Oxford University Press
198 Madison Avenue, New York, NY 10016, United States of America

British Library Cataloguing in Publication Data
Data available

Library of Congress Control Number: 2017930522

ISBN 978–0–19–875583–8

For Ann, Frederick, and Helen

General Editor's Introduction

This monograph challenges some key assumptions held by criminal lawyers about the actual boundaries and the proper boundaries of the criminal law. Should the criminal law be used to penalize those who fail to comply with the taxation regime? That simple question dissolves into more detailed and more complex questions—whether there should be criminal offences of non-compliance and, if so, which wrongs should be criminalized; and whether those offences should be used as the stock response to the targeted non-compliers, or whether the criminal law should be deployed as the last resort after various civil and other mechanisms. Peter Alldridge approaches these issues through rigorous analysis of the distinction between tax avoidance and tax evasion, through a sustained critique of the chaotic state of the relevant English criminal law (common law and legislation), and through a searching assessment of the machinery of prosecution. He demonstrates the importance of studying procedure, raising questions about the special powers available to those investigating tax non-compliance in relation to such issues as search, the privilege against self-incrimination, and legal professional privilege. Thus the core issues on which this monograph shines its scholarly light are not only questions of criminal law and of criminal procedure, but questions about the interaction of the two at a practical level and at a normative level.

Andrew Ashworth

Preface and Acknowledgements

This is a study of the group of criminal offences of tax evasion. Only a small proportion of instances of these crimes that come to the attention of the authorities are prosecuted. The book considers tax evasion against the background of growing concerns, arising from the financial crisis of 2007–8, about financial crime. These concerns have generated demands for more, more vigorous, and more punitive responses, amplified by the publicity around *HSBC Suisse* and the *Panama Papers*. Expressions of outrage in the debates around the election of 2015 and the EU referendum in 2016 regarding the positions of large international companies and rich individuals renew recognition of the difficulties, risks, and expenses of bringing prosecutions in this area and raise considerations as to whether the traditional criminal procedure and punishment is the best way in which to deal with financial crime.

Tax evasion law and practice have never been simple, but four further connected developments have made them more complex. First, the insertion into the traditionally understood distinction between evasion and avoidance of an intermediate notion of 'aggressive avoidance' has given rise to pressure for a realignment of categories. Second, the increasingly important international dimension arising from the abrogation of the 'Revenue Rule' has thrown attention into some murky corners, including those identified in the scandals. Third, the changing role of the professions has generated scrutiny of the possibility of imposing criminal liability upon them, and also of the boundaries of privilege. Fourth, the growth of the anti-money laundering industry, and its move into tax evasion, have meant that tax offences have moved to the forefront of the assault upon the proceeds of crime, if only because this is the only area in which the sums of money involved might come close to those whose recovery was first promised by the industry.

The prosecution structures have altered over years. The history is of different treatment, until recently, of crimes falling under the respective jurisdictions of Customs and Excise and the Inland Revenue, and of the assimilation of the two branches one to another in this century. The many changes reflect tensions in the relationship between investigation and prosecution functions and as to how the lines of accountability work, consistently, with a practically operable structure. Most disappointingly, some of them have been driven by priorities elsewhere, with operative factors only of marginal significance to the prosecution of tax evasion.

Collection of material stopped on 1 June 2016, and although it has been possible to insert some later references at proof stage to what will be the Criminal Finances Act 2017, its final form was not known. The text was submitted after the EU referendum, but before even the earliest legal consequences were known. In any event, efforts to deal with evasion on an international basis will continue, and their success will depend more upon the levels of commitment of the main players than the forum in which their collaboration occurs.

In the production of the text I have incurred numerous debts. Amongst colleagues, Richard Walters and Bob Ferguson read and made very helpful comments on drafts. Librarians at the Institute of Advanced Legal Studies went well beyond what one might reasonably expect, and, when approached, HMRC fielded enquiries very well. Ann Mumford first piqued my interest in the subject, read the text, and has given tremendous support throughout.

Errors and omissions that remain are my own responsibility.

London, 30 June 2016

Table of Contents

Table of Cases xv
Table of Statutes xxv
Table of Statutory Instruments xxvii
Table of EU Legislation xxix
Table of International Instruments xxxi
List of Abbreviations xxxiii

1 Introduction 1

2 Crimes of Evasion—History and Theory 7
A Short History 7
Customs and Excise 8
Customs 8
Excise 9
Smuggling to Evade Duty 11
The Relationship between Customs and Excise Duties and Other Taxes 14
Precursors of Income Tax 14
Income Tax 15
What Is Wrong with Tax Evasion? 17
The Nature of the Wrong 18
Conscientious Refusers and Tax Resisters 20
Advisers and Customers 21
Complicity of Corporations 24

3 Avoidance and Evasion 25
Avoidance 26
The Jurisprudence of Tax Avoidance and Statutory Interpretation 28
Avoidance—Remedies 31
Evasion—Remedies 34
Blurring the Line between Avoidance and Evasion 34
The *HSBC Suisse* (2015) and Mossack Fonseca (*Panama Papers*) (2016) Scandals 37

4 Criminal Evasion of Duties and Taxes 41
Types and Interrelationships of Criminal Offences 41
Common Law and Statutory Offences 41

Specific or General Offences? 43
Vague or Precise Definitions? 45
Tax-specific or Not? Mutually Exclusive or Overlapping Offences? 46
The Existing Criminal Charges 47
Smuggling Offences 47
The 'Tax Perjury' Offence 48
The Major Smuggling Offences 48
Evasion of Income Tax 50
The Early Statutory Offences 52
Cheating the Revenue 53
Conduct 55
Mental state 56
The Statutory Offence of Fraudulent Evasion 57
The Overseas Evasion Offence 57
Value Added Tax 58
Inheritance Tax and Corporation Tax 59
Stamp Duty and Stamp Duty Land Tax 60
Offences Ancillary to Tax Evasion 60
After the substantive offence—the customs handling offence 61
Tax Credit Fraud 63
Council Tax Fraud and Council Tax Benefit Fraud 64
Rulings, Guidance, Abuse of Process, Exclusion of Evidence 64
Sentencing 66
Concluding—Offence Definitions and Reform Options 69

5 Investigation and Prosecution Structures 71
Models in Criminal Procedure 71
Philips and the Crown Prosecution Service 72
Enquiries and Reports 74
Glidewell 74
Gower–Hammond 75
Butterfield 76
O'Donnell 78
Organizing the Prosecutions 81
Conclusion 82

6 Investigatory Powers 83
Investigatory Functions and Powers of HMRC 83
Dawn Raids and the Legacy of *Rossminster* 83
The Keith Committee 85

Conduct of Tax Investigations 86
Civil Investigations 86
Customs Searches 88
Criminal Investigations by HMRC 88
Obtaining Information from the Taxpayer 88
Confidential and Privileged Information 91
The Privilege against Self-incrimination in Tax Law 91
Evasive answers and limitations upon questions 97
Legal Advice Privilege—Lawyers and Other Tax Advisers 98
Litigation Privilege 100
Absolute or defeasible? 101
Legal advice privilege and non-lawyers 102
What is 'legal' advice? 104
Does LPP extend to companies? 104
Advice to individual and to corporate clients 105
In-house lawyers 105
Must the lawyer be an English lawyer? 106
The 'Iniquity Exception' 107
The Mechanics of LPP: (i) Resolution of Disputes 110
The Mechanics of LPP: (ii) The Execution of Tax Fraud Searches 111
Obtaining Information Otherwise than From the Taxpayer 113
Taxpayer Confidentiality 115
Conclusions 116

7 **Prosecution and Its Alternatives** 119
The Prosecution Decision 119
Publicity Without Prosecution? 122
Judicial Review of Prosecution Decisions 122
Deal-making 124
The Hansard Procedure 126
Code of Practice 9 130
Contractual Disclosure Facilities 131
Offshore Disclosure Facilities 132
Switzerland 133
Deferred Prosecution Agreements 134
The Civil Penalties Regime 135
The Modern Penalty Provisions 137
Procedure, and Burden and Standard of Proof 138
The Human Rights Aspects of Civil Penalties 139
Civil Actions 142

8 The International Element 143
International Aspects of Tax Evasion 143
Offshore 146
The International Response to Scandals 148
Specific Offences of Offshore Evasion 151
Failure to Prevent Offences 153
Extradition for Tax Evasion 154
Evidence-gathering 155
Conclusion 155

9 Problems at the Intersections of Tax and Criminal Law 157
Taxing the Proceeds of Crime 157
Income Tax 157
Deductions for Illegal Expenses? 159
Confiscating the Proceeds of Tax Evasion 161
Deductions from Confiscation Orders 165
Do Confiscation Orders Affect Tax Liability (and *Vice Versa*)? 167
Confiscation or Compensation Orders? 168
Who Gets the Money? Incentivized Criminal Law Enforcement 168
Laundering the Proceeds of Tax Evasion 170
Tax Offences and the Identification of their Proceeds 174
The Substantive Laundering Offences 175
The Proceeds of Crime Act Tax Jurisdiction 179
Double Counting 183
Forfeitures and Other *In Rem* Seizures 184
Forfeitures 184
Cash Forfeiture 184
Unexplained Wealth Orders 187
Conclusions 188

10 Should More Alleged Tax Evaders Be Prosecuted? 189

Bibliography 193
Index 211

Table of Cases

A (Children) (Conjoined Twins: Medical Treatment) (No 1), Re [2001] Fam 147 65
Ahmed v Revenue and Customs Commissioners [2013] EWHC 2241 (Admin) 186
Air Canada v United Kingdom (1995) 20 EHRR 150 184
Airedale NHS Trust v Bland [1993] AC 789; [1993] 1 All ER 821 65
Akzo Nobel Chemicals Ltd v European Commission (C-550/07 P) [2011] 2 AC 338; [2011] All ER (EC) 1107 105
Al Fayed v Advocate General for Scotland [2004] STC 1703 64
Alfred Crompton Amusement Machines Ltd v Customs and Excise Commissioners (No 2) [1972] 2 QB 102; [1972] 2 All ER 353 105
Allen v United Kingdom (Admissibility) (76574/01) 74 TC 263; (2002) 35 EHRR CD289 96
Allgemeine Gold- und Silberscheideanstalt AG (AGOSI) v United Kingdom (1987) 9 EHRR 1 184
Amps v Director of Border Revenue [2013] UKFTT 570 (TC) 184
Angus v United Kingdom Border Agency [2011] EWHC 461 (Admin); [2011] Lloyd's Rep FC 329 186
AP v Switzerland (1998) 26 EHRR 541 140
Astall and another v Revenue and Customs Commissioners [2009] EWCA Civ 1010; [2010] STC 137 32
Atherton, Re [1912] 2 KB 251 91
Attorney General v Observer Ltd [1990] 1 AC 109 107
Attorney General's Reference (No 1 of 1975) [1975] QB 773; [1975] 2 All ER 684 21
Attorney General's Reference (No 1 of 1981) [1982] QB 848; (1982) 75 Cr App R 45 . . . . . . 49, 50
Attorney General's Reference (No 1 of 1998) (1999) 163 JP 390, *The Times*, October 2, 1998 49
Attorney General's Reference (No 3 of 1999) [2001] 2 AC 91; [2001] 1 Cr App R 34 113
Attorney General's References (Nos 86 and 87 of 1999) [2001] 1 Cr App R (S) 141 66
Attorney-General v Casey [1930] IR 163 135
Attorney-General v Johnstone (1926) 136 LT 31 136
Attorney-General v Till [1909] 1 KB 694 136
Attorney-General v Till [1910] AC 50 136
Ayrshire Pullman Motor Services v Inland Revenue (1929) 14 TC 754 29

B v Auckland District Law Society [2003] UKPC 38; [2003] 2 AC 736 101
Balabel v Air India [1988] Ch 317 104
Barclays Mercantile Business Finance Ltd v Mawson [2004] UKHL 51; [2005] 1 AC 684 32
Beghal v Director of Public Prosecutions [2015] UKSC 49; [2016] AC 88 . . . . 91, 92, 132
Bendenoun v France (1994) 18 EHRR 54 . . . . 139, 141
Berd v Lovelace (1577) Cary 62; 21 ER 33 98
Bishopsgate Investment Management Ltd v Maxwell [1993] Ch 1 91
Black Nominees v Nicol [1975] STC 372; 50 TC 229 27
Blank v Canada (Minister for Justice) [2006] SCC 39 101
Bolkiah v KPMG (A Firm) [1999] 2 AC 222 113
Bowman v Fels [2005] EWCA Civ 226; [2005] 2 Cr App R 19 . . . . 99, 110, 114
Brown v Stott [2003] 1 AC 681; [2001] 2 All ER 97 . . . . 93, 94
Butt v HM Customs and *Excise* [2001] EWHC Admin 1066 187

C v C [2008] 1 FLR 115 109
C&E Comrs v City of London Magistrates [2000] 1 WLR 2020; [2000] 4 All ER 763 141
C's Application for Judicial Review, Re [2009] UKHL 15; [2009] 1 AC 908 114
Camezind v Switzerland (1999) 28 EHRR 458 185
Capone v United States, 56 F 2d 927 (1931), cert denied, 286 US 553 (1932) 158
Channa v Revenue and Customs Commissioners [2013] UKFTT 499 137
Chic Fashions (West Wales) Ltd v Jones [1968] 2 QB 299; [1968] 1 All ER 229 84
Chicago Holdings Ltd v Cooper [2005] EWHC 3466 107
Commissioner v Wilcox 327 US 404 (1946) 159
Cooper v Slade (1858) 6 HL Cas 746 53
Council of the European Union v Bank Mellat ECJ (Fifth Chamber), 18 February 2016, Case C-176/13 P 171
Crown of Leon (Owners) v Lords Commissioners of the Admiralty [1921] 1 KB 595 9
Customs and Excise Commissioners v Air Canada [1989] QB 234; [1989] 2 All ER 22 184
Customs and Excise Commissioners v Air Canada (CA) [1991] 2 QB 446; [1991] 2 WLR 344; [1991] 1 All ER 570 184
Customs and Excise Commissioners v Everwine Ltd [2003] EWCA Civ 953 48
Customs and Excise Commissioners v Ghiselli Unreported 1999 WL 33101332 48
Customs and Excise Commissioners v Total Network SL [2008] UKHL 19; [2008] 1 AC 1174 . . . . . 2, 142

Davis v Germany [2013] EWHC 710 155
Dennis v Codrington (1579) Cary 100; 21 ER 53 98
Department for Work and Pensions v Richards [2005] EWCA Crim 491 165
DPP v Kilbourne [1973] AC 729; [1973] 1 All ER 440 53
DPP v Ray [1974] AC 370; [1973] 3 All ER 131 163
DPP v Turner [1974] AC 357; [1973] 3 All ER 124 . . . . . 50, 163
Duncan, decd, In re [1968] P 306 106

Einberger v Hauptzollamt Freiburg [1984] ECR 1177 159
EL v Switzerland (1997) 3 BHRC 348; [2000] WTLR 873 140
Engel v Netherlands (No 1) (1976) 1 EHRR 647 139
Eustice v Barclays Bank [1995] 1 WLR 1156 (CA) 108

Fenech v SOCA [2013] UKFTT 555 . . . . . 182, 183
Film Partners No 35 LLP v Revenue and Customs Commissioners [2015] EWCA Civ 95 . . . . . 31, 32
Fitzwilliam v IRC [1993] 1 WLR 1189; [1993] 3 All ER 184 35
Flanagan, Moyles and Stennett v Commissioners for HMRC [2014] UKFTT 175 36
Fletcher v Chief Constable of Leicestershire [2013] EWHC 3357 (Admin); [2014] Lloyd's Rep FC 60 185
Forbes v Director of the Assets Recovery Agency [2007] STC (SCD) 1; [2006] STI 2510 183
Funke v France (1993) 16 EHRR 297 92

Gammon v Roach [1983] RPC 1 109
Garner v US 424 US 648 (1976) 158
Georgiou (t/a Mario's Chippery) v United Kingdom (40042/98) [2001] STC 80 140
Ghani v Jones [1970] 1 QB 693; [1969] 3 All ER 1700 84
Glantz v Finland [2014] STC 2263 140
Gold Nuts Ltd and Others v Commissioners for Her Majesty's Revenue & Customs [2016] UKFTT 82 (TC); [2016] Lloyd's Rep FC Plus 24 . . . . . 88, 131
Goodie v Ontario (Ministry of Correctional Services) [2006] 2 SCR 32 101

Government of India v Taylor [1955] AC 491 . . . . 52, 143
Great Atlantic Insurance Co v Home Insurance Co [1981] 1 WLR 529. 106
Greenough v Gaskell (1833) 1 My & K 98; 39 ER 618 98
Gregory v Helvering 239 US 465 (1935) 31
Griffiths v JP Harrison (Watford) Ltd [1963] AC 1 27

Han & Yau v HMRC [2001] EWCA Civ 1048; [2001] 1 WLR 2253. . . . . 128, 141
Hanson v Revenue and Customs Commissioners [2012] UKFTT 314 (TC);
[2012] WTLR 1769 (FTT (Tax)). 137
Harding v Revenue and Customs Commissioners [2013] UKUT 575 (TCC); [2014] STC 891 137
Harper v Director of the Assets Recovery Agency [2005] STC (SCD) 874; [2005] STI 1906 183
Hayes v Duggan [1929] 1 IR 406 159
Hertel v Canada [2010] EWHC 2305 (Admin) 155
Higgins v National Crime Agency [2015] UKFTT 46 (TC). 183
HM v Germany (Admissibility) (62512/00) 8 ITL Rep. 206; (2005) 41 EHRR SE15. 140
HMRC v UBS [2016] UKSC 13 114
Holland v United States (1954) 348 US 121 180
Horncastle v United Kingdom (2015) 60 EHRR 31. 95
Houston v MacDonald 1989 SLT 276; 1988 SCCR 611. 57

Ibrahim v R [1914] UKPC 1; [1914] AC 599 127
Impositions del Roy (1606) 12 Co Rep 64; [1607] EWHC KB J23; 77 ER 1342. 9
Ingenious Games LLP, Inside Track Productions LLP, Ingenious Film Partners 2 LLP v Commissioners for Her Majesty's Revenue and Customs [2015] UKUT 105 31
IRC v Aken [1990] 1 WLR 1374; [1990] STC 497 159
IRC v Duke of Westminster [1936] AC 1 28
IRC v Hinchy [1959] 2 QB 357; [1959] 2 All ER 512 136
IRC v Hinchy [1960] AC 748; [1960] 1 All ER 505. 136
IRC v McGuckian [1997] 1 WLR 991 27
IRC v Paget [1938] 2 KB 25; 21 TC 677 27
IRC v Scottish Provident Institution [2004] UKHL 52; [2004] 1 WLR 3172. 32
IRC v Willoughby [1997] AC 1071. 27
Ireland v European Commission (2016) ECLI:EU:T:2016:227 150

Jalloh v Germany (2007) 44 EHRR 32; 20 BHRC 575. 94
James v United States 366 US 213 (1961) 159
JB v Switzerland 3 ITL Rep 663; [2001] *Crim LR* 748. 96
JSC BTA Bank v Ablyazov [2014] EWHC 2788 (Comm). 109
Jussila v Finland [2006] A/73053/01; [2009] STC 29 140

Khan (t/a Greyhound Dry Cleaners) v Customs and Excise Commissioners [2005]
EWHC 653 (Ch); [2005] STC 1271. 130
Khan v Director of the Assets Recovery Agency [2006] STC (SCD) 154; [2006] STI 593. 182
Khawaja v Revenue and Customs Commissioners [2013] UKUT 353 (TCC);
[2014] STC 150. 138
Khodorkovskiy v Russia (2014) 59 EHRR 7. . . . . 45, 99
King of the Hellenes v Brostrom (1923) 16 Ll L Rep 167 . . . . 5, 52
King v United Kingdom (13881/02) [2005] STC 438; (2005) 41 EHRR 29. 96
King v United Kingdom (Admissibility) (No.1) (13881/02) 5 ITL Rep 963;
(2003) 37 EHRR CD1 96
King v Walden (Inspector of Taxes) [2001] STC 822; [2001] BPIR 1012 141

Kittel v Belgium (C-439/04) [2008] STC 1537; [2006] ECR I-6161 137
Kuwait Airways Corp v Iraqi Airways Co (No 6) [2005] EWCA Civ 286; [2005] 1 WLR 2734 107

Lawrence v Campbell (1859) 4 Drew 485; 62 ER 186.................... 106
Lindsay v Customs and Excise Commissioners [2002] EWCA Civ 267 .... 13, 184
London Borough of Brent v Estate of Kane [2014] EWHC 4564 (Ch) 109
Lord Advocate v McLaren (1905) 7 F 984; 5 TC 110 136
Lynch v National Crime Agency [2014] UKFTT 1088 (TC) (FTT (Tax)) 183

Macfarlan v Rolt (1872) LR 14 Eq 580.................... 106
Mann v Nash [1932] 1 KB 752 159
Mansworth v Jelley [2002] EWCA Civ 1829; [2003] STC 53.................... 64
Martin v Commissioners for HMRC [2015] UKUT 0161 (TCC) 167
Matrix Securities Ltd v Theodore Goddard [1998] STC 1; [1997] BTC 578.................... 64
Mauro v Government of the United States of America [2009] EWHC 150 (Admin) 57, 155
McE, Re [2009] UKHL 15; [2009] 1 AC 908 109
McKnight (Inspector of Taxes) v Sheppard [1999] 1 WLR 1333; 71 TC 419.................... 161
McLaren Racing Ltd v Revenue and Customs Commissioners [2014] UKUT 269 (TCC); [2014] STC 2417.................... 161
Mobilx Ltd (In Administration) v Revenue and Customs Commissioners [2010] EWCA Civ 517; [2010] STC 1436.................... 58
MPC v Charles [1977] AC 177; [1976] 3 All ER 112.................... 163

N J Cowan v Revenue & Customs [2013] UKFTT 604 (TC).................... 86
N v S and the National Crime Agency [2015] EWHC 3248.................... 65
National Coal Board v Gamble (1958) 42 Cr App R 240 21
Nationwide Building Society v Various Solicitors (No 1) [1999] PNLR 52 at 72 109
Newstead v Frost [1980] 1 WLR 135; 53 TC 525.................... 27
Niemietz v Germany (1992) 16 EHRR 97 112
Norris v Government of the United States of America and others [2007] EWHC 71 (Admin); [2007] 2 All ER 29.................... 43

O'Halloran v *United Kingdom, Francis v United Kingdom* (2008) 46 EHRR 21; 24 BHRC 380.................... 94, 95
O'Rourke v Derbyshire [1920] AC 581 107
Öztürk v Germany [1984] ECHR 8544/79.................... 139

P v P (Ancillary Relief: Proceeds of Crime) [2003] EWHC Fam 2260; [2004] Fam 1 110
PA Holdings Ltd v Revenue and Customs Commissioners [2011] EWCA Civ 1414; [2012] STC 582 32
Paget; ex p Official Receiver, Re [1927] 2 Ch 85.................... 91
Parissis and Others v Revenue & Customs [2011] UKFTT 218 (TC) 87
Pendle v HMRC [2015] UKFTT 27 (TC).................... 141
Pendragon plc and others v Commissioners for HMRC [2015] UKSC 37.................... 31
Polok v Customs and Excise Commissioners [2002] EWHC 156; [2002] STC 361 159
Practice Note (Judges' Rules) [1964] 1 WLR 152 71
Preston v IRC [1985] AC 835; [1985] STC 282.................... 124

R (AM) v Director of Public Prosecutions [2012] EWHC 470 (Admin) 65
R (Churchouse) v IRC [2003] EWHC 681 Admin; [2003] STC 629 113

R (Faisaltex Ltd) v Preston Crown Court [2008] EWHC 2832 (Admin); [2009] 1 Cr App R 37 112
R (on the application of Anand) v Revenue and Customs Commissioners [2012] EWHC 2989 (Admin); [2013] CP Rep 2. 90
R (on the application of Bermingham) v Director of the SFO [2006] EWHC 200 (Admin); [2007] QB 727 124
R (on the application of Boughton) v HM Treasury [2005] EWHC 1914 (Admin); [2006] EWCA Civ 504; [2006] BTC 460 20
R (on the application of Colin McKenzie) v Director of the Serious Fraud Office [2016] EWHC 102 (Admin) 113
R (on the application of Commissioners of HMRC) v Crown Court at Kingston [2001] EWHC Admin 581 . . . . 37, 155
R (on the application of Corner House Research) v Director of the Serious Fraud Office [2008] UKHL 60; [2009] 1 AC 756 124
R (on the application of Crittenden) v National Parking Adjudication Service [2006] EWCA 1786 (Civ) . . . .
R (on the application of Crittenden) v National Parking Adjudication Service [2006] EWHC 2170 (Admin) 169
R (on the application of Derrin Brother Properties Ltd) v Revenue and Customs Commissioners [2014] EWHC 1152 (Admin) [2014] STC 2238. 87
R (on the application of Faisal Kaiyam) v Secretary of State for Justice [2014] UKSC 66; [2015] 2 WLR 76 95
R (on the application of Ford) v Financial Services Authority (Johnson and Owen, Interested Parties) [2011] EWHC 2583 (Admin) 105
R (on the application of H) v IRC [2002] EWHC 2164 (Admin); [2002] STC 1354. 111
R (on the application of Hallinan Blackburn-Gittings & Nott (A Firm)) v Middlesex Guildhall Crown Court [2004] EWHC 2726 (Admin); [2005] 1 WLR 766. 107
R (on the application of Hely-Hutchinson v HMRC [2015] EWHC 3261 (Admin) 64
R (on the application of Herron) v The Parking Adjudicator [2009] EWHC 1702 (Admin). 169
R (on the application of Hunt) v Criminal Cases Review Commission (IRC, interested party) [2001] QB 1108; [2000] STC 1110. 45
R (on the application of Ingenious Media Holdings Plc & Anr) v HMRC [2013] EWHC 3258 (Admin); [2014] STC 673 116
R (on the application of Ingenious Media Holdings Plc & Anr) v HMRC [2015] EWCA Civ 173 . . . . 27, 116
R (on the application of McCann) v Kensington & Chelsea LBC [2002] UKHL 39; [2003] 1 AC 787 141
R (on the application of Prudential plc) v Special Commissioner of Income Tax [2013] UKSC 1; [2013] 2 AC 185 . . . . 98, 102
R (on the application of Redknapp) v Commissioner of the City of London Police [2008] EWHC 1177 (Admin); [2009] 1 WLR 2091. . . . . 35, 51, 90, 121
R (on the application of the Director of the Assets Recovery Agency) v Green [2005] EWHC 3168 186
R (on the application of Wilkinson) v Director of Public Prosecutions [2006] EWHC 3012 (Admin). 62
R (Rawlinson & Hunter Trustees) v Central Criminal Court; R (Tchenguiz) v Director of the Serious Fraud Office [2012] EWHC 2254 (Admin); [2013] 1 WLR 1634; [2013] Lloyd's Rep FC 132 112
R v Absolam (1989) 88 Cr App R 332 129
R v Ahmad (CA) [2012] EWCA Crim 391; [2012] 1 WLR 2335. 162
R v Ahmad, R v Fields [2014] UKSC 36; [2015] AC 29 166

R v Allen [2001] UKHL 45; [2002] 1 AC 509 . . . . . 95, 123, 127
R v Asif [1985] Crim LR 679 59
R v Asutaits, Daily Telegraph, 10 July 2012 159
R v Ayres [1984] AC 447 73
R v Bajwa [2011] EWCA Crim 1093; [2012] 1 WLR 601 163
R v Barker [1941] 2 KB 381; [1941] 3 All ER 33 127
R v Beardall & Lord [2006] EWCA Crim 577 77
R v Bell [2011] EWCA Crim 6 49
R v Bembridge (1783) 3 Doug KB 327; 22 State Tr 1 54
R v Bradbury, R v Edlin (1920) [1956] 2 QB 262n 54
R v Bradbury, R v Edlin [1921] 1 KB 562; (1921) 15 Cr App R 76 . . . . . 54, 57
R v Caippara (1988) 87 Cr App R 316 49
R v Central Criminal Court, ex p Francis & Francis (A Firm) [1989] AC 346; (1989) 88 Cr App R 213 108
R v Charlton [1996] STC 1418 35
R v Chesterfield Justices ex p Bramley [2000] QB 576 111
R v Chief Constable of Lancashire ex p Parker [1993] QB 577 90
R v Choudhury (Khaled) [1996] STC 1163; [1996] 2 Cr App R 484 59
R v Citrone and another [1998] STC 29; [1999] *Crim LR* 327 159
R v Coulson 2000 WL 989462 56
R v Cowley-Hurlock [2014] EWCA Crim 170 53
R v Cox & Railton (1884) 14 QBD 153 . . . . . 107, 108
R v Da Silva [2006] EWCA Crim 1654; [2007] 1 WLR 303 114
R v Derby Magistrates' Court, ex p B [1996] AC 487 . . . . . 98, 101
R v Dimsey; R v Allen (CA) [1999] STC 846 55
R v Dimsey; R v Allen [2000] 1 Cr App R (S) 497 168
R v *Dimsey; R v Allen* [2001] UKHL 46; [2002] 1 AC 509 35
R v Director of the Serious Fraud Office, ex p Smith [1993] AC 1; [1992] 3 All ER 456 92
R v Doncaster [2008] EWCA Crim 5 130
R v Doran and others, 8 June 2000 75
R v Dosanjh [1998] 3 All ER 618; [1999] 1 Cr App R 371 67
R v Dosanjh [2014] 1 WLR 1780 43
R v DPP, ex p Chaudhary [1995] 1 Cr App R 136 123
R v DPP, ex p Manning [2001] QB 330 123
R v Eddishaw [2014] EWCA Crim 2783; [2015] Lloyd's Rep FC 212 . . . . . 49, 166
R v Edwards [2004] EWCA 2923; [2005] 2 Cr App R (S) 160 167
R v Ellames [1974] 1 WLR 1391; 60 Cr App R 7 (CA) 61
R v Ellis (1987) 84 Cr App R 235; [1987] Crim LR 44 49
R v Feely [1973] QB 530 56
R v Fields, R v Ahmad [2014] UKSC 36; [2015] AC 299 . . . . . 164, 165
R v Forbes [2001] UKHL 40; [2002] 2 AC 512 49
R v Gabriel [2006] All ER (D) 26 178
R v Gell & Others [2003] EWCA Crim 123 77
R v GH [2015] UKSC 24; [2015] 2 Cr App R 12 . . . . . 62, 177
R v Ghosh [1982] QB 1053; 75 Cr App R 154 . . . . . 35, 56
R v Gill (Sewa Singh) [2003] EWCA Crim 2256; [2004] 1 WLR 469 129
R v Goodwin (John Charles) (C-3/97) European Court of Justice (First Chamber) [1998] QB 883; [1998] STC 699 59
R v Goodwin (John Charles) [1997] STC 22; [1997] BTC 5226 . . . . . 62, 159
R v Governor of Pentonville Prison, ex p Osman (1990) 90 Cr App R 281, DC 99
R v Hancock (1995) 16 Cr App R (S) 187 66

R v Harvey [2013] EWCA Crim 1104 165
R v Harvey [2015] UKSC 73; [2016] 1 Cr App R (S) 60 . . . . 164, 165, 183
R v Hayes [2015] EWCA Crim 1944 . . . . 51, 126
R v Hayley Bevan Savill and Leighton, Birmingham Crown Court, June 24, 2016. 36
R v Heneghan [2003] EWCA Crim 397 67
R v Hertfordshire CC, ex p Green Environmental Industries Ltd [2000] 2 AC 412; [2000] 1 All ER 773. . . . . 93, 131
R v Hirani [2008] EWCA Crim 1463 64
R v Hood Barrs [1943] 1 KB 455; [1943] 1 All ER 665 52
R v Horncastle [2009] UKSC 14; [2010] 2 AC 373 95
R v Horseferry Road Magistrates' Court, ex p Bennett [1994] 1 AC 42. . . . . 44, 65
R v Hudson [1956] 2 QB 252; 40 Cr App Rep 55 . . . . 54, 55
R v Hunt [1994] *Crim LR* 747 42
R v Hunt [1995] STC 819; (1995) 16 Cr App R (S) 87 . . . . 42, 55
R v Innospec plc [2010] EW Misc 7 (EWCC) 124
R v IRC, ex p Allen [1997] STC 1141. 122
R v IRC, ex p Matrix Securities Ltd [1994] 1 WLR 334; [1994] 1 All ER 769. 64
R v IRC, ex p Mead and another [1993] 1 All ER 772; [1992] STC 482. . . . . 120, 122
R v IRC, ex p MFK Underwriting Agents Ltd [1990] 1 WLR 1545 at 1569; [1990] 1 All ER 91 100
R v IRC, ex p National Federation of Self Employed and Small Businesses Ltd [1982] AC 617 . . . 124
R v IRC, ex p Rossminster Ltd [1979] 3 All ER 385; [1979] STC 688 84
R v IRC, ex p Rossminster Ltd [1980] AC 952; (1980) 70 Cr App R 157. . . . . 35, 83, 87
R v J [2004] UKHL 42; [2005] 1 AC 562 44
R v Jakeman (1983) 76 Cr App R 223; [1983] Crim LR 104 50
R v Jones (1703) 2 Raym 1013; 92 ER 174. 19
R v K [2009] EWCA Crim 1640; [2010] QB 343 . . . . 92, 96
R v Kakkad (Freshkumar) [2015] EWCA Crim 385; [2015] 1 WLR 4162 164
R v Keenan [1990] 2 QB 54; (1990) 90 Cr App R 1. 129
R v Kuchhadia [2015] EWCA Crim 1252; [2015] Lloyd's Rep FC 526 178
R v Leaf (Ian) (Unreported, December 1, 2005) (Crown Ct) 155
R v Less, The Times, 30 March 1993; 1993 WL 965668 55
R v Lewis (Somerset Assizes, 1922). 163
R v Loosely [2001] UKHL 53; [2001] 1 WLR 2060 . . . . 93, 114
R v Louca [2013] EWCA Crim 2090; [2014] 2 Cr App R(S) 9 165
R v Mavji [1987] 1 WLR 1388; 84 Cr App R 34. 55
R v Maxwell [2010] UKSC 48; [2011] 1 WLR 1837 44
R v Middlesex Guildhall Crown Court ex p Tamosius & Partners [2000] 1 WLR 453; [1999] STC 1077 84
R v Mitchell [1994] Crim LR 66. 59
R v Montila [2004] UKHL 50; [2004] 1 WLR 3141 177
R v Mulligan [1990] STC 220 . . . . 54, 55
R v Natji [2002] EWCA Crim 271; [2002] 1 WLR 2337 191
R v Neal (John Frederick) [1984] 3 All ER 156; (1983) 77 Cr App R 283. 48
R v Nolan (Tracey) [2012] EWCA Crim 671; [2012] Lloyd's Rep FC 498 63
R v O'Connor [1980] *Crim LR* 43. 53
R v Perrin & Faichney [2012] EWCA Crim 1729; [2012] EWCA Crim 1730 . . . . 21, 67, 189
R v Phillips [2007] EWCA Crim 485 44
R v Price (1990) 90 Cr App R 409 56
R v Quillan [2015] EWCA Crim 538; [2015] Lloyd's Rep FC Plus 20. . . . . 30, 35
R v Redford (1988) 89 Cr App Rep 1 . . . . 54, 55

R v Rollins [2010] UKSC 39; [2010] 1 WLR 1922 . . . . 44, 73, 81, 123
R v Royle [1971] 1 WLR 1764 163
R v Russell [2014] EWCA Crim 1747. . . . . 54, 64
R v Seymour [1983] 2 AC 493 46
R v Shahid [2009] EWCA Crim 831; [2009] 2 Cr App R (S) 105 54
R v Smith (DR) [1974] QB 354; [1974] 1 All ER 632 178
R v Sood [1998] 2 Cr App R 355; (1999) 47 BMLR 166. 53
R v Special Commissioner and another, ex p Morgan Grenfell & Co Ltd [2002] UKHL 21; [2003] 1 AC 563 . . . . 98, 99
R v Stannard [2002] EWCA Crim 458. 31
R v Sturgess [2009] EWCA Crim 169. 54
R v Taaffe [1984] AC 539; [1984] 1 All ER 747. 50
R v Takkar [2011] All ER (D) 217 58
R v Tatham [2014] EWCA Crim 226; [2014] Lloyd's Rep FC 354. . . . . 49, 164
R v Terry [1984] AC 374 62
R v Thornhill [1980] 2 Cr App R (S) 320 66
R v Timmins [2005] EWCA Crim 2909; [2006] 1 Cr App R 18 44
R v Tompkins (1978) 67 Cr App R 181. 113
R v Vreones [1891] 1 QB 360 54
R v Walsh (1990) 91 Cr App R 161 129
R v Waya [2012] UKSC 51; [2013] 1 AC 294 . . . . 166, 167
R v Werner [1998] STC 550. . . . . 122, 123
R v William, William & William [2013] EWCA Crim 1262. 178
Ramsay (CA) - WT Ramsay Ltd v IRC [1979] 3 All ER 213; [1979] STC 582 . . . . 29, 35
Ramsay (WT) Ltd v IRC, Eilbeck (Inspector of Taxes) v Rawling [1982] AC 300. . . . . 27, 31
Revenue and Customs Commissioners v Crossman [2007] EWHC 1585 (Ch); [2008] 1 All ER 483. 168
Revenue and Customs Commissioners' Application (Approval to Serve 308 Notices on Financial Instititutions), Re (TC 174) [2009] UKFTT 224 (TC); [2009] SFTD 780 87
Revenue and Customs Commissioners' Application (Section 20(3) Notice: Plc), Re (SpC 647) [2008] STC (SCD) 358; [2007] STI 2851 s 102
Revenue and Customs Prosecution Office v Duffy [2008] EWHC 848 (Admin); [2008] 2 Cr App R (S) 103; [2008] *Criminal Law Review* 734. 168
Reynolds v MPC [1985] 1 QB 881 111
Rose v Director of the Assets Recovery Agency [2006] STC (SCD) 472; [2006] STI 1631. 183

Saunders v United Kingdom (1996) 23 EHRR 313. 92
SC BTA Bank v Ablyazov [2014] EWHC 2788; [2014] Lloyd's Rep FC Plus 56. 107
Secretary of State for the Home Department v Tuncel [2012] EWHC 402; [2012] Lloyd's Rep FC 475. 186
Serious Fraud Office v Standard Bank [2016] 1 Lloyd's Law Reports: Financial Crime Plus 121 134
Shannon v United Kingdom (2006) 42 EHRR 31 96
Sharkey v Revenue and Customs [2005] STC (SCD) 336; [2005] STI 223. 141
Sharkey v Revenue and Customs [2006] EWHC 300 (Ch); [2006] STC 2026. 141
Smiths Potato Estates v Bolland [1948] AC 508; 30 TC 267 161
SOCA v Bosworth [2010] All ER (D) 273. 178
Southern (Inspector of Taxes) v AB [1933] 1 KB 713 159
State of Norway's Application, Re [1990] 1 AC 723 155
SW (and CR) v United Kingdom (A/355-B) [1996] 1 FLR 434; (1996) 21 EHRR 363. . . . . 45, 55
Sweeney v Westminster Magistrates' Court [2014] EWHC 2068 (Admin) 90

Tamosius v United Kingdom (Admissibility) [2002] STC 1307; [2003] BTC 169. 112
Tchenguiz and others v Director of the Serious Fraud Office [2013] EWHC 2297 100
Tesco Supermarkets Ltd v Nattrass [1971] UKHL 1; [1972] AC 153 . . . . 37, 207
Testa v Revenue and Customs Commissioners [2013] UKFTT 151 (TC); [2013] SFTD 723. . . . 137
Thoburn v Sunderland City Council [2003] QB 151 169
Three Rivers District Council and Others v Governor and Company of the Bank of England (No 5) [2003] EWCA Civ 474; [2003] QB 1556. 106
Three Rivers District Council and Others v Governor and Company of the Bank of England (No 6) [2004] UKHL 48; [2005] 1 AC 610. . . . . 98, 104
Tinsley v Milligan [1994] 1 AC 340 60

United States v Capone 93 F2d 840 (1937), cert. denied, 303 US 651; 82 LEd 1112; 58 SCt 750 (1938) 158
Upjohn Co v United States (1981) 449 US 383. 98
US v Daugerdas 757 F Supp 2d 364 (SDNY 2012) 22
US v Stein 435 F Supp 2d 330 (SDNY 2006) 22
US v Sullivan 274 US 259 (1927) 158

Walsh Automation (Europe) Ltd v Bridgeman [2002] EWHC 1344 (QB) 109
Webster v Crown Prosecution Service [2014] EWHC 2516 (Admin) 123
Westmoreland Investments Ltd v MacNiven (HMIT) [2001] UKHL 6; [2003] 1 AC 311 27
Wiese v UK Border Agency [2012] EWHC 2549. 186
Woodward and Hiscox v IRC (1932) 18 TC 43 159
Woolwich Equitable Building Society Respondents v IRC [1993] AC 70. 2

Yukos Universal Ltd (Isle of Man) v The Russian Federation Permanent Court of Arbitration Case No AA 227 (2014). 37
Yukos v Russia [2011] STC 1988; (2012) 54 EHRR 19 . . . . 35, 37

Table of Statutes

Alcoholic Liquor Duties Act 1979 166
Bill of Rights 1689 (1 W & M c 2) 2, 9, 56, 169
Births and Deaths Registration Act 1953 . . . 95
Borders, Citizenship and Immigration Act 2009 80
Bretton Woods Agreements Act 1945. 184
Bribery Act 2010 . . . . 65, 154
Commissioners for Revenue and Customs Act 2005 (CRCA) 8, 78 113, 115, 126,
Companies Act 2006 144
Company Directors Disqualification Act 1986 68
Confirmation of Liberties; Charters and Statutes, Exportation of Gold, Silver, Leaving the Realm, &c Act, 1381 (5 R 2 c 3) 7
Corporation Tax Act 2009 16
Corporation Tax Act 2010 . . . . 16, 64
Counter-Terrorism Act 2008 171
Crime and Courts Act 2013. . . . 115, 134, 179
Criminal Attempts Act 1981 61
Criminal Evidence Act 1965 81
Criminal Justice (International Co-operation) Act 1990. 185
Criminal Justice Act 1988 53
Criminal Justice Act 1993 . . . . 54, 151,
Criminal Justice Act 2003 . . . . . . 53, 74, 125,
Criminal Justice and Police Act 2001 . . . . . 89, 111, 112
Criminal Justice and Public Order Act 1994 86
Criminal Law Act 1977 . . . . 54, 55, 177
Customs and Excise Act 1787 (27 Geo 3 c 13). 10
Customs and Excise Act 1952 . . . . . . 67, 126,
Customs and Excise Act 1979 48
Customs and Excise Management Act 1979 (CEMA) 10, 19, 47, 48, 49, 61, 62, 67, 88, 113, 127, 164, 184,
Customs, &c Act 1833 (3 & 4 W 4 c 52). . . 11
Drug Trafficking Act 1994 185
Duties on Income Act 1799 (39 Geo 3 c 13). 16
Enterprise Act 2002 161
Environmental Protection Act 1990. 93
Exchange Control Act 1947. 184
Excise Act 1660 (12 Ch 2 c 23) 10
Excise Act 1723 (10 Geo 1 c 10) 10
Excise Ordinance 1643. 10
Exportation Act 1697. 11
Exportations, etc Act 1802 (43 Geo 3 c 12) 16
Extradition Act 2003 155
F(No 2)A 1992 27
F(No 2)A 1997 27
F(No 2)A 2015 150
FA 1894. 59
FA 1908. 10
FA 1910. 57
FA 1942. 127
FA 1960. . . . . 27, 52, 136
FA 1965. . . . . 27, 59
FA 1978. 84
FA 1986. 59
FA 1988. 67
FA 1989. 116
FA 1992. 159
FA 1993. 159
FA 1994. 46
FA 1996. 46
FA 1997. 46
FA 2000. . . . . 46, 57
FA 2001. 46
FA 2002. 160
FA 2003. . . . . 46, 60
FA 2009. . . . . 5, 22, 122, 137
FA 2012. 46
FA 2013. . . . . 33, 36
FA 2014. . . . . 22, 27
FA 2015. . . . . 138, 150
FA 2016. . . . . 30, 35, 36, 151, 153, 154, 191,
Financial Services (Banking Reform) Act 2013 51
Forgery Act 1913 111
Forgery and Counterfeiting Act 1981. . . 44, 48

Fraud Act 2006 . . . . . . 19, 42, 43, 44, 61, 62, 64, 66, 67, 86, 163
Hearth Money Act 1688 (3 J 2 c 10) 15
Human Rights Act 1998 . . . . 126, 128
Income and Corporation Taxes Act 1970 . . . 16
Income and Corporation Taxes Act 1988 . . . . 16, 159, 160
Income Tax (Earnings and Pensions) Act 2003 16
Income Tax (Employments) Act 1943 16
Income Tax (Trading and Other Income) Act 2005 . . . . 16, 159, 160
Income Tax Act 1803 (43 Geo 3 c 122) 16
Income Tax Act 1806 (46 Geo 3 c 65) 16
Income Tax Act 1842 . . . . 16, 28 52, 135
Income Tax Act 1952 . . . . . 16, 43, 52, 57, 135
Income Tax Act 2007 16
Inland Revenue Regulation Act 1890 113
Insolvency Act 1986 108
Investigatory Powers Act 2016 . . . . 95, 114
Legal Services Act 2007 99
Matrimonial Causes Act 1973 92
Merchant Shipping Act 1794 (34 Geo 3 c 68) 11
Navigation Act 1660 (12 Ch 2 c 18) 11
Navigation Act 1849 (12 & 13 Vict c 29) . . 13
Navigation Ordinance 1651 11
Offences against Customs or Excise Act 1745 (19 Geo 2 c 34) 12
Perjury Act 1911 53
Police and Criminal Evidence Act 1984 (PACE) 72, 84, 85, 87, 88, 89, 90, 93, 99, 108, 111, 112, 114, 126, 127, 129, 130, 131
Proceeds of Crime Act 2002 (POCA) 16, 65, 86, 89, 109, 110, 114, 132, 138, 142, 159, 165, 166, 167, 169, 174, 175, 176, 177, 178, 179, 180, 182, 183, 185, 187
Powers of Criminal Courts Act 1973 168
Policing and Crime Act 2009 186
Prosecution of Offences Act 1985 . . . . 44, 73, 74, 75
Public Interest Disclosure Act 1998 114
Recruiting Act 1778 (18 Geo 3 c 53) 13
Regulation of Investigatory Powers Act 2000 . . . . 77, 95, 114
Road Traffic Act 1988 93
Serious Crime Act 2007 . . . . 54, 181
Serious Organised Crime and Police Act 2005 . . . . 67, 89, 90, 91, 99, 125
Ship Money Act 1640 (16 Ch 1 c 14) 9
Shipping Act 1786 (26 Geo 3 c 60) 11
Small Business, Enterprise and Employment Act 2015 144
Smuggling, etc Act 1779 (19 Geo 3 c 69) . . . 13
Social Security Administration Act 1992 . . . . 50, 63
Stamp Duties on Cards and Dice Act 1828 (9 Geo 4 c 18) 60
Stamp Duty Administration Act 1891 60
Statute Law Revision Act 1867 13
Tax Credits Act 2002 63
Taxation (International and Other Provisions) Act 2010 . . . . 16, 57, 144
Taxation Act 1662 (13 & 14 Ch 2 c 10) 15
Taxation Act 1695 (7 & 8 W 3 c 18) 15
Taxation Act 1756 (29 Geo 2 c 13) 60
Taxation Act 1798 (38 Geo 3 c 16) 16
Taxation of Capital Gains Act 1992 64
Taxes Management Act 1970 (TMA) 52, 55, 57, 58, 60, 61, 65, 66, 67, 83, 86, 88, 89, 95, 99, 102, 111, 112, 127, 128, 135, 136, 140, 151, 152, 153, 161
Tenures Abolition Act 1660 (12 Ch 2 c 23) 10
Terrorism Act 2000 . . . . 86, 131
Terrorism Act 2006 61
Theft Act 1978 163
Value Added Tax Act 1983 58
Value Added Tax Act 1994 (VATA) . . . 58, 59, 61, 62, 66, 67, 137, 142
Vehicle Excise and Registration Act 1994 . . . 62
Vehicles (Excise) Act 1971 62
Welfare Reform Act 2012 64
Winchester Assize of 1203–4 9
Youth Justice and Criminal Evidence Act 1999 93

Table of Statutory Instruments

Criminal Procedure Rules 2015 SI 1490 . . . 45
European Convention on Extradition (Fiscal Offences) Order 1993 SI 2663 . . . 155
European Convention on Extradition (Fiscal Offences) Order 2001 SI 1453 . . . 155
Exchange Control (General Exemption) Order 1979 SI 1660 . . . 184
Family Proceedings Rules 1991 SI 1247 . . . 92
Information Notice: Resolution of Disputes as to Privileged Communications Regulations 2009 SI 1916 . . . 110
Money Laundering Regulations 2007 SI 2157 . . . 174
Penalties, Offshore Income etc. (Designation of Territories) (Amendment) Order 2013 SI 1618 . . . 138
Penalties, Offshore Income etc. (Designation of Territories) Order 2011 SI 976 . . . 138
Police and Criminal Evidence Act 1984 (Application to Revenue and Customs) Order 2007 (Amendment) Order 2010 SI 360 . . . 89
Police and Criminal Evidence Act 1984 (Application to Revenue and Customs) Order 2007 (Amendment) Order 2014 SI 788 . . . 89
Police and Criminal Evidence Act 1984 (Application to Revenue and Customs) Order 2007 SI 3175 . . . 89
Police and Criminal Evidence Act 1984 (Application to Revenue and Customs) Order 2015 SI 1783 . . . 89
Proceeds of Crime Act 2002 (Cash Searches: Code of Practice) Order 2008 SI 947 . . . 185
Proceeds of Crime Act 2002 (Recovery of Cash in Summary Proceedings: Minimum Amount) Order 2006 SI 1699 . . . 185
Proceeds of Crime Act 2002 and Money Laundering Regulations 2003 (Amendment) Order 2006 SI 308 . . . 109
Public Bodies (Merger of the Director of Public Prosecutions and the Director of Revenue and Customs Prosecutions) Order 2014 SI 834 . . . 81
The Proceeds of Crime Act 2002 (Cash Searches: Code of Practice) Order 2016 SI 208 . . . 185

Table of EU Legislation

Directive 2014/107/EU 150
Directive 2015/849/EU (Fourth Money Laundering Directive) 103
Directive 91/308/EEC (First Money Laundering Directive) 171

Table of International Instruments

Convention for the Suppression of the Financing of Terrorism (1999) 171
Convention on International Trade in Endangered Species of Wild Fauna and Flora 80
European Convention on Extradition ETS 24 1957 155
International Monetary Fund (Cmd 6546, 1945) Articles of Agreement. . . 184
OECD Convention on Combating Bribery of Foreign Public Officials in International Business Transactions, Paris, 17 December 1997 (Cm 3994) 159
OECD Convention on Mutual Administrative Assistance in Tax Matters 149
OECD, Recommendation of the Council on Tax Measures for Further Combating Bribery of Foreign Public Officials in International Business Transactions Adopted on 25 May 2009 160
OECD, Recommendation on the Tax Deductibility of Bribes of Foreign Public Officials, adopted on 11 April 1996, C(96)27/FINAL. 160
UN Convention Against Illicit Traffic in Narcotic Drugs and Psychotropic Substances (Vienna Convention) 1998. . . . . 170, 171, 175, 176
United Nations Convention against Corruption (UNCAC) (2005) 160
United Nations Convention against Transnational Organized Crime (Palermo Convention 2004). . . . 171, 175
United Nations Security Council Resolutions 1737 (2006) and 1747 (2007). 171

List of Abbreviations

A1P1	First Protocol to Article 1 of the ECHR
AML	Anti-money laundering
ARA	Assets Recovery Agency
ARIS	Asset Recovery Incentivization Scheme
BEPS	Base erosion and profit shifting
CDDF	Crown Dependencies Disclosure Facilities
CDF	Contractual Disclosure Facility
CEMA	Customs and Excise Management Act 1979
CEPO	Customs and Excise Prosecutions Office
CFG	Central Fraud Group
CFT	Countering the financing of terrorism
CGT	Capital gains tax
CPS	Crown Prosecution Service
CTT	Capital transfer tax
DPA	Deferred Prosecution Agreements
DPP	Director of Public Prosecutions
DWP	Department for Work and Pensions
EAW	European Arrest Warrant
ECHR	European Convention on Human Rights
ECJ	European Court of Justice
ECtHR	European Court of Human Rights
EOI	Exchange of information
FA	Finance Act
FATCA	Foreign Account Tax Compliance Act
FATF	Financial Action Task Force
FCA	Financial Conduct Authority
FTT	First-tier Tribunal
GAAR	General Anti-abuse Rule
HMC&E	HM Customs and Excise
HMRC	HM Revenue and Customs
IMF	International Monetary Fund

IRS	Internal Revenue Service
LAP	Legal advice privilege
LDF	Liechtenstein Disclosure Facility
LPP	Legal professional privilege
MTIC	Missing trader intra-community
NCA	National Crime Agency
NCIS	National Criminal Intelligence Service
NICs	National Insurance contributions
OECD	Organisation for Economic Co-operation and Development
OFC	Offshore financial centre
PACE	Police and Criminal Evidence Act 1984
POCA	Proceeds of Crime Act 2002
PwC	PricewaterhouseCoopers
RCD	Revenue and Customs Division
RCPO	Revenue and Customs Prosecution Office
SFO	Serious Fraud Office
SOCA	Serious Organised Crime Agency
TMA	Taxes Management Act 1970
UKBA	UK Border Agency
UWO	Unexplained wealth order
VAT	Value added tax
VATA	Value Added Tax Act 1994

1
Introduction

Fifty years ago, criminal law and taxation were areas of law discrete from one another and both relatively autonomous from other areas of law. This book describes their increasing integration. For students of criminal law, tax evasion raises important questions. It prompts us to consider whether there is anything distinctive about criminal law as a means of inducing compliance to the obligation upon citizens to pay taxes, and, conversely, whether there is anything distinctive about tax evasion as a crime.

One of the consequences of the concentration of traditional criminal law scholarship upon the gravest crimes is that there may not appear to be many plausible responses to reprehensible behaviour other than to criminalize and, in the event of the offence being committed, appropriate evidence being available, and so on, to prosecute. Yet for the vast majority of crimes on the statute book a case could be made for treatment other than criminalization, and, in a significant proportion of cases where the behaviour is criminal, for treatment other than prosecution. Tax evasion falls within these categories. It is possible to imagine a wide range of ways of dealing with it. There is a continuum from prosecution being more or less automatic; through being selective on one or more of a range of priorities, perhaps with a presumption against; to non-prosecution. There could be (there has been) a jurisdiction in which tax evasion is not a criminal matter at all, or, if criminal, then confined to the lesser ranks of criminality.

Criminal prosecution has never been the preferred enforcement response to a direct tax fraud. Her Majesty's Revenue & Customs' (HMRC's) policy for the criminal investigation powers and safeguards is the (circular) one that '[c]riminal [i]nvestigation will be reserved for cases where HMRC needs to send a strong deterrent message or where the conduct involved is such that only a criminal sanction is appropriate'.[1] The standard reason given by

[1] <https://www.gov.uk/government/publications/criminal-investigation/hmrc-criminal-investigation-policy>

tax-collection agencies for leaning against prosecution is that, were they to devote too many resources to prosecutions, they would be sidetracked from their primary task of raising revenue. This claim is bolstered by the consideration that there are powerful mechanisms whereby tax can be collected and penalties imposed without recourse to the criminal courts.

Where tax evasion stands relative to other crimes has always been contentious. Is it worse than other frauds because the victim is the State (that is, everyone), or is it not so bad because the victim is unknown? Is it less of a priority for prosecutors because the Revenue has at its disposal a range of other mechanisms for getting the money, including the imposition of administrative penalties? Or is it more of a priority because the overall sums involved are so large, because of the need to make examples, and because the victim is everyone? These questions would be difficult enough if we knew more as to the effects of the respective policies. In fact, very little reliable information is available as to the effect of these responses on the behaviour of the particular taxpayers involved, or upon the taxpaying public more generally.

The book will deal with crimes to do with tax, predominantly tax evasion. Increasingly the criminal justice system is becoming involved with taxation not only in dealing with evasion and its prosecution, but also at later stages, when charges of laundering the proceeds of evasion, and/or proceedings for the confiscation or civil recovery of the proceeds of tax evasion, are brought. The book considers crimes of evasion in respect of all UK taxes and duties, but will deal preponderantly with evasion of income tax, customs and excise duty, value added tax, capital gains tax, and corporation tax. It will not attempt to furnish an exhaustive list of taxes, partly at least because the point at which something becomes a tax is sometimes unclear.[2]

The substantive criminal law of taxation—the patchwork of specific offences—is a mess. It provides prosecutors with a huge legal armoury, most of which is seldom if ever deployed. It is in need of rationalization, but it has no real *lacunae*. Where the taxpayer, the full facts of whose affairs are known, has lied or failed to disclose information so as to pay less tax, s/he will be criminally liable in one or more of a range of ways. There are ample powers to acquire and generate evidence and strong sentencing options. The question

[2] For example, for the purposes of the 'levying Money for or to the Use of the Crowne by pretence of Prerogative without Grant of Parlyament' clause of Article 4 of the Bill of Rights 1689 (1 W & M c 2)—see, eg, *Customs and Excise Commissioners v Total Network SL* [2008] UKHL 19; [2008] 1 AC 1174; *Woolwich Equitable Building Society Respondents v IRC* [1993] AC 70. On some accounts, for example, repayments on student loans, or road and bridge tolls, are taxes.

is usually about priorities, due process, and the danger of 'overkill' in the criminal justice system.

The book will assess the extent to which tax prosecutions are, and should be, like, and how unlike, other prosecutions. It will address a range of types of question and issue, as follows.

Analytical questions: Substantively, what sort of a crime is tax evasion? How is its gravity to be assessed relative to other offences? What should the standard be for criminal liability? How should it be punished and what other dispositions should be contemplated?

Procedural and evidential questions: Setting the limits of the right of the state to information against the right of the taxpayer to financial privacy and to communicate confidentially with his/her legal adviser, and providing for one jurisdiction to acquire information from another as to the affairs of a taxpayer.

Institutional questions: Whose job is it to be to decide what type of proceedings (prosecutions, or proceedings in place of prosecution, or negotiations) are to be brought? What guidance and what incentives and resources are they to be given? What is to be the relationship between that agency and the officials who conduct the investigation? Is it to be someone whose agency has a financial interest in the outcome? What agencies are to be charged with making the decisions and bringing the proceedings? Is that office to be integrated within the prosecution system, or within the system for collecting taxes, or to stand separately from both? Is the priority and the default for whichever agency it is to be to prosecute or to get the money? There have been changes in the enforcement structures driven by considerations of convenience, by the consequential effects of the failings of bodies central to frontier enforcement but tangential to revenue-raising, and, doubtless, by resources. These changes reflect underlying theoretical questions about the relationships of both investigator to prosecutor and civil to criminal enforcement.

Teleological questions: What are the objectives of the procedure? Are they efficient tax collection, or retribution, denunciation, deterrence (general and/or specific), or what? And if deterrence is one of the objectives, what is the significance of publicity? By reference to what criteria should taxpayers be selected for prosecution? Should they always be the taxpayers in default themselves, or (on occasion) their advisers or the financial institutions they use? Is it legitimate to select people in the public eye for prosecution? Should taxpayers be able to pay more to HMRC in order to reduce the publicity to be given to their actions? Is there an optimal level of tax evasion prosecutions? And if there is, is it to be assessed by reference only to comparisons between tax evasion cases and other financial crimes, or is it legitimate also to take into account the alternative to prosecution (which, in the case of tax evasion, can be expensive)? What role, if any, does the public appetite for prosecution play in this area?

Questions of organizational culture: Whether tax prosecutors are to be housed in an office of tax collectors or of general prosecutors is of crucial importance. This bears on what is regarded as success. What sorts of things will bring them career rewards? What are the measures by which the performance of individuals is assessed?

At heart these amount to a set of questions about the relationship between the system for dealing with tax crimes and the system for dealing with other crimes, from the definitions of offences, through the policing and other investigative structures, to the prosecutors and the courts. It is possible to envisage, at every point in the criminal justice process, an entirely separate or an entirely integrated system for tax offences, and most steps on the continuum in-between.

The structural alterations that have been made in the twenty-first century follow from the merger of Customs and Excise and Inland Revenue in 2005. The Revenue and Customs Prosecution Office (RCPO) was established as a body independent from HMRC at that time, then was abolished in 2009.[3] In its stead a Revenue and Customs prosecutions body was placed within the Crown Prosecution Service, perhaps implying that the people who perform prosecution functions for HMRC are primarily prosecutors, and not primarily tax collectors. Countervailing pressure has been placed upon *all* prosecutors to have greater regard to the revenue implications of their behaviour. In particular, the introduction of the Asset Recovery Incentivization Scheme (ARIS),[4] under which the prosecution agency will receive a proportion of any confiscated assets, has the effect of making the Crown Prosecution Service (CPS) more like a tax-collection body. That is, the institutional changes of the first decade of the twenty-first century may be less significant than a general convergence in the approaches of prosecutors and tax collectors, amplifying the significance of the financial consequences of the behaviour and the responses made by prosecutors, and narrowing the differences between civil and criminal routes.

Relationships with other agencies: The relationship between whoever investigates and prosecutes tax crimes and those who prosecute other financial crimes—the Financial Conduct Authority (FCA) (previously the Financial

[3] See Chapter 7, section entitled 'The Civil Penalties Regime'.
[4] See Chapter 9, section entitled 'Confiscating the Proceeds of Tax Evasion'.

Services Authority), the National Crime Agency (NCA) (previously NCIS and then SOCA), and the Serious Fraud Office (SFO)—and, if there ever were to be an overarching Economic Crime Agency, with that. There are questions of demarcation and exchange of information, and occasional conflicts of interest.

The international dimension: Tax and criminal law were two of the last vestiges of state sovereignty in the 'Westphalian' mode. In the days when the 'Revenue Rule' held sway, there would have been little to say about international aspects of tax evasion. One jurisdiction would not help another collect tax, or enforce any associated laws.[5] Mutual assistance in gathering evidence of evasion had not been thought of and extradition for tax offences was unthinkable.[6] The international aspects of tax have increasingly come to the fore. 'Secrecy jurisdictions'[7] and other tax havens have given rise to narratives of multinational companies avoiding taxes by allocating their income to the jurisdiction that provides the most beneficial outcomes, and of multinational companies or rich individuals benefiting from the use of frequently anonymized offshore accounts.[8] The current preferred 'tax justice' remedy—exchange of information (EOI)—challenges established ideas on taxpayer confidentiality.

Much of the book will deal with criminal liability. Civil penalties are part of the alternative dispositions available to the tax authorities. Compared to prosecution, the advantages to HMRC are that proceedings for civil penalties are simpler, cheaper, quicker, have advantageous evidential rules (burden and standard of proof, admissibility), and are more predictable (because the vicissitudes of jury trial are avoided). Civil penalties can also be seen as a softer option, and, before 2009,[9] were a means of avoiding publicity.

The years since 1980 have given growing importance to confiscation, and revived importance to forfeiture. While the emphasis of proceeds of crime enforcement was upon the trade in drugs, and there were alternative powerful mechanisms for recovering tax lost through evasion, little attention was paid to the use of proceeds of crime law in the tax arena. As the sums promised from drugs and other sources failed to materialize, and with renewed

[5] 'It is perfectly elementary that a foreign government cannot come here—nor will the courts of other countries allow our government to go there—and sue a person found in that jurisdiction for taxes levied and which he is declared to be liable to by the country to which he belongs.' (*King of the Hellenes v Brostrom* (1923) 16 Ll L Rep 167 (Rowlatt J).

[6] See Chapter 8.

[7] Young, Mary Alice, *Banking Secrecy and Offshore Financial Centres: Money Laundering and Offshore Banking* (London: Routledge, 2012).

[8] Murphy, Richard, *The Joy of Tax* (London: Bantam, 2015).

[9] FA 2009 s 94.

attention being given to tobacco smuggling and to missing trader intra-community (MTIC) frauds, proceeds of crime law has increasingly been invoked in the area of tax.

The recurrent questions, then, are as to whether, and if so in what ways and to what extent, tax offences are different from other criminal offences.

2

Crimes of Evasion—History and Theory

A Short History

There are two major, radically variant, historical sources supplying the basis for an account of criminal law as a means by which to enforce tax laws. On the one hand is the mailed gauntlet of those charged with the collection of customs and excise duties and, latterly, VAT; and, on the other, the kid glove of the Inland Revenue, collecting income tax and most other domestic taxes. The idea of customs law as establishing a semi-permeable membrane through which contraband should not pass forms the basis of modern customs seizure and prosecution powers. Border laws are strong and rough-and-ready, to deal with people on the move, and are as much concerned with border control as with revenue-raising. When caught in breach of border controls, the earliest economic criminals—smugglers and currency offenders—were treated very harshly. Heavy criminal sanctions and forfeiture provisions against smugglers were in place from the reign of Richard II.[1] The eighteenth-century history of customs law, in particular, is punctuated by the gibbeted remains of hanged smugglers.[2]

Methods of collecting domestic taxes were frequently also harsh, but the emphasis was always on the acquisition of the property by the State, rather than the use of the criminal law against non-payers. This approach developed with the income tax in the Victorian era.[3] The main objective of domestic tax law enforcement was to get the money, giving the taxpayer every chance to pay (or even to negotiate the liability down) and avoid the criminal justice pathway. Even into the twenty-first century, very few evaders of income or

[1] Confirmation of Liberties; Charters and Statutes, Exportation of Gold, Silver, Leaving the Realm, &c Act, 1381 (5 R 2 c 3).

[2] Webb, Simon, *Execution: A History of Capital Punishment in Britain* (Stroud: The History Press, 2011) 27.

[3] And see this chapter, section entitled 'Income Tax'.

other domestic taxes[4] hear the clang of the prison gates behind them. The eventual merger[5] of Customs and Excise with the Inland Revenue, against the background of their discrete historical bases, internal cultures, and legal powers, was pithily described by the *Financial Times* as 'crossing the C&E terrier with the IR retriever', and it does seem that the continued less favourable treatment of evaders of VAT than of evaders of income tax is partly due to this history.[6]

Customs and Excise

The early history of tax and crime deals first with customs and then with excise duties. The history of HM Customs and Excise (HMC&E)[7] from their inception until the merger of the revenue collection agencies[8] is of the three major functions discharged by Customs and Excise, namely tax collection, criminal law enforcement, and frontier control. The emphases in the priorities of Customs and Excise as between these functions has varied over time.

Customs

Customs duties were established by the King, and smuggling was regarded as a combination of *lèse-majesté* and theft from the King.[9] In 1203 King

[4] Not that there is consistency in this regard. Anecdotally at least, excise duty and VAT evasion attract heavier penalties than income tax evasion.

[5] This book will use the expression 'merger'. This is the word used, for example, in the announcement, as part of the 2004 Budget, that the two agencies were to be combined (HC Debates, 17 March 2004 Col 331), and in contemporaneous discussions, for example McFall, John (Chair), Treasury Committee, *The Merger of Customs & Excise and the Inland Revenue*, Ninth Report of Session 2003–04, HC 556. See also, however, Lord Goldsmith QC A-G, HL Debates, 7 February 2005 Col 587: '[w]hen we talk about forming HMRC, we talk about "integration". Integration is not the same as a merger: it is a more fundamental change that brings services together to produce new and better solutions. But the goal is not integration for its own sake. Integration in parts of the business that share customers or functions—such as Customs' work on VAT and Inland Revenue's work on direct taxes—can deliver real benefits, and here it will be pursued with vigour.'

[6] 'The Joys of Crossing a Terrier with a Retriever', *Financial Times*, 9 July 2004.

[7] And see Atton, H, and H Holland, *The King's Customs* (London: Frank Cass & Co Ltd, 1967); Carson, Edward, *The Ancient and Rightful Customs: A History of the English Customs Service* (London: Faber and Faber, 1972); Smith, Graham, *Something to Declare: 1000 Years of Customs and Excise* (London: Chambers Harrap, 1980).

[8] Commissioners for Revenue and Customs Act 2005.

[9] And see Ashworth, William J, *Customs and Excise Trade, Production, and Consumption in England 1640–1845* (Oxford: Oxford University Press, 2003).

John established by prerogative a customs service, operating on a national scale and responsible directly to the Crown.[10] At all the ports, he required commissioners to account to him for the revenue, and he divided the control between assessment, collection, and accounting to guard against bribery or collusion.[11] To facilitate surveillance, goods were only to be landed or shipped at approved quays.[12] The Book of Rates, the forerunner of present-day tariffs, was produced, and many articles other than the original subjects (wine and wool) were then made liable to duty.[13] The rates were determined by the King, sometimes with, often without, the authority of Parliament. When James I wished to increase revenue and, being unable to get Parliament to raise the rates, decided he would revise the valuation of goods in the published Books, a merchant argued that no increase in taxation could be imposed without the consent of Parliament. The court held that the King acted within his prerogative.[14] Upon the Restoration, parliamentary control over taxation was affirmed and subsequently embodied in the Bill of Rights.[15] Instead of appointing his own collectors, the King might subcontract—selling the rights to the Customs duties for a fee, often substantial, to a 'farmer' who would then undertake the collection with his own staff. This system was open to abuse, with bribery and extortion causing loss of revenue.

Excise

'Customs' was not the only taxation on goods. Excise, 'a hateful tax',[16] was of purely parliamentary origin and was first imposed by the Long Parliament

[10] Winchester Assize of 1203–4; Carson, n 7 at 16; Butterfield, *Review of criminal investigations and prosecutions conducted by HM Customs and Excise by the Hon Mr Justice Butterfield* (HM Treasury, 2003) para 1.4.

[11] Carson, n 7, at 16.

[12] For consideration of the 'Survey of the Port of Southampton', commissioned by Elizabeth I in 1565 in an effort to deter illicit trading in English ports, see Parker, Leanna T, 'Southampton's Sixteenth-century Illicit Trade: An Examination of the 1565 Port Survey' (2015) 27 *International Journal of Maritime History* 268–84.

[13] Gras, NSB, 'The Tudor "Books of Rates": A Chapter in the History of the English Customs' (1912) 26 *Quarterly Journal of Economics* 766–75; Carson, n 7 at 26 *et seq*.

[14] *Impositions del Roy* (1606) 12 Co Rep 64; [1607] EWHC KB J23; 77 ER 1342. See also *Ship Money, Case of* (1637) 3 State Trials 826, a case 'reversed by the Battle of Naseby': *Crown of Leon (Owners) v Lords Commissioners of the Admiralty* [1921] 1 KB 595 at 607–08 per Earl of Reading CJ (it had been reversed more prosaically by the Ship Money Act 1640 (16 Ch 1 c 14)).

[15] Bill of Rights 1689 (1 W & M c 2) Article 4.

[16] 'Excise—a hateful tax levied upon commodities, and adjudged not by the common judges of property, but wretches hired by those to whom excise is paid': Johnson, Samuel, *A Dictionary of the English Language* (1755).

in 1643,[17] to provide money for the parliamentary forces engaged in war against the Crown. Excises were initially managed directly by a Board of Commissioners in the same manner as the Customs. Excise was a type of tax on domestic consumption. During the years of the Civil War, it covered many different items, but it was reduced ten years later to cover just chocolate, coffee, tea, beer, and spirits. It was an effective way of raising revenue, so successive governments introduced, repealed, and re-introduced excise duty on various items, including essentials such as salt, leather, and soap.[18]

Part of the constitutional settlement at the Restoration was that one half of the total Excise revenue should be made over to Charles II for the term of his natural life, and the other half to him or his heirs forever (as compensation for the loss to the Crown of their rights to feudal dues).[19] The whole of the Excise was therefore in the King's hands. In 1671, Charles II created the Board of Customs—an official body responsible for the collection of Customs duties.[20] In 1787, the hereditary Excise was abolished, the Crown was provided with a Civil List, and all duties were thereafter accounted to the Consolidated Fund.[21]

The Excise was unpopular, partly because the hated 'right of entry'[22] to inspect premises and produce had to be exercised more often in the Excise than in the Customs. Excise penalties were severe. In 1849 the Board of Excise combined with the Board of Stamps and Taxes to become the Board of Inland Revenue. At that time there was pressure for the Board of Customs to merge with the Board of Inland Revenue to administer all general taxation collection. This did not come about. Instead, sixty years after the creation of the Board of Inland Revenue, the collection and management of excise duties was transferred to the Commissioners of Customs.[23] The Board of Customs was amalgamated with that of Excise by Order in Council and renamed the

[17] Ordinance for the speedy raising and levying of moneys by way of charge or impost upon several commodities, Excise Ordinance 1643.

[18] O'Brien, Patrick K, and Philip Hunt, 'The Emergence and Consolidation of Excises in the English Fiscal System before the Glorious Revolution' [1997] *British Tax Review* 35–58.

[19] Excise Act 1660 (12 Ch 2 c 23) and Tenures Abolition Act 1660 (12 Ch 2 c 23). Carson, n 7 at 41.

[20] See Butterfield, n 10 para 1.5; Leftwich, BR, 'The Later History and Administration of the Customs Revenue in England (1671–1814)' (1930) 13 *Transactions of the Royal Historical Society (Fourth Series)* 187–203.

[21] Customs and Excise Act 1787 (27 Geo 3 c 13).

[22] The Customs power of entry was originally a prerogative power. The Excise powers were imposed duty by duty until Excise Act 1723 (10 Geo 1 c 10), the progenitors of CEMA s 161. A review in 2014 found thirty-nine statutory entry powers held by HMRC, of which thirty were reviewed and five found wanting. HMRC, *Report on Our Powers of Entry* (London: HMRC, 2014).

[23] FA 1908 s 4.

Board of Customs and Excise.[24] That remained the position into the twenty-first century.

Smuggling to Evade Duty

Initially, the Customs Service existed only passively to collect the duties at the ports, and not to prevent smuggling or to act against smugglers.[25] The development of awareness of smuggling and the growth of economic protectionism forced a wider remit. Protectionism in Britain was at its strongest from the Restoration till the mid-nineteenth century.[26] The Rump Parliament passed the first Navigation Ordinance,[27] requiring goods brought to England to be carried in English ships, navigated by English crews and captains.[28] The Navigation Act 1660[29] re-enacted the Ordinance and gave more work to the Customs, enforcing the requirement of certificates on produce carried only on British ships.[30] In 1614, export of wool was made completely illegal.[31] In 1661, it was made punishable by death. Smugglers subsequently began arming themselves. In turn, they were faced with armed prevention in the form of the British Army. In 1697, eight 'owlers' (illegal exporters) were earmarked for solemn impeachment. They escaped by making a full confession and paying a total of £20,000 in fines.[32] Parliament then forbade anyone who lived within a fifteen-mile distance from the sea from buying wool unless he could produce documentary evidence that he intended to sell it inland from the 'exclusion zone'.[33]

During the seventeenth and eighteenth centuries illegal trade increased.[34] Smugglers always commanded some sympathy, both on brute economic

[24] See Butterfield, n 10, and refer to this chapter, section entitled 'Butterfield'.

[25] And see Carson, n 7, at 55 *et seq*.

[26] Davis, Ralph, 'The Rise of Protection in England, 1689–1786' (1966) 19 *Economic History Review* 306–17.

[27] Navigation Ordinance 1651.

[28] Earlier laws, starting with 5 R II c 3, restricted imports and exports to people and ships of the King's liege. See also Shipping Act 1786 (26 Geo 3 c 60), Merchant Shipping Act 1794 (34 Geo 3 c 68), and Customs, &c Act 1833 (3 & 4 W 4 c 52). There is a full account of the Acts in Chitty, Joseph, *Wyndham Beawes's Lex Mercatoria* (London: Rivington, 6th edn, 1813) vol 1, especially at p 83 *et seq*. I am grateful to Michael Lobban for drawing this valuable source to my attention. See also Reeves, John, *A History of the Law of Shipping and Navigation* (London: Brooke, 1792).

[29] Navigation Act 1660 (12 Ch 2 c 18).

[30] Carson, n 7 at 42.

[31] After 1614 export of wool from England was prohibited and export of finished clothing was encouraged: Hill, Christopher, *Reformation to Industrial Revolution* (Harmondsworth: Penguin Books, 1969) 88.

[32] McLynn, Frank, *Crime and Punishment in Eighteenth Century England* (London: Routledge, 3rd edn, 2013) 172 *et seq*.

[33] Exportation Act 1697.

[34] See McLynn, n 32.

considerations, because of the benefits they brought to their local area, and on loftier philosophical grounds, because they were romanticized into the embodiment of free trade.[35] Adam Smith[36] and Beccaria[37] both expressed admiration for them. For Smith the smuggler was:

> *[A] person who, though no doubt highly blameable for violating the laws of his country, is frequently incapable of violating those of natural justice, and would have been, in every respect, an excellent citizen had not the laws of his country made that a crime which nature never intended to be so.*[38]

In the eighteenth century the duty on imports and exports rose, smuggling increased, and the efforts of the State to suppress it grew.[39] The Offences against Customs or Excise Act 1745,[40] an integral part of the 'Bloody Code', established the severest penalties, initially for a period of seven years. The death penalty was available for running contraband, assembling to run goods, or harbouring smugglers,[41] though few executions actually took place.[42] Smugglers convicted of killing officers were to be gibbeted. Collective fines were imposed on the relevant county for unresolved offences.[43] A system of

[35] Hence the expression 'freetrader', meaning 'smuggler': '[t]here is something amusing about the old meaning of the word Freetrader. For a Freetrader used to mean a smuggler. There is something pleasing about the picture of all those men with top-hats and side-whiskers rolling kegs of rum into a romantic cave. There is something very satisfactory about the image of John Bright in a red cap with pistols at his belt, or Cobden swaggering in sea boots with a cutlass in his teeth.' Chesterton, GK, 'Our Note Book', *Illustrated London News*, 25 June 1921. And see Andreas, Peter, 'Smuggling Wars: Law Enforcement and Law Evasion in a Changing World' (1998) 4 *Transnational Organized Crime* 75–90.

[36] Like Chaucer, a customs collector himself: Anderson, Gary M, William F Shughart, and Robert D Tollison, 'Adam Smith in the Customhouse' (1985) 93 *Journal of Political Economy* 740–59.

[37] Beccaria, Cesare, *Of Crimes and Punishments* (1764) (ed Adolph Caso) (Boston: International Pocket Library, 2nd edn) ch 33. And see Woolrych, Humphry William, *The History and Results of the Present Capital Punishments in England* (London: Saunders and Benning, 1832) ch 2.

[38] Smith, Adam, *The Wealth of Nations* (ed RH Campbell, AS Skinner, and WB Todd) (Oxford: Oxford University Press, 3rd edn, 1976) Book V Chapter II. 'James Holt, the smuggler, behaved very penitently, but did not seem convinced his sentence was just, or that smuggling merited death. Amongst his last words were "It is very hard to be hanged for smuggling"': (1752) 21 *London Magazine: or, Gentleman's Monthly Intelligencer* 335, quoted in Emsley, Clive, *Crime and Society in England, 1750–1900* (London: Routledge, 3rd edn, 2010) 266. Very similar remarks were attributed to Rodrigo Gularte on his execution for drug-smuggling in Indonesia in April 2015: *The Guardian*, 30 April 2015, <https://www.theguardian.com/world/2015/apr/30/brazilian-executed-by-indonesia-was-hearing-voices-all-the-time>.

[39] McLynn, n 32, p 177 *et seq*.

[40] Offences against Customs or Excise Act 1745 (19 Geo 2 c 34).

[41] And see Winslow, Cal, 'Sussex Smugglers' in Hay, Douglas et al (eds), *Albion's Fatal Tree* (London: Penguin, 1975) and Monod, Paul, 'Dangerous Merchandise: Smuggling, Jacobitism, and Commercial Culture in Southeast England, 1690–1760' (1991) 30 *Journal of British Studies* 150–82.

[42] See Woolrych, n 37.

[43] £100 for an officer killed by smugglers, £40 for an officer wounded—s 6.

outlawry was introduced under which names of known smugglers were published in the *London Gazette*, these men to surrender within forty days or be judged guilty.[44] A £500 reward was available to anyone turning in a gazetted smuggler.[45] The Smuggling &c Act 1779[46] amended the 1745 Act and added penalties for goods carried in vessels over 200 tons.[47] Boats with more than four oars were forbidden.[48] Penalties were imposed on gaolers allowing smugglers to escape.[49] At some periods in history, particularly during the American Revolution, smugglers could redeem their crimes by finding men to serve in the army and navy. One landsman and one seaman could compound a £500 penalty, and two of each could redeem all penalties, however great.[50]

Although the death penalty for smuggling was not formally abolished until 1867,[51] Britain adopted a free-trade policy in the 1840s, repealed the Navigations Acts[52] and reduced import duties significantly, and so made smuggling to evade excise duty no longer so profitable an occupation. For the century to 1950, smuggling was not a major legislative or enforcement priority. The period since the 1960s has seen a rise in the smuggling of forbidden items (preponderantly drugs) and also, particularly since the 1980s, of items (tobacco, alcohol) on which the duty payable differs in different parts of the EU. With the relaxation on the amounts of alcoholic drinks and tobacco that could be imported, and the ease of importation, this sort of excise fraud again became a significant drain on the Exchequer. Losses to the Treasury are thought to be substantial,[53] so the prevention of tobacco- and alcohol-smuggling is a priority for the UK government.[54]

[44] S 10. [45] S 10. [46] Smuggling, etc Act 1779 (19 Geo 3 c 69). [47] S 2.
[48] S 3. [49] S 15.

[50] Recruiting Act 1778 (18 Geo 3 c 53) (an early combination of rehabilitation of offenders, diversion, and state interest).

[51] Statute Law Revision Act 1867, repealing the 1745 Act.

[52] Navigation Act 1849 (12 & 13 Vict c 29).

[53] Taylor, Martin, *Report on Tobacco Smuggling* 1999, <https://www.govuk/government/publications/taylor-report-on-tobacco-smuggling>.

[54] Vaz, Keith (Chair), Home Affairs Committee, *Tobacco Smuggling*, First Report of Session 2014–15; HMIC, *Proceeds of Crime: An Inspection of HMRC's Performance in Addressing the Recovery of the Proceeds of Crime from Tax and Duty Evasion and Benefit Fraud* (London: TSO, 2011). And see van Duyne, Petrus, 'Organizing Cigarette Smuggling and Policy Making, Ending Up in Smoke' (2003) 39 *Crime, Law and Social Change* 285–317; Hornsby, Rob, and Dick Hobbs, 'A Zone of Ambiguity: The Political Economy of Cigarette Bootlegging' (2007) 47 *British Journal of Criminology* 551–71; Griffiths, Hugh, 'Smoking Guns: European Cigarette Smuggling in the 1990s' (2004) 6 *Global Crime* 185–200. In *Lindsay v Customs and Excise Commissioners* [2002] EWCA Civ 267 para 19 the sums lost by the UK were said by a customs officer to be £3.8 billion per annum in tobacco alone. In March 2016 HMRC announced that by more rigorous enforcement it had halved the losses to UK £2.1bn in the year 2014–15: 'HMRC Hails Huge Cut in UK Tobacco Fraud', *The Observer*, 5 March 2016.

The Relationship between Customs and Excise Duties and Other Taxes

Customs law safeguards the integrity of the nation by preventing the entry of contraband substances. It also collects duties on goods whose entry into the jurisdiction is lawful if and only if the appropriate declaration is made and duty paid. Where smuggling takes place, it is because the only reason for the importation is to profit by evading the tax, so there is little difference in practice between items apprehended at customs that fall within the categories of dutiable goods and of contraband. There is a social hygiene function in attempting to prevent harmful things (whether weapons, pornography, or drugs) entering the country. The prohibitions upon imports and exports might also be for economic reasons. Protectionism is usually implemented by tariffs, not by prohibitions, but the agency responsible for the borders[55] must also oversee import and export licences, which are needed for import and export of military and paramilitary goods, dual-use and technology, artworks, plants and animals, medicines, and chemicals. Restrictions also apply to certain destinations—in particular those to which trade sanctions and arms embargoes apply.

Precursors of Income Tax

Excise in its various forms remained the major source of revenue until the end of the seventeenth century. Various other taxes were tried under the Plantagenets, Tudors, and Stuarts. During the period from Richard II to the end of the seventeenth century, the poll tax was levied intermittently. It was a lay subsidy (a tax on the movable property of most of the population) to help fund war. It had first been levied in 1275 and continued, under different names, until the seventeenth century. People were taxed a percentage of the assessed value of their movable goods. That percentage varied from year to year and place to place, and which goods could be taxed differed between urban and rural locations. Ultimately, the inefficiency of its collection—receipts routinely fell far short of expected revenues—prompted the government to abandon the poll tax. It was last levied in 1698.

[55] For a time (2009–13) the UK Borders Agency, now again the Home Office through Border Force.

The hearth tax, introduced in 1662,[56] levied two shillings on every hearth in a family dwelling (which were easier to count than persons). This was a heavier, more permanent, and more regressive tax than the poll tax proper; the intrusive entry of tax inspectors into private homes to count hearths was unpopular, and was repealed after the Glorious Revolution.[57] The hearth tax was replaced in 1695 by a 'window tax', which had the advantage that inspectors could count windows from outside homes, and so no right of entry was required.[58]

Until the middle of the eighteenth century, fraud *in general* was not considered as a separate form of criminal wrongdoing,[59] and the taxes then applied were not triggered so much by a declaration by the taxpayer as by inspection by the authorities. If the authorities, having inspected, were aware that there was a window or a hearth or a person, then, in principle, the tax was chargeable and was levied. No possibility arose of evasion as a separate category. This is what changed with the advent of income tax.

Income Tax

For many years, opposition to the introduction of any income tax flowed from the belief that the disclosure of personal income represented an unacceptable governmental intrusion into private matters, and a potential threat to personal liberty.[60] The interest of paying for wars eventually took precedence.[61]

The British income tax was a direct outcome of the gigantic struggle against France. The reason of its introduction can be grasped only when we understand the fiscal situation of the day. Like that of most other countries, the English revenue system of the eighteenth century had come to consist almost exclusively of customs and excises. The mediaeval system of taxes on property and produce had shrunk to very small dimensions, and the old general property tax had long become virtually nothing but a land tax.[62]

[56] Taxation Act 1662 (13 & 14 Ch 2 c 10). See Ward, WR, 'The Administration of the Window and Assessed Taxes, 1696–1798' (1952) 67 *English Historical Review* 522–42; Glantz, Andrew E, 'A Tax on Light and Air: Impact of the Window Duty on Tax Administration and Architecture, 1696–1851' (2008) 15 *Penn History Review* 1–23.

[57] Hearth Money Act 1688 (3 J 2 c 10).

[58] Taxation Act 1695 (7 & 8 W 3 c 18).

[59] Hall, Jerome, *Theft, Law and Society* (Bloomington IN: Bobbs Merrill, 2nd edn, 1952) Ch 2.

[60] Mill, John Stuart, *Principles of Political Economy* (1848) Book V Chapter 3, section 5.

[61] 'Princes do in times of action get new taxes, and remit them not in peace' (Donne, *Love's Growth* in Robbins, Robin (ed), *The Poems of John Donne: Volume One* (London: Routledge, 2014) 110.

[62] Seligman, ERA, *The Income Tax: A Study of the History, Theory, and Practice of Income Taxation at Home and Abroad* (New York: Macmillan, 1911) Preface. And see Monroe, HH, *Intolerable Inquisition? Reflections on the Law of Tax* (London: Stevens, 1981) Ch 1.

After an earlier, temporary use of the tax to finance the Napoleonic wars,[63] income tax was reintroduced in the UK by Peel in 1842,[64] using the schedular structure devised for Addington's earlier (1803)[65] revision of Pitt's original (1798) imposition of the tax.[66] There have been periodical consolidating Acts,[67] assessments, and reassessments.[68] Deduction at source for employment income was introduced during the Second World War[69] and a rewrite programme operated in the early 2000s,[70] but the essential structure of taxation by reference to source,[71] rather than by reference to increase in wealth, remains.

The basis upon which income tax was charged was not inspection or demonstration but declaration, and that gave rise to the possibility of evasion by failing to make an accurate declaration. The Revenue's treatment of income tax evasion developed during the nineteenth and twentieth centuries, and from an early stage prosecution was a low priority.[72] Williams suggests that prosecutions were avoided because of the perceived difficulty in proving guilt:

[63] Hope-Jones, Arthur, *Income Tax in the Napoleonic Wars* (Cambridge: Cambridge University Press, 1939); Duties on Income Act 1799 (39 Geo 3 c 13), Income Tax Act 1803 (43 Geo 3 c 122), and Income Tax Act 1806 (46 Geo 3 c 65). Taxation Act 1798 (38 Geo 3 c 16); Exportations, etc Act 1802 (43 Geo 3 c 12). See Sabine, BEV, *History of Income Tax* (London: George Allen & Unwin, 1966) ch 4; Daunton, MJ, *Trusting Leviathan: The Politics of Taxation in Britain, 1799–1914* (Cambridge: Cambridge University Press, 2001).

[64] Income Tax Act 1842.

[65] Income Tax Act 1803 (43 Geo 3 c 122). See Farnsworth, A, 'Addington, Author of the Modern Income Tax' (1950) 66 *Law Quarterly Review* 358; Avery Jones, John, 'The Sources of Addington's Income Tax' in Tiley, John (ed), *Studies in the History of Tax Law, Volume One* (Oxford: Hart, 2004) 1.

[66] Jeffrey-Cook, John, 'William Pitt and His Taxes' [2010] *British Tax Review* 376.

[67] Income Tax Act 1842, Income Tax Act 1918, Income Tax Act 1952, Income and Corporation Taxes Act 1970, Income and Corporation Taxes Act 1988.

[68] Macmillan (Chair), *Report of the Income Tax Codification Committee* (London: Cmd 5131, 1936); Radcliffe, Lord (Chair), *Royal Commission on the Taxation of Profits and Income*, Final Report (London: Cmd 9474, 1956).

[69] Income Tax (Employments) Act 1943. PAYE had been piloted by Churchill's Chancellor, Sir Kingsley Wood, from 1940 to 1941. Its full introduction, which places the administration and collection of the taxes of employees in the hands of the employer, meant that the Revenue received the money earlier and that the possibility of fraud or non-payment was reduced. Braithwaite, John, *Markets in Vice, Markets in Virtue* (Oxford: Oxford University Press, 2005) 162 describes deduction at source as 'the single most important innovation in the history of tax compliance'. Note the difference in VAT frauds, where, frequently, the recipient of the money is also the collector of the tax.

[70] Giving rise to the Income Tax (Earnings and Pensions) Act 2003, Income Tax (Trading and Other Income) Act 2005, Income Tax Act 2007, Corporation Tax Act 2009, Corporation Tax Act 2010, and Taxation (International and Other Provisions) Act 2010.

[71] Subject to the POCA Part 7 jurisdiction, which does not require a source or a year of assessment to be identified. See Chapter 9, section entitled 'The Proceeds of Crime Tax Jurisdiction'.

[72] See Colley, Robert, 'The Arabian Bird: A Study of Income Tax Evasion in Mid-Victorian Britain' [2001] *British Tax Review* 207–21; Colley, Robert, 'Mid Victorian Employees and the Taxman: A Study in Information Gathering by the State in 1860' (2001) 21 *Oxford Journal of Legal Studies* 593–608; Colley, Robert, 'Railways and the Mid-Victorian Income Tax' (2003) 24 *Journal of Transport History* 78–102.

When Sir Francis Gore, the Board's Solicitor, argued quite vigorously in his evidence to Ritchie that flagrant evaders might be prosecuted in the police court (the ancestor of the modern magistrates' court) for fraud, his colleagues felt that the fear of such a fate would simply mean that all taxpayers under enquiry would refuse to answer questions and take their chance. Even Gayler[73] *thought that fraud would be too hard to prove in a criminal court.*[74]

It is not clear from the sources how tax evasion differs in this regard from any other offence requiring proof of dishonesty, but the idea took root early, and has continued, that income tax liabilities are not best enforced by prosecutorial vigour. A certain deference in the Revenue's approach to the taxpayer might also be responsible.[75]

What Is Wrong with Tax Evasion?

Perceptions of tax evasion have altered over time.[76] Students of crime only began to consider white-collar crimes as a significant part of their remit after Sutherland's work.[77] Even when white-collar crime had been so recognized, it was a further step to treat tax evasion as a crime.[78] For many years, tax evasion, particularly under-declaration for the purposes of income tax, was thought of as a victimless crime or a crime with only remote, intangible harms. Accounts were developed that it was a crime acceptable in the middle class,[79] in this

[73] William Gayler (1846–1907), Chief Inspector of Stamps & Taxes (footnote added).

[74] Williams, David, 'Surveying Taxes, 1900–14' [2005] *British Tax Review* 222 at 240.

[75] In the days (1929–73) when the higher rates of income tax were called 'surtax', letters from the Inland Revenue to male taxpayers dealing with income tax were addressed to 'Mr AB Taxpayer', and those dealing with surtax to 'AB Taxpayer, Esq'.

[76] Karlinsky, Stewart, Hughlene Burton, and Cindy Blanthorne, 'Perceptions of Tax Evasion as a Crime' (2004) 2 *E-Journal of Tax Research* 226–40.

[77] Sutherland, EH, 'White-collar Criminality' (1940) 5 *American Sociological Review* 1–12; Sutherland, Edwin, *White Collar Crime* (New York: Dryden Press, 1949); Sutherland, EH, *White Collar Crime: The Uncut Version* (New Haven: Yale University Press, 1983).

[78] Moohr, Geraldine Szott, 'Tax Evasion as White Collar Fraud' (2009) 9 *Houston Business & Tax Law Journal* 207–445.

[79] Monroe (n 62) refers (at 69) to the passage in Act Two of Gilbert & Sullivan's *Ruddigore* (1887) in which the protagonist, attempting to commit a crime a day, 'confesses' to having submitted a false tax return, but is told that this is too trivial to count. The dialogue is as follows:

> Robin Oakapple. On Tuesday I made a false income tax return.
>
> All. Ha! ha!
>
> First Ghost. That's nothing.
>
> Second Ghost. Nothing at all.
>
> Third Ghost. Everybody does that.
>
> Fourth Ghost. It's expected of you.

sense not unlike those applied to drink-driving in the 1970s.[80] Those narratives and the low prosecution rate were mutually reinforcing. Tax evasion was not prosecuted because it was not thought serious, and it was not thought serious because it was not prosecuted.

The Nature of the Wrong

A crime without a known victim is not necessarily a victimless crime.[81] Attempts are occasionally made to quantify the amounts lost nationally[82] or globally through tax fraud.[83] If the public purse is deprived of money by tax evasion, that will have the effects either that the tax burden will fall elsewhere or that the government will be unable to carry out planned expenditure. There are also consequential effects to taxpayers being seen to 'get away' without paying tax. Most obviously, others might imitate freeriders.

The nature of the wrong should shape the definitions of the crime(s). The literature distinguishes various accounts as to the wrong in tax evasion. Green's account of the wrong in tax evasion is that it is a form of cheating.[84] In the case of evasion by failure to declare, this is fairly accurate. It does not describe the gist of the other types of evasion so closely. The wrong in tax evasion might be characterized in one or more of the following ways.

(i) A failure of citizenship: one way in which to characterize tax evasion is as freeriding—attempting to receive the benefits of citizenship without paying the subscription. This kind of account is not limited to evasion but is also applied, particularly in wartime and at other times of crisis, to avoidance.
(ii) A form of perjury: the idea here is that the taxpayer making a return or other declaration is in a position of particular solemnity with a heightened obligation to tell the truth.

[80] Hatfield, Michael, 'Tax Lawyers, Tax Defiance, and the Ethics of Casual Conversation' (2011) 10 *Florida Tax Review* 2010–26; Morris, Donald, *Tax Cheating: Illegal—But Is It Immoral?* (Albany, NY: SUNY Press, 2012).

[81] And see 'Prosecuting Tax Evasion', Speech by Keir Starmer QC, Director of Public Prosecutions 23 January 2013, in Chapter 10.

[82] See HMIC, n 54.

[83] Cebula, Richard J, and Edgar L Feige, 'America's Unreported Economy: Measuring the Size, Growth and Determinants of Income Tax Evasion in the US' (2012) 57 *Crime, Law and Social Change* 265–85.

[84] Green, Stuart, *Lying, Cheating and Stealing* (Oxford: Oxford University Press, 2005). See also Green, Stuart, 'Moral Ambiguity in White Collar Criminal Law' (2004) 18 *Notre Dame Journal of Law, Ethics & Public Policy* 501; Green, Stuart P, 'What is Wrong with Tax Evasion?' (2008) 9 *Houston Bus & Tax Legal Journal* 221.

(iii) A form of fraud: the taxpayer increases his/her wealth by deliberately failing to comply with his/her obligations, usually in circumstances attracting adjectives like 'dishonest' and 'fraudulent'.
(iv) A form of theft. The tax evader steals money from the exchequer. The money in his/her hands is not ever 'really' his/hers.

There are elements of each of these ideas both in the history of the treatment of evasion and in the definitions of crimes of evasion. The freeriding argument is mostly used when expressing outrage. As a backlash against evasion gained in strength during 2015, a French judge, sentencing to prison the first of the *HSBC Suisse* evaders to be convicted in France, described the woman's conduct as 'a threat to public order and to the republican pact',[85] very much recalling the treatment of early smugglers.[86] While the 'perjury' aspect still holds a distinct place in in the United States,[87] and is still evident in some of the UK statutory offences,[88] it has faded somewhat in the UK,[89] partly at least as a result of changes in attitudes to the uttering of untruths when not in a special position of obligation to tell the truth. The distinction between 'tax fraud' (on the one hand) and 'tax perjury' is still current in the US literature, and there are subtle differences according to which version is pursued. In particular, as for matters of proof, there has always tended to be a heightened level of scrutiny, including requirements for corroboration of the evidence, where the charge is of perjury than is the case for other crimes. Second, the harm in tax perjury is slightly different. It is the false swearing. The defendant who makes a true declaration believing it to be false might not be fraudulent, but this would be a version of tax perjury. The distinction dates from a time when, without more, *caveat emptor* governed and a person could say whatever was to his/her financial advantage. Nothing, without more, was criminal about lying when one's financial interests were at stake.[90]

[85] 'Affaire HSBC: prison ferme pour Arlette Ricci', *Le Monde*, 14 April 2015. <www.lemonde.fr/economie/article/2015/04/13/affaire-hsbc-prison-ferme-pour-arlette-ricci_4615042_3234.html>. The use of the expression 'Pacte republicain' is most telling because of its significance in French constitutional discourse. It connotes equal treatment for all, within the terms especially of Article 2 of the French Constitution.

[86] See this chapter, section entitled 'Customs'.

[87] The relevant legislation is set out in Brown, Logan, and Aurash Jamali, 'Tax Violations' (2014) 51 *American Criminal Law Review* 1751.

[88] CEMA ss 167 and 168, which is rarely, if ever, charged. See Chapter 4, section entitled 'The "Tax Perjury" Offence'.

[89] See CEMA s 167.

[90] 'Shall we indict one man for making a fool of another?' Holt CJ in *R v Jones* (1703) 2 Raym 1013; 92 ER 174. Ormerod, David, 'The Fraud Act 2006—Criminalizing Lying?' [2007] *Criminal Law Review* 193.

Some kinds of tax evasion look very similar to insurance frauds; for example, where D claims a rebate for tax that has not been paid, which is the essence of many missing trader and tax credit frauds. Others, for analogous reasons, appear to be akin to benefit frauds. The 'theft' model is clearest in those crimes where the crime is committed by a person whose task is to collect the tax—most clearly in the case of VAT. A person charged with collecting VAT and then handing it over to the authorities commits a crime of the nature of embezzlement when s/he retains the money and appropriates it to his/her own ends.

An account of the moral aspects of evasion needs also to consider whether there is any sustainable distinction to be made between acts and omissions—between false representations, on the one hand, and failures to undeceive, on the other. The 'acts and omissions' doctrine in English criminal law worked reasonably well for a non-mechanized society. It has no real place in areas where one party is completely dependent upon the other for support or information. The duty to furnish information to the tax authorities should make any distinction between acts and omissions irrelevant. In the context of taxation there is no moral difference between lying to Her Majesty's Revenue and Customs (HMRC), on the one hand, and deliberately failing to undeceive them when there is a duty to inform them correctly, on the other.[91]

Conscientious Refusers and Tax Resisters

Not all tax evasion is for financial benefit. From time to time taxpayers refuse to pay all or part of tax to which they are assessed in order to draw attention to their objections to the purposes for which the money is then spent.[92] Perhaps for this reason, the (US) IRS now prefers the term 'tax defier', to describe a person who 'seeks to deny and defy the fundamental validity of the tax laws'.[93] The end of the era that Daunton identified with 'just taxes' has given rise

[91] Duff, RA, Lindsay Farmer, SE Marshall, Massimo Renzo, and Victor Tadros, 'Introduction' in Duff, RA et al (eds), *Criminalization: The Political Morality of the Criminal Law* (Oxford: Oxford University Press, 2014) 25, draw attention to HMRC policy as a test for criminalization.

[92] See *R (on the application of Boughton) v HM Treasury* [2005] EWHC 1914 (Admin): [2006] EWCA Civ 504; [2006] BTC 460 (Quakers). The actor Wesley Snipes was sentenced to prison after making such claims in 2008: 'Wesley Snipes Gets 3 Years for Not Filing Tax Returns', *New York Times*, 25 April 2008, at C3.

[93] Braithwaite, Valerie A, *Defiance in Taxation and Governance: Resisting and Dismissing Authority in a Democracy* (Cheltenham: Edward Elgar Publishing, 2009); Braithwaite, Valerie, 'Resistant and Dismissive Defiance towards Tax Authorities' in Crawford, Adam, and Anthea Hucklesby (eds), *Legitimacy and Compliance in Criminal Justice* (London: Routledge, 2012) 91. And see Delalande, Nicolas, and Romain Huret, 'Tax Resistance: A Global History?' (2013) 25 *Journal of Policy History* 301–7.

to radical questioning of the legitimacy of taxation.[94] In particular, the Tea Party movement in the United States objects not so much to the policy of the government on any one specific issue, but to the fact of the appropriation.[95] Conversely, growing publicity given to the mechanism whereby the wealthy avoid and sometimes evade tax has given rise to anger among those who do pay it. The (US) constitutional law claims made by such taxpayers may generate publicity but, in legal terms, are largely implausible.[96]

Advisers and Customers

Two areas in which the liability, and the blameworthiness of accomplices, come up for consideration are, first, the liability of advisers and financial institutions for the crimes of their advisees and clients, and second, and more mundanely, the liability of those who make cash payments to contractors knowing or suspecting that the reason they pay cash is that the contractors under-declare income for the purpose of taxation.

On one account the moral gravity of the ancillary offences is a function of the main offence, but the extent of the accomplice's culpability can vary infinitely. Where the accomplice is involved in more than one offence, his/her role can be far more than simply to render assistance and is closer to that of an instigator, which is not a distinct category in English law. This can be the case where tax advisers procure the act of evasion by a number of their advisees,[97] or a bank offers services to thousands, far more actively than the usual passive model of retail banking.[98] Because the mental state for conviction as an accomplice is so widely drawn in English law,[99] without any exclusions for 'normal business dealing', 'what everyone else does', or similar,[100] the bank employee who wrote that an HSBC client wished money to be in a particular

[94] Daunton, Martin, *Just Taxes* (Cambridge: Cambridge University Press, 2002).

[95] Huret, Romain D, *American Tax Resisters* (Cambridge, MA: Harvard University Press, 2014).

[96] Kornhauser, Marjorie E, 'For God and Country: Taxing Conscience' [1999] *Wisconsin Law Review* 939–1016.

[97] *R v Perrin & Faichney* [2012] EWCA Crim 1729; [2012] EWCA Crim 1730; [2012] EWCA Crim 1730, para 46.

[98] This was the burden of the *HSBC Suisse* scandal in 2015: see Chapter 3, section entitled 'The *HSBC Suisse* (2015) and Mossack Fonseca (*Panama Papers*) (2016) Scandals'.

[99] Simester, AP, 'The Mental Element in Complicity' (2006) 122 *Law Quarterly Review* 578; Ormerod, David, and Karl Laird, *Smith & Hogan's Criminal Law* (Oxford: Oxford University Press, 14th edn, 2015) 211. Compare Kwon, Michelle M, 'The Criminality of Tax Planning' (2015) 18 *Florida Tax Review* 153.

[100] *National Coal Board v Gamble* (1958) 42 Cr App R 240; *Attorney General's Reference (No 1 of 1975)* [1975] QB 773; [1975] 2 All ER 684.

place 'for ESD reasons'[101] might fall within the scope of criminal liability as an accomplice to cheating by the client.

The suggestion that lawyers or financial institutions might bear more of the moral or legal responsibility for evasion undertaken by their clients is taking hold.[102] The traditional representation is of a passive industry, responding only to requests from clients. One of the matters that has been brought more clearly into the light in recent years is that the involvement both of professionals and of financial institutions has been far more active than had previously been thought. When it became clear that *HSBC Suisse* had been actively colluding in large-scale tax avoidance, and very possibly evasion, by clients, there were calls for reform of the law. Few, if any, of the taxpayers whose money is the subject of the disclosures in the *Panama Papers* would have sent it where it went without professional advice.

The Code of Practice on taxation for banks (which, anecdotally[103] at least, appears to have been effective) was introduced 'for banks only, as banks have historically undertaken and promoted tax avoidance and their behaviour in this activity was typically more aggressive than that of companies in other sectors'.[104] The Code of Practice has been given statutory elements.[105] Under the Code, banks have an obligation not to promote avoidance.[106]

A change in enforcement practices was made in the United States in the middle of the first decade of this century:

> *[T]he government began focusing its criminal resources on the professionals who advised and enabled their clients to evade or avoid taxes. Thus, instead of pursuing taxpayers who claimed hundreds of millions of dollars in phony losses, the government decided to go after the accounting firms, law firms, and professionals who advised these taxpayers.*[107]

[101] That is, with a view to evading tax under the European Savings Directive: this is a quotation from an HSBC Suisse official to a client. 'HSBC Files: Swiss Bank Aggressively Pushed Way for Clients to Avoid New Tax', *The Guardian*, 10 February 2015.

[102] And see Schumacher, Scott A, 'Magnifying Deterrence by Prosecuting Professionals' (2014) 89 *Indiana Law Journal* 511.

[103] Collier, Richard, 'Intentions, Banks, Politics and the Law: The UK Code of Practice on Taxation for Banks' [2014] *British Tax Review* 478 at n 78 quotes with approval the following: 'Such is the heightened state of paranoia in the banks at the moment that any tax planning which could be erosive of the UK tax base—including some fairly anodyne transactions—tends to get killed off pretty quickly, if not by a nervous internal committee, then following a friendly chat with HMRC in advance of implementation. The legality or effectiveness of the proposed transactions does not come into it.' Lethaby, H, 'Reflections on Tax and the City' (2014) 1220 *Tax Journal* 10, 11.

[104] HMRC, *Strengthening the Code of Practice on Taxation for Banks* (May 2013).

[105] FA 2014 Part 6 (s 185 *et seq*).

[106] <www.gov.uk/government/uploads/system/uploads/attachment_data/file/408674/yield_stats.pdf>.

[107] Schumacher, n 102, citing *US v Daugerdas* 757 F Supp 2d 364 (SDNY 2012); and *US v Stein* 435 F Supp 2d 330 (SDNY 2006).

The US government targeted some of the biggest players, entering into a Deferred Prosecution Agreement with UBS, Switzerland's largest bank, and indicting some of its bankers. In 2012, the government indicted Switzerland's oldest bank, Wegelin Bank, and three of its partners, even though the bank had no US office. As a result of the indictment, the bank ceased to exist as an independent entity within a month. Wegelin pleaded guilty to tax crimes in January 2013, and formally ceased operation.[108]

This leaves open the questions of when a professional adviser will be personally criminally liable and whether proceeding against advisers would be a worthwhile prosecution strategy. Given the apparent successes in the US, and given that decisions in this area need to be driven by results, it merits further consideration. The Finance Act 2016 contains (non-criminal) penalty provisions directed against enablers and there will be further changes to criminal law in the Criminal Finance Bill. Professional bodies may also have a role to play.[109]

Underpinning the discussions about the legal liability of the adviser is an issue about the role of the professional. The traditional characterization is of the professional (lawyer, tax adviser, accountant) having an overriding loyalty to the client, and no duty to inform the State of wrongdoing by the client of which the professional became aware. Ideas that s/he might have some kind of function as 'gatekeeper'[110] or even 'whistleblower' involve significant changes to this view.[111] These matters bear on the extent of privilege.[112]

What of the more quotidian practice of paying some tradespeople in cash, knowing or suspecting that they will not make a full declaration for the purposes of their own liability? The transaction may be badged as a discount 'for cash' or 'discount for prompt payment' or some similar euphemism. Consumers do not seem to be prosecuted, but it is difficult to see what conceivable defence there might be to a charge of complicity in evasion. In the case where the tradesperson is convicted, the colluding customer will, in theory, be liable as an accomplice to whatever tax evasion offence is committed. Of the many areas of under- or non-prosecuted crimes, this is one of the

[108] 'Swiss Bank Wegelin to Close after US Tax Evasion Fine', <http://www.bbc.co.uk/news/business-20907359>.

[109] 'Despite the evidence of fraudulent schemes, no *firm* has ever been disciplined by any professional accountancy body': Prem Sikka, *The Guardian*, 8 December 2012.

[110] Perkins, Rachelle Holmes, 'The Tax Lawyer as Gatekeeper' (2010) 49 *University of Louisville Law Review* 185–230.

[111] Cramton, Roger C, 'The Lawyer as Whistleblower: Confidentiality and the Government Lawyer' (1991) 5 *Georgetown Journal of Legal Ethics* 291–315.

[112] See Chapter 6, section entitled 'Legal Advice Privilege: Lawyers and Other Tax Advisers'.

most striking. Evasion might be reduced if the consumers were not regarded as immune.

Complicity of Corporations

A further avenue is to consider the possibility of imposing criminal liability onto corporations. The 'industrial scale' of the *avoidance* in which large accountancy firms engage[113] does not necessarily imply criminal guilt. It is notoriously difficult under English law to convict a corporation of anything, let alone a crime involving quite a complex mental state.[114] The government announced in September 2015 that it would not carry further any reform of English law dealing with the criminal liability of corporations. At the time of writing it is unclear whether the changes elsewhere will reverse this decision.

[113] Hodge, Margaret (Chair), Public Accounts Committee, *Tax Avoidance: The Role of Large Accountancy Firms*, Forty-fourth Report of Session 2012–13, HC 870 (2013) 8, Hodge, Margaret (Chair), Public Accounts Committee, *Tax Avoidance: The Role of Large Accountancy Firms (Follow-up)*, Thirty-eighth Report of 2014–15, HC 860.

[114] *Tesco Supermarkets Ltd v Nattrass* [1971] UKHL 1; [1972] AC 153.

3

Avoidance and Evasion

It would facilitate financial planning by government if taxes—other than those imposed deliberately to achieve some change in behaviour—could be imposed so as to have no effect on the behaviour of taxpayers. It does not work like that. Taxpayers and their advisers read taxing provisions and attempt to devise ways not to have to pay. McBarnet[1] holds that the process of legislation, followed by the generation of avoidance mechanisms, followed by the blocking of particular avoidance routes and the search for others, is not so much a failure by lawmakers, law enforcers, and judges to put in place bullet-proof law as an inevitable dynamic process involving 'constructive compliance' by taxpayers and a continuing attempt by legislation not to be left too far behind. This is not to say that draftspeople, legislators, and judges make no difference. They do.[2] It is simply to say that legislators can never make avoidance impossible, only more difficult.

Over the years the idea has developed that there is a valid distinction to be made between avoidance—ordering one's affairs so as not to fall within the charge to tax or so as to reduce it—which is lawful, and evasion, usually by deception, which is not. The avoider attempts to comply with the law and the evader seeks to benefit from not complying.

[1] Expressed particularly in McBarnet, Doreen, 'Law, Policy, and Legal Avoidance: Can Law Effectively Implement Egalitarian Policies' (1988) 15 *Journal of Legal Studies* 113; McBarnet, Doreen, 'Legitimate Rackets: Tax Evasion, Tax Avoidance, and the Boundaries of Legality' (1992) 3 *Journal of Human Justice* 56–74; McBarnet, Doreen, 'It's Not What You Do But the Way That You Do It: Tax Evasion, Tax Avoidance and the Boundaries of Deviance' in D Downes (ed), *Unravelling Criminal Justice* (London: Macmillan, 1992) 247–68.

[2] Freedman, Judith, 'Improving (Not Perfecting) Tax Legislation: Rules and Principles Revisited' [2010] *British Tax Review* 717.

Avoidance

Leaving aside the group of taxes that are intended to affect behaviour—taxes on tobacco, alcohol, or harmful foodstuffs and on environmentally damaging conduct (diesel oil, landfill)—and various other 'nudges',[3] the underpinning assumption of most taxes is that they work best if they do not affect the way in which people behave, and that if the tax does affect taxpayer behaviour, in particular by giving rise to behaviour directed towards avoidance, then that is a problem. Ideally, for example, the Revenue would want income tax to operate so as not to affect the transactions by which people acquire income, or how they are categorized. If the effect of taxing income is that taxpayers attempt to recategorize their transactions to be classified as capital and not as income then the tax is, to that extent, a failure. Sometimes undesirable consequences are not foreseen. For example, one of the consequences of the window tax was a rise in the incidence of ailments associated with poor ventilation,[4] and the 'gin craze' in the eighteenth century was partly caused by changes in the rules relating to the importation of French brandy.[5]

Many early avoidance mechanisms were directed against taxes upon death and to keep property in families.[6] The modern history of tax avoidance begins with the introduction of supertax in 1909, giving rise to many devices by which taxpayers divested themselves of income.[7] Since then, avoiders and anti-avoidance legislation have come in waves. Wealthy individuals transferred income-producing assets to overseas bodies or individuals, and taxes on transfer of assets abroad and legislation were introduced in response.[8]

[3] Thaler, Richard H and Cass R Sunstein, *Nudge: Improving Decisions about Health, Wealth, and Happiness* (New Haven, CT: Yale University Press, 2008); Sunstein, Cass R, 'Nudges, Agency, and Abstraction: A Reply to Critics' (2015) 6 *Review of Philosophy and Psychology* 511–29.

[4] Stebbings, Chantal, 'Public Health Imperatives and Taxation Policy: The Window Tax as an Early Paradigm in English Law' in John Tiley (ed), *Studies in the History of Tax Law, Volume 5* (Oxford: Hart Publishing, 2011) ch 2.

[5] Dillon, Patrick, *The Much-lamented Death of Madam Geneva: The Eighteenth-century Gin Craze* (London: Review, 2002).

[6] Hence the development of the trust: Holdsworth, Sir William, *History of English Law*, 2nd edn (London: Methuen, 1937) vol VI p 641 and Stopforth, David, 'Settlements and the Avoidance of Tax on Income—The Period to 1920' [1990] *British Tax Review* 225.

[7] Troup, Edward, 'Unacceptable Discretion: Countering Tax Avoidance and Preserving the Rights of the Individual' (1992) 13 *Fiscal Studies* 128–38; Stopforth, David, '1922–36: Halcyon Days for the Tax Avoider' [1992] *British Tax Review* 88–105.

[8] Parrot, David, and John F Avery Jones, 'Seven Appeals and an Acquittal: The Singer Family and Their Tax Cases' [2008] *British Tax Review* 56.

Before the introduction of the capital gains tax it became popular to badge sales as giving rise to capital rather than income, to avoid income tax.[9] In the 1950s and 1960s much avoidance took the form of dividend-stripping,[10] and overseas partnerships were adopted by film and pop stars to shield overseas income.[11] In the 1960s transactions in securities rules were introduced, to prevent dividend-stripping and other schemes converting income into capital. Advisers' successes in circumventing each new set of anti-avoidance measures resulted in the enactment of a wide-ranging anti-avoidance measure[12] aimed at 'transactions in securities' generally.

In 1965, corporation tax and capital gains tax (CGT) were introduced, partly as anti-avoidance measures.[13] Corporation tax was to stop dividend-stripping and CGT to stop schemes that involved manipulation of the boundary between income and capital.[14] In the 1980s the *Ramsay*[15] case gave rise to a 'principle' that transactions with no underlying justification other than the tax advantages they generated could be ignored for the purposes of computing liability to tax. The 1990s saw the *Willoughby*,[16] *McGuckian*,[17] and *Westmoreland*[18] cases. Legislation directed towards incentives for the British film industry gave rise to the film schemes.[19] The sums involved in all these schemes are huge. Film schemes alone were said to make a difference to Her Majesty's Revenue and Customs (HMRC) of £5 billion per annum.[20] Follower notices were introduced in 2014.[21] A follower notice can be given to a person who has used an avoidance scheme that has been shown in another person's litigation to be ineffective. The follower notice tells the taxpayer that they may be liable to a penalty of up to 50 per cent of the tax and/or National Insurance contributions (NICs) in dispute if they do not amend their return or settle their dispute.

[9] *IRC v Paget* [1938] 2 KB 25; 21 TC 677.

[10] And see *Griffiths v JP Harrison (Watford) Ltd* [1963] AC 1.

[11] *Newstead v Frost* [1980] 1 WLR 135; 53 TC 525 and *Black Nominees v Nicol* [1975] STC 372; 50 TC 229.

[12] FA 1960 s 28.

[13] FA 1965 Part III and Part IV respectively. Whiting, RC, 'Ideology and Reform in Labour's Tax Strategy, 1964–1970' (1998) 41 *Historical Journal* 1121–40.

[14] Lazar, Leonard, 'Finance Act 1965: The Capital Gains Tax' (1966) 29 *Modern Law Review* 181.

[15] *Ramsay (WT) Ltd v IRC, Eilbeck (Inspector of Taxes) v Rawling* [1982] AC 300.

[16] *IRC v Willoughby* [1997] AC 1071.

[17] *IRC v McGuckian* [1997] 1 WLR 991.

[18] *Westmoreland Investments Ltd v MacNiven* (HMIT) [2001] UKHL 6; [2003] 1 AC 311.

[19] Under F(No 2)A 1992 s 42 and F(No 2)A 1997 s 48.

[20] Sir Robin Jacob in *R (on the application of Ingenious Media Holdings Plc & Anr) v HMRC* [2015] EWCA Civ 173.

[21] FA 2014 Part 4.

So far as concerns personal taxation,[22] attention in the UK is directed against the tax status of those who are not domiciled in the UK ('non-doms')[23] and do not fall within the charge to income tax. In the area of corporate taxation, profit-shifting—that is, arranging the finances of an international organization so that the profits are expressed to arise where the greatest fiscal advantage may be had—is the major issue. Underlying both is the problem of identification of the beneficial owner of trusts or 'shell companies' anywhere in the world, which can be vehicles either for illegal obtained money or for money which would be taxed if declared.

The Jurisprudence of Tax Avoidance and Statutory Interpretation

Tax law is not an area of legal learning separate from all others.[24] It is made up of the same things—legislation, cases, law-enforcement officials, lawyers, and subjects—as other areas, and is susceptible to the same analytical devices and techniques. The area of avoidance has become a test case for the interpretation of statutes.[25] The principle in the *Duke of Westminster's* case is that

Every man is entitled, if he can, to order his affairs so as that the tax attaching ... is less ... If he succeeds in ordering them so as to secure this result, then, however unappreciative the Commissioners of Inland Revenue or his fellow taxpayers may be of his ingenuity, he cannot be compelled to pay an increased tax.[26]

[22] And see Gravelle, Jane G, *Tax Havens: International Tax Avoidance and Evasion* Congressional Research Service 7-5700 (2014), 20 *et seq.*

[23] HM Treasury, *Reform of the Taxation of Non-domiciled Individuals: A Consultation* (HM Treasury, 2011); HM Treasury, *Reform of the Taxation of Non-domiciled Individuals: Responses to Consultation* (HM Treasury, 2011).

[24] Wilkie, J Scott, and Peter W Hogg, 'Tax Law within the Larger Legal System' (2015) 52 *Osgoode Hall Law Journal* 460–90.

[25] The literature is enormous. See Farnsworth, A, 'The Income Tax Act, 1842—A Century of Judicial Interpretation' (1942) 58 *Law Quarterly Review* 314–33; Rice, Ralph S, 'Judicial Techniques in Combating Tax Avoidance' (1953) 51 *Michigan Law Review* 1021–52; Wheatcroft, GSA, 'The Attitude of the Legislature and the Courts to Tax Avoidance' (1955) 18 *Modern Law Review* 20; Freedman, Judith, 'Interpreting Tax Statutes: Tax Avoidance and the Intention of Parliament' (2007) 123 *Law Quarterly Review* 53.

[26] *IRC v Duke of Westminster* [1936] AC 1, 19–20 per Lord Tomlin. The circumstances are described in detail in Likhovski, Assaf, 'Tax Law and Public Opinion: Explaining IRC v Duke of Westminster' in Tiley, John (ed), *Studies in the History of Tax Law, Volume 2* (Oxford: Hart, 2007) 183. See also Lord Clyde, when Lord President: 'No man in the country is under the smallest obligation, moral or other, so to arrange his legal relations to his business or property as to enable the Inland Revenue to put the largest possible shovel in his stores. The Inland Revenue is not slow, and quite rightly, to take every advantage which is open to it under the Taxing Statutes for the purposes of depleting the taxpayer's pocket. And the taxpayer is in like manner entitled to be astute to prevent,

Once the *Westminster* principle is granted in unattenuated form (that is, with no consideration for avoidance, 'aggressive' or otherwise), talk of fairness makes no sense and there is no sustainable distinction between the mechanisms by which a person orders his/her affairs so as to fall outside the charge to tax. It might be that the corporation domiciled in jurisdiction A that does most of its trading in jurisdiction B pays little tax in jurisdiction B. It might be that multinational corporations are able to shift profits to jurisdictions where the tax position is more favourable. It might be that interest on offshore bank accounts is not taxable until remitted. If these are problems, the law should be changed.

At various times the *Westminster* principle has been criticized or limited,[27] and the traditional distinction between illegal tax evasion and legal tax avoidance[28] (or planning, or mitigation) has been complicated by the efforts of the authorities to have some forms of avoidance seen as unacceptable even if they satisfy the letter of the law.[29] This is the basis of the claim made by the 'tax justice' movement. It bears especially upon international tax law, where the concern, so far as concerns individual taxpayers, is the status of 'non-doms' and, as concerns corporations, is profit-shifting mechanisms.

In modern political discourse, attempts are made to differentiate acceptable from unacceptable avoidance by reference to the test of whether or not it was performed 'aggressively'. There has been much discussion of 'aggressive' tax avoidance measures and the evils attached to them. The problem is that, like that between 'harmful' and 'non-harmful' tax competition,[30] the difference between 'aggressive' and 'non-aggressive' tax avoidance is by no means clear.[31]

so far as he honestly can, the depletion of his means by the Inland Revenue': *Ayrshire Pullman Motor Services v Inland Revenue* (1929) 14 TC 754, 764.

[27] See Templeman LJ in *Ramsay (CA)—WT Ramsay Ltd v IRC* [1979] 3 All ER 213; [1979] STC 582.

[28] HL Debates, 24 May 2006: WA111-2 (Lord McKenzie of Luton, government spokesperson in the House of Lords for HM Treasury).

[29] Gammie, Malcolm, 'Moral Taxation, Immoral Avoidance—What Role for the Law?' [2013] *British Tax Review* 577.

[30] See Chapter 8, section entitled 'International Aspects of Tax Evasion', and OECD, *Harmful Tax Competition: An Emerging Global Issue* (Paris: OECD, 1998); Genschel, Philipp, and Peter Schwarz, 'Tax Competition: A Literature Review' (2011) 9 *Socio-Economic Review* 339–70.

[31] The distinction is used by the OECD's Aggressive Tax Planning (ATP) Steering Group: <http://www.oecd.org/tax/exchange-of-tax-information/atp.htm>. Aggressive tax planning consists in taking advantage of the technicalities of a tax system or of mismatches between two or more tax systems for the purpose of reducing tax liability. The EU has published an Action Plan to fight against aggressive tax planning and tax evasion. See [2015] (3) *British Tax Review* and Calderón Carrero, José Manuel, and Alberto Quintas Seara, 'The Concept of "Aggressive Tax Planning" Launched by the OECD and the EU Commission in the BEPS Era: Redefining the Border between Legitimate and Illegitimate Tax Planning' (2016) 44 *Intertax* 206–26.

Insufficient attention has been given hitherto to 'non-aggressive avoidance'. Until we have a clearly articulated notion of non-aggressive versus aggressive avoidance (other than simply as ad hoc badges of approval and disapproval), it will be difficult to make a tenable distinction work in criminal law.[32] In late 2014, the UK government floated a proposal for a crime of offshore avoidance,[33] but when the issue arose again[34] the possibility of a *crime* of *avoidance*—aggressive or otherwise—had faded from the picture.[35]

Avoidance has developed its own lexicon, somewhat at odds with the rule of law. Such expressions as 'playing the system', 'skating on thin ice', and 'sailing close to the wind' reflect an ambivalence towards the activity. In a March 2015 White Paper, George Osborne and Danny Alexander, then respectively Chancellor and Chief Secretary, exhorted us to 'play by the rules'.[36] The response of those seeking to minimize their liability to tax might well be that playing by the rules is exactly what they are doing. During the *HSBC Suisse* scandal, coinages such as 'vanilla'[37] and 'mild' were offered to defend particular forms of avoidance. Other euphemisms include 'tax planning' and 'structuring transactions'. Conversely, the avoidance against which action should be taken was 'aggressive' and to be uttered in the same breath as 'evasion'.[38]

The UK government uses the following account to differentiate evasion and avoidance:[39]

Tax evasion is always illegal. It is when people or businesses deliberately do not declare and account for the taxes that they owe. It includes the hidden economy, where people conceal their presence or taxable sources of income. Tax avoidance involves bending the rules of the tax system to gain a tax advantage that Parliament never intended. It often involves contrived, artificial transactions that serve little or no purpose other than to produce this advantage. It involves operating within the letter—but not the spirit—of the law. Most tax avoidance schemes simply do not work, and those who engage in it can find they pay more than the tax they attempted to save once HMRC has successfully challenged them. Tax planning involves using tax reliefs for the purpose for which they were intended, for example, claiming tax relief on capital investment, or saving via ISAs or for retirement by making contributions to a pension scheme. However, tax reliefs can be used excessively or

[32] And note *R v Quillan* [2015] EWCA Crim 538; [2015] Lloyd's Rep FC Plus 20.

[33] HMIC, *Proceeds of Crime: An Inspection of HMRC's Performance in Addressing the Recovery of the Proceeds of Crime from Tax and Duty Evasion and Benefit Fraud* (London: TSO, 2011).

[34] In HM Treasury, *Tackling Tax Evasion and Avoidance* (Cm 9047, 2015) 4.

[35] Yet the idea of (civil) sanctions for avoidance continues: HMRC, *Strengthening Sanctions for Tax Avoidance—A Consultation on Detailed Proposals* (HMRC, 2015). FA 2016 Part 10.

[36] HM Treasury, n 34, at 4.

[37] Lord Fink, 'Tax Avoidance Is Normal in British Society', *The Guardian*, 12 February 2015: <https://www.theguardian.com/business/2015/feb/12/lord-fink-tax-avoidance-is-normal-in-british-society>.

[38] David Cameron, HC Debates, 11 February 2015: Column 774.

[39] HM Treasury, n 34, at 4.

aggressively, by others than those intended to benefit from them or in ways that clearly go beyond the intention of Parliament.[40]

That is, the distinction is made by reference to the enormously slippery concept of parliamentary intention. The problem with this approach is that standard constitutional doctrine holds that there is one way and one way only by which for Parliament to make its intentions clear, and that that is by the enactment of legislation.

Avoidance—Remedies

Within any tax system, the remedy for avoidance is usually taken to be specific and general anti-avoidance provisions. Attempts to distinguish acceptable from unacceptable avoidance have been made worldwide by reference to the form as opposed to the substance of the transaction,[41] to its 'commercial reality',[42] to 'shams',[43] or to motive and the idea of abuse of rights.[44] In the period opened by *Ramsay*,[45] the courts undertook the curious jurisprudence of looking for the 'spirit' of a set of rules,[46] distinct from what the rules say.[47]

[40] And see National Audit Office, *Tackling Tax Fraud: How HMRC Responds to Tax Evasion, the Hidden Economy and Criminal Attacks* (HC 610, 2015–16).

[41] *Gregory v Helvering* 239 US 465 (1935). At the Federal Appeals Court level, Learned Hand J had said, 'any one may so arrange his affairs that his taxes shall be as low as possible; he is not bound to choose that pattern which will best pay the Treasury; there is not even a patriotic duty to increase one's taxes'. *Helvering v Gregory*, 69 F 2d at 810–11.

[42] *Film Partners No 35 LLP v Revenue and Customs Commissioners* [2015] EWCA Civ 95.

[43] *R v Stannard* [2002] EWCA Crim 458; *Ingenious Games LLP, Inside Track Productions LLP, Ingenious Film Partners 2 LLP v Commissioners for Her Majesty's Revenue and Customs* [2015] UKUT 105 (TCC).

[44] Frommel, Stefan, 'L'abus de droit en droit fiscal britannique' (1991) 43 *Revue internationale de droit comparé* 585–625 and the essays in de la Feria, Rita, and Stefan Vogenauer (eds), *Prohibition of Abuse of Law: A New General Principle of EU Law?* (Oxford: Hart, 2011); Bowler, Tracey, *Countering Tax Avoidance in the UK: Which Way Forward?* TLRC Discussion Paper No. 7 (London: IFS, 2009) section 12. And see *Pendragon plc and others v Commissioners for HMRC* [2015] UKSC 37, in which the Supreme Court applied the doctrine of abuse of law to strike down schemes designed to avoid VAT, which implements EU Directives and to which the EU law of *abus de droit* applies.

[45] *Ramsay (WT) Ltd v IRC, Eilbeck (Inspector of Taxes) v Rawling* [1982] AC 300.

[46] And see (for the EU) a similar elision, Communication from the Commission to the European Parliament and the Council on tax transparency to fight tax evasion and avoidance, COM(2015) 136.

[47] The Code of Practice on Taxation for Banks (<https://www.gov.uk/government/collections/the-code-of-practice-on-taxation-for-banks>) also refers to this spirit, commencing: 'The Government expects that banking groups, their subsidiaries, and their branches operating in the UK, will comply with the spirit, as well as the letter, of tax law, discerning and following the intentions of Parliament.'

In *Barclays Mercantile Business Finance Ltd v Mawson*[48] the House of Lords affirmed:

The modern approach to statutory construction is to have regard to the purpose of a particular provision and interpret its language, so far as possible, in a way which best gives effect to that purpose.

After that decision Lord Hoffmann seemed to be under the impression that there would be no more talk of such a 'Ramsay principle',[49] but later cases and documents cited it, and there was always scope for using *dicta* in the contemporaneous (to *Barclays*) case of *IRC v Scottish Provident Institution*[50] to support the view that some notions derived from *Ramsay* survive. *Film Partners No 35 LLP v Revenue and Customs Commissioners*[51] provided further authority citing *Ramsay* and its 'principle' favourably, and the revival was completed by *UBS AG v Commissioners for HMRC*,[52] in which Lord Reed affirmed that the 'principle' was one of the purposive interpretation of statutes. He said:

Rather than dealing with the arguments in the way in which they were presented, in terms of broader and narrower versions of a 'Ramsay' approach, it seems to me to be preferable to begin with the interpretation of the legislation, and the fundamental question whether it can be given a purposive interpretation going beyond its literal terms: that is to say, whether a 'Ramsay' approach is possible at all, and if so, the purposive construction on which it is to be based. If those issues are determined in the Revenue's favour, the question next arises how, on its proper interpretation, the legislation is to be applied to the facts. It is at that stage that what have been described as the broad and the narrow approaches require to be considered.[53]

[48] *Barclays Mercantile Business Finance Ltd v Mawson* [2004] UKHL 51; [2005] 1 AC 684 at para 28.

[49] Hoffmann, Lord, 'Tax Avoidance' [2005] *British Tax Review* 197 at 203. 'The primacy of the construction of the particular taxing provision and the illegitimacy of rules of general application has been reaffirmed by the recent decision of the House in *Barclays Mercantile Business Finance Ltd v Mawson*. Indeed it may be said that this case has killed off the *Ramsay* doctrine as a special theory of revenue law and subsumed it within the general theory of the interpretation of statutes, perhaps the interpretation of utterances of any kind.' Nonetheless, HMRC (*EIM12010*—'PAYE avoidance: application of the Ramsay principle') and many judges in lower courts still refer to it and apply or disapply it. Higher courts seem more disposed to adopt Lord Hoffmann's account of the principle—eg *Astall and another v Revenue and Customs Commissioners* [2009] EWCA Civ 1010; [2010] STC 137; see Freedman, Judith, 'Lord Hoffmann, Tax Law and Principles' in Davies, Paul, and Justine Pila, *The Jurisprudence of Lord Hoffmann* (Oxford: Hart, 2015) 269; *PA Holdings Ltd v Revenue and Customs Commissioners* [2011] EWCA Civ 1414; [2012] STC 582.

[50] *IRC v Scottish Provident Institution* [2004] UKHL 52; [2004] 1 WLR 3172, at para 23.

[51] *Film Partners No 35 LLP v Revenue and Customs Commissioners* [2015] EWCA Civ 95.

[52] *UBS AG v Commissioners for HMRC* [2016] UKSC 13. On appeal from [2014] EWCA Civ 452.

[53] Para 72.

Many anti-avoidance provisions involve 'deeming'—the creation of the legal fiction that, where they have no commercial purpose, or are not at arm's length, or have a substance different from their form, or appeal to the 'spirit' of particular provisions, particular transactions did not happen or have an effect specified by the provision. 'Deeming' is accepted as a necessity in some areas of tax law. It is far more problematic in criminal law, because it seems wrong to punish someone because of something that is only deemed to have happened.[54] Usually, and constitutionally, anti-avoidance provisions are found in legislation. In English law there is a category of tax avoidance scheme that has specifically to be drawn to the attention of the Revenue before it is implemented.[55] Following consultations,[56] a general anti-abuse rule was put in place in the United Kingdom by the Finance Act 2013,[57] and one effect of that may well be in time to diminish the number of references to the 'Ramsay principle'.[58] More sophisticated classifications[59] have been offered for different purposes, but the fundamental distinction remains and follows from the rule of law. The taxpayer who sets out to reduce his/her liability by lawful means is, and should be, in a different position from s/he who seeks to do so by unlawful means. In the wake of Amazon, Google,[60] Starbucks, *HSBC Suisse*, the *Panama Papers*, and so on the thrust of anti-avoidance work has been on international devices of avoidance, and the 'remedy' is identification of beneficial ownership of property together with exchange of information between jurisdictions.[61]

[54] And see Alldridge, Peter, 'Some Uses of Legal Fictions in Criminal Law' in Twining, William, and Maksymilian Del Mar (eds), *Legal Fictions in Theory and Practice* (Dordrecht: Springer, 2015) 367–84.

[55] Disclosure of Tax Avoidance Schemes (DOTAS). See Devereux, Michael, Judith Freedman, and John Vella, *Review of DOTAS and the Tax Avoidance Landscape* (Oxford: Oxford University Press, 2012).

[56] HMRC, *A General Anti-abuse Rule* (GAAR) consultation document, June 2012.

[57] FA 2013 Part V s 206 *et seq*. It does not apply to VAT. And see HMRC, *Strengthening Sanctions for Tax Avoidance* (HMRC, 2015); Seely, Antony, *Tax Avoidance: A General Anti-Abuse Rule* (HC Library Standard Note: SN6265 2015).

[58] See Gammie, Malcolm, 'Moral Taxation, Immoral Avoidance—What Role for the Law?' [2013] *British Tax Review* 577.

[59] Eg HMRC, *Measuring Tax Gaps* (London: HMRC, 2015). 'Tax gap' denotes the disparity between tax that taxpayers are liable to pay and tax actually paid.

[60] A settlement was reached in the UK with Google. The French authorities adopted a less conciliatory line: 'Google Offices Raided in Paris as Prosecutors Announce Fraud Probe', *The Guardian*, 24 May 2016.

[61] See Chapter 8, section entitled 'International Aspects of Tax Evasion'.

Evasion—Remedies

Whereas the standard remedy in the case of avoidance is to change the rule—to put in place anti-avoidance provisions or similar, or change the tax consequences of actions—the standard 'solutions' to any crime are to invest in detection and enforcement, raise the penalties, and change the rules of evidence so as to make it easier for convictions to be achieved. All these are possible, but there is no clear reason to do any of these for tax evasion rather than other crimes. More specifically to tax evasion, there are policies within the framework of 'situational crime prevention'.[62] First, where possible, taxes should be structured so as for them to be collected at source. Second, relevant entities should be required to report payments. Third, transparency requirements should be imposed on banks and other financial institutions. Fourth, enforcement should be firmer and more consistent. That is, with sufficient monitoring, reporting, and disclosure, the problems would diminish. So far as concerns the use of 'offshore' to hide money from taxation, the real problems are the mechanisms of secrecy which conceal or obscure beneficial ownership of property.

Blurring the Line between Avoidance and Evasion

The traditional approach to evasion and avoidance is that they are two different phenomena, requiring different approaches. Avoidance is lawful, evasion is criminal, and that is the end of it. Although the boundary between avoidance and evasion is clearly drawn by reference to what is legal and what is illegal, the distinction between the two is not so easily drawn in behavioural terms.[63] Attention to financial crime arising from the crisis following the collapse of Lehman Brothers, coupled with increased attention to the mechanisms used by international companies to reduce their tax liabilities, has led to increased attention being given to the financial sector, and the possibility of increased use being made there of the criminal law. The traditionally accepted version of the distinction between avoidance and evasion, by reference to the lawfulness or unlawfulness of the conduct, has been threatened in at least six ways.

First, the limits of the criminal offence of cheating the public revenue[64] are so indistinct, and depend so heavily upon the notion of dishonesty in

[62] Middleton, David, and Michael Levi, 'Let Sleeping Lawyers Lie: Organized Crime, Lawyers and the Regulation of Legal Services' (2015) 55 *British Journal of Criminology* 647–68.

[63] HC Library, 'Tax Avoidance: A General Anti-Abuse Rule', Standard Note: SN6265 5 August 2014.

[64] See Chapter 4, section entitled 'Cheating the Revenue'.

Ghosh,[65] that the evasion offences may be used to extend to cases which might previously have been called avoidance.[66] Second, investigations into avoidance may be carried on in such a way as to suggest that some very serious crime is involved when it might not be. *Rossminster*,[67] in which no criminal charges followed a (lawful) dawn raid, and the unlawful raid at the home of the football manager Harry Redknapp,[68] are cases in point. Third, statutory extensions to the criminal law of evasion might make the distinction between evasion and avoidance otherwise than on the basis of the mental state of the defendant. In particular, the idea that there could be a non-deliberate evasion[69] is a radical departure. If one could evade by mistake but only avoid deliberately, it is difficult to see why evasion should be regarded more seriously than avoidance.

Fourth, there are those who talk about evaders and avoiders as though they are in the same category. Successive governments have announced that they oppose 'tax evasion and aggressive tax avoidance'.[70] This habit is not restricted to the media or to politicians,[71] but can also be heard from judges[72] and academics.[73] This blurring of categories should be resisted.[74] While the

[65] *R v Ghosh* [1982] QB 1053; 75 Cr App R 154; Chapter 4, section entitled 'Mental State'.

[66] *R v Charlton* [1996] STC 1418. Bridges, Martyn, Paul Atkinson, Robert Rhodes, and Rowan Bosworth-Davies, '*Regina v Charlton, Cunningham, Kitchen and Wheeler* [1995]' (1999) 2 *Journal of Money Laundering Control* 197–208; *Yukos v Russia* [2011] STC 1988; (2012) 54 EHRR 19.

[67] *R v IRC, ex p Rossminster Ltd* [1980] AC 952; (1980) 70 Cr App R 157; Chapter 6, section entitled 'Dawn Raids and the Legacy of *Rossminster*'. See also *R v Dimsey; R v Allen* [2001] UKHL 46; [2002] 1 AC 509.

[68] *R (on the application of Redknapp) v Commissioner of the City of London Police* [2008] EWHC 1177 (Admin); [2009] 1 WLR 2091.

[69] FA 2016 Part 10. See Chapter 8, section entitled 'Specific Offences of Offshore Evasion'.

[70] 'I do feel strongly about tax evasion and aggressive tax avoidance': David Cameron, HC Debates, 11 February 2015 Col 776. The elision probably comes from the OECD. In 2016 it emerged that Mr Cameron had benefited from a Panamanian fund established by his father.

[71] Watson, Roland, 'PM Seeks Global Action to Tackle Tax Avoiders', *The Times*, 25 April 2013: '[David Cameron] urged Europe's leaders to use next month's EU summit in Brussels to agree new rules and help to restore public confidence in European tax systems. "Tax evasion and aggressive tax avoidance are global problems that require truly global solutions," Mr Cameron said. "Otherwise tax evaders will simply play the system." ' 'Playing the system' is a standard condemnation of avoidance. It lies especially badly in the mouths of those responsible for the system being as it is.

[72] Lord Templeman in *Fitzwilliam v IRC* [1993] 1 WLR 1189; [1993] 3 All ER 184 stated (at 1226): 'I regard tax-avoidance schemes of the kind invented and implemented in the present case as no better than attempts to cheat the revenue.' See also his judgment in *Ramsay (CA)—WT Ramsay Ltd v IRC* [1979] 3 All ER 213; [1979] STC 582 and, extra-judicially, Templeman, Lord, 'Tax and the Taxpayer' (2001) 117 *Law Quarterly Review* 575.

[73] McBarnet, 'Legitimate Rackets', n 1.

[74] See *R v Quillan* [2015] EWCA Crim 538; [2015] Lloyd's Rep FC Plus 20, in which the Court of Appeal was critical of prosecution attempts to present as a sham a scheme involving the claiming of relief at source on pension contributions.

same kinds of prescriptions—usually based around transparency and making information available—can militate against both, the development of the category of disapproved 'aggressive'[75] avoidance is, in this context, problematic. 'We disapprove of tax avoidance so we should prosecute more tax evaders' is a *non sequitur*.

Fifth, the same people (tax advisers and financial institutions) might be involved both in avoidance and evasion. The clientele of tax advisers may well care for little but seeing the liability to taxation reduced. Take, for example, the reliance placed by Chris Moyles, a DJ, on the false factual proposition that he was a used-car dealer for the purposes of a tax avoidance scheme.[76] Or take the example of Amazon, whose tax avoidance relied on the factual assertion that its Luxembourg and UK entities have operations neatly split into trading on the one hand and auxiliary functions on the other, when in reality the operations of the two companies are so mixed up together that one of them has been found liable for the other's tort.[77] A fraud can be set up to resemble an avoidance scheme.[78]

Sixth, the decision to attach civil penalties to the General Anti-Abuse Rule (GAAR) is a further muddying of the water, by juxtaposing 'penalties' and 'avoidance'. The GAAR as enacted[79] applied to arrangements which are abusive, and the response was an adjustment to the tax liability. Penalties were then put in place where a taxpayer submits a return, claim, or document to HMRC that includes arrangements which are later found to come within the scope of the GAAR.[80] A more principled approach would have been only to adjust the liability to tax.[81]

While the line between avoidance and evasion has certainly been blurred a few times,[82] it should be sustained. Those who want to equate avoidance and evasion should pay attention to where this may lead. Russian law does not differentiate between evasion and avoidance. The original tax proceedings against Yukos were driven by a number of factors, including a crackdown on avoidance by using the favourable tax position of a particular area

[75] 'Aggressive tax avoidance is the practice of seeking to minimise a tax bill by attempting to comply with the letter of the law whilst avoiding its purpose or spirit.' Jenkins, Rhys, and Peter Newell, 'CSR, Tax and Development' (2013) 34 *Third World Quarterly* 378.

[76] The 'Working Wheels' scheme: *Flanagan, Moyles and Stennett v Commissioners for HMRC* [2014] UKFTT 175 (TC). Another scheme, 'Liberty', began in 2005 and was closed down in 2009.

[77] David Quentin's Tax and Law Blog, 27 February 2015, <http://dqtax.tumblr.com/page/2>.

[78] *R v Hayley Bevan Savill and Leighton*, Birmingham Crown Court 24 June 2016.

[79] FA 2013 Part 5 and Schedule 43.

[80] FA 2013 Part 5 and Schedule 43, FA 2016 Part 10.

[81] Under FA 2013 s 209.

[82] See Chapter 4.

of Russia, which subsequently was held to fall foul of Article 6. In *Yukos v Russia*[83] the European Court of Human Rights (ECtHR) held that, although having a basis in law, the pace of enforcement measures used by the Russian tax authorities against Yukos (a company which had consequently gone into liquidation), and the failure of the authorities to have sufficient regard to the economic and social implications of those measures on the company and its stakeholders, meant that the authorities had failed to strike a fair balance between the legitimate aim of enforcing a tax liability and the measures employed to achieve that aim. This followed from treating evasion and avoidance as not being differentiable.

It is, moreover, possible to overcomplicate the avoidance/evasion distinction. While it is unhelpful (because circular) to say that the difference between evasion and avoidance is 'the thickness of a prison wall',[84] there is a simple test that does differentiate. There are technical matters to be dealt with in the definitions, but the irreducible core is that if the taxpayer lies to the Revenue with a view to reducing his/her liability, then that is evasion. If the taxpayer does not lie, however much his/her conduct might attract opprobrium, it is not.[85] Many anti-evasion measures are consequently directed to ensuring full disclosure by the taxpayer so as to prevent *suggestio falsi* by *supressio veri*.

The *HSBC Suisse* (2015) and Mossack Fonseca (*Panama Papers*) (2016) Scandals

In 2006–7, Hervé Falciani began surreptitiously extracting client data from inside *HSBC Suisse*. In December 2008 he was arrested in Geneva, was bailed, and fled to France with the files. HSBC revealed that data had been stolen from its Swiss arm affecting 30,000 accounts. In January 2009 French authorities refused a Swiss extradition request and launched their own investigation into the data. Early in 2010, French tax authorities began informing other tax authorities around the world of the existence of the HSBC files. In April

[83] See n 66. And see *Yukos Universal Ltd (Isle of Man) v The Russian Federation*, Permanent Court of Arbitration Case No AA 227 (2014). The litigation continues: 'Dutch Court Rejects $50bn Yukos Award against Russia', *Financial Times*, 20 April 2016.

[84] Generally attributed to Denis Healey, Chancellor of the Exchequer 1974–9: Elliffe, Craig, 'The Thickness of a Prison Wall—When Does Tax Avoidance Become a Criminal Offence?' (2011) 17 *New Zealand Business Law Quarterly* 441–66, cites 'Holes in the Net: Tax Avoidance' (2000) 354 *The Economist* 8152–63, 186.

[85] And see *R (on the application of the Commissioners of HMRC) v Crown Court at Kingston* [2001] EWHC Admin 581 at para 2 (Burnton LJ).

2010 HMRC received the HSBC files.[86] In July 2010 the *Financial Times* reported that HSBC had asked the French courts to prevent the country's tax authority handing files to HMRC.[87] In September 2011 Dave Hartnett, head of HMRC, informed the House of Commons Treasury select committee: 'I think the whole nation probably knows that our department has a disc from the Swiss—from the Geneva branch of a major UK bank—with 6,000 names, all ripe for investigation.'[88] It turned out that HMRC was in the process of acting on information from the Falciani list, which it received from the French in 2010, of 130,000 potential tax evaders using the Geneva branch of HSBC. HMRC identified from this list 3,600 potentially non-compliant UK taxpayers. It recovered £135 million of unpaid taxes and penalties and has secured one criminal conviction.[89]

In November 2014, French judges placed HSBC under official investigation for 'illicit financial and banking practices'. Belgium charged HSBC with money laundering and fraud in connection with its Swiss arm and sought to reclaim €540 million in taxes from HSBC accounts. Argentina charged HSBC with aiding tax evasion via its Swiss arm. In February 2015, media organizations around the world, working under the co-ordination of the International Consortium of Investigative Journalists, began to publish revelations from the leaked files. In March 2015 the French financial state prosecutor formally requested that *HSBC Suisse* be sent to criminal trial over tax fraud allegations.[90] In April 2015 France widened its HSBC Swiss bank inquiry to the global holding company[91] and Arlette Ricci was convicted in France of evasion.[92] In June 2015 HSBC paid out £27.8 million (SFr 40 million)

[86] There seems to have been an issue at this stage as to whether the information could be used in a prosecution. Even if the relevant provision (Article 27 of the UK–France Double Taxation Treaty) prevented the use of information secured under it—a strained construction—it would have been possible for HMRC to acquire the information in such a way as to allow its use in a prosecution.

[87] 'Denials Continue Despite MPs Hearing of HSBC Tax Evasion Claims in 2011', *The Guardian*, 13 March 2015. <https://www.theguardian.com/news/2015/feb/11/denials-continue-despite-mps-hearing-of-hsbc-tax-evasion-claims-in-2011>.

[88] In January 2013, six months after retiring from HMRC, Hartnett joined HSBC as a consultant.

[89] Hodge, Margaret (Chair), Public Accounts Committee, *Improving Tax Collection,* Fiftieth Report of Session 2014–15, paras 9–11 and qq 16–18. The conviction was of Michael Shanly. See Chapter 10.

[90] 'Affaire HSBC: prison ferme pour Arlette Ricci', *Le Monde*, 14 April 2015. <http://www.lemonde.fr/evasion-fiscale/article/2015/04/13/affaire-hsbc-prison-ferme-pour-arlette-ricci_4615042_4862750.html>.

[91] 'France Widens HSBC Swiss Bank Inquiry to Global Holding Company', *The Guardian*, 9 April 2015.

[92] *Le Monde*, n 90.

over money laundering claims.[93] It is undoubtedly the case that during the period to which the records relate, the bank was the repository for huge sums. The total amount of money acquired by the State in England and Wales by confiscating the proceeds of crime in any given year is about £150 million.[94] This pales into insignificance compared to the amounts stashed in just one bank in just one country.

These events brought to the fore the range of issues raised by avoidance, evasion, and offshore. In the febrile perielectoral period it did appear that *HSBC Suisse* might generate significant change, but the initial sound and fury turned out to signify little. Then in March 2016, leaks from the Panamanian company-formation agent Mossack Fonseca, again co-ordinated by the International Consortium of Investigative Journalists, drew worldwide attention. They disclosed that the firm had been providing offshore legal services, frequently as a company-formation agent, to a range of people, some of whom were avoiding taxes and some evading taxes, some of whom were in breach of sanctions and others of whom were laundering the proceeds of crime.[95] Mossack Fonseca incorporated companies in offshore jurisdictions as well as administering offshore firms on an ongoing basis on behalf of its clients.

These leaks showed the widespread use among the world's elite of devices intended to anonymize the beneficial ownership of property.[96] One attraction to the investors was that under Panamanian laws, as previously it had stood, it was possible to control a company with bearer shares (that is, documents which entitle their holder to exercise shareholder rights, without a register or any other means by which to identify the beneficial owner). By no means did all the business relate to Panama, however. Many of the companies formed by Mossack Fonseca were registered in the British Virgin Islands.

As with all such scandals, the response of those in power is to promise a clampdown, and the UK, EU, US, and Organisation for Economic Co-operation and Development (OECD) all proposed action.[97] If there is to be significant change it will be by the establishment of registers of beneficial

[93] 'Geneva Prosecutor Agrees to Close Investigation into HSBC in Return for the Financial Settlement', *The Guardian*, 4 June 2015.

[94] National Audit Office, *Confiscation Orders* (HC 738, 2013–14) 4.

[95] And see 'What Are the Panama Papers? A Guide to History's Biggest Data Leak', *The Guardian*, 4 April 2016. <https://www.theguardian.com/news/2016/apr/03/what-you-need-to-know- about-the-panama-papers>.

[96] It turned out that David Cameron's father had operated such a company in Panama.

[97] 'Panama Papers: US Launches Crackdown on International Tax Evasion', *The Guardian*, 5 May 2016.

ownership of all legal entities and comprehensive and automatic exchange of information between jurisdictions on an international level, along the lines proposed by the OECD.[98]

HSBC Suisse and the *Panama Papers* have once again drawn attention to the issues surrounding the relationship between tax evasion and avoidance. Both are enormously important just in terms of sheer volume. We may not like either, but we should dislike them for different reasons. Attempts to equate 'aggressive' or any other form of avoidance with evasion should be resisted.

[98] See Chapter 10.

4

Criminal Evasion of Duties and Taxes

Types and Interrelationships of Criminal Offences

There are several oppositions that may describe the manner in which criminal offences are defined in any given jurisdiction, and these can be seen in the offences of tax evasion. Offences might be:

(i) common law offences or offences created by statute; and/or
(ii) specific or general offences; and/or
(iii) overlapping or mutually exclusive offences; and/or
(iv) tightly or vaguely drawn offences.

Common Law and Statutory Offences

The history of the movement for codification in criminal law has as its underpinning the idea that it would be better, both practically and constitutionally, if all criminal offences were to be set out in a code—or at least in some exhaustive set of statutes. It would be so practically, because it would be easier, both for lawyers and, ideally, for citizens, to find out what the law is. It would be so constitutionally, because decisions as to the extent of the criminal law would then be made principally by Parliament, which is what should happen in a democracy. The examples of the catch-all offences in Stalin's and Hitler's codes[1] show that it is the substance of the offences, not so much whether or not they are embodied in statute, that makes vague offences objectionable, but in any event matters so important as the definitions of our most serious crimes should be dealt with by Parliament and not be the results of judges making law.

[1] See Preuss, Lawrence, 'Punishment by Analogy in National Socialist Penal Law' (1936) 26 *Journal of Criminal Law and Criminology* 847; Hall, Jerome, 'Nulla Poena Sine Lege' (1937) 47 *Yale Legal Journal* 165.

Ambivalence about common law offences in this area is seen clearly in relation to the Theft Act 1968, apparently written as a comprehensive code yet retaining the two common law offences of conspiracy to defraud and cheat, the latter only so far as it relates to revenue fraud. 'Cheat' is the common law offence that remains central to tax evasion prosecutions. Sir John Smith said that the Criminal Law Revision Committee, when it considered theft,[2] wanted the offence of cheat to be abolished, but the Revenue did not concur,[3] and that was why cheat, which had been developed for reasons other than tax, was then abolished except so far as concerned its application to tax.

In spite of various efforts, from the Utilitarians to the Law Commission,[4] to codify English criminal law altogether, or at least to make particular areas of it subject to a comprehensive statute, the history of the law of theft has a strong, resilient thread running through it that Parliament should not express that entire body of law in a statute. The common law 'catch-all' offences have remained attractive to legislators, who doubt their own capacity to describe in advance the entirety of the dishonest conduct they wish to criminalize. In particular, despite various proposals[5] (in particular the attempt during the enactment of the Fraud Act 2006[6] to abolish conspiracy to defraud,[7] and the restrictions placed by the Theft Act 1968 upon cheat), fear of the unforeseen dishonest act has led to the retention of the common law offences of conspiracy to defraud and cheat. Notwithstanding the view, expressed by the Law Commission and others, that the offence has 'no place in a coherent criminal law',[8] and Lord Lloyd of Berwick's 'instinctive dislike ... of these catch-all

[2] Criminal Law Revision Committee, Eighth Report, *Theft and Related Offences*, Cmnd 2977 (1966).

[3] *R v Hunt* [1995] STC 819; (1995) 16 Cr App R (S) 87 noted by JCS at *R v Hunt* [1994] *Criminal Law Review* 747.

[4] Kadish, Sanford H, 'Codifiers of the Criminal Law: Wechsler's Predecessors' (1978) 78 *Columbia Law Review* 1098–144; Smith, KJM, *Lawyers, Legislators, and Theorists: Developments in English Criminal Jurisprudence 1800–1957* (Oxford: Oxford University Press, 1998); Farmer, Lindsay, 'Reconstructing the English Codification Debate: The Criminal Law Commissioners, 1833–45' (2000) *Law and History Review* 397–426. The project embodied in Law Commission Report No 177, *A Criminal Code for England and Wales* (1989) was finally abandoned in 2008: Law Commission Report No 311, *Tenth Programme of Law Reform* (2008).

[5] Law Commission Working Paper No 56, *Conspiracy to Defraud* (1974); Law Commission Report No 228, *Conspiracy to Defraud* (1994); Law Commission Consultation Paper No 155, *Legislating the Criminal Code: Fraud and Deception* (1999); Law Commission Report No 276, *Fraud* (Cm 5560, 2002).

[6] HC Debates, 12 Jun 2006 Col 543 (Vera Baird QC, S-G).

[7] And see Fraud Act 2006 explanatory notes, para 6: conspiracy to defraud retained 'for the time being'.

[8] Law Commission Report No 276, *Fraud* (Cm 5560, 2002).

offences such as conspiracy to defraud',[9] Parliament has repeatedly refused to take the plunge and place the matter entirely on a statutory footing.[10]

In *Dosanjh*[11] the Court of Appeal held that, since Parliament had expressly retained the common law offence of cheating the Revenue, with a penalty at large—despite putting in place the statutory offences of fraud and fraudulent evasion of value added tax (VAT), to which maximum penalties applied, and also despite imposing a maximum penalty for the common law offence of conspiracy to defraud[12]—cheating the Revenue retained its 'established role' in the prosecution of revenue offences, which was to 'supplement the statutory framework' by providing the appropriate charge for the most serious and unusual revenue frauds where the statutory framework would not adequately reflect the criminality involved and where an unrestricted sentence was more appropriate.[13]

Specific or General Offences?

Whether specific offences can provide a useful supplement to general ones is something considered from time to time. Thus, for example, in the case of manslaughter, there are arguments about the value of having specific offences to deal with various specific manifestations where death is caused by non-aggressive acts.[14] It seems to have been the trend at the time of the enactment of the Theft Act 1968 to favour fewer, and more general, offences dealing with fraud.[15] This is, however, nothing more than a matter of fashion, and the pendulum may now be swinging the other way.

General offences govern all areas of activity. Specific ones govern only particular areas. Thus, for example, manslaughter may be committed by any person in any way, but causing death by dangerous driving can only be committed by someone driving on public roads. In the context of tax evasion, the 'general offence' is usually a fraud offence and the specific offences are ones

[9] HL Debates, 22 June 2005 Col 1665. Conspiracy to defraud also survived the *Post-legislative Assessment of the Fraud Act 2006 carried out by the Ministry of Justice. Memorandum to the Justice Select Committee* (Cm 8372, 2012).

[10] 'Whether the Law Commission or academics like it or not, the broad umbrella offence of conspiracy to defraud is and has been for a long time part of our law.' *Norris v Government of the United States of America and others* [2007] EWHC 71 (Admin); [2007] 2 All ER 29 para 98 (Auld LJ).

[11] *R v Dosanjh* [2014] 1 WLR 1780.

[12] Ten years' imprisonment: Criminal Justice Act 1987 s 12(3).

[13] Para 32 *et seq.*

[14] Clarkson, Christopher MV, and Sally Cunningham (eds), *Criminal Liability for Non-aggressive Death* (Farnham: Ashgate, 2013).

[15] Hence its repeal of Income Tax Act 1952 s 505: Theft Act 1968 Schedule 3.

that can only be committed in respect of taxation, but there are also offences that are specific to one or more taxes.

There is no reason in principle why defendants in cases of tax evasion could not be charged, according to the facts of the individual cases, with general criminal offences, such as those under the Fraud Act 2006, false accounting or suppression of documents under the Theft Act 1968,[16] offences under the Forgery and Counterfeiting Act 1981, or the general offence of conspiracy to defraud.[17] While the 'abuse of process' doctrine[18] might inhibit some prosecutions where criminal offences overlap,[19] the existence of the more specific offence does not necessarily prevent the more general charge being brought. The Theft Act 1968[20] seems to have been written on the basis that it was to provide an incomplete but general code of property offences, and that no specific statutory offence was required for tax evasion, or some other particular areas,[21] and that prosecutions for tax evasion should be brought under its provisions.[22]

Since the move towards more general offences signalled in the Theft Act 1968, things have moved on. There has been a change of emphasis in the expression of criminal prohibitions away from the greatest possible generality. The landscape changed with two important developments. First, the move, in the Prosecution of Offences Act 1985, away from the historical root of the English prosecutions system—that all prosecutions are private—gave rise to rules that particular agencies should have powers to prosecute specific offences,[23] and that for others there could be a 'lead' prosecuting authority. The Prosecutors' Conventions 2009[24] operate best if as many as possible of the offences as to which there may be lack of clarity can be allocated in advance to specific bodies, and that is facilitated by having specific offences.

Second, the age of regulation, from about 1980 onwards, has given rise to the advent of regulatory bodies with prosecuting powers alongside powers to

[16] Theft Act 1968 ss 17 and 20.

[17] See this chapter, section entitled 'Common Law and Statutory Offences'.

[18] *R v Horseferry Road Magistrates' Court, ex p Bennett* [1994] 1 AC 42; *R v Maxwell* [2010] UKSC 48; [2011] 1 WLR 1837.

[19] *R v J* [2004] UKHL 42; [2005] 1 AC 562. Distinguished in *R v Phillips* [2007] EWCA Crim 485 and *R v Timmins* [2005] EWCA Crim 2909; [2006] 1 Cr App R 18. See Mirfield, Peter, 'A Challenge to the Declaratory Theory of Law' (2008) 124 *Law Quarterly Review* 190–5.

[20] Criminal Law Revision Committee, Eighth Report, *Theft and Related Offences*, Cmnd 2977 (1966).

[21] Hence the repeals in Schedule 3 of the Act.

[22] Usually deception offences (ss 15 and 16) or false accounting (s 17).

[23] Notwithstanding the difficulties in this area created by *R v Rollins* [2010] UKSC 39; [2010] 1 WLR 1922.

[24] <http://www.cps.gov.uk/legal/p_to_r/prosecutors__convention/>.

impose 'regulatory' fines. These agencies' powers of prosecution should be circumscribed in some way. If there is to be an agency charged with bringing tax prosecutions, separate from that which brings 'general' prosecutions (that is, the Crown Prosecution Service (CPS)), that agency's brief will need to be limited, either to tax prosecutions or to tax prosecutions plus some other designated offences. One way in which to accomplish that objective is to have separate offences, at least as the default for tax prosecutions, and to designate Her Majesty's Revenue and Customs (HMRC) the lead investigator and prosecutor for them.[25] The alternative approach would be to have a single agency dealing with economic crime, and not to differentiate tax evasion from other frauds. Both strategies are assisted by having specific tax offences, so as a consequence of these changes the established preference for offences specifically dealing with tax has been cemented.

Vague or Precise Definitions?

Vague definitions, and in particular the principle of analogy, may offend against the principle *nulla poena sine lege*[26] or Article 7 of the European Convention on Human Rights (ECHR).[27] Typically, though not necessarily, statutory offences are more precisely defined than common law ones. Both conspiracy to defraud and conspiracy to cheat have been criticized for their vagueness, but that is what makes them so attractive to prosecuting bodies. Instead of having to draft numerous specific counts and risk the effect of the rules on duplicity, one catch-all charge is very appealing.[28]

So far as concerns statutory offences, the normal rule, itself honoured more in the breach, that criminal statutes are to be construed strictly, has two supplementary and mutually countervailing influences. First, the 'purposive interpretation' line adopted, for example, in the *UBS* case[29] will frequently militate

[25] On the power of HMRC to prosecute see *R (on the application of Hunt) v Criminal Cases Review Commission (IRC, interested party)* [2001] QB 1108; [2000] STC 1110.

[26] See n 1.

[27] Though there is considerable scope for extension of existing offences on foreseeable lines. See *SW (and CR) v United Kingdom* (A/355-B) [1996] 1 FLR 434; (1996) 21 EHRR 363 and *Khodorkovskiy v Russia* (2014) 59 EHRR 7.

[28] A count on an indictment is bad for duplicity where it discloses allegations of more than one offence. Criminal Procedure Rules 2015 SI 1490 para 10.2(2) relaxes the rule so that '(2) More than one incident of the commission of the offence may be included in a count if those incidents taken together amount to a course of conduct having regard to the time, place or purpose of commission.' The view amongst prosecutors still seems to be that for fraud by representation there should be one charge per representation, but in conspiracy no representation is necessary and the issue is unresolved.

[29] *UBS AG v Commissioners for HMRC* [2016] UKSC 13.

towards holding that a statute does impose liability to taxation. Second, the influence of human rights considerations—not merely Article 7, but also the First Protocol to Article 1 (A1P1) of the ECHR—can have an impact.

Tax-specific or Not? Mutually Exclusive or Overlapping Offences?

Whether the enactment of a specific statutory offence excludes a pre-existing more general statutory or common law offence from a field will always present a question of construction of the relevant statute. Common law offences may be excluded expressly or impliedly, but the mere fact that legislation is in the same area does not necessarily exclude common law offences.[30] Whereas the common law offence of cheating the Revenue applies across all taxes, statutory offences apply each to its designated tax. This implies, for example, that it is a good defence to a charge of evasion of VAT in an importation case that the tax evaded was actually customs duty and not VAT.

When new taxes are put in place, crimes of evasion specific to those taxes are frequently, but not always, also put in place. Although the taxpayer's ability to regulate his/her conduct so as to comply with the law is not affected by whether or not s/he is able to know in advance whether evasion of a particular tax constitutes a specific statutory offence or a general common law one, it should be easier than it is to identify all the statutory evasion offences. There are no separate offences in respect of capital gains tax, inheritance tax, corporation tax, or the diverted profits tax, but in addition to evasion of income tax, customs, and VAT,[31] there *are* specific offences dealing with insurance premium tax,[32] landfill tax,[33] gaming duty,[34] climate change levy,[35] aggregates levy,[36] machine games duty,[37] and stamp duty land tax.[38] The reason for this appears to be that there is no summary jurisdiction for cheat, and it was thought important to have offences of evasion triable in magistrates' courts for these offences but not, apparently, evasion of corporation tax, inheritance tax, or the diverted profits tax. If—and the experience of the 'Grabiner' offence seems to suggest otherwise—magistrates' courts have a significant role to play in this area, neater solutions to that particular problem might have been to give magistrates' courts jurisdiction over cheat, or to

[30] *R v Seymour* [1983] 2 AC 493 (manslaughter and offences of causing death by driving).
[31] See this chapter, section entitled 'Common Law and Statutory Offences'.
[32] FA 1994 Schedule 7 Part IV. [33] FA 1996 Schedule 5 Part IV.
[34] FA 1997 Schedule 1. [35] FA 2000 Schedule 6 Part VIII.
[36] FA 2001 Schedule 6 Part 1. [37] FA 2012 Schedule 24. [38] FA 2003 s 95.

place the offence of cheat on a statutory footing, or to have a general statutory evasion applying to all taxes on a list, perhaps in a statutory schedule, that could be updated as and when necessary.

The Existing Criminal Charges

Rather than a single statute setting out a general tax evasion offence, with, perhaps, preparatory and consequential offences, there is a range of offences—some statutory, some common law, some widely defined, some quite specific. There are some offences to which the general law of complicity applies, some to which statutory forms of complicity are added that either replace or supplement the general offences, some which have specific offences of dealing with the property that is their subject matter, and some to which only the general law of 'post-crime' liability applies. Some taxes have their own evasion offences. Others do not and fall back on the common law of cheat, or general fraud offences.[39]

For anyone interested in the rational development of criminal law, or even legal aesthetics, this cannot be a satisfactory state of affairs. It might have been hoped that the renewed interest in tax evasion prosecutions signalled by the change in the CPS policy in 2013[40] and the *HSBC Suisse* scandal[41] would generate pressure for a set of offences expressed and organized on more rational grounds. There is much to be said for having one statute setting out the crimes of evasion, for those crimes to apply to evasion of all taxes, and, if there is to be an hierarchy of tax evasion, setting out those taxes whose evasion is most and whose least serious, and the other aggravating and mitigating factors. Inertia does, however, exert its own influence.

Smuggling Offences

Smuggling nowadays is charged under Part XII of the Customs and Excise Management Act 1979 (CEMA), which contains a series of offences.

[39] See this chapter, section entitled 'Specific or General Offences?'.

[40] And see 'Prosecuting Tax Evasion', Speech by Keir Starmer QC, Director of Public Prosecutions, 23 January 2013, <http://www.cps.govuk/news/articles/prosecuting_tax_evasion/>: see Chapter 10.

[41] See Chapter 3, section entitled 'The *HSBC Suisse* (2015) and Mossack Fonseca (*Panama Papers*) (2016) Scandals'.

The 'Tax Perjury' Offence

Ss 167 and 168 of CEMA set out the offence of making an untrue declaration. The offence is committed where the defendant 'knowingly or recklessly' makes a representation or statement which is untrue in any material particular 'for any purpose of any assigned matter' (that is, for the purposes of determining customs and excise liability). A lesser, strict liability offence[42] deals with such statements when not made 'knowingly or recklessly'. Section 167 is not used so much as a regular charge but is used to found forfeiture claims.[43] There is also a counterfeiting provision whose existence raises questions of overlap and redundancy.[44] If this offence were not available there would always be the possibility of a (more general) counterfeiting charge.[45]

The Major Smuggling Offences

The major provision under which smuggling charges are brought (whether for evasion of duty or for smuggling items that are entirely prohibited, for example drugs) is s 170 of CEMA, which includes two major sets of offences, both of wide scope. Section 170(1) relates to the smuggled goods. It puts in place the offences of knowing acquisition of possession contraband goods[46] and knowingly being concerned in 'carrying, removing, depositing, harbouring, keeping or concealing or in any manner dealing with any such goods',[47] in both cases 'with intent to defraud Her Majesty of any duty payable on the goods or to evade any such prohibition or restriction with respect to the goods'. Section 170(2) deals with the evaded duty. It is an offence knowingly to be concerned in any fraudulent evasion or attempt at evasion (a) of any duty chargeable on the goods; or (b) of any prohibition or restriction for the time being in force with respect to the goods under or by virtue of any enactment; or (c) of any provision of the Customs and Excise Acts 1979 applicable to the goods. There is a forfeiture provision.[48] Section 170(2) is wider in scope than s 170(1) on its wording and cannot be construed as applying only to those engaged in the initial illegal importation.[49] The elements of the s 170(2) offence are as follows.

[42] S 167(3).

[43] *Customs and Excise Commissioners v Everwine Ltd* [2003] EWCA Civ 953; *Customs and Excise Commissioners v Ghiselli* Unreported 1999 WL 33101332.

[44] CEMA s 168.

[45] Under the Forgery and Counterfeiting Act 1981.

[46] CEMA s 170(1)(a).

[47] CEMA s 170(1)(b).

[48] CEMA s 170(6).

[49] *R v Neal (John Frederick)* [1984] 3 All ER 156; (1983) 77 Cr App R 283.

Duty: The duty must be payable.[50] Liability to pay duty on goods which are imported arises at the 'duty point'.[51] If D is wrong in believing that duty is in fact payable, liability may arise for attempts, but confiscation proceedings are not available, there being no benefit.

Concerned: It is possible for a person to be 'concerned' in the fraudulent evasion without taking any actual steps to bring about the importation. If uncertainty over whether the importation would actually take place allowed D to escape liability, the effect of s 170(2)(b) would be weakened as it would not be unusual for such an enterprise to be subject to uncertainty.[52] To keep an unsolicited consignment of imported drugs may amount to being knowingly concerned in evasion of the prohibition on their importation.[53] Fraudulent evasion of the prohibition on the importation of goods requires dishonest conduct deliberately intended to evade the prohibition: there is no necessity for the prosecution to prove acts of deceit practised on a customs officer.[54]

Knowingly: 'Knowingly' in s 170 of CEMA means knowing that a fraudulent evasion of a prohibition against importing goods was taking place. For the purposes of a conviction for being knowingly concerned in the fraudulent evasion of a prohibition on the importation of goods, the prosecution does not have to prove that the defendant was aware of the exact nature of the goods he was importing, but only that he was aware that the goods he was importing were prohibited.[55] Thus a person was guilty of being knowingly concerned in the fraudulent evasion of the prohibition against the importation of a controlled drug where he mistakenly believed the goods to be pornographic films subject to a prohibition against importation.[56] 'Knowingly

[50] *R v Bell* [2011] EWCA Crim 6 (appeals against confiscation orders were allowed where the appellants, who had pleaded guilty to being knowingly concerned in the fraudulent evasion of the duty chargeable on cigarettes, had not been liable to pay the duty themselves and therefore had not obtained a pecuniary advantage in relation to it). But see *R v Tatham* [2014] EWCA Crim 226; [2014] Lloyd's Rep FC 354 and *R v Eddishaw* [2014] EWCA Crim 2783; [2015] Lloyd's Rep FC 212.

[51] In the case of smuggled tobacco, when goods are being smuggled into the UK with the intention of avoiding the payment of any duty due on them, the evasion will take place when the vessel enters the limits of the port: *R v B* [2011] EWCA Crim 1093; [2012] 1 WLR 601.

[52] *Attorney General's Reference (No 1 of 1998)* (1999) 163 JP 390; *The Times*, 2 October 1998; *R v Caippara* (1988) 87 Cr App R 316.

[53] *R v Caippara* (1988) 87 Cr App R 316. C's sister sent him from Bolivia a package containing cocaine. Customs officers intercepted the package in England, and substituted baking powder for the cocaine. C accepted the package as his. He kept the powder, assuming it to be cocaine. He was convicted under s 107(2), because the importation was complete by the time of the interception and the substitution of the baking powder made no difference.

[54] *Attorney General's Reference (No 1 of 1981)* [1982] QB 848; (1982) 75 Cr App R 45.

[55] *R v Forbes* [2001] UKHL 40; [2002] 2 AC 512.

[56] *R v Ellis* (1987) 84 Cr App R 235; [1987] Crim LR 44.

concerned' involved not merely knowledge of a smuggling operation but also knowledge that the substance in question was one the importation of which was prohibited; where a man's state of mind and knowledge were ingredients of the offence charged, he was to be judged on the facts as he believed them to be.[57] 'Knowingly' is to be judged at the time of the involvement, not that of the importation.[58]

'To be concerned' is a formulation which implies that the defendant is guilty without the prosecution having to allege and prove the precise role s/he undertook in the commission of the offence. Section 170(2) could not be construed as applying only to those engaged in the initial illegal importation. It means that the prosecution need not specify in the indictment that the defendant's own conduct is able to be described by the verb in the prohibition.

Evasion: 'Evade' was defined in a Theft Act 1968 case as follows:

[a]n obligation is evaded if by some contrivance the debtor avoids or gets out of fulfilling or performing his obligation. In the days when such things happened, a welshing bookmaker not only evaded his pursuers, he also evaded his obligations. Evasion does not necessarily mean permanent escape. If the bookmaker evaded his pursuers on Monday, the fact that he is caught and made to pay up on Tuesday does not alter the fact that he evaded his obligations on Monday. Unlike reducing and deferring an obligation, evading an obligation is a unilateral operation. It leaves the obligation untouched and does not connote any activity on the part of the creditor. When the evasion ceases he can seek to recover the debt in any way open to him.[59]

'Fraudulent evasion' imports the *Ghosh* notion of dishonesty.[60]

Evasion of Income Tax

Prosecutions for income tax evasion have always been proportionately rare, compared, for example, to social security or insurance frauds.[61] During the nineteenth and twentieth centuries, civil sanctions were the preferred option against evaders and the only criminal prosecutions were in the most egregious

[57] *R v Taaffe* [1984] AC 539; [1984] 1 All ER 747.

[58] *R v Jakeman* (1983) 76 Cr App R 223; [1983] Crim LR 104.

[59] *DPP v Turner* [1974] AC 357; [1973] 3 All ER 124 at 127, HL, per Lord Reid.

[60] *Attorney General's Reference (No 1 of 1981)* [1982] QB 848; (1982) 75 Cr App R 45 was decided shortly before *Ghosh* but refers to dishonesty. On dishonesty see this chapter, section entitled 'Concluding—Offence Definitions and Reform Options'.

[61] Usually of making a false representation to obtain benefit, contrary to s 111A(1a), or failing to notify a change of circumstances to obtain benefit, contrary to s 111A(1A) Social Security Administration Act 1992.

cases—typically where there had been a 'Hansard procedure'[62] enquiry[63] during which the taxpayer lied, particularly when the defendant had a high public profile.[64] The Grabiner Report concluded in 2000 that 'for tax evasion, the current system seems to work well'.[65] Three main reasons are usually given for the Revenue's historical aversion to prosecution: first, that the overriding objective of the Inland Revenue was to collect taxes in order to finance wars and build schools and hospitals, and that it should get involved in the expensive collateral use of the criminal law only where so to do would contribute towards its success in raising revenue; second, that the Revenue has such extensive powers to secure the money from the taxpayer, including the ability to impose penalties at its own instance, that it did not need the criminal sanction; and third, that under the rules of evidence on the charges then applicable, it was unusually difficult to secure convictions.

In the past twenty-five years the public statements of the HMRC position regarding prosecution for evasion have altered, for five main reasons. First, there has been a shift in public perceptions of tax evasion. The financial crisis of 2007–8 has directed attention towards crimes in the financial markets. Although these were not principally tax crimes,[66] an enhanced public appetite for the prosecution of financial criminals will undoubtedly include enthusiasm for increased prosecution rates in respect of tax crimes. Second, there have been institutional changes. The way in which tax prosecutions are organized has been altered so that there are now people the main part of whose job, and the major function of the institution for which they work, it is to bring these prosecutions. Prosecution is no longer an adjunct to tax collection. Third, there has been a change in the financial incentives for prosecution as against other dispositions, which has made prosecution a more lucrative option to HMRC. Fourth, globalization has prompted a shift in approaches to tax evasion. The

[62] See Chapter 7, section entitled 'The Hansard Procedure'.

[63] The author was approached by the makers of a drama series set in the late 1950s and early 1960s for a plot line in which one of the characters was at serious risk of imprisonment in England for tax fraud. The Hansard procedure was incorporated into the plot. See Lionsgate Inc, *Mad Men* Series Five, Episodes 11 ('The Other Woman') and 12 ('Commissions and Fees').

[64] Noteworthy are the successful prosecution of the Jockey Lester Piggott in 1987, the unsuccessful prosecution of the comedian Ken Dodd in 1989, and the costly (£8 million—*Daily Telegraph*, 9 February 2012) failed prosecution of football manager Harry Redknapp in 2012, also after an unlawful search was conducted: *R (on the application of Redknapp) v Commissioner of the City of London Police* [2008] EWHC 1177 (Admin); [2009] 1 WLR 2091.

[65] HM Treasury, *The Informal Economy: The Grabiner Report* (London: HM Treasury, 2000).

[66] In addition to reckless borrowing and lending, which has only since been criminalized (Financial Services (Banking Reform) Act 2013 s 36), criminal proceedings were brought (belatedly) for market manipulation offences in respect of the LIBOR (*R v Hayes* [2015] EWCA Crim 1944) and other rate manipulation scandals.

traditional 'Westphalian' doctrine was embodied in the 'Revenue Rule' that one country would not assist another in the enforcement of its tax law,[67] so tax offences tended not to be covered by extradition treaties and arrangements for mutual legal assistance. The fact that tax offences are now covered by international agreements makes a significant difference. Fifth, the substantive and procedural law has changed to make it easier to secure convictions. Until 2000, all prosecutions had to be brought in the Crown Court. The idea (not wholly successful) of the 'Grabiner' offence was to use magistrates' courts more. The current HMRC prosecution policy[68] and its consequences will be evaluated presently.[69]

The Early Statutory Offences

In spite of there being little enthusiasm until much later for prosecutions of tax evaders,[70] making a fraudulent income tax return was criminal from the outset, and was characterized in the early statutes as a form of perjury.[71] Section 180 of the Income Tax Act 1842 made it an offence:

if any Person, upon any Examination on Oath or Affirmation, or in any Affidavit, Deposition, or Affirmation authorized by this Act, shall wilfully and corruptly give false Evidence, or shall wilfully and corruptly swear or affirm any Matter or Thing which shall be false or untrue.

That is, the essence of the original statutory offence was not so much intent to defraud (although the adverb 'corruptly' does appear) but rather swearing falsely. The taxpayer completing a return, or giving evidence before the Special Commissioners,[72] was placed in a position of solemn obligation to tell

[67] *King of the Hellenes v Brostrom* (1923) 16 Ll L Rep 167, see Chapter 1; Lord Keith of Avonholm in *Government of India v Taylor* [1955] AC 491 at 511. And see Harris, Peter and David Oliver, *International Commercial Tax* (Cambridge: Cambridge University Press, 2010) at 466, and Chapter 8 of this book.

[68] HMRC Criminal Investigation Policy (2015, <http://www.hmrc.govuk/prosecutions/crim-inv-policy.htm>, accessed 5 April 2016). For an apologia see Fisher, Jonathan, 'HSBC, Tax Evasion and Criminal Prosecution' (2015) *Tax Journal* 1253, 2 March 2015, <https://www.taxjournal.com/articles/hsbc-tax-evasion-and-criminal-prosecution-02032015>.

[69] See Chapter 10.

[70] Williams, David, 'Surveying Taxes, 1900–14' [2005] *British Tax Review* 222 at 240–1. On the earlier use of the law for reasons which attracted suspicion from employers see Colley, Robert, 'Mid Victorian Employees and the Taxman: A Study in Information Gathering by the State in 1860' (2001) 21 *Oxford Journal of Legal Studies* 593–608.

[71] Income Tax Act 1842 s 55 seems to have contemplated a less serious crime (maximum penalty £50) for failure by third parties to furnish required information. S 55 was re-enacted by Income Tax Act 1918 s 107, re-enacted by Income Tax Act 1952 s 25(3) *et seq*, repealed and replaced by FA 1960 s 46, and consolidated as s 98 TMA, which has been subject to many amendments. (I am grateful to Richard Walters for drawing this sequence to my attention.)

[72] *R v Hood Barrs* [1943] 1 KB 455; [1943] 1 All ER 665, CCA.

the truth, and, where s/he failed, was treated as a perjurer. When s 180 was repealed and re-enacted in 1911,[73] it remained a form of perjury—indeed more so, since it was then expressed in the Perjury Act 1911, and operated under the particularly onerous rules on proof of perjury.[74] Prosecutions do not seem to have been encouraged by the facts that the adverb 'corruptly', whose meaning was much debated in the context of bribery offences,[75] no longer appears (as it did in the earlier legislation confined to tax), and that 'knowingly and wilfully' does not import motive.[76]

Section 5 of the Perjury Act 1911 imposed a maximum prison term of two years, together with or alternatively to a fine, for materially false statements knowingly and wilfully made in documents required by an Act of Parliament. It eventually came to be thought in England[77] to be a better route to a criminal conviction for evaders. Even so, the first prosecution reported under this Act was not until 1916, by which time public feeling may have been less sympathetic to tax evasion because of the War and, in any event, the star of cheat was in the ascendant. The defendant in this case received four months' imprisonment.[78] It appears that the requirement for supplementary evidence[79] presented difficulties to prosecutors. This would have been more of a problem before relaxations upon the admissibility of hearsay evidence[80] than it would currently. Although s 5 remains in force and is used in other contexts,[81] it is no longer used in tax evasion cases.

Cheating the Revenue

Cheat has developed from obscure common law origins[82] and, in spite of the availability at all relevant times of appropriate statutory offences,

[73] Perjury Act 1911 s 5.

[74] In which regard the 1911 Act restated the common law: Lord Hailsham of St Marylebone in *DPP v Kilbourne* [1973] AC 729; [1973] 1 All ER 440; [1973] AC at 740.

[75] Competing meanings of 'corruptly', from *Cooper v Slade* (1858) 6 HL Cas 746 forward, are set out in Law Commission Consultation Paper No 145, *Legislating the Criminal Code: Corruption* (1997) para 4.13 *et seq*.

[76] *R v Sood* [1998] 2 Cr App R 355; (1999) 47 BMLR 166.

[77] It did not apply in Scotland or Ireland.

[78] Williams, n 70, 222 at 240, citing [1916] QR at 247 and adding that an additional charge of conspiracy to defraud had not been pursued.

[79] Introduced by Perjury Act 1911 s 13. It is not, strictly speaking, a corroboration requirement. The provision states: 'A person shall not be liable to be convicted of any offence against this Act, or of any offence declared by any other Act to be perjury or subornation of perjury, or to be punishable as perjury or subornation of perjury solely upon the evidence of one witness as to the falsity or any statement alleged to be false.' See *R v O'Connor* [1980] *Criminal Law Review* 43.

[80] Criminal Evidence Act 1965; Criminal Justice Act 1988; Criminal Justice Act 2003.

[81] *R v Cowley-Hurlock* [2014] EWCA Crim 170.

[82] And see Watchful, 'Common Law Revenue Offences' [1956] *British Tax Review* 119; Ormerod, David, 'Cheating the Public Revenue' [1998] *Criminal Law Review* 627–45.

has come to be the principal weapon in the hands of prosecutors dealing with tax evasion.[83] Cheat is a common law offence, deriving from the institutional writers[84] and some rather unclear case law. It is not limited to income tax.[85] To contemporary eyes, the early cases[86] that gave it rise to look more like conspiracy to defraud or misconduct in public office, a matter under review by the Law Commission.[87] *Vreones*,[88] an important case in the development of the crime, involved a charge of cheat where conspiracy to defraud was unavailable as a charge because the accused were married, and married people could not be convicted of conspiring one with another.[89] Cheat came to be the standard charge for evasion in the period after the First World War.[90]

The offence of cheating the public revenue is a Group A offence within the Criminal Justice Act 1993[91] and is a 'serious offence' for the purposes of the Serious Crime Prevention Order provisions.[92] In the light of its origins, it is striking that it was abolished in 1968, 'except as regards offences relating to the public revenue',[93] but so far as the public revenue is concerned it remains indictable only even though statutory offences could be charged on the facts.[94]

The offence may be committed by, for example, submitting to the inspector of taxes incorrect accounts and a certificate of disclosure, knowing them to be false, with intent to defraud the Revenue, or by causing a false tax document to

[83] See the account of the statutory offence in this chapter, section entitled 'The Statutory Offence of Fraudulent Evasion'.

[84] 1 Hawk PC 322; 2 East PC 821.

[85] There appears to be no guidance on the extent of 'the public revenue' for these purposes, but it has been applied to benefits and to local government finances, and hence to council tax fraud and council tax benefit fraud: *R v Russell* [2014] EWCA Crim 1747; *R v Shahid* [2009] EWCA Crim 831; [2009] 2 Cr App R (S) 105; *R v Sturgess* [2009] EWCA Crim 169.

[86] Especially *R v Bembridge* (1783) 3 Doug KB 327; 22 State Tr 1 as explained in *R v Hudson* [1956] 2 QB 252; 40 Cr App Rep 55. On *Bembridge* itself see Horder, Jeremy, *Rex v Bembridge* (1783) in Mares, Henry, Phil Handler, and Ian Williams (eds), *Landmark Cases in Criminal Law* (Oxford: Bloomsbury, 2017) 81–101.

[87] Law Commission, *Misconduct in Public Office Issues Paper 1: The Current Law* (2016).

[88] *R v Vreones* [1891] 1 QB 360.

[89] A common law rule given statutory form in Criminal Law Act 1977 s 2(2).

[90] According to Sir Reginald Manningham-Buller QC, A-G, *arguendo* in *R v Hudson* [1956] 2 QB 252; 40 Cr App Rep 55 at 257, the charge of cheat had been first used in 1917 and subsequently, successfully, in a hundred cases since then (that is, an average of two or three cases per year). And see Watchful, n 82; *R v Bradbury, R v Edlin* (1920) [1956] 2 QB 262n (and on another point *R v Bradbury, R v Edlin* [1921] 1 KB 562; (1921) 15 Cr App R 76, CCA).

[91] Pt I (ss 1–6) (see s 1, and para 355).

[92] Serious Crime Act 2007 Pt 1 (ss 1–43): see s 2(2)(a), Schedule 1 para 8(5).

[93] Theft Act 1968 s 32(1)(a).

[94] Theft Act 1968 s 32(2). *R v Redford* (1988) 89 Cr App Rep 1, CA. See also *R v Mulligan* [1990] STC 220, CA.

be delivered with such intent.[95] Cheat does not require any positive act of deception either by words or conduct, but may include any form of conduct (including an omission by the defendant to do what he was legally obliged to do).[96] In this respect the offence is, however, no broader than the 'Grabiner' offence whose definition states specifically that an omission will suffice.[97] Fraud on the public revenue is indictable, even though the particular fraud might not have been indictable had it been a fraud on one individual by another.[98]

The act must be performed with intent to defraud the revenue which results in diverting money from the revenue and in depriving the revenue of money to which it is entitled.[99] The offence of cheating the public revenue is a 'conduct offence' and consequently the prosecution does not have to prove that the defendant caused actual loss.[100] The existence of the common law offence of cheat implies that conspiring to cheat is an offence.[101] There were suggestions[102] that cheat might offend Article 7 of the ECHR, but as the jurisprudence of Article 7 has developed, it has become clear that the offence would apparently have to be considerably vaguer even than it is to fall foul.[103] The common law offence of cheat is, in practice, reserved for serious offences rather than conventional cases. Taxi drivers who under-declare, when charged at all, are charged under the (summary) 'Grabiner' offence.

Conduct

The modern definition of cheat was set out in *R v Less*:[104]

Cheating can include any form of fraudulent conduct which results in diverting money from the Revenue and in depriving the Revenue of the money to which it is

[95] *R v Hudson* [1956] 2 QB 252; 40 Cr App Rep 55.

[96] *R v Mavji* [1987] 1 WLR 1388; 84 Cr App R 34 and *R v Dimsey; R v Allen* (CA) [1999] STC 846, 859, per Laws LJ.

[97] TMA s 106A(4).

[98] *R v Hudson*; see this chapter, section entitled 'Cheating the Revenue'.

[99] *R v Mavji* [1987] 1 WLR 1388, 84 Cr App R 34, CA (conviction for cheating public revenue upheld where defendant had fraudulently failed to make VAT returns and to pay VAT due); applied in *R v Redford* (1988) 89 Cr App Rep 1, CA.

[100] *R v Hunt* [1995] STC 819; (1995) 16 Cr App R (S) 87; [1994] *Criminal Law Review* 747, CA.

[101] Criminal Law Act 1977. *R v Mulligan* [1990] STC 220. When the *HSBC Suisse* scandal broke, Lord (Ken) MacDonald QC, a former DPP, suggested it could have been deployed against the bank: 'HSBC Should Face UK Criminal Charges, Says Former Public Prosecutor', *The Observer*, 22 February 2015.

[102] Virgo, Graham, 'Cheating the Public Revenue: Fictions and Human Rights' (2002) 61 *Cambridge Law Journal* 47.

[103] *SW (and CR) v United Kingdom* (A/355-B) [1996] 1 FLR 434; (1996) 21 EHRR 363 (court removes marital rape immunity: no violation).

[104] *R v Less, The Times*, 30 March 1993; 1993 WL 965668.

entitled.[105] *It has, of course, to be fraudulent conduct. That is to say, deliberate conduct by the defendant to prejudice, or take the risk of prejudicing, the Revenue's right to the tax in question, knowing that he has no right to do so.*

Mental state

The mental state required for cheating the revenue is that the defendant must be held by the jury to have been dishonest in the sense defined in *Ghosh*:[106]

> *You must first of all decide whether according to the ordinary standards of reasonable and decent people as determined by yourselves what was done in respect of the non-payment of tax was dishonest. If it was not dishonest by those standards that is the end of the matter and the prosecution fails. If it was dishonest by those standards then you must consider a further question. That is to say, whether the defendant himself must have realized what he was doing was those standard of reasonable and decent people dishonest. If your answer to that second question, if you come to it, is, 'Yes, we are sure', then convict. If your answer is, 'No', or, 'We are not sure', then acquit.*[107]

Actual *Ghosh* directions are not necessary in all cases, and can be misleading.[108] The *Ghosh* test might not be perfect, but it has proved a workable test for juries to apply in most Theft Act and Fraud Act areas.[109] The fundamental difficulty in applying it in the area of tax evasion is that it is designed to apply *ex post*. *Ghosh* does not provide any basis upon which for a lawyer to advise a client considering a possible course of action, and this is a scenario which may well develop in tax evasion.

The oddness of the declaratory theory of the common law—the idea that when a judge states the law in a common law area, s/he states what always has been the law—is demonstrated by the fact that the common law offence of cheat has acquired a component—dishonesty in the *Ghosh* sense—deriving from an interpretation placed in 1981 upon a statute enacted in 1968. A further lingering peculiarity of cheat is that a nation that prosecuted a civil war to place taxation on a statutory basis[110] has on numerous occasions fought shy of putting the definitions of the crimes of tax evasion on a similar footing.

[105] In *Rossminster*, Lord Denning MR in the Court of Appeal mentioned 'the common law offence of making a false statement relating to income tax in an attempt to defraud the revenue, which is dealt with in Archbold, *Criminal Pleading Evidence & Practice*, 40th ed, para 3547' ([1980] AC at 978). This is not an offence distinct from cheat, nor is cheat specific to income tax.

[106] *R v Ghosh* [1982] QB 1053; 75 Cr App R 154.

[107] This is the direction in *Less*, n 104.

[108] *R v Price* (1990) 90 Cr App R 409; *R v Coulson* 2000 WL 989462.

[109] It had quickly replaced the earlier (and widely criticized) *Feely (R v Feely* [1973] QB 530) test.

[110] Bill of Rights 1689 (1 W & M c 2) Article 4.

The Statutory Offence of Fraudulent Evasion

From 1910,[111] there was a statutory summary offence of knowingly making a false statement for the purpose of obtaining any allowance, reduction, rebate, or repayment in respect of any duty,[112] but it does not seem to have been widely used and the provision was repealed for England and Wales by the Theft Act 1968.[113] It remains in force in Scotland.[114] The Grabiner Report[115] recommended the (re-)creation of a specific summary statutory offence. It suggested that this offence could be based on the offences of fraudulent evasion that already existed for VAT[116] and in respect of National Insurance contributions, and should be triable either way. In consequence, in 2000, a statutory offence of fraudulent evasion of income tax was put in place.[117] The provision was subsequently relocated.[118] It has not proved a tremendous success. Prosecuting 'Grabiners' (as they are known)—most frequently under-declaration by taxi drivers and construction workers[119]—is expensive, and a bench of lay magistrates may not be best placed to understand the necessary evidence. The elements are that the defendant be: (a) 'knowingly concerned' in the (b) 'fraudulent evasion' of income tax by him or any other person. The meaning of these expressions is as for their use in other 'fraudulent evasion' offences.[120]

The Overseas Evasion Offence

In consequence of growing concern about overseas evasion, and in particular the *HSBC Suisse* scandal, pressure grew for legislation dealing specifically with offshore evasion. The Finance Act 2016 inserted provisions in the Taxes

[111] FA 1910 s 94. Consolidated so far as concerns tax, Income Tax Act 1918 s 227, Income Tax Act 1952 s 505.

[112] And see *R v Bradbury, R v Edlin* [1921] 1 KB 562; (1921) 15 Cr App R 76.

[113] Theft Act 1968 Schedule 3 Part 1.

[114] Consolidated again by TMA s 107. On prosecution powers see *Houston v MacDonald* 1989 SLT 276; 1988 SCCR 611.

[115] *Grabiner Report*, n 65.

[116] See this chapter, section entitled 'Value Added Tax'.

[117] FA 2000 s 144. And see Salter, David, 'Some Thoughts on Fraudulent Evasion of Income Tax' [2002] *British Tax Review* 489; Ormerod, David, 'Summary Evasion of Income Tax' [2002] *Criminal Law Review* 3–24. And see *Mauro v Government of the United States of America* [2009] EWHC 150 (Admin).

[118] To be TMA s 106A: Taxation (International and Other Provisions) Act 2010 Schedule 7, Part 16.

[119] Sigala, Maria, *Social Norms, Occupational Groups and Income Tax Evasion: A Survey in the UK Construction Industry* (Maidenhead: Open University, 2000).

[120] See this chapter, section entitled 'The Statutory Offence of Fraudulent Evasion'.

Management Act 1970 (TMA) to create an offence for which it is not necessary to show either intention or dishonesty. It will be considered later.[121]

Value Added Tax

As value added tax (VAT) was to be based on transactions and invoices, in which Customs and Excise had greater experience than the Inland Revenue, the control of the tax was laid to the Commissioners of Customs and Excise.[122] The relevant legislation was last consolidated in 1994[123] and has been amended textually thereafter. VAT accounts for about 20 per cent of the UK's total tax receipts,[124] and losses as a consequence of fraud, particularly missing trader intra-community (MTIC) frauds, have been substantial. Perhaps because of this, and perhaps because of the use of Customs and Excise in the collection of VAT rather than the Inland Revenue, VAT frauds have tended to be prosecuted proportionately more than other evasion offences.[125] HMRC lists and describes various types of VAT frauds.[126] Particular attention has been given to MTIC frauds.

The classical form of a MTIC fraud takes place where goods, usually of high value, are imported from the European Community into this country, without the addition of VAT because they are zero rated. They are then sold on to a United Kingdom company. The importer of the goods charges VAT on this sale but fails to account for it to Customs and diverts it. The goods then become the subject of a series of onward sales in the United Kingdom, which may generate small VAT liabilities on the mark-up which are duly paid. At the end of this chain, the goods are exported and VAT reclaimed from Customs. In many cases, the goods that are the subject of the apparent importations do not exist, and if they do exist are never imported, but documents purporting to evidence their sale and purchase are produced. Whether the goods do or do not exist is irrelevant to the fraud (which involves the re-export or apparent re-export of the goods).[127]

One response by HMRC to suspected MTIC fraud is not to pay the money claimed, and that has generated its own case law.[128] As elsewhere, the tax must be payable and points of domestic and EU law will arise as

[121] See Chapter 8. [122] Value Added Tax Act 1983 Schedule 7.

[123] Value Added Tax Act 1994 (VATA).

[124] HMRC Tax and NIC receipts June 2016.

[125] And see Leigh, Edward (Chair), Public Accounts Committee, *Tackling VAT Fraud*, Thirty-Sixth Report (HC 512, 2004).

[126] VATF23000. [127] *R v Takkar* [2011] All ER (D) 217.

[128] *Mobilx Ltd (In Administration) v Revenue and Customs Commissioners* [2010] EWCA Civ 517; [2010] STC 1436.

to the original liability.[129] Where the criminal offences are used for these or other VAT frauds,[130] the 'fraudulent evasion' offence of VAT[131] covers knowingly being concerned in, or in the taking of steps with a view to, the fraudulent evasion of VAT by him or any other person. The deception offence penalizes the production with intent to deceive or use of false documents, or making false statements.[132]

Subsection 72(8) contains a further offence, where HMRC is unable to specify the particulars of an offence.[133]

(8) Where a person's conduct during any specified period must have involved the commission by him of one or more offences under the preceding provisions of this section, then, whether or not the particulars of that offence or those offences are known, he shall, by virtue of this subsection, be guilty of an offence.

This is of jurisprudential significance. The provision seems to create an offence to which the normal procedural constraints upon prosecutions do not apply. Compelling the prosecution to allege particulars is a corollary of the rule of law. The defendant should be told in reasonably precise terms the wrong which is alleged against him/herself. This kind of erosion of the normal due process is what tends to happen in the offences to prevent which there is most concern. Sir John Smith[134] suggested that

[Section 72(8)] appears to be designed to meet the case where the jury is sure that the defendant committed an offence under [subsection (1) or subsection (3)] but is unable to say which. The necessity for the unanimity of the jury is no less than in any other criminal offence.

Inheritance Tax and Corporation Tax

The single estate duty was put in place in 1894.[135] Capital transfer tax (CTT) replaced it in 1975. The tax was charged both on transfers upon death and *inter vivos*. CTT was renamed inheritance tax in 1986.[136] The most common inheritance tax frauds are to do with the valuation of the estate. Corporation tax was introduced in 1965.[137] There is no specific evasion offence for either

[129] Eg *R v Goodwin (John Charles)* (C-3/97) European Court of Justice (First Chamber) [1998] QB 883; [1998] STC 699.

[130] Ie those under VATA s 72. [131] S 72(1). [132] VATA s 72(3).

[133] There is also a 'handling' offence: VATA s 72(10)—and see this chapter, section entitled 'After the substantive offence—the customs handling offence'.

[134] Note to *R v Choudhury (Khaled)* [1996] STC 1163; [1996] 2 Cr App R 484 [1996] *Criminal Law Review* 657, mentioning *R v Asif* [1985] *Criminal Law Review* 679 and *R v Mitchell* [1994] *Criminal Law Review* 66, all decided under s 39(3) of the 1983 Act, which was in identical terms to VATA s 72(8).

[135] FA 1894 Part 1. [136] FA 1986 s 100. [137] FA 1965 Part IV.

tax. Where criminal proceedings are used, they are charged as cheating the Revenue or under one of the non-tax-specific offences.

Stamp Duty and Stamp Duty Land Tax

Stamp duty was a tax upon various types of documents and transactions.[138] In the United Kingdom, stamp duty was a form of tax charged on instruments (that is, written documents),[139] and historically required a physical stamp to be attached to or impressed upon the instrument in question.[140] Stamp duty land tax is imposed, among other things, on house sales. The transaction is charged at what now[141] is a progressive rate. Under the previous regime, the entirety of the transaction was taxed at one rate, the rates being in bands according to the value of the property. This led to an evasion technique being adopted of over-valuing the contents, which were not subject to stamp duty, and undervaluing the real property.[142] From 2003, save on particular stock or marketable securities,[143] stamp duty was abolished. Stamp duty land tax was put in place on land transactions. It carries its own offence of fraudulent evasion,[144] written in terms identical (save for the word 'income') to that now in the TMA dealing with income tax.[145] There is an additional offence of assisting in the preparation of an incorrect return.[146] As elsewhere, the common law cheat offence could also be used.

Offences Ancillary to Tax Evasion

The range of substantive offences dealing with tax evasion is hardly neat and consistent, but it is as nothing compared to the ad hoc provisions in respect of offences ancillary to them. The normal range of offences of complicity and assisting and encouraging[147] apply to all the offences just described,

[138] For whose history see Oats, Lynne, and Pauline Sadler, '"This Great Crisis in the Republick of Letters"—The Introduction in 1712 of Stamp Duties on Newspapers and Pamphlets' [2002] *British Tax Review* 353.

[139] Stamp Duty Administration Act 1891 s 13 still applies only to documents kept overseas. It is more a forgery offence than one of evasion.

[140] From the Taxation Act 1756 (29 Geo 2 c 13), playing cards carried the duty, shown by an elaborate stamp on the Ace of Spades, forging which was made capital under Stamp Duties on Cards and Dice Act 1828 (9 Geo 4 c 18) s 35.

[141] As a result of changes announced by the 2014 Autumn Statement.

[142] And see, eg, *Tinsley v Milligan* [1994] 1 AC 340.

[143] Stamp duty reserve tax was created in 1986. FA 2003 s 125.

[144] FA 2003 s 95.

[145] See this chapter, section entitled 'The Statutory Offence of Fraudulent Evasion'. The definition in FA 2003 s 121 states that the meaning of the word 'tax' is restricted to stamp duty land tax.

[146] FA 2003 s 96.

[147] Ormerod, David, and Karl Laird, *Smith & Hogan's Criminal Law* (Oxford: Oxford University Press, 14th edn, 2015) 184 *et seq*.

and extended accessorial liability[148] is imposed by a set of specific statutory offences. These offences vary from tax to tax. It is also, and more generally, an offence to go equipped to cheat.[149] Proof is required that the defendant had the article for the purpose or with the intention that it be used in the course of or in connection with the offence, but if that is shown then a general intention to commit fraud will suffice.[150]

It is an offence to take steps preparatory to the fraudulent evasion of excise duty.[151] It is an offence not merely knowingly to be concerned to take steps with a view to the fraudulent evasion of VAT, but also, and more specifically, to produce, furnish, send, or otherwise make a document.[152] There is no offence relating to income tax, CGT, or corporation tax equivalent to the Customs and Excise 'preparatory steps' offence,[153] but many of the definitions of the statutory evasion offences include knowingly 'taking ... steps with a view to, the fraudulent evasion of [whatever the tax is]'. So long as more than one person is involved, conspiracy to cheat or to defraud can always be charged for behaviour before the substantive offence.

In its extension of the law of attempts (which introduces liability only when there is an act 'more than merely preparatory to the commission of' the offence[154]), the CEMA offence is the forerunner of the equivalent offence in respect of the offence of terrorism,[155] an indication of the seriousness with which excise offences have always been regarded. There are supplementary offences[156] involving falsification of documents that one has been required to produce or deliver (forgery or fraud offences).[157]

After the substantive offence—the customs handling offence

There are some tax offences akin to that of handling stolen goods.[158] They are directed against dealing in the proceeds of tax evasion, either by, for example,

[148] And see Law Commission Consultation Paper No 183, *Conspiracy and Attempts* (HMSO, 2007) Appendix C for a list of such offences. Clarkson, Christopher, 'Attempt: The Conduct Requirement' (2009) 29 *Oxford Journal of Legal Studies* 25–41.

[149] Theft Act 1968 s 25; and see Ormerod, David, and David Williams, *Smith's Law of Theft* (Oxford: Oxford University Press, 9th edn, 2007) ch 9, and also possession of articles for fraud (Fraud Act 2006 s 6) and making or supplying articles for use in frauds (s 7).

[150] *R v Ellames* [1974] 1 WLR 1391; 60 Cr App R 7 (CA).

[151] CEMA s 170B, inserted by F(No 2)A 1992 Schedule 2 para 8.

[152] VATA s 72(3). [153] CEMA s 170B. [154] Criminal Attempts Act 1981 s 1.

[155] Terrorism Act 2006 s 5. See Hodgson, Jacqueline, and Victor Tadros, 'How to Make a Terrorist Out of Nothing' (2009) 72 *Modern Law Review* 984–98.

[156] TMA s 20BB. [157] And compare CEMA s 167(3).

[158] And since Theft Act 1968 s 24(4) includes property obtained by fraud within the definition of handling, and since most tax evasion will constitution Fraud Act 2006 crimes, even where there is no specific 'handling' offence, there might be one under the Theft Act. On the theory of handling

handling contraband goods that have been smuggled, or by receiving the financial benefits of evasion. The growth of the crime of money laundering has given rise to a shift in emphasis between the predicate offence and the act of laundering.[159]

It is a summary offence to handle goods that are subject to unpaid excise duty.[160] There may be arguments about whether the tax is actually payable.[161] If it is not, then liability can be imposed for inchoate offences. 'No fault' defences are provided for a person who acted in accordance with the directions of, or with the consent of, the proper officer,[162] or was not liable or believed on reasonable grounds that there was no liability, or that it had been discharged.[163] Unlike the Theft Act handling offence,[164] neither 'dishonesty' nor any other 'positive' mental state (such as 'fraudulently' or 'knowingly') is required. Under the VAT provisions, there is an offence of acquiring possession of or dealing with any goods, or accepting the supply of any services, having reason to believe that VAT in their regard has been or will be evaded.[165]

There is an argument, in the pejorative sense 'academic', that if the tax offences were to be considered as falling within the Fraud Act 2006, then any property thereby would be subject to the crime of handling stolen goods.[166] While most probably correct, that claim has been made redundant by the addition to this area of money laundering offences. Even though Lord Toulson in *R v GH*[167] discouraged the use of laundering charges where previously handling would have been used, laundering offences are being used increasingly in the case of tax evasion, and it is doubtful whether the CEMA crime or the Theft Act 1968 handling offence would be charged nowadays because of the greater ease of establishing money laundering, whose relationship to tax evasion will be given extended attention later.[168] *R v Terry*[169] held that 'fraudulently'[170] was not to be confined to an intent to deprive a person

see Green, Stuart P, 'Thieving and Receiving: Overcriminalizing the Possession of Stolen Property' (2011) 14 *New Criminal Law Review* 35–54.

159 And see Alldridge, Peter, *What Went Wrong with Money Laundering Law?* (London: Palgrave, 2016).

160 CEMA s 170A.

161 *R v Goodwin (John Charles)* [1997] STC 22; [1997] BTC 5226 (counterfeit perfume still subject to VAT): compare cases cited in this chapter, section entitled 'The Major Smuggling Offences'.

162 S 170A(2)(a). 163 S 170A(2)(b). 164 Theft Act 1968 s 22.

165 VATA s 72(10). 166 Theft Act 1968 s 24(4).

167 *R v GH* [2015] UKSC 24; [2015] 2 Cr App R 12 at para 49, citing *R (on the application of Wilkinson) v Director of Public Prosecutions* [2006] EWHC 3012 (Admin).

168 See Chapter 9, section entitled 'Laundering the Proceeds of Tax Evasion'.

169 *R v Terry* [1984] AC 374.

170 In section 26(1) of the Vehicles (Excise) Act 1971, now Vehicle Excise and Registration Act 1994 ss 44–45.

of an economic advantage or inflict economic loss on him, but included an intent to deceive a person responsible for a public duty into doing something that he otherwise would not have done or refraining from doing something that he otherwise would have done.

Tax Credit Fraud

There is a long-standing impression, both in the UK and elsewhere,[171] that at the major points in the criminal justice system (investigation, charge, trial, and punishment),[172] the treatment of tax evaders is less harsh than that of those who commit social security frauds. At the national level, things have happened since Cook's ground-breaking study.[173] There are now more widespread use of civil penalties for benefit fraud, more tax evasion prosecutions, and proportionately fewer prosecutions for benefit fraud.

There is a statutory offence of knowingly being concerned in any fraudulent activity undertaken with a view to obtaining payments of a tax credit.[174] This offence arises from the transfer of many benefits from the field of social security to that of taxation. As with the equivalent benefits offences,[175] the existence of these offences does not prevent a charge of cheating the public revenue. In order to prove 'fraudulent activity' for the purposes of the Tax Credits Act 2002, an offender had to behave in a manner calculated to achieve false benefits payments. A passive receipt of funds and a deliberate failure to notify the benefits agency of an overpayment, while dishonest, falls short of fraudulent activity.[176] Investigations are performed by the Department for

[171] McKeever, Grainne, 'Social Citizenship and Social Security Fraud in the UK and Australia' (2012) 46 *Social Policy & Administration* 465–82; Marriott, Lisa, 'Justice and the Justice System: A Comparison of Tax Evasion and Welfare Fraud in Australia and New Zealand' (2013) 22 *Griffith Law Review* 403; Marriott, Lisa, 'An Investigation of Attitudes towards Tax Evasion and Welfare Fraud in New Zealand' (2015) *Australian & New Zealand Journal of Criminology*, published online before print.

[172] Rowlingson, Karen et al, *Social Security Fraud* (London: Stationery Office, 1997). See also Vincent, J et al, *Choosing Advice on Benefits*, DSS Research Report No.35 (London: HMSO, 1995); SPARK Research, *A Review of the DWP Benefit Fraud Sanctions Scheme* (London: Department of Work and Pensions, 2004) 41–5; DWP, *Beating Fraud is Everyone's Business: Securing the Future*, Cm 4012 (London: TSO, 1998) 26.

[173] Cook, Dee, *Rich Law, Poor Law: Differential Response to Tax and Supplementary Benefit Fraud* (Milton Keynes: Open University Press, 1989).

[174] Tax Credits Act 2002 s 35.

[175] Social Security Administration Act 1992 s 111 (delay, obstruction etc of inspector), s 111A (dishonest representations for obtaining benefit etc), and s 112 (false representations for obtaining benefit etc).

[176] *R v Nolan (Tracey)* [2012] EWCA Crim 671; [2012] Lloyd's Rep FC 498.

Work and Pensions (DWP). Responsibility for prosecutions for tax credits offences was placed in the hands of the CPS in 2012, which was a move towards closer alignment of the treatment of benefits fraud and tax fraud.[177]

Council Tax Fraud and Council Tax Benefit Fraud

At the level of local government, council tax fraud (this is usually by falsely claiming the discount for living alone) is investigated and, where prosecuted, prosecuted by the same organization, in the same proportions, with the same results as council tax benefit fraud (falsely claiming council tax benefit, which is means-tested). That makes a good deal of sense. There are no specific offences but benefits frauds and tax frauds are treated equally, with offences charged either as frauds (under the Fraud Act 2006 or conspiracy to defraud) or cheat.[178] That is, at the local level, and perhaps by chance, a conclusion seems to have been reached that that might do well nationally.

Rulings, Guidance, Abuse of Process, Exclusion of Evidence

If criminal liability is to be imposed, the taxpayer should be in a position to know that that is a possibility. John Gardner has argued that 'those of us about to commit a criminal wrong should be put on stark notice that that is what we are about to do'.[179] There is no system of binding 'revenue rulings'[180] in the United Kingdom.[181] The Revenue may lawfully disown advice given by its staff which it subsequently decides was incorrect,[182] and may (indeed must) also renege upon agreements made *ultra vires* to limit taxpayers' liability.[183]

[177] Welfare Reform Act 2012 s 124.

[178] *R v Hirani* [2008] EWCA Crim 1463, *R v Russell* [2014] EWCA Crim 1747; Chapter 3.

[179] Gardner, John, 'Wrongs and Faults', in Simester, AP (ed), *Appraising Strict Liability* (Oxford: Oxford University Press, 2005) at 69–70.

[180] A procedure by which the taxpayer can be informed in advance, so as to bind the Revenue, of the tax consequences of particular transactions.

[181] But see eg Corporation Tax Act 2010 ss 748, 749 or Taxation of Capital Gains Act 1992 s 138.

[182] *R v IRC, ex p Matrix Securities Ltd* [1994] 1 WLR 334; [1994] 1 All ER 769. A subsequent legal action against the lawyers failed: *Matrix Securities Ltd v Theodore Goddard* [1998] STC 1; [1997] BTC 578. In *R v IRC, ex p MFK Underwriting Agents Ltd* [1990] 1 WLR 1545 at 1569; [1990] 1 All ER 91, Bingham LJ stated that a taxpayer's only legitimate expectation is prima facie that she will be taxed according to statute, not a concession or a wrong view of the law. See Daly, Stephen, 'Recent Developments in Tax Law: *Vires* Revisited' (2016) 2 *Public Law* 190–8, discussing the saga of *Mansworth v Jelley* [2002] EWCA Civ 1829; [2003] STC 53. A judicial review of HMRC's actions pertaining to the fallout from this case was heard in the High Court: see *R (on the application of Hely-Hutchinson v HMRC* [2015] EWHC 3261 (Admin).

[183] *Al Fayed v Advocate General for Scotland* [2004] STC 1703.

It is not possible, in general, to apply to the court for a declaration that particular conduct either will or will not amount to a criminal offence. The actor is thus placed in the position of acting at his/her peril.[184] There appears to be an exception to enable lawyers to represent their clients.[185]

If the defendant does rely upon official statements, however, two further defences to any evasion charges will be available. First, the defendant will be able to claim that it constitutes an abuse of process to bring the proceedings.[186] Second, the defendant will be able to claim not to be dishonest for the purposes of any evasion offence requiring dishonesty. The fact that the taxpayer acted in good faith on the basis of advice from HMRC should be sufficient to negative dishonesty or fraudulent intent for the purposes of an evasion offence.[187]

When the Aaronson Committee considered the introduction of revenue rulings as part of the system for militating against abusive avoidance, various organizations raised the possibility of introducing rulings.[188] All this may be seen as an allocation of risk. The risk of having to pay a good deal of tax is, however, one thing, and it may well be defensible to place that risk on someone who chooses to put their money in a Swiss bank. The risk of being fined, or even going to jail, is another thing entirely.

The way in which additional certainty might be brought to the definitions of offences upon which people might rely is the publication of guidance as to how to comply. This is how the 'adequate procedures' defence under s 9 of the Bribery Act 2010 has been dealt with.[189] The idea is that even if a legally enforceable court order cannot be obtained, particular conduct will not be the subject of a successful criminal prosecution if the defendant can show compliance with the guidance. It is unclear whether the 'failure to prevent' corporate offence in the Criminal Finances Bill 2017 will be accompanied by analogous guidance.

[184] *Airedale NHS Trust v Bland* [1993] AC 789; [1993] 1 All ER 821, CA: compare on this point *A (Children) (Conjoined Twins: Medical Treatment) (No 1), Re* [2001] Fam 147. Ashworth, Andrew, 'Testing Fidelity to Legal Values: Official Involvement and Criminal Justice' (2000) 63 *Modern Law Review* 633, at 635–42.

[185] *R (AM) v Director of Public Prosecutions* [2012] EWHC 470 (Admin) (an assisted dying case), *N v S and the National Crime Agency* [2015] EWHC 3248 (a POCA case, but one where there was no *lis inter partes*).

[186] *R v Horseferry Road Magistrates' Court, ex p Bennett* [1994] 1 AC 42. Choo, Andrew L-T, *Abuse of Process and Judicial Stays of Criminal Proceedings* (Oxford: Oxford University Press, 2008).

[187] It will not necessarily negative negligence for the purposes of TMA s 106A.

[188] Seely, Antony, *Tax Avoidance: A General Anti-abuse Rule* (HC Library Standard Note: SN6265, 2015).

[189] The Ministry of Justice published guidance about procedures which relevant commercial organizations can put into place to prevent persons associated with them from bribing (section 9 of the Bribery Act 2010), in particular as to how corporations might satisfy the 'adequate procedures' defence under Bribery Act 2010 s 7: Alldridge, Peter, 'The Bribery Act 2010—Guidance to Corporations' (2012) 6 *Law and Financial Markets Review* 140–4.

Sentencing

The usual range of considerations as to deterrence, retribution, and denunciation bear upon the sentencing of evasion. So far as concerns retribution, there is no distinction to be made between the treatment of tax evasion and the equivalent 'non-tax' offence.[190] So far as concerns deterrence and denunciation the critical issues are as to the operation of the alternative mechanisms that are available in tax cases but not elsewhere.

Among judges and legislators, opinions differ greatly as to appropriate sentences for tax evasion. An early study[191] asked US federal judges to assign sentences for a diverse set of hypothetical cases. The recommended sentences varied widely. One tax evasion case drew recommendations as lenient as a six-month suspended prison sentence, and as harsh as a five-year prison sentence with a $20,000 fine. Although (perhaps because) the rate of prosecution has always been very low, when there is a conviction for serious tax fraud, the rhetoric of the courts has always been that imprisonment is almost inevitable. In *Dolan and Cormack*,[192] a false-invoicing case, Lord Lane CJ stated that 'except in extraordinary circumstances, an immediate custodial sentence is necessary to make it perfectly plain to others that this sort of activity must not be embarked upon and to discourage others from embarking upon this highly anti-social activity, which, of course, rebounds unfavourably on all honest taxpayers'.[193]

Sentencing of evasion is now covered by guidelines issued by the Sentencing Council for England and Wales,[194] which adopts for the relevant offences[195] the format of a range of degrees of harm and culpability and gain/loss and a range of aggravating and mitigating factors.[196] The procedure is to assess the culpability and the harm (loss caused or intended, in this case to the Revenue). The section on revenue fraud[197] deals with conspiracy to defraud and all the

[190] See Chapter 4.

[191] 'Disparity of Sentences for Sixth, Seventh and Eighth Judicial Circuits' (1962) 30 *Federal Rules of Decision* 401–505.

[192] *R v Dolan and Cormack* (1981) 3 Cr App R (S) 139. See also *R v Hancock* (1995) 16 Cr App R (S) 187.

[193] And see *R v Thornhill* [1980] 2 Cr App R (S) 320.

[194] Sentencing Council, *Fraud, Bribery and Money Laundering Offences: Definitive Guidelines* (2014) 19 *et seq*.

[195] TMA s 106A; CEMA ss 50, 170, and 170B; VATA s 72.

[196] Those set out in the Guidance do not differ markedly from those in the previous authority, *Attorney General's References (Nos 86 and 87 of 1999)* [2001] 1 Cr App R (S) 141.

[197] At 19 *et seq*, dealing with the following offences: conspiracy to defraud, fraud (Fraud Act 2006 s 1), false accounting (Theft Act 1968 s 17), fraudulent evasion of VAT, false statement for

major statutory offences.[198] A further table deals with cheating the Revenue when the sums involved extend into millions.[199] Where the offending is on the most serious scale, involving sums significantly higher than the starting point in category 1, sentences of fifteen years and above may be appropriate. A court sentencing a person convicted of an offence of cheating the public revenue may also make a financial reporting order in respect of him.[200]

The factors bearing upon the seriousness of the offence include:[201] first, the sophisticated nature of the fraud; second, the exploitation of a scheme (designed in the case in question to promote vocational training); third, a breach of trust; fourth, the fraudulent obtaining of money pursuant to the scheme coupled with the suppression of profits; fifth, the amount of loss to the Revenue; sixth, the personal benefit to each defendant; and, seventh, the concealment of the fraudulent nature of the claims at audit.

Giving judgment in the 'Operation Reciprocal' case in the Court of Appeal in 2013,[202] Lady Justice Rafferty quoted these aggravating factors with approval and identified three other cases to give 'an illustration of judicial cast of mind'.[203] 'There is a place for deterrent sentencing. Large scale frauds on the Revenue involve potentially enormous profits. Condign punishment can be expected. A complex web is difficult to detect and very expensive to prosecute.'[204]

So far as concerns Customs and Excise offences, the 'war on drugs' drove sentences upwards. The maximum penalty under s 170(2) of CEMA[205] was raised in 1988 from two to seven years.[206] Partly, probably, because of its

VAT purposes, conduct amounting to an offence under VATA s 72, fraudulent evasion of income tax (TMA s 106A), fraudulent evasion of excise duty and improper importation of goods (CEMA ss 50, 170, and 170B), cheating the public revenue.

[198] Fraud Act 2006 s 1, false accounting (Theft Act 1968 s 17), fraudulent evasion of VAT or making a false statement for VAT purposes, fraudulent evasion of income tax, fraudulent evasion of excise duty, improper importation of goods (CEMA ss 50, 170, and 170B).

[199] Table 3 p 23.

[200] Serious Organised Crime and Police Act 2005 s 76(3)(k). Following conviction for a listed offence a financial reporting order is made, in addition to sentencing or otherwise dealing with the person, if it is satisfied that the risk of D committing another listed offence is 'sufficiently high' to justify making it. The FRO requires bodies with whom the subject holds account to report activity, usually to the NCA.

[201] These are taken from *Attorney General's References Nos 86 and 87 of 1999* [2001] 1 Cr App R (S) 141.

[202] *R v Perrin & Faichney* [2012] EWCA Crim 1729; [2012] EWCA Crim 1730. I am grateful to the CPS for furnishing details of this case.

[203] Para 54, quoted by Keir Starmer DPP in his speech 'Prosecuting Tax Evasion', 23 January 2013, considered in Chapter 10.

[204] Para 52.

[205] Re-enacting Customs and Excise Act 1952 s 304.

[206] FA 1988 s 12. See *R v Dosanjh* [1998] 3 All ER 618; [1999] 1 Cr App R 371, considered in *R v Heneghan* [2003] EWCA Crim 397.

collection having been by Customs and Excise, prosecution policy and sentencing both seem to be harsher where VAT is concerned than income tax. While on paper the sanctions are harsh, it is difficult to track individual cases otherwise than via newspaper reports, and it should be noted that Michael Shanly,[207] the *HSBC Suisse* defendant (presumably selected from a range of possible defendants as the one most likely to yield both a conviction and exemplary treatment), avoided a custodial sentence and received a fine within the range that would have been applicable had civil penalties been imposed.[208]

There are three categories of culpability. High culpability is identified by various descriptors (a leading role where offending is part of a group activity; involvement of others through pressure/influence; abuse of position of power or trust or responsibility; sophisticated nature of offence/significant planning; and fraudulent activity conducted over a sustained period of time). Medium culpability is identified largely by the absence of factors rendering the culpability high or lesser, but also by the defendant taking on a significant role where offending is part of a group activity. Lesser culpability is ascribed to those involved through coercion, intimidation, or exploitation, not being motivated by personal gain, where the offence is an opportunistic one; where the defendant performed a limited function under direction; or where there is limited awareness or understanding of extent of fraudulent activity. Harm bands are calculated by reference to the gain or intended gain to the offender or the loss or intended loss to HMRC.[209] According to HMRC, of those sentenced to imprisonment for evasion (171 in 2011 and 220 in 2014), the average time served fell from 41.3 months in 2011 to 17.7 months in 2014.[210] It is unclear how many of these are tax credit fraud cases.

The usual range of non-custodial sanctions applies to tax evasion offences. One to which special attention should be drawn is the possibility of disqualification from holding directorships,[211] which is used as a sanction for VAT fraud.

[207] See Chapter 3, section entitled 'The *HSBC Suisse* (2015) and Mossack Fonseca (*Panama Papers*) (2016) Scandals'.

[208] See Chapter 7, section 'The Civil Penalties Regime'.

[209] Category 1 £50 million or more, starting point based on £80 million; Category 2 £10 million–£50 million, starting point based on £30 million; Category 3 £2 million–£10 million, starting point based on £5 million; Category 4 £500,000–£2 million, starting point based on £1 million; Category 5 £100,000–£500,000, starting point based on £300,000; Category 6 £20,000–£100,000, starting point based on £50,000; Category 7 less than £20,000, starting point based on £12,500.

[210] 'More UK Tax Evaders Going to Jail but Prison Terms Are Falling', *Financial Times*, 1 June 2015.

[211] Company Directors Disqualification Act 1986.

Concluding—Offence Definitions and Reform Options

So far as concerns the substance of the offences, there do not appear to be gaps, and while the absence of any operative organizing principles in the offences in this area is to be regretted, it does not appear to do much harm. Offences have arisen ad hoc. Many of them are not used by prosecutors. Classification of offences by reference to the specific tax evaded has arisen because whenever a new tax is put in place, an offence or series of offences might be put in place to counter evasion. It would be better to have broadly drafted offences applying to whichever taxes are put in place, or which appear on a designated list. There have been changes in fashion, both among prosecutors and draftspeople, as to how these matters are to be dealt with.

A range of things might be done about the organization of evasion offences. It would be possible (a) to abolish tax-specific offences and rely on the general ones; (b) to place cheat on a statutory basis, triable either way, while abolishing the other statutory evasion offences; (c) to place cheat on a statutory basis, triable either way, but retain or reorganize the statutory evasion offences; (d) as the Keith Committee recommended, to have a set of specific statutory criminal offences of dishonesty in respect of Inland Revenue taxes;[212] or (e) to do nothing, because the current patchwork range of offences does little harm. There is something to be said for each of these, but no overwhelming case for any.

In theft law generally, *Ghosh* seems to be embedded, and although it is a matter on which it is difficult for a person to take advice in advance of acting, there does not seem to be any appetite for its replacement, or suggestions for alternatives.[213] So far as concerns its application in tax evasion, however, a radical approach would be to dispense entirely with the requirement of dishonesty, but instead not to allow conviction without a deception. The provisions of s 2 of the Theft Act 1968 (stating that claim of right, or belief in consent, or belief in the impossibility of finding the real owner of the property in question each negatives dishonesty) only apply to theft and its derivatives,[214] and

[212] Board of Inland Revenue, *The Inland Revenue and the Taxpayer: Proposals in Response to the Recommendations of the Keith Committee on Income Tax, Capital Gains Tax and Corporation Tax* (London: HMSO, 1986) citing Keith para 6.8.2 and recommendation 70.

[213] Thus Griew, Edward, 'Dishonesty: The Objections to Feely and Ghosh' [1985] *Criminal Law Review* 341, Halpin, Andrew, 'The Test for Dishonesty' [1996] *Criminal Law Review* 283, and Glazebrook, Peter, 'Revising the Theft Acts' (1993) 52 *Cambridge Law Journal* 191 seem not to have precipitated action.

[214] Theft Act 1968 s 1(3).

its provisions. In fraud law generally, the notion of dishonesty adds something because it is possible to imagine non-dishonest deceptions. These are cases, for example, where there might be a claim of right. If tax evasion were confined to knowing or reckless deception of HMRC, it is difficult to imagine that the requirement of dishonesty would add anything, and so the requirement of dishonesty could be dispensed with. It was suggested earlier[215] that the essence of evasion, as a differentiation from avoidance, and because of the obligation to respond, is the lie to HMRC. If a definition along those lines—making a statement to the Revenue knowing it to be untrue or being reckless as to whether or not it is untrue—were adopted, reverting to the idea of tax perjury as providing the gravamen of the offence, then it would be possible to eliminate 'dishonesty' from the definition of tax evasion, and that might be a worthwhile simplification.

[215] See Chapter 3, end of section entitled 'Blurring the Line between Avoidance and Evasion'.

5

Investigation and Prosecution Structures

Models in Criminal Procedure

This chapter will deal with enforcement structures in tax prosecutions—which body prosecutes, with what incentives and under what constraints, and how its power and duties relate to other prosecuting bodies, especially those in the area of financial crime.[1] Two of the critical turning points in criminal procedure are those at which investigation becomes accusation, and at which accusation becomes prosecution.[2] From the point of view of the person under investigation, at these junctures s/he moves from being a suspect to being an accused, and then to being a defendant. As this process takes place, the defendant is accorded increasing rights to defend him/herself. From the point of view of the State, its agents move from being investigators, to being accusers, to being prosecutors, and classical theory requires that those roles should be discharged by different people. There are some consequences of the distinction between investigator and prosecutor. For example, the rule that a defendant may not be questioned after charge,[3] and its corollary that s/he

[1] Button, Mark, 'Fraud Investigation and the "Flawed Architecture" of Counter Fraud Entities in the United Kingdom' (2011) 39 *International Journal of Law, Crime and Justice* 249–65.

[2] And see Damaska, Mirjan, *The Faces of Justice and State Authority* (New Haven, CT: Yale University Press, 1986); Moohr, Geraldine Szott, 'Prosecutorial Power in an Adversarial System: Lessons from Current White Collar Cases and the Inquisitorial Model' (2004) 8 *Buffalo Criminal Law Review* 165–220.

[3] On the history see McBarnet, Doreen, 'The Royal Commission and the Judges' Rules' (1981) 8 *British Journal of Law and Society* 109–17; Garoupa, Nuno, Anthony Ogus, and Andrew Sanders, 'The Investigation and Prosecution of Regulatory Offences: Is There an Economic Case for Integration?' (2011) 70 *Criminal Law Journal* 229–59. The most recent non-statutory formulation was *Practice Note (Judges' Rules)* [1964] 1 WLR 152. The Philips Commission (Philips, Sir Cyril (Chair), *Royal Commission on Criminal Procedure* (Cmnd 8092, 1981)) para 4.114 approved it. See now PACE *Code of Practice for the Detention, Treatment and Questioning of Persons by Police Officers* (2012) para 16.5, 'A detainee may not be interviewed about an offence after they have been charged'; for an exception for terrorist suspects, see Walker, Clive, 'Post-charge Questioning of Suspects' [2008] *Criminal Law Review* 509–24.

must be brought before a court as soon as possible after charge,[4] is more than a statement of the different roles of the relevant state agencies; it also symbolically asserts the constitutional significance of charge.[5] The other major issue with which these models deal is judicial control over the investigator. In the classic adversarial model, police behaviour is controlled retrospectively from the point of trial, with the principal mechanism of control being the exclusion of evidence. In the classic inquisitorial model, in contrast, contemporaneous judicial supervision is the major safeguard against oppression of the accused.

Philips and the Crown Prosecution Service

In English law, the degree of compliance with either major model, and the connection between investigation and accusation, has varied over time.[6] The Royal Commission on Criminal Procedure[7] identified as a guiding principle the separation of investigative and prosecutorial functions.[8] The 'Philips principle' was developed as a reaction to a system rooted in private prosecution, in which one person might be victim, investigator, and prosecutor.

Independence of the prosecutor from the investigator and from the government was valued, for four major sets of reasons.[9] First, the usual crisis management reasons applied. Bad things had happened: change—any change—was therefore necessary. Second, for the elimination of corruption (whether 'noble cause' or regular) and mistakes, a 'fresh pair of eyes' is valuable. An investigator might form and become wedded to a particular view of a case, and that is a reason why s/he should not be involved in decision-making on the conduct of the prosecution. Independence of the prosecutor from the investigator excludes the investigator from any involvement in decisions as to whether or not to halt a prosecution. Third, it was thought a waste of police

[4] PACE s 46.

[5] And see the discussion, in the context of the introduction of post-charge questioning of terrorism suspects, in Joint Committee on Human Rights (Ninth Report), *Counter-terrorism Policy and Human Rights (Eighth Report): Counter-terrorism Bill* (2008) para 22 *et seq*.

[6] Brants, Chrisje, and Allard Ringnalda, *Issues of Convergence: Inquisitorial Prosecution in England and Wales?* (Nijmegen: Wolf Legal Publishers, 2011).

[7] Philips, n 3. And see Fisher, Sir Henry (Chair), *Report of an Inquiry into the Circumstances Leading to the Trial of Three Persons on Charges Arising out of the Death of Maxwell Confait and the Fire at 27 Doggett Road, London SE6* (London: HMSO, 1977).

[8] And see Home Office, *An Independent Prosecution Service for England and Wales* (Cmnd 9074, 1983).

[9] And see Sanders, Andrew, 'An Independent Crown Prosecution Service?' [1986] *Criminal Law Review* 16; Garoupa, Ogus, and Sanders, n 3.

time to have them spending more time than necessary on prosecution work. Someone would have to do it, and as an issue of effectiveness and efficiency as between different public services, it was better that some organization other than the police do it. Fourth, investigation and prosecution are different functions requiring different skills.

There are obvious answers to the first three. Crisis management required that something be done, but did not dictate anything in particular. As to the second, the fact that the investigator has been involved from an early point in the proceedings might be thought a reason why s/he brings particular knowledge and skills to bear. Where the investigator might have formed and become wedded to a particular view of the case, that will frequently be a useful thing, because s/he will have reviewed the evidence. The third and fourth are not arguments about principles at all: they are about resource allocation. Investigation and prosecution are only to a certain extent different functions requiring different skills: it is impossible to investigate or prosecute without having some idea about both investigating and prosecuting.

When the Crown Prosecution Service (CPS) was introduced,[10] the 'Philips principle' was adopted. The governing model was that the police would investigate, and, when there was enough evidence, charge and send the file to the CPS, whose job would be to check that appropriate charges had been laid, determine whether prosecution was appropriate, and, if so, prosecute. The CPS, in the early days, did not advise on charge or get involved in the investigation. The 'Philips principle' was never really a principle but more a defeasible preference, and it was developed in response to particular events. There was always something to be said for closer integration of police and prosecutors, particularly in areas where legal expertise is required at the point of charge.[11] The Philips Commission itself said that the 'pure theory of separation could not work in practice'.[12]

No sooner had the 'Philips principle' been identified and accepted than it was departed from, in two directions. First, when the CPS was established it was not given a monopoly on prosecutions.[13] This not only retained private prosecutions, but also implied that regulatory agencies could bring what were, in effect, private prosecutions.[14] Second, when the Roskill Report[15] gave rise

[10] Prosecution of Offences Act 1985.

[11] For example, where searches are conducted: see Chapter 6.

[12] Para 6.31.

[13] Prosecution of Offences Act 1985 s 6.

[14] *R v Rollins* [2010] UKSC 39; [2010] 1 WLR 1922.

[15] Roskill, Lord (Chair), *Fraud Trials Committee Report*, 1986. Even though its terms of reference were to do with the restrictions on the use of a charge of conspiracy to defraud in the light of the decision in *R v Ayres* [1984] AC 447 and subsequent cases, it threw its net more widely, to include the fallout from Johnson Matthey, Lloyds, Guinness, and Blue Arrow.

to the establishment of the Serious Fraud Office (SFO),[16] it was established on an entirely different model, with police and other investigators working alongside prosecutors. Even before the creation of the CPS, the particular difficulties of prosecuting frauds had given rise to concern, and the concern had led to the proposal for a system for the investigation and prosecution of serious frauds, itself arising from unsuccessful prosecutions.

The theory of separation between investigator and prosecutor until the point of charge relied upon the assumption that police at least had sufficient expertise in *what* to charge. In practice, in many cases they did not and from an early point, the CPS began to advise on charge. Lord Justice Auld drew attention to some of the practical deficiencies[17] of operating a rigid demarcation and recommended earlier and more direct involvement by the CPS, especially that the CPS should decide upon the charge in all but trivial cases and those cases where a 'holding charge' was used.[18] The relevant law was changed shortly afterwards.[19]

Enquiries and Reports

In the period of the separate existence of Inland Revenue and Customs and Excise, the bodies responsible for prosecutions developed their own cultures and practices, and they were not untouched by scandal. It should be no surprise, therefore, that the issues have been considered frequently by official and semi-official committees. This concern was not limited to Customs and Excise, but must also be seen in the context of the development of prosecutions more generally since the Prosecution of Offences Act 1985.

Glidewell

Owing to concerns in the early years of the CPS about its organization and efficiency, the government commissioned a review of it, chaired by Sir Iain Glidewell, whose Report was published in June

[16] Criminal Justice Act 1987.

[17] Brownlee, Ian, 'The Statutory Charging Scheme in England & Wales: Towards a Unified Prosecution System?' [2004] *Criminal Law Review* 896 at 897.

[18] Auld LJ, *A Review of the Criminal Courts of England and Wales* (Lord Chancellor's Department, September 2001) 412.

[19] Criminal Justice Act 2003 ss 28–30 and Schedule 2, introducing the 'statutory charging scheme'. See Brownlee, n 17 and Ashworth, Andrew, 'Developments in the Public Prosecutor's Office in England and Wales' (2000) 8 *European Journal of Crime Criminal Law and Criminal Justice* 257.

1998.[20] This Report recommended closer working between police and CPS lawyers. It proposed that Criminal Justice Units be headed by a CPS lawyer with mainly CPS staff. Because the units would need to be able to call on the police to take action in obtaining more evidence, a senior officer would need to be part of each unit, which would be housed in or near the relevant police station.[21] The Report also recommended the re-establishment of small groups of Special Casework Lawyers who would be available to provide early advice to the police.[22]

Gower–Hammond

The next official review arose from the conduct of Customs and Excise prosecutions. In June 2000 the government published the report[23] of an inquiry by Judge Gerald Butler QC into the prosecution of the case of *Doran and Others*,[24] which had been stayed by the judge because of a failure of disclosure by the prosecution. Recommendations 26 and 27 in the Butler Report were as follows:

Consideration should be given as to whether or not prosecutions at present conducted by Customs should continue to be conducted by this, or by another prosecuting authority. If Customs are to continue as a prosecuting authority, there should be an independent inspectorate established. This might be made an extension of the powers and duties of the current CPS inspectorate.

In its response to the Butler Report, the government agreed that consideration should be given to this and established a Review to examine the relevant issues and to make recommendations.[25] The system of accountability for prosecutions conducted by the CPS was and is that the Attorney-General answer to Parliament.[26] The system that then operated in Customs and Excise involved a great deal of local autonomy. A Customs and Excise investigator might take a case through to court (as could a police officer, before the Prosecution of Offences Act 1985). The Customs and Excise Solicitor's

[20] Glidewell, Sir Iain (chair), *The Review of the Crown Prosecution Service: A Report* (London: HMSO, 1998) Cm 3960.

[21] Para 29. [22] Chapter 9, paras 32 and 33.

[23] Gower, J, and A Hammond, *Review of Prosecutions Conducted by the Solicitor's Office of HM Customs and Excise* (2000). HL Debates, 8 June 2000 Col 172W (Lord Williams of Mostyn QC A-G).

[24] *R v Doran and others*, 8 June 2000; White, Robin, 'Investigators and Prosecutors, or Desperately Seeking Scotland: Reformulation of the Philips Principle' (2006) 69 *Modern Law Review* 143.

[25] The terms of reference are at HL Debates, 8 June 2000: vol 613 cc 172–3, 172WA.

[26] Beith, Sir Alan (Chair), Justice Committee, *The Crown Prosecution Service: Gatekeeper of the Criminal Justice System,* Ninth Report of Session 2008–09 Ev 61.

Department, which had overall control of Customs and Excise prosecutions, was accountable to the Commissioners of Customs and Excise, *not* to the Director of Public Prosecutions or to the Attorney-General, for the conduct of prosecutions. So far as concerned accountability, the Gower–Hammond Report proposed a change in the line of accountability, so that the prosecutor should not be accountable to the Board of Customs and Excise but rather to the Attorney-General,[27] and that while the Solicitor's Office should remain part of Customs and Excise, in relation to his prosecution function, the Solicitor should be accountable to the Attorney-General and not to the Commissioners or their chairman.

As concerned the implications for Customs and Excise prosecutions, Gower–Hammond rejected the idea of the 'Philips principle' as a '"Shibboleth", that is, a set of rules which must always be followed to the letter if a criminal justice system is to command the confidence of the public'.[28] Gower–Hammond stated it had never been suggested that the way the work of the SFO is arranged had led to unfairness or prejudiced the impartiality of the lawyers' decisions on evidential sufficiency and the public interest in relation to whether or not to prosecute. In making these decisions the lawyers are governed by the Code for Crown Prosecutors.[29]

The Gower–Hammond Review identified the need for prosecutors to be independent of investigators, to ensure that they felt able to exercise their professional judgment when dealing with their cases. It recommended that the Customs and Excise Prosecutions Group should be given greater autonomy within HM Customs and Excise's (HMC&E) Solicitor's Office, and that it should have its own budget and be accountable to the Attorney-General alone. The Prosecutions Group was renamed the Customs and Excise Prosecutions Office (CEPO). A memorandum of understanding was then agreed, setting out the relationship between the Attorney-General, the CEPO, and the Commissioners of Customs and Excise, under which Customs and Excise investigating officers and local staff no longer had audience rights in magistrates' courts.

Butterfield

A further crisis arose from the collapse late in 2002 of a bonded warehouse fraud trial, as a consequence of material non-disclosure by the Customs

[27] Recommendations 26 and 27. [28] Para 4.16.

[29] Gower, J, and A Hammond, *Review of Prosecutions Conducted by the Solicitor's Office of HM Customs and Excise* (2000) at paras 4.16–4.20.

and Excise prosecutors of information relating to a 'participating informant'.[30] The Customs officers misled the court by not telling the defence that the warehouse owner was actually an informant, thus denying the accused a fair trial. Of thirteen prosecutions, involving 109 accused, there were no convictions. In some of the cases no evidence was offered, in some acquittals were directed, in some the jury acquitted, and in some convictions were quashed, some even following guilty pleas. Lengthy abuse of process proceedings followed. The legal aid bill was estimated at £20 million, and the duty foregone by 'letting loads run' at £668 million.[31] In January 2003 HMC&E did not seek to resist the appeal in the Court of Appeal (Criminal Division) of *R v Gell and others*[32] (known as the 'Stockade' cases).[33]

In response, the Butterfield Review[34] dealt with HMC&E (as it was then) prosecutions. Two of the issues highlighted by the review were (a) that the officers responsible for the investigation had also been responsible for the conduct of the prosecution, and (b) the 'tripartite' arrangement as a particular feature of HMC&E prosecutions. Under the arrangement, the investigators decided what matters to investigate, HMC&E solicitors decided if there was sufficient evidence, and (most significantly) administrators decided whether to prosecute.[35] This scheme had probably emerged because, as both a revenue and a regulatory body, HMC&E commonly used 'compounding, seizure, forfeiture and civil penalties' as alternatives to prosecution, and this required that it retain control of the case from the opening of the investigation until the end of the punishment.[36] Butterfield found that one of the factors contributing to the problems identified in the cases whose collapse gave rise to the enquiry was the lack of independence of Customs and Excise prosecutors from Customs and Excise investigators, and recommended the establishment of a system of prosecutors independent of the investigatory branch.

[30] Regulation of Investigatory Powers Act 2000 Part II and s 26 and s 29. See White, n 24, at 162 *et seq*. Further fallout was seen in *R v Beardall & Lord* [2006] EWCA Crim 577.

[31] White, n 24, at 163.

[32] *R v Gell & Others* [2003] EWCA Crim 123.

[33] Garoupa, Ogus, and Sanders, n 3, 241, writing before the abolition of RCPO, drew attention to Butterfield and the events that led to it and suggested that the reason for the foundation of RCPO was that the previous arrangements were ineffective.

[34] Butterfield, *Review of Criminal Investigations and Prosecutions Conducted by HM Customs and Excise by the Hon Mr Justice Butterfield* (HM Treasury, 2003).

[35] White, n 24, at 162, quoting the Gower–Hammond Review, n 29, paras 3.7–3.14 and 5.10.

[36] See Chapter 7, end of section entitled 'Deal-making'.

O'Donnell

With the prosecutorial conduct of Customs and Excise having fallen under considerable criticism, the next significant event was the more general review of revenue collecting bodies which led to the merger of Customs and Excise and Inland Revenue.[37] The change was not driven primarily by the scandals concerning prosecutions that had attracted the attention of the four reviews of which Butterfield was the latest, but more by an apparent desire for administrative neatness and savings of resources. The merger of the Inland Revenue and Customs and Excise was announced by Gordon Brown in the 2004 Budget[38] and effected by the Commissioners for Revenue and Customs Act 2005, which created Her Majesty's Revenue and Customs (HMRC); gave it ancillary powers to do anything necessary, expedient, incidental, or conducive to its powers;[39] and permitted the Treasury only to give directions of a general nature.[40]

Organization of prosecutions did not figure much in the O'Donnell Review, but the resulting legislation did make provision for their reform.[41] If, as Butterfield had recommended, Customs and Excise needed independent prosecutors, and if, as O'Donnell recommended, Customs and Excise was to be merged with the Inland Revenue, then it followed that the merged body needed independent prosecutors. Hence the establishment of the Revenue and Customs Prosecution Office (RCPO), independent of the newly established HMRC.[42] Introducing the legislation, Lord Goldsmith, the Attorney-General, emphasized the element of independent scrutiny that was introduced and the power to prosecute cases generated by the (then) new Serious Organised Crime Agency (SOCA).[43]

The short-lived RCPO was consequently launched in April 2005, but was then incorporated into the CPS in January 2010. The merger of the CPS and RCPO, 'in order to deliver enhanced prosecution services to the public',[44] was

[37] O'Donnell, Gus, *Financing Britain's Future: A Review of the Revenue Departments* (HM Treasury, March 2004, Cm 6163).

[38] Gordon Brown emphasized the gains in efficiency and effectiveness that the new structure would bring: HC Debates, 17 March 2004 Col 331. And see McFall, John (Chair), Treasury Committee, Ninth Report of Session 2003–04, *The Merger of Customs & Excise and the Inland Revenue*, HC 556.

[39] Commissioners for Revenue and Customs Act 2005 s 9.

[40] S 11.

[41] S 34 *et seq*.

[42] And see HC Standing Committee E, 13 January 2005 3rd Sitting, cols 96 and 98 (John Healey, Economic Secretary to the Treasury).

[43] HL Debates, 7 February 2005 Column 587. The RCPO did not have a monopoly upon tax prosecutions. HMRC could itself commence them, whereupon the RCPO would be obliged to take them over: Commissioners for Revenue and Customs Act 2005 s 35(1)(b).

[44] Beith, n 26, Evidence, HC 128.

announced in April 2009 by the then Attorney-General, Baroness Scotland QC.[45] Work to consolidate the merger took place throughout the remainder of 2009.[46] The merger was said to have taken place without loss of jobs.[47] By April 2010 the incorporation of the RCPO within the CPS was being presented as having been a success.[48] The reasons given for the switch were written to make it seem that all had been planned from the outset. In Parliament the minister said: '[t]he purpose of the merger was to create a strengthened prosecution service, to safeguard and improve the high-quality work done by both organizations in serious and complex cases and to provide efficiency savings. Those objectives have to a large extent been achieved.'[49] A Home Office document stated:

> *The merger took place against a background of criminals operating increasingly across both functional and national boundaries, with a consequent need for prosecutors to be able to operate more collaboratively and more internationally. The aim was to provide an enhanced international capability, a specialist tax prosecution service and a joint prosecution approach to cross-border crime, together with efficiencies achieved by minimising duplication and driving economies of scale.*[50]

What really happened? Behind the bland presentation of the 'dramatic structural change'[51] involved in the creation and then the dissolution of RCPO within such a short time, two matters are not mentioned in the official statements. First, the most serious practical issue was staffing. RCPO prosecutors were initially drawn from the merger of the CEPO (which was itself established in 2003 from the previous HMC&E Solicitor's Office) and the Inland Revenue Crime Group. Criminal prosecutors could not easily be recruited from the CPS or tax lawyers from HMRC. Also, in the area of direct tax, criminal prosecutions were seen as a lot of effort for little reward. As the

[45] And see Scotland, Patricia, 'Creating a Modern Public Prosecution Service: Our New Contract with the Community', keynote speech at RCPO Conference, 6 May 2009.

[46] And see also Scotland, Patricia, 'Delivering an Excellent Public Prosecution Service', speech at University of Sussex, 3 February 2010.

[47] HL Debates, 24 February 2014 Col GC271 (Lord Faulks).

[48] 'Finally, a key recommendation of the Butterfield Report, that the prosecution function of HM Customs and Excise should be carried out by a wholly independent prosecuting authority to restore confidence in fair and effective prosecutions, has been implemented successfully under the leadership of David Green QC. The Revenue and Customs Prosecutions Office, established in 2005, now forms an important part of the Crown Prosecution Service under the Director of Public Prosecutions.' Vera Baird QC S-G, HC Debates, 6 April 2010 Col 138WS.

[49] HL Debates, 24 February 2014 Col GC271 (Lord Faulks).

[50] Home Office Consultation Paper CP6/2012, *Public Bodies Act 2011: Consultation on an Order to Give Legal Effect to the Administrative Merger of the Crown Prosecution Service and Revenue and Customs Prosecutions Office* (Cm 8250, 2012), para 19.

[51] RCPO Annual Report 2008–09, 8.

CPS was supplying most of the staff on secondment, it was thought better in management terms that the CPS take over the whole enterprise. Secondments are difficult to operate because there are always questions as to how the reporting line 'really' works.

Second, the principal institutional change in the RCPO's workload was the effects of the establishment and then the dissolution of the UK Border Agency (UKBA). Although it prosecuted a range of offences,[52] the majority of RCPO cases originally involved drug-trafficking prosecutions, which might not have been thought appropriate for a specialist revenue-centred organization, drugs cases typically yielding no tax. The UKBA was established in December 2009 in order better to integrate border control, which deals with the processing of people and goods crossing the border and 'protective security at the border'.[53] On its inception the UKBA took over investigation of all non-fiscal smuggling offences. This left the RCPO with comparatively few substantial cases. The UKBA was abolished in March 2013 as a result of successive scandals unrelated to prosecutions.[54] At that point drug smuggling prosecutions did not revert to the RCPO, but the Serious Organised Crime Agency (SOCA, now NCA) took over the detection and prosecution of drug smuggling. Border Force, part of the Home Office, now exercises concurrent jurisdiction over drug smuggling and prosecutions are conducted by the CPS,[55] and this was the collateral event of which the end of the RCPO was an inevitable consequence.

The mechanisms adopted for the termination of the RCPO were first administrative and only subsequently legal. After consultations,[56] the administrative decision was given legal effect by a statutory instrument. The directorship of the RCPO, to which some residual powers attached, continued after the end of the RCPO itself, but was held by the Director of Public Prosecutions (DPP). The post of Director of RCPO was then merged with

[52] It dealt with cases of fraud in relation to direct taxes (income tax, capital gains tax, inheritance tax, corporation tax) and indirect taxes (mainly VAT—notably multi-million pound MTIC frauds), tax credits, drug smuggling and money laundering, cases involving United Nations trade sanctions, conflict diamonds, and breaches of the Convention on International Trade in Endangered Species of Wild Fauna and Flora (Washington Convention).

[53] Cabinet Office, *Security in a Global Hub—Establishing the UK's New Border Arrangements* (London: Cabinet Office, 2009).

[54] Vaz, Keith (Chair), Home Affairs Committee, *The Work of the UK Border Agency*, Fourteenth Report of 2012–13.

[55] Borders, Citizenship and Immigration Act 2009 s 7.

[56] Consultation Paper CP6/2012, *Public Bodies Act 2011: Consultation on an Order to Give Legal Effect to the Administrative Merger of the Crown Prosecution Service and Revenue and Customs Prosecutions Office* (Cm 8250, 2012). The government response is Ministry of Justice, *Public Bodies Act 2011: Government Response on the Consultation CPR13/2012 to Give Legal Effect to the Administrative Merger* (Cm 8422, 2012).

that of the DPP in 2014.[57] The Revenue and Customs Division (RCD), a specialist division within the CPS, was established to provide a specialist tax and revenue prosecution service together with expertise in the prosecution of arms-dealing and sanctions violations. The RCD prosecuted all cases on behalf of HMRC. It merged with the Fraud Prosecution Division of the CPS in April 2010 to form the Central Fraud Group (CFG). The CFG prosecutes cases in England and Wales investigated by HMRC and, where expertise in fiscal matters is required, by the police or other investigators. The CFG also prosecutes all criminal cases relating to benefits and child maintenance legislation which are investigated by the Department of Work and Pensions (DWP), and advises on the conduct of financial investigations; the law; practice and procedure relating to restraint, confiscation, and receivership; and the enforcement of confiscation orders. HMRC has responsibility for investigating all fiscal crimes, which involve activities such as direct and indirect tax evasion, excise duty fraud, and tax credit fraud. The CFG also handles other casework investigated by HMRC, involving serious non-fiscal crimes such as illegal arms trafficking, certain breaches of sanctions legislation, and associated money laundering. In theory, tax prosecutions may also be brought by the SFO or even the Financial Conduct Authority (FCA), but these things rarely happen.[58]

Organizing the Prosecutions

We might need more prosecutions,[59] but, in addition to considerations about costs and alternatives to prosecutions, prosecution rates should only be increased if some clear conditions are satisfied as to how they are to be brought. The first is that appropriate resources are made available. Second, the enforcement personnel must be offered a future other than in the private sector. If there are to be more tax prosecutions, someone has to bring them. It is a skilled job. Reliance upon the 'revolving door'—the idea that lawyers might spend their twenties and perhaps early thirties in public service and then go into more lucrative private practice—might provide some, but not the whole, of the answer. If tax prosecution is to be regarded as an important job, then tax prosecutors need to be offered a rewarding career. This implies that they should not feel lesser either than other prosecutors or other tax collectors. Third, the lines

[57] Public Bodies (Merger of the Director of Public Prosecutions and the Director of Revenue and Customs Prosecutions) Order 2014 SI 834.

[58] *R v Rollins* [2010] UKSC 39; [2010] 1 WLR 1922.

[59] See Chapter 10.

of accountability must be clear and should, in particular, avoid the problems to which Butterfield drew attention.

Conclusion

Policy on tax prosecutions has always manifested ambivalence. On the one hand, evasion is denounced and powers are in place equal to those of the most serious crimes. On the other, rates of prosecution are low, and, compared to the number of prosecutions, the rate of conviction in contested cases is also less than for other serious property offences. The changes over years in the governing structures reflect this uncertainty.

It is neither possible nor desirable to operate the 'Philips principle' in the case of tax evasion, nor, in all probability, in any area where complex issues of substantive law and of evidence need to be resolved at the outset of the investigation. There may have been, and there may still be, good reasons to differentiate between tax and any other prosecutions. Alignment of Customs and Excise and Inland Revenue functions is welcome. The frequent changes of prosecution structures and the alphabet soup of acronyms reflect partly that this is what happens in bureaucracies, and partly a real conflict between the purity of the 'Philips principle' and the case, based on efficiency and resource allocation, for its attenuation.

6

Investigatory Powers

Investigatory Functions and Powers of HMRC

Dawn Raids and the Legacy of *Rossminster*

The *Rossminster* affair[1] casts a long shadow over all subsequent discussion of Her Majesty's Revenue and Customs' (HMRC's) powers of entry and search.[2] During a period of high taxation, particularly of 'unearned' income, various schemes were marketed the effect of which was to reduce a taxpayer's liability. *Rossminster* was the creature of Roy Tucker and Ron Plummer, both qualified accountants and ex-employees of one of the largest accountancy firms. They dealt in 'off-the-peg' avoidance schemes and for five years made themselves, and their clients, recipients of tax savings to the extent of hundreds of millions of pounds. In the mid-1970s the Revenue began a well-publicized attack on both evasion and avoidance. Retrospective legislation was enacted in 1978[3] which defeated some schemes already operating (and paid for).

At 7am on 13 July 1979 came the famous raid, followed by protracted litigation. Suspecting that some tax fraud had been committed, a senior revenue officer placed information before a circuit judge, in consequence of which he obtained search warrants[4] for named revenue officers to search specified premises and seize anything which they had reasonable cause to believe might be required as evidence in proceedings in respect of a tax fraud. Teams of revenue officers accompanied by police officers arrived at the premises, including those of the applicants, and, having gained entry, searched those

[1] *R v IRC, ex p Rossminster Ltd* [1980] AC 952; (1980) 70 Cr App R 157.

[2] Tutt, Nigel, *The Tax Raiders: The Rossminster Affair* (London: Financial Training, 1985); Gillard, Michael, *In the Name of Charity: The Rossminster Affair* (London: Chatto & Windus, 1987). And see Walters, John, 'Revenue Raids' [1998] *British Tax Review* 213 and Brown, B, 'Inland Revenue Powers of Search' [1999] *British Tax Review* 16.

[3] FA 1978 s 31.

[4] In accordance with s 20C TMA.

Criminal Justice and Taxation. First Edition. Peter Alldridge. © Peter Alldridge 2017. First published 2017 by Oxford University Press.

premises.[5] They seized anything which, they claimed, they had reasonable cause to believe might be required as evidence of a tax fraud,[6] but they did not inform the applicants of the offences suspected or of the persons suspected of having committed them. The warrant contained no such particulars.[7] Tucker was subsequently fined for failing to return five desk diaries,[8] but no criminal tax evasion charges were ever brought.[9]

Lord Denning, never one for understatement on the liberty of the subject, compared the raid with the treatment of Wilkes denounced by Lord Camden, and also the Spanish Inquisition.[10] Reversing the Court of Appeal's decision, but without enthusiasm, the House of Lords held that the warrants, which conferred the power to enter and search premises regardless of their ownership, were strictly and exactly within the very wide authority of the statute. Once a warrant had validly been issued under s 20C, the occupants had no right to be told at that stage what offences were alleged to have been committed, who were alleged to have committed them, or what the 'reasonable ground' was which the judge was satisfied existed for suspecting that an offence had been committed involving fraud relating to tax.

Under s 20C(3), the existence of 'reasonable cause to believe' that any things found on the premises might be required as evidence for the purposes of proceedings in respect of the suspected offences was a question of fact to be tried on the evidence, and on the question whether such a belief existed in respect of individual documents seized, the evidence fell short of supporting the final declaration which alone could be granted against the Crown. At that time, the law of search with warrants was governed by unsatisfactory common law authorities,[11] and the provision of clearer tests was one of the recommendations of the Philips Commission subsequently given effect in Part 1 of the Police and Criminal Evidence Act 1984 (PACE).

[5] 'It was a military style operation.' Lord Denning MR, [1980] AC at 968.

[6] As Moses J put it: 'No one concerned at the revenue's powers of seizure could forget that in 1979, when searching for needles indicative of tax fraud the Revenue took haystacks from the homes of Mr Plummer and Mr Tucker, amongst others.' *R v Middlesex Guildhall Crown Court ex p Tamosius & Partners* [2000] 1 WLR 453; [1999] STC 1077; [2000] 1 WLR at 459.

[7] Which would have been required for a search by the police under the common law of warrants: *Chic Fashions (West Wales) Ltd v Jones* [1968] 2 QB 299; [1968] 1 All ER 229.

[8] *R v IRC, ex p Rossminster Ltd* [1979] 3 All ER 385; [1979] STC 688. See Levi, Michael, *Regulating Fraud* (London: Routledge Revivals, 2014) 168.

[9] Sabine, Basil, 'Life and Taxes 1932–1992. Part 3: 1965–1992: Reform, Rossminster and Reductions' [1993] *British Tax Review* 504.

[10] At 970.

[11] *Chic Fashions (West Wales) Ltd v Jones* [1968] 2 QB 299; [1968] 1 All ER 229, *Ghani v Jones* [1970] 1 QB 693; [1969] 3 All ER 1700.

The Keith Committee

Rightly or wrongly, the lingering impression created around *Rossminster* is one of overbearing abuse of State power. So far as concerned investigation of criminal tax evasion, there was never any good reason why the investigatory powers should differ significantly from those for other frauds. There might be very few cases in which dawn raids upon domestic premises could be justified,[12] but the power had to be retained. The Keith Committee was appointed by the Chancellor of the Exchequer (Sir Geoffrey Howe) in 1980[13] and published the last (fourth) volume of its report in 1985. Since the earlier volumes dealt with the powers of search and seizure at common law they did not have the benefit, as a comparator, of the PACE structure of powers and constraints.[14] At that time, police investigatory powers were ill-defined and the Philips Commission[15] was deliberating upon them.

The Committee laboured intensively[16] and produced numerous significant recommendations. Considering the search powers accorded to revenue agents, Keith emphasized the concerns both of the profession and the population as a whole about the scope of the search powers and the potential for their abuse, but nonetheless recommended their extension.[17] The governing assumption at that time seems to have been that tax searches ought not to be assimilated to criminal searches more generally.[18] The government response was generally favourable. Many of the recommendations were able to be implemented without legislation, and many of those which did require legislation saw it enacted.[19]

The fundamental question that was not fully considered by Keith was whether there was any justification for having different powers for the investigation of tax fraud from those for other crimes. The law on the powers

[12] Levi, Michael, *Regulating Fraud* (London: Routledge Revivals, 2014) 157.

[13] Terms of reference and composition at HC Debates, 17 July 1980, vol 988 cc 683–4W.

[14] The earlier (Whitelaw) Police and Criminal Evidence Bill 1983 fell at the (June 1983) election: the 1984 (Brittan) Act was thus the second bite at the Philips cherry.

[15] See Chapter 5, section entitled 'Philips and the CPS'.

[16] Keith of Kinkel, Lord (Chair), *The Enforcement Powers of the Revenue Departments*. Volumes 1 and 2 (Cmnd 8822, March 1983) dealt with income tax, corporation tax, capital gains tax, and value added tax. Volume 3 (Keith of Kinkel, Lord (Chair), *The Enforcement Powers of the Revenue Departments* (Cmnd 9120, Jan 1984) dealt with the remaining Inland Revenue taxes, namely development land tax, petroleum revenue tax, capital transfer tax, and stamp duties. Volume 4 (Keith of Kinkel, Lord (Chair), *The Enforcement Powers of the Revenue Departments* (Cmnd 9440, Feb 1985)) dealt with the remaining taxes and duties under the care and management of Customs and Excise.

[17] Keith of Kinkel, Lord (Chair), n 15, Vols 1 and 2, at para 9.23.7.

[18] See, for a contemporary response, Gammie, Malcolm, and John Kay, 'Taxation, Authority and Discretion' (1983) 4 *Fiscal Studies* 46–61.

[19] The government response was Board of Inland Revenue, *The Inland Revenue and the Taxpayer: Proposals in Response to the Recommendations of the Keith Committee on Income Tax, Capital Gains Tax and Corporation Tax* (London: HMSO, 1986). There is a table at 155 *et seq* of the recommendations and the government responses.

of criminal investigation of tax evasion under consideration in *Rossminster*[20] lasted until 2008, when the assimilation began of the powers of the Inland Revenue and Customs and Excise (HMC&E), on the one hand, and tax powers and criminal justice powers, on the other.

Conduct of Tax Investigations

The modern law of tax investigations has at least had some wrinkles ironed out.[21] The law has moved from being relatively autonomous of other fields to mirroring much more closely the criminal model. The starting point is that without more, a citizen does not have to answer a question posed to him/her by a police officer or any other person before the citizen is arrested. There may be consequences, at a subsequent trial, of failure to answer;[22] there are exceptional cases in which there is an obligation to disclose information;[23] and there are cases where people who occupy particular roles, in distinction from the rest of the population, have an obligation to disclose information;[24] but the general rule is that there is no obligation to respond. The obligation to make a tax return[25] and to pay taxes is what makes tax law different.

Civil Investigations

The procedure for civil tax investigations is now set out in Schedule 36 of the Finance Act 2008, which gives HMRC powers to gather information, to examine documents, and to inspect business premises and the assets and documents on those premises. These powers apply to all major taxes except excise duties.[26] They apply to information or documents 'reasonably required' by HMRC[27] for the purpose of checking the taxpayer's tax position.[28]

[20] TMA s 20 *et seq*.

[21] And see McLaughlin, Mark (ed), *HMRC Investigations Handbook 2015–16* (London: Bloomsbury, 2015).

[22] Most of which arise under Criminal Justice and Public Order Act 1994 ss 34–39, or, in this context, Fraud Act 2006 s 13.

[23] Terrorism Act 2000 s 39.

[24] For example, the duties of disclosure applying to the regulated sector under POCA.

[25] TMA ss 7 and 8.

[26] Paras 63, 64(2), and 84.

[27] 'The weight of authority is that the burden of proof in relation to the "reasonably required" test in Sch 36 notices rests on the appellant, and not on HMRC.' *Mathew v Commissioners for HMRC* [2015] UKFTT 0139 (TC). See also *N J Cowan v Revenue & Customs* [2013] UKFTT 604 (TC).

[28] FA 2008, Schedule 36, para 1. That is, not extending to 'fishing expeditions'.

Usually a tax investigation will begin informally. If an informal approach proves unsatisfactory, a tax inspector has power to serve a notice ('taxpayer notice') requiring the taxpayer to produce information and documents.[29] Once the material has been delivered up, HMRC may take as long as is reasonable to examine it.[30] Notices may also, with the tribunal's approval,[31] be served on third parties[32] and can override Article 8 claims by the third parties.[33] The taxpayer must be informed, unless the tribunal so determines, of requirements imposed on third parties. HMRC may not serve a notice on a named third party without either prior approval of the First-tier Tribunal (FTT) or the agreement of the taxpayer. When the identity of the people concerned is not known, this can still be done. The Tribunal has previously given its approval for the Revenue and Customs Commissioners to serve a generic notice to 308 financial institutions requiring them all to disclose information relating to offshore accounts held by customers with addresses in the United Kingdom.[34] No court order is required for a taxpayer notice, but the HMRC officer may get the approval of the Tribunal, in which case the penalty for *deliberate* obstruction is available.[35] There are additional powers to remove or to take copies of documents,[36] and to mark assets and record information.[37] The taxpayer has a right of appeal against a notice served on himself for information other than his statutory records, unless HMRC has first sought the approval of the FTT.[38] HMRC must obtain the approval of the FTT before serving a notice in relation to a person or class of persons whose identity is unknown. There is a power to enter and inspect business premises,[39] but not private dwellings, which had been one of the grounds for the objections to the Inland Revenue behaviour in *Rossminster*.[40] Private dwellings may only be entered if the PACE procedures are satisfied.

[29] FA 2008, Schedule 36 para 1. Documents are deemed to be in a person's power if they can obtain them by influence or otherwise, and without great expense, from another person even where that person has the legal right to refuse to produce them: *Parissis and Others v Revenue & Customs* [2011] UKFTT 218 (TC).

[30] *Jacques v Revenue and Customs Commissioners* [2007] STC (SCD) 166; [2007] STI 263.

[31] Para 3. [32] Para 2.

[33] *R (on the application of Derrin Brother Properties Ltd) v Revenue and Customs Commissioners* [2014] EWHC 1152 (Admin) [2014] STC 2238.

[34] *Revenue and Customs Commissioners' Application (Approval to Serve 308 Notices on Financial Institutions), Re* (TC 174) [2009] UKFTT 224 (TC); [2009] SFTD 780.

[35] Paras 13 and 39. [36] Para 16. [37] Para 17. [38] Para 29.

[39] Para 10.

[40] *R v IRC, ex p Rossminster Ltd* [1980] AC 952; (1980) 70 Cr App R 157; see this chapter, section entitled 'Dawn Raids and the Legacy of *Rossminster*'.

The sorts of due process constraints which apply in the case of suspected crime did not apply in the case of enquiries from tax agencies under their civil powers, which, on the received account, had another purpose, that of determining the extent of the taxpayer's liability. To what extent, if at all, may HMRC use the civil powers to collect evidence and then subsequently use them in a criminal prosecution? In *Gold Nuts Ltd and Others v Commissioners for Her Majesty's Revenue & Customs*,[41] the FTT held that if HMRC was using the civil enquiries procedure for the dominant purpose of obtaining information to allow it to decide whether or not to prosecute the taxpayer, that would be *ultra vires* the Schedule.[42] This issue requires consideration at a higher level, but the reasoning in *Gold Nuts* appears sound.

Customs Searches

Customs and Excise has its own history.[43] The Customs and Excise Management Act 1979 (CEMA) s 118C allows a Justice of the Peace to issue a search warrant which allows officers to enter and search premises and persons for the purpose of removing documents and other items, such as goods or false stamps, if they are considered evidence of a fraud offence. There is a specific search power[44] in relation to ss 167 and 170 of CEMA where fraud is suspected both in respect of documents and other items. HMRC officers are subject to the PACE Code of Practice B when exercising this power.[45] HMRC inherited from HMC&E numerous other powers of entry.[46]

Criminal Investigations by HMRC

Obtaining Information from the Taxpayer

Until 2007, there were different rules on criminal investigations for the Inland Revenue and Customs and Excise, and the powers available to HMC&E[47] were more extensive than those of the Inland Revenue.[48] The standard

[41] *Gold Nuts Ltd and Others v Commissioners for Her Majesty's Revenue & Customs* [2016] UKFTT 82 (TC); [2016] Lloyd's Rep FC Plus 24.

[42] At para 91.

[43] And see Butterfield, *Review of Criminal Investigations and Prosecutions Conducted by HM Customs and Excise by the Hon Mr Justice Butterfield* (HM Treasury, 2003), para 1.7 *et seq.*

[44] CEMA s 118(5).

[45] HMRC, *Report on Our Powers of Entry* (London: HMRC, 2014), para 4.3.19.

[46] Ibid. [47] Under CEMA. [48] Under TMA.

criminal justice procedure for a police investigation, set out in PACE and its Codes of Practice, with provision for searches, arrests, and interrogation, only applied to HMC&E and the procedures to be followed in an investigation under the *aegis* of the Inland Revenue were those laid down in successive incarnations of ss 19A–20D of the Taxes Management Act 1970 (TMA). In addition to (civil) tax law powers,[49] HMRC is granted criminal investigation powers by PACE,[50] the Serious Organised Crime and Police Act 2005, the Proceeds of Crime Act 2002,[51] and the Criminal Justice and Police Act 2001.[52]

HMRC may enter and search premises, require the production of documentation, seize items or require relevant material to be handed over, and arrest persons. The Finance Act 2007[53] had the effect of aligning the rules on searches and seizures by HMRC to those governing the police (and, where they were involved, the Serious Fraud Office (SFO)). It applied PACE to HMRC so as to provide consistent powers to be used in criminal investigations in England and Wales. Section 114 of PACE now applies consistently to HMRC. An Order,[54] and subsequent amendments and consolidation,[55] applied[56] most of the provisions of PACE to all investigations conducted and persons detained by HMRC.

Not all the powers in PACE are available to HMRC. HMRC may not take fingerprints, charge, detain, release, or bail suspects.[57] Some of the powers in PACE are modified for HMRC. For example, a search warrant may allow HMRC to search persons found on the premises without the need for arrest. This allows HMRC to search a bookkeeper who is not considered a suspect but who may have evidence in a briefcase or laptop when a company's premises are searched but no arrest is made. PACE ss 14A and 14B[58] disapply the rules on special procedure and excluded material from the case where the investigation is by HMRC.

[49] See this chapter, section entitled 'Civil Investigations'.

[50] PACE ss 8, 17, 19, 24, and Schedule 1.

[51] POCA s 389.

[52] Criminal Justice and Police Act 2001 ss 1 and 50.

[53] FA 2007 s 82.

[54] Police and Criminal Evidence Act 1984 (Application to Revenue and Customs) Order 2007 SI 3175, Schedule 2(1), para 1, art 3(2).

[55] Police and Criminal Evidence Act 1984 (Application to Revenue and Customs) Order 2007 (Amendment) Order 2010 SI 360; Police and Criminal Evidence Act 1984 (Application to Revenue and Customs) Order 2007 (Amendment) Order 2014 SI 788. See now Police and Criminal Evidence Act 1984 (Application to Revenue and Customs) Order 2015 SI 1783, consolidating and extending.

[56] With variations set out in the schedules to the 2015 Order.

[57] Police and Criminal Evidence Act 1984 (Application to Revenue and Customs) Order 2015 SI 1783 art 4.

[58] Police and Criminal Evidence Act 1984 (Application to Revenue and Customs) Order 2015 SI 1783 art 6.

The investigatory powers available to police and to members of the SFO in the investigation of tax crime are the same as their respective powers in respect of any other crime. When—rarely in tax cases—the investigation is conducted by the SFO, responses may be required, even after charge. It is an offence not to comply, or to furnish misleading information in response to a request.[59]

Under PACE, and unlike the provisions under consideration in *Rossminster*,[60] warrants to enter and search premises must provide sufficient information about the relevance and value of the evidence sought.[61] The courts have emphasized many times that the issue of a search warrant is never a routine operation. The authorities have failed many times to fulfil the statutory criteria for searches.[62] Recurrent issues are: the lack of specificity in the information provided to the court; the process by which the warrant decision was made; and the fact that the warrant did not sufficiently describe the offence or offences being investigated or the type and nature of the material sought in the search.[63]

Sections 60–70 of the Serious Organised Crime and Police Act 2005 conferred powers, in respect of designated offences, on the relevant Directors (now the Director of Public Prosecutions (DPP) and the Director of Border Revenue) to issue disclosure notices[64] and production orders.[65] That is, in respect of the evidence sought under these orders, HMRC may be empowered to proceed without a court order. So far as these provisions create exceptions to the applications of the privilege against self-incrimination, as with the Criminal Justice Act 1987 or any other clear statutory abrogation of the privilege, the privilege does not apply, but evidence thereby acquired is not admissible,[66] unless the charge is a false statement offence.[67]

At the theoretical level, the amendments to PACE implied that the role of the tax investigator conducting a criminal investigation dealing with

[59] Criminal Justice Act 1987 s 2(23) and 2(14).

[60] See this chapter, section entitled 'Dawn Raids and the Legacy of *Rossminster*'.

[61] *R (on the application of Redknapp) v Commissioner of the City of London Police* [2008] EWHC 1177 (Admin); [2009] 1 WLR 2091; *R (on the application of Anand) v Revenue and Customs Commissioners* [2012] EWHC 2989 (Admin); [2013] CP Rep 2.

[62] *R v Chief Constable of Lancashire ex p Parker* [1993] QB 577; *R (on the application of Anand) v Revenue and Customs Commissioners* [2012] EWHC 2989 (Admin); [2013] CP Rep 2; [2013] Lloyd's Rep FC 278. See Fisher, Jonathan, 'Unwarranted Conduct' (2012) 8 *Tax Journal* 1145.

[63] *Sweeney v Westminster Magistrates' Court* [2014] EWHC 2068 (Admin).

[64] S 62.

[65] S 63.

[66] Serious Organised Crime and Police Act 2005 s 65, as with Criminal Justice Act 1987 s 8(2). There are exceptions in s 65(2) mirroring Criminal Justice Act 1987 s 8(2).

[67] Serious Organised Crime and Police Act 2005 s 67, Perjury Act 1911 s 5 or False Oaths (Scotland) Act 1933 s 2.

allegations of criminal evasion shifted from that of a hybrid between a police officer and a seeker after truth to that unambiguously, of a police officer, and the procedure by which the information was acquired in criminal tax investigations moved from being partly inquisitorial (to ascertain and impose the correct tax liability) and partly adversarial to being unambiguously adversarial. Tax evasion was thus aligned to serious fraud and other very serious property offences[68] and was brought within the 'organized crime' agenda which is driving much criminal justice policy. While there are so few prosecutions and while those that yield convictions generate such low sentences, this is further evidence of ambivalence, bordering upon doublethink, towards evasion.

Confidential and Privileged Information

There are two major claims that the taxpayer might want to make to bar access to information in his/her possession—the privilege against self-incrimination and legal professional privilege.

The Privilege against Self-incrimination in Tax Law

Requests from the state for information from a person might arise as part of an investigation into suspected crime by that person, or for other reasons to do with the administration of the country, or both. In the context of taxation, the request for information may be either to investigate suspected evasion or simply properly to assess the taxpayer's liability. In the case where the question is a part of a criminal investigation, procedural constraints are appropriate—that the suspect be warned that s/he is a suspect and that information provided by him/her might be used against him/her, that the possibility of access to legal advice be considered, that s/he have access to medical care where appropriate, that s/he be entitled to know something of the evidence against him/her, and so on.

The privilege against self-incrimination[69] is a mysterious but long-established[70] feature of the common law. It is not absolute.[71] As a creature of

[68] The list is at Serious Organised Crime and Police Act 2005 s 61. The offences are the serious property offences—theft, fraud, laundering, and their inchoate forms.

[69] And see Choo, Andrew L-T, *The Privilege against Self-incrimination and Criminal Justice* (Oxford: Hart Publishing, 2013); Redmayne, Mike, 'Rethinking the Privilege against Self-incrimination' (2007) 27 *Oxford Journal of Legal Studies* 209–32.

[70] *Beghal v Director of Public Prosecutions* [2015] UKSC 49; [2016] AC 88 at para 60. Gray, Charles M, RH Helmholz, John H Langbein, and Eben Moglen, *The Privilege against Self-incrimination: Its Origins and Development* (Chicago, IL: University of Chicago Press, 1997).

[71] *Paget; ex p Official Receiver, Re* [1927] 2 Ch 85, approving a decision of Phillimore J in *Atherton, Re* [1912] 2 KB 251. See also *Bishopsgate Investment Management Ltd v Maxwell* [1993] Ch 1.

common law, it may be removed or restricted by an appropriately worded statute.[72] It has never been available, for example, in bankruptcy proceedings,[73] in which the person involved asks to be released from liabilities and can be compelled to make fuller disclosure than could otherwise be required. The bankrupt has the option of remaining undischarged until the debts are paid.

If the privilege against self-incrimination were nothing but a testimonial privilege—dealing only, and to the extent that it does, with courtroom testimony—then it would have no application to tax returns and other information required by the tax authorities. It has, however, extended far more widely. At the time (the late 1940s) when the European Convention was written, the privilege against self-incrimination was not a uniform, or even a common, feature of many of the systems of criminal justice it was written to govern. In particular, the privilege had no part in any system based on the Napoleonic Code of Criminal Procedure, which granted extensive powers to investigating magistrates and gave few rights to suspects. There was consequently no explicit mention of self-incrimination in Article 6 of the European Convention on Human Rights (ECHR), which deals with fair trial rights.

The incorporation of the privilege in any form into the protections of Article 6 therefore came as something of a surprise.[74] In *Funke v France*[75] the defendant was fined in a French court for failing to produce bank statements demanded, under statutory powers, by customs officers. The Court, differing from the Commission, held that there had been a breach of Article 6(1). The reasoning of the Court was very briefly, and not very well, expressed.[76] The pronouncements of the court grew more sybillic in *Saunders v United Kingdom*,[77] where the applicant had been obliged under threat of imprisonment to give answers to questions posed by an inspector enquiring into a company takeover. He gave the answers and they were subsequently used in criminal proceedings against him. The European Court of Human Rights (ECtHR) held, for reasons which again could have been more clearly expressed,[78] that

[72] *R v Director of the Serious Fraud Office, ex p Smith* [1993] AC 1; [1992] 3 All ER 456. The Matrimonial Causes Act 1973 and Family Proceedings Rules 1991 SI 1247 are such provisions: *R v K* [2009] EWCA Crim 1640; [2010] QB 343. See also *Beghal v Director of Public* Prosecutions [2015] UKSC 49; [2016] AC 88.

[73] For the US see Tarvin, Tim, 'The Privilege Against Self-incrimination in Bankruptcy and the Plight of the Debtor' (2014) 44 *Seton Hall Law Review* 47.

[74] 'Unexpected and faltering': Ashworth, Andrew, 'Self-incrimination in European Human Rights Law—A Pregnant Pragmatism' (2008) 30 *Cardozo Law Review* 751, 752.

[75] *Funke v France* (1993) 16 EHRR 297.

[76] Para 44.

[77] *Saunders v United Kingdom* (1996) 23 EHRR 313.

[78] The core of the judgment is at paras 68–76.

the privilege against self-incrimination was part of the protection offered by Article 6 of the Convention. The response of the UK government was to put in place legislation[79] which had the effect of compelling, under threat of imprisonment, a person in the situation of Saunders to respond, but which then prevented the use of the answers in subsequent criminal proceedings. These provisions amended the law in many, but not all, cases where a person was obliged to provide the state with information.

An early case dealing with an area not covered by the statutory changes, but where the application of *Saunders* was restricted and the privilege was nonetheless held not to apply, was *R v Hertfordshire CC, ex p Green Environmental Industries Ltd.*[80] Medical waste appeared to have been disposed of unlawfully, and in such a way as to endanger anyone who had been involved in the disposal. A notice served under s 71(2) of the Environmental Protection Act 1990 required the company on which it was served to furnish particulars of all persons, companies, or hospitals which had supplied clinical waste to Green and of the persons who carried waste on its behalf. The company sought to rely upon *Saunders*, since to give the information would tend to expose them to prosecution for offences under the Environmental Protection Act 1990. The House of Lords held that it could not. Giving the only speech, Lord Hoffmann said that the restriction of a defendant's right not to incriminate himself would not infringe his right to a fair trial provided that the compulsion under which the information was obtained was of a moderate nature and the use of the evidence obtained represented a proportionate response to a pressing social need. Evidence gained by this compulsion might be excluded in the exercise of the general discretion under s 78 of PACE, and, as with some other areas,[81] s 78 served, without any further mandatory exclusionary rule, to satisfy the United Kingdom's obligations under Article 6. That is, the distinction between areas where the State needs the information for criminal prosecution and those where it needs it for other purposes still bears.

More problematically yet, in *Brown v Stott*[82] the Judicial Committee of the Privy Council held that *Saunders* did not give the privilege to someone charged with driving while over the prescribed blood-alcohol limit, who had been required[83] to state who drove her car to the supermarket at which

[79] Youth Justice and Criminal Evidence Act 1999 s 59 and Schedule 3.

[80] *R v Hertfordshire CC, ex p Green Environmental Industries Ltd* [2000] 2 AC 412; [2000] 1 All ER 773.

[81] *R v Loosely* [2001] UKHL 53; [2001] 1 WLR 2060.

[82] *Brown v Stott* [2003] 1 AC 681; [2001] 2 All ER 97.

[83] Under Road Traffic Act 1988 s 172.

she was apprehended. The reasoning in the judgment of Lord Bingham is not satisfactory. He advanced[84] a number of reasons why *Saunders* did not govern. Three are relevant in the context of tax evasion. First, there was the 'one simple question' argument. This is the claim that the obligations upon the defendant differed from those upon Saunders because she was only being asked (by the notice under s 172) one question—to name the driver of the car. Second, there was the argument that the answer would not, without more, be incriminatory. Here the argument is that the individual item of evidence (the statement that she was driving the car) would not, taken on its own (in this case without evidence of her intoxication), be incriminatory, because something more was required (in this case, the evidence of blood alcohol level). This does not provide a workable distinction. It will frequently be a matter of chance whether one item of evidence taken on its own will suffice to prove guilt, and usually it will not. Last came the 'specific regulatory regime' argument.[85] This is the claim that when a citizen engages in a regulated activity governed by a set of rules that is specific to it, s/he enters into an arrangement equivalent to a contract with the State, by which the citizen gives up the right not to incriminate him/herself in that regard, while acquiring the privilege of taking part in the activity. The model is a contractual one: by applying for a driving licence or other permit, a person subjects him/herself to obligations beyond those applying to those who do not engage in that particular area of activity. While this seems to provide a good account of the rationale for the privilege, and its application or non-application in various areas,[86] the obvious difficulty is that it would give a result in *Saunders* opposite to that reached by the ECtHR. Becoming a company director is an example *par excellence* of subjecting oneself to a specific regime. It may just as easily be argued that it is entirely legitimate that the State should be able to impose duties upon those who apply for the privileges of limited liability as it is upon those who apply for driving licences.[87] The ECtHR subsequently followed *Brown v Stott*, hardly more satisfactorily.[88] The effort not to express disapproval of *Saunders* made the task far more difficult than it would have been had the court been less deferential. It may be that the more flexible rules of precedent as between

[84] [2003] 1 AC 681 at 705. [85] Ibid. [86] *Green*, n 80.

[87] And compare the treatment of legal advice privilege for corporations: see this chapter, section entitled 'Does LPP Extend to Companies?'.

[88] *O'Halloran v United Kingdom, Francis v United Kingdom* (2008) 46 EHRR 21; 24 BHRC 380; *Jalloh v Germany* (2007) 44 EHRR 32; 20 BHRC 575 (forcible administration of emetics to induce production of evidence of drugs—article 3 violation).

the Supreme Court and the ECtHR adopted since that time[89] might have made the issues easier.

How does this relate to tax evasion? The taxpayer called upon to complete a tax return is under an obligation to furnish information to the State.[90] HMRC has power to impose penalties without recourse to the courts,[91] whether for late submission of a tax return or for failure to furnish information requested.[92] May the taxpayer assert that to give the information would tend to incriminate him/herself (and consequently decline)? Is the obligation of the taxpayer like the obligation of the driver (*Brown*), that of the toxic waste contractor (*Green*), or that of the company director (*Saunders*)? It has long been apparent that *Saunders* can hardly be allowed to lead to the conclusion that all compulsory powers requiring information or documents to be supplied are contrary to Article 6, but where and how is the line to be drawn? Ashworth's view is that the exigencies of taxation and other important administrative demands for information should be regarded as the exceptional cases to a wide-ranging privilege.[93] The alternative view might be a more contractual model of the privilege against self-incrimination, which examines the issue partly from the point of view of criminal justice fairness, but also having regard to the duties of citizenship. There are few duties attaching solely to living in the UK. There are duties to respond to a census; to register, if required, for military service; and for the registration of births and deaths.[94] The duty to make a tax return, when required, is such a duty.[95]

Even though the reasons for the conclusion may vary, there is general agreement that the privilege against self-incrimination is not available in the case of tax authorities' requests for information.[96] Lord Bingham's 'regulating a specific field' argument[97] might even make the availability of the privilege vary according to the precise nature of the tax liability in question. A return for income tax or capital gains tax does not make such complex demands as the questioning to which Saunders was subject. The threat is very similar to that faced by Saunders. The regulatory framework does not govern the whole range of citizens, but only

[89] *R (on the application of Faisal Kaiyam) v Secretary of State for Justice* [2014] UKSC 66; [2015] 2 WLR 76; *R v Horncastle* [2009] UKSC 14; [2010] 2 AC 373; *Horncastle v United Kingdom* (2015) 60 EHRR 31.

[90] TMA s 8.

[91] And see Chapter 7, section entitled 'The Civil Penalties Regime'.

[92] FA 2008 Schedule 36 para 39.

[93] At 773.

[94] Births and Deaths Registration Act 1953 s 36.

[95] Regulation of Investigatory Powers Act 2000 s 49 and its replacement in the Investigatory Powers Act 2016 make similar provision for the compelled disclosure of computer passwords.

[96] *R v Allen* [2001] UKHL 45; [2002] 1 AC 509.

[97] This justification for the privilege was approved in *O'Halloran v United Kingdom, Francis v United Kingdom* (2008) 46 EHRR 21; 24 BHRC 380.

those upon whom the obligation to make a return falls. The registration regime for VAT, on the other hand, might very well fall within that 'regulatory regime' account, so that one who registers could be regarded as subjecting themselves to enquiries above those to which other citizens are subject.

In *R v Allen*, the House of Lords was dismissive of the suggestion that the privilege was available as a response to a tax return:

> *the present case is one which relates to the obligation of a citizen to pay taxes and to his duty not to cheat the revenue. It is self-evident that the payment of taxes, fixed by the legislature, is essential for the functioning of any democratic state. It is also self-evident that to ensure the due payment of taxes the state must have power to require its citizens to inform it of the amount of their annual income, and to have sanctions available to enforce the provision of that information.*[98]

The ECtHR jurisprudence on Article 6 and the privilege is itself unsatisfactory. In *JB v Switzerland*,[99] the penalty for failing to submit documents required by the tax authorities was some £700–800 and the court held that this amounted to improper compulsion, was an attempt to obtain evidence 'in defiance of the will of the person charged', and fell foul of *Saunders*. In *Shannon v United Kingdom*,[100] the ECtHR held there had been a violation of Article 6 where the applicant had been required to attend an interview with financial investigators and had then been compelled to answer questions in connection with events in respect of which he had already been charged. This was not compatible with his right not to incriminate himself. In *King v United Kingdom*,[101] the ECtHR did not admit the complaint for other reasons, but, so far as concerned the relationship between a tax return and the Article 6.2 and 6.3 rights, was clear that the sanction for failure to complete a return was only financial; it distinguished *Saunders* and *JB v Switzerland* and approved *Allen v United Kingdom*.[102]

When the information is provided for purposes other than the determination of liability to tax, the privilege against self-incrimination may be available. In *R v K*[103] the court held that a criminal prosecution for

[98] At para 29 per Lord Hutton. An application to the ECtHR was refused: *Allen v United Kingdom (Admissibility)* (76574/01) 74 TC 263; (2002) 35 EHRR CD289.

[99] *JB v Switzerland* 3 ITL Rep 663; [2001] *Criminal Law Review* 748.

[100] *Shannon v United Kingdom* (2006) 42 EHRR 31. And see Berger, Mark, 'Self-incrimination and the European Court of Human Rights: Procedural Issues in the Enforcement of the Right to Silence' (2007) 5 *European Human Rights Law Review* 514–33.

[101] *King v United Kingdom (Admissibility) (No 1)* (13881/02) 5 ITL Rep 963; (2003) 37 EHRR CD1. Decided subsequently on the issue of delay in *King v United Kingdom* (13881/02) [2005] STC 438; (2005) 41 EHRR 29.

[102] *Allen v United Kingdom (Admissibility)* (76574/01) 74 TC 263; (2002) 35 EHRR CD289.

[103] *R v K* [2009] EWCA Crim 1640; [2010] QB 343.

cheating the Revenue could not be based on admissions made in a form in which the defendant disclosed assets, or otherwise under compulsion, within financial remedy proceedings (although in some circumstances other evidence might exist to permit a prosecution for tax evasion). In the course of divorce proceedings, he had signed a declaration-of-assets form, which a party is obliged to make truthfully under threat of imprisonment, in which he disclosed the existence of various bank accounts and investment portfolios in Switzerland and Liechtenstein. He had not declared them to HMRC.

The court held that the nature of the compulsion which might be applied to enforce compliance with the obligation to disclose information of an incriminating nature was severe, since a wilful refusal to comply would amount to a contempt of court, which might attract the not insignificant sanction of imprisonment. The social purpose for which the Crown sought to adduce evidence in such criminal proceedings was the suppression of tax evasion—which was an important social objective—but the admission of evidence obtained from the defendant under threat of imprisonment was not a reasonable and proportionate response to that social need, and the use of the defendant's admissions in the ancillary relief proceedings would deprive the defendant of the fair trial to which he was entitled under Article 6 of the Convention. They therefore had to be excluded by the judge in the exercise of his powers under s 78 of PACE. This is an indication that only direct questions from HMRC will displace the privilege against self-incrimination.

Evasive answers and limitations upon questions

What if the defendant has furnished enough information to enable an assessment to be made of his/her liability to tax, but refuses to answer questions as fully, or as is required, by HMRC? There may be good reasons, other than that it is acquired by crime, why the taxpayer might not want to make a statement about his/her source of income. A commercial sex worker, for example, might experience less difficulty obtaining a mortgage, for which s/he may need to supply a copy of a tax return, if s/he describes herself on the return (and the mortgage application) as an 'executive stress consultant' rather than as a 'prostitute'. Now of course prostitution is not per se criminal, but a drug dealer might describe him/herself similarly euphemistically. So long as no tax advantage comes from how the taxpayer describes his/her occupation, and so long as the return does not contain an out-and-out lie, it does not seem to make any difference how s/he describes him/herself. In any event, HMRC can always simply raise an assessment, and leave the burden on the taxpayer to show it to be incorrect.

Legal Advice Privilege—Lawyers and Other Tax Advisers

The relationship between a professional legal adviser and a client is confidential, and that confidentiality rests upon an express or implied contractual obligation. It is protected more closely than any other relationship of confidence, such as those of clients with bankers or accountants, or patients with doctors. Legal professional privilege (LPP) is a general term governing two distinct privileges (legal advice privilege and litigation privilege) which may arise in respect of communications between lawyers and their clients.[104] Legal advice privilege (LAP) exists to ensure that there is what Justice Rehnquist called 'full and frank communication between attorneys and their clients', which 'promote[s] broader public interests in the observance of law and administration of justice'.[105] LPP is a creature of common law, which was developed by the judges in cases going back at least to the sixteenth century.[106] Its history[107] is set out in the opinion of Lord Taylor of Gosforth CJ in *R v Derby Magistrates' Court, ex p B*.[108] Most authorities[109] have it that its rationale was first coherently characterized in a judgment by Lord Brougham LC in *Greenough v Gaskell*[110] and that it is well stated by Lord Hoffmann in *R (on the application of Morgan Grenfell & Co Ltd) v Special Commissioners of Income Tax*:[111]

> *First, LPP is a fundamental human right long established in the common law. It is a necessary corollary of the right of any person to obtain skilled advice about the law. Such advice cannot be effectively obtained unless the client is able to put all the facts before the adviser without fear that they may afterwards be disclosed and used to his prejudice ...*

[104] Passmore, C, 'The Future of Legal Professional Privilege' (1993) 3 *International Journal of Evidence and Proof* 71–86.

[105] Rehnquist CJ in *Upjohn Co v United States* (1981) 449 US 383, 389, quoted by Lord Scott in *Three Rivers District Council and Others v Governor and Company of the Bank of England (No 6)* [2004] UKHL 48; [2005] 1 AC 610 at para 31.

[106] *Berd v Lovelace* (1577) Cary 62; 21 ER 33 (solicitor) and *Dennis v Codrington* (1579) Cary 100; 21 ER 53 (barrister).

[107] Hazard, GC, 'An Historical Perspective on the Attorney–Client Privilege' (1978) 66 *California Law Review* 1061. Litigation privilege seems to have developed later—see per Lord Carswell in *Three Rivers (No 6)*, n 105, para 96.

[108] *R v Derby Magistrates' Court, ex p B* [1996] AC 487, 504–5.

[109] By, eg, Lord Neuberger in *R (on the application of Prudential plc) v Special Commissioner of Income Tax* [2013] UKSC 1; [2013] 2 AC 185 para 23.

[110] *Greenough v Gaskell* (1833) 1 My & K 98; 39 ER 618 (client confidentiality protects a solicitor in an action alleging fraud by the solicitor from production of documents in his possession which might well determine the matter).

[111] *R v Special Commissioner and another, ex p Morgan Grenfell & Co Ltd* [2002] UKHL 21; [2003] 1 AC 563, paras 7–8. And see Dixon, Dennis, 'Legal Professional Privilege and Advice from Non-lawyers' [2010] *British Tax Review* 83.

Secondly, the courts will ordinarily construe general words in a statute, although literally capable of having some startling or unreasonable consequence, such as overriding fundamental human rights, as not having been intended to do so. An intention to override such rights must be expressly stated or appear by necessary implication.

Legal professional privilege is protected by Article 6.1 and 6.3(c) of the European Convention, and, while it is not absolute, any interference with privileged material should be justified by a pressing need and subjected to the strictest scrutiny by the court.[112] LPP is expressly preserved in some enactments,[113] but is a common law principle and, leaving aside considerations of human rights, is capable of being superseded by statute. However, in *Bowman v Fels* Brooke LJ described access to private and confidential legal advice as 'a fundamental principle not lightly to be interfered with',[114] and the Supreme Court indicated in *Morgan Grenfell*[115] that legislation would not be interpreted to reduce legal professional privilege other than where there are very clear words so doing; consequently, the legislation under consideration[116] could not be invoked to force anyone to produce documents to which LPP attached. It is still clearer where LPP is specifically protected.[117] LPP protects the client from the production of documents, but once the documents are produced it does not affect their admissibility in evidence.[118]

It is misleading to think of the interaction between the client and his/her lawyers as a consultation from which one answer will inexorably and mechanistically ensue. There might well be a conference in which a team of lawyers are assembled and express differing points of view. Part of the reason for LPP is that these conferences should be candid and confidential.

The literature and the case law of LPP does not differentiate between civil and criminal law. Implicit in the accounts is the idea that if there is privilege then there is privilege and it is absolute, whether the client is discussing with the lawyer the legal consequences of a particular future company merger or a defence to a charge of murder. In contentious civil cases the overwhelming probability is that there will be a settlement before the matter reaches court.

[112] *Khodorkovskiy v Russia* (2014) 59 EHRR 7.

[113] PACE, FA 2008 Schedule 36 para 23, Serious Organised Crime and Police Act 2005 s 64, Legal Services Act 2007 s 190.

[114] *Bowman v Fels* [2005] EWCA Civ 226; [2005] 2 Cr App R 19 para 74.

[115] *R v Special Commissioner and another, ex p Morgan Grenfell & Co Ltd* [2002] UKHL 21; [2003] 1 AC 563.

[116] TMA s 20, now FA 2008 Schedule 36 para 23.

[117] The Criminal Justice Act 1987 does not apply where LPP is available: s 2(9). LPP is a defence to a disclosure order under Serious Organised Crime and Police Act 2005 s 64.

[118] *R v Governor of Pentonville Prison, ex p Osman* (1990) 90 Cr App R 281, DC.

In criminal cases this is not usually the case, and the role of the professional is different.[119] It may be that reconsideration of whether or not the privilege is defeasible will generate further enquiry into the different values of the various claims to privilege.

The question remains what the privilege exists for. It is quite plausible to suggest, when referring to *ex ante* lawyering—giving the client advice as to the legal consequences of various possible courses of action—that the privilege exists to ensure the client's compliance to the law, and that the extent of privilege is consequently limited by that purpose.[120] When referring to *ex post* lawyering—working through the legal consequences of events that have already taken place, so as to optimize or mitigate their effects for the client—the position is different. Whatever has happened has happened, and the role of the lawyer cannot be wholly a compliance task. When the events have happened it might be possible to imagine that the lawyer is an alter ego of the client with legal knowledge, accepting, where necessary, that the client may not have behaved well. When the events have not happened, however, it is less easy to ground a claim to privilege on the basis that the client wanted to behave unlawfully and then obtain the most favourable outcome.

Litigation Privilege

Preparation for litigation of any sort generates a separate but frequently overlapping legal professional privilege—litigation privilege. Litigation privilege protects communications between a lawyer and a third party, such as an investigator, adjuster, or medical adviser, when the dominant purpose[121] of the communication is ongoing or anticipated litigation. Tax advice given by lawyers will normally be covered by LAP. In the case of tax avoidance schemes whose chances of success depend upon the outcome of litigation, it might also be assumed that all communications, from the very outset, would be prepared with a view to litigation, and so litigation privilege might also be available.

There are four major issues of principle involved in describing the extent of LPP:

[119] And see this chapter, section entitled 'Legal Advice Privilege—Lawyers and Other Tax Advisers'.

[120] Loughrey, Joan, 'Legal Advice Privilege and the Corporate Client' (2005) 9 *International Journal of Evidence and Proof* 183–203; Higgins, Andrew, 'Corporate Abuse of Legal Professional Privilege' (2008) 27 *Civil Justice Quarterly* 377–406; Higgins, Andrew, 'Legal Advice Privilege and Its Relevance to Corporations' (2010) 73 *Modern Law Review* 371–98; Loughrey, Joan, *Corporate Lawyers and Corporate Governance* (Cambridge: Cambridge University Press, 2011) 173 *et seq.*

[121] *Tchenguiz and others v Director of the Serious Fraud Office* [2013] EWHC 2297.

(i) Is LPP absolute or defeasible, and if defeasible, by what?
(ii) Does it apply to lawyers only or to anyone giving advice on the legal position of the client?
(iii) How is 'legal' differentiated from 'non-legal' advice?
(iv) Does LPP extend to corporations?[122]

Absolute or defeasible?

As a matter of English law it is clear that where LPP applies, and has not been removed by statute,[123] it is not defeasible. Lord Taylor CJ said of the argument for a 'balancing exercise', setting off the claim of the holder of LPP against some countervailing interest:

> *[I]f a balancing exercise was ever required in the case of legal professional privilege, it was performed once and for all in the 16th century, and since then has applied across the board in every case, irrespective of the client's individual merits.*[124]

Whether LPP is defeasible or not should turn on the rationale for the privilege. It has been suggested, at least because of the advent of corporations since the sixteenth century, that this 'once and for all' should be subject to reappraisal.[125] In particular where the party claiming the privilege is a corporation, it should be remembered that limited liability is itself a privilege, and it may be made available at a price, and there would be no overwhelming human rights or other argument that the price should not include attenuation of legal professional privilege. The Supreme Court of Canada, for example, held in *Blank v Canada (Minister for Justice)*[126] that LPP was defeasible where absolutely necessary. Section 112 of the Investigatory Powers Act 2016 allows the interception of communications between lawyer and client when there are 'exceptional and compelling circumstances that make it necessary to authorise' it.

[122] Higgins, Andrew, 'Corporate Abuse of Legal Professional Privilege' (2008) 27 *Civil Justice Quarterly* 377–406.

[123] *C's Application for Judicial Review, Re* [2009] UKHL 15; [2009] 1 AC 908; *RE v United Kingdom* (62498/11) European Court of Human Rights, 27 October 2016.

[124] *R v Derby Magistrates' Court, Ex p B* [1996] AC 487 at 507. See also *B v Auckland District Law Society* [2003] UKPC 38; [2003] 2 AC 736; compare *Goodie v Ontario (Ministry of Correctional Services)* [2006] 2 SCR 32 LAP, displaced where 'absolutely necessary'.

[125] Loughrey, JM, 'An Unsatisfactory Stalemate: *R (on the application of Prudential plc) v Special Commissioner of Income Tax*' (2014) 18 *International Journal of Evidence and Proof* 65–77.

[126] *Blank v Canada (Minister for Justice)* [2006] SCC 39; Ives, Dale E, and Stephen GA Pitel, 'Filling in the Blanks for Litigation Privilege: *Blank v Canada (Minister for Justice)*' (2007) *International Journal of Evidence and Proof* 49.

Legal advice privilege and non-lawyers

What exactly is it that gives rise to the protection? Is it a particular qualification or a particular function? In *R (on the application of Prudential Plc) v Special Commissioner of Income Tax*,[127] the extent of the privilege was in issue. In 2004, PricewaterhouseCoopers ('PwC'), a form of accountants, devised a marketed tax avoidance scheme. PwC adapted the scheme for the benefit of the Prudential group of companies, who implemented the scheme through a series of transactions. The inspector of taxes considered it necessary to look into the details of the transactions and so served notices[128] on Prudential giving them the opportunity to make available specified classes of documents. Prudential refused to disclose certain documents on the ground of legal advice privilege, because they related to the seeking (by Prudential) and the giving (by PwC) of legal advice in connection with the transactions.

The Supreme Court held, by a majority of five to two (Lords Clarke and Sumption dissenting), that legal advice privilege did not extend to accountants. Lord Neuberger, for the majority, relied upon the received understanding of the privilege[129] and a number of more specific reasons in rejecting what he acknowledged to be the force of the argument of principle advanced by the dissentients. There are substantive technical reasons to be given in support of the decision in *Prudential*. Among the most important of these are, first, that the Keith Committee[130] proceeded on the clear basis that LAP was limited to communications with a client's lawyers and did not extend to communications with their tax accountants, even where these communications involve the seeking and giving of legal advice.[131] It did recommend change, but the recommendation was not implemented. The second reason is that in its deliberations on the Finance Act 2008,[132] in effect renewing the legislation in question, the Parliamentary Select Committee declined to extend LAP

[127] *R (on the application of Prudential plc) v Special Commissioner of Income Tax* [2013] UKSC 1; [2013] 2 AC 185. And see Higgins, Andrew, and Adrian Zuckerman, '*Re Prudential plc* [2013] UKSC 1: The Supreme Court Leaves to Parliament the Issue of Privilege for Tax Advice by Accountants, What Parliament Should do is Restrict Privilege for Tax Advice Given by Lawyers' (2013) 32 *Civil Justice Quarterly* 313. See also Dixon, n 111.

[128] Under TMA s 20B(1), now FA 2008 Sched 36, but in relevant respects unchanged.

[129] For example, in *Revenue and Customs Commissioners' Application (Section 20(3) Notice: Plc), Re (SpC 647)* [2008] STC (SCD) 358; [2007] STI 2851 s.

[130] Keith of Kinkel, Lord (Chair), n 15, Vols 1 and 2, Chapter 26.

[131] Lord Neuberger at para 33, citing Keith Report para 6.6.9 and recommendation 97, which recommended change. The government response to Keith—Board of Inland Revenue, *The Inland Revenue and the Taxpayer: Proposals in Response to the Recommendations of the Keith Committee on Income Tax, Capital Gains Tax and Corporation Tax* (London: HMSO, 1986)—took the view (at 165) that further consideration was necessary.

[132] HC Debates, 10 June 2008 Cols 606–8.

to tax advice given by accountants through an amendment to what became paragraph 23 of Schedule 36 to the 2008 Act.[133]

In 1983, when the Keith Committee recommended that LPP should be extended to communications in connection with tax advice given by expert accountants, it included two qualifications. The first was that the privilege should be overridden where it 'would ... unreasonably impede the ascertainment of facts necessary to the proper determination of the taxpayer's tax liabilities, being facts not otherwise capable of ascertainment'.[134] The second was that LAP should not extend to advice given by in-house professional advisers.[135] In a standard judicial response to rational arguments for change, Lord Neuberger in *Prudential* said that it would be open to Parliament to impose such types of restriction or condition: it would not realistically be open to the courts.[136] Lord Sumption and Lord Clarke argued (as the majority tended to concede) that as a matter of principle there was no reason to restrict the privilege. Lord Clarke expressed the argument of principle very clearly:

> *[A]s I see it, that principle can readily be seen by taking a simple example. Suppose that two individuals, A and B, have the same problem, the solution to which depends upon an application of the legal principles of taxation law to the same, or substantially the same, facts. Suppose that A seeks advice from, say, Freshfields, and that B seeks advice from, say, PricewaterhouseCoopers. Each asks the same question and gives an account of what are substantially the same facts to the person from whom the advice is sought. Each is receiving legal advice. The question for decision in this appeal is whether the information given and the advice received are privileged as legal advice. Are both A and B entitled to claim the privilege and refuse to disclose to HMRC the information and the advice?*
>
> *In my opinion, the only principled answer to that question is yes.*[137]

As a matter of principle, that is indeed the end of the matter. There is no tenable distinction to be made, and the decision in *Prudential* is to be regretted and should be reversed by statute.

In addition to the kinds of arguments considered in the *Prudential* case, a competition argument has arisen from time to time. It states that to restrict absolute LPP to members of the legal profession places its members at a competitive advantage as against other tax professionals, and that this ought not to be permitted.[138] Recital (10) to the Fourth Money Laundering Directive[139]

[133] Lord Neuberger at para 36.

[134] Keith of Kinkel, Lord, n 15, Vols 1 and 2, para 26.6.5.

[135] Para 26.6.13.

[136] Lord Neuberger at para 65.

[137] Paras 140–1.

[138] And see Office of Fair Trading, *Competition in Professions: A Report by the Director General of Fair Trading* (2001) para 47, available at <http://webarchive.nationalarchives.gov.uk/20140402142426/http:/www.oft.gov.uk/shared_oft/reports/professional_bodies/oft328.pdf>.

[139] Directive 2015/849/EU (Fourth Money Laundering Directive).

stipulates that directly comparable services ought to be treated in the same manner when practised by any of the professionals covered by the Directive, and there are clear competition law arguments against differentiation by qualification rather than by function.

What is 'legal' advice?

It may be difficult to distinguish legal advice from more general commercial or prudential advice, and this issue will frequently arise where the advice in question relates to liability to tax. The taxpayer might very well take the view that the tax outcome of a proposed course of action is one of the things to be taken into account in determining whether or not it is commercially worthwhile. In *Three Rivers District Council and Others v Governor and Company of the Bank of England (No 6)*[140] the House of Lords gave 'legal advice' a fairly wide reading, overruling the Court of Appeal and holding that it extended to advice as to what should prudently and sensibly be done in a 'relevant legal context',[141] which would include the presentation of a case to an inquiry[142] by someone whose conduct might be criticized by it. In consequence, communications between the Bank's inquiry unit and its lawyers were privileged when they dealt with the presentation to the inquiry of its case that its discharge of its public law obligations under the Banking Acts was not deserving of criticism.[143]

Does LPP extend to companies?

The claims made for LPP give rise to particular difficulties in the corporate context. In the *Prudential* case it was the company's privilege. It was difficult to see how, in the circumstances which had arisen, it needed it. It has been argued with considerable force[144] that simply to treat a corporation as acquiring, with its legal personality, the same rights as a natural person is a mistake, and that the balancing exercise to which Lord Taylor referred may at least need to be reconsidered so as to deal with the advent of the limited liability company.[145] Public and large private companies in particular already have sufficient incentives to obtain accurate legal advice about their affairs

[140] *Three Rivers District Council and Others v Governor and Company of the Bank of England (No 6)* [2004] UKHL 48; [2005] 1 AC 610.

[141] *Balabel v Air India* [1988] Ch 317 at 330 (Lord Taylor CJ).

[142] Bingham, T (Chair), *Inquiry into the Collapse of BCCI* (HC 198, 1992).

[143] At paras 34–8; 43–5 (Lord Scott).

[144] Loughrey, n 120.

[145] Higgins, Andrew, *Legal Professional Privilege for Corporations: A Guide to Four Major Common Law Jurisdictions* (Oxford: Oxford University Press, 2014).

even without a privilege. There are also sound policy reasons for restricting the right of corporations to claim legal advice privilege, given its costs to the administration of justice.

Advice to individual and to corporate clients

In order for the privilege to be held jointly, either there must be a joint retainer, or an individual claiming joint legal professional privilege with others would need to establish that the legal advice had been sought in an individual capacity, that s/he had made his capacity clear to the lawyer, that those with whom the joint privilege was claimed had appreciated the legal position, and that the communications were confidential.[146]

In-house lawyers

Does it matter whether the lawyer in question is 'in-house' or from an independent firm?[147] The traditional position in English law is that the privilege applies in both cases.[148] Lord Denning justified the result primarily on the ground that, although a corporation's communications with an in-house legal adviser were internal to the corporation, nevertheless the adviser was performing the same function as the lawyer in independent practice. The Keith Committee recommended change, but this proposal was not taken up.[149] In EU competition law investigations by the European Commission there is a difference. Communications with in-house lawyers are not extended the privilege,[150] apparently because recognition of LPP is based upon the idea of the independent lawyer as collaborating in the administration of justice. Employed lawyers, on the other hand, were thought less able to deal with conflicts of interest between the interests of justice and those of the client/employer.

[146] *R (on the application of Ford) v Financial Services Authority (Johnson and Owen, Interested Parties)* [2011] EWHC 2583 (Admin).

[147] Bastin, Lucas, 'Should "Independence" of In-house Counsel Be a Condition Precedent to a Claim of Legal Professional Privilege in Respect of Communications between Them and Their Employer Clients?' [2011] *Civil Justice Quarterly* 33.

[148] *Alfred Crompton Amusement Machines Ltd v Customs and Excise Commissioners (No 2)* [1972] 2 QB 102; [1972] 2 All ER 353 per Lord Denning MR at 129. *Prudential*, n 127, at paras 63 (Lord Neuberger) and 123 (Lord Sumption, dissenting, but not on this point).

[149] Keith, 6.6.9 and recommendation 97, response that 'further consideration [is] necessary' in Board of Inland Revenue, *The Inland Revenue and the Taxpayer: Proposals in Response to the Recommendations of the Keith Committee on Income Tax, Capital Gains Tax and Corporation Tax* (London: HMSO, 1986) 165.

[150] *Akzo Nobel Chemicals Ltd v European Commission (C-550/07 P)* [2011] 2 AC 338; [2011] All ER (EC) 1107.

The practical consequence of the decision will be that in-house lawyers will communicate about competition matters, whenever possible, orally. Critics of the judgment have not been slow to point out that in-house lawyers have an important role to play in ensuring compliance with EU competition law and that this decision makes this important prophylactic task more difficult. External lawyers may be pleased by the judgment because it could push more business their way. They have been given an advantage over their in-house colleagues that multinational corporations with deep pockets will not be slow to exploit.[151]

Must the lawyer be an English lawyer?

Relevant communications with foreign lawyers have for many years attracted the same privilege. In *Lawrence v Campbell*,[152] privilege was claimed in English litigation for communications between a Scottish client and a Scottish solicitor practising in London. Sir Richard Kindersley V-C held that 'the same principle that would justify an Englishman consulting his English solicitor would justify a Scotchman consulting a Scotch solicitor'.[153] It is difficult to see why this should be the case. The logical consequence of the view that there is something special, for these purposes, about having specific legal qualifications in England and Wales should be that foreign qualifications do not count for these purposes, even though much tax law is the same in Scotland. Inclusion of foreign lawyers gives rise to a difficult consideration of which legal qualifications were, and which were not, transferable. This particular issue should be resolved as a part of a wider reform of LAP.

In the *Three Rivers* litigation,[154] the Court of Appeal[155] held that that LAP, unlike litigation privilege, applied only to communications between a client and his legal advisers, to documents evidencing such communications, and to documents that were intended to be such communications even if not in fact communicated.[156] The House of Lords declined to address that issue.

[151] Pattenden, Rosemary, 'Legal Professional Privilege' (2011) *International Journal of Evidence and Proof* 79; Stefanelli, Justine N, 'Expanding Azko Nobel' (2013) 62 *International & Comparative Law Quarterly* 485.

[152] *Lawrence v Campbell* (1859) 4 Drew 485; 62 ER 186, *Macfarlan v Rolt* (1872) LR 14 Eq 580; *Duncan, decd, In re* [1968] P 306; *Great Atlantic Insurance Co v Home Insurance Co* [1981] 1 WLR 529, 535–6, cited in *Prudential* at para 123 by Lord Sumption, dissenting, but not on this point.

[153] At 491.

[154] And see Zuckerman, Adrian, 'A Colossal Wreck—The BCCI –Three Rivers Litigation' (2006) 25 *Civil Justice Quarterly* 287–311.

[155] *Three Rivers District Council and Others v Governor and Company of the Bank of England (No 5)* [2003] EWCA Civ 474; [2003] QB 1556.

[156] Stockdale, Michael and Rebecca Mitchell, 'Who Is the Client? An Exploration of Legal Professional Privilege in the Corporate Context' (2006) 27 *Company Lawyer* 110–18.

The 'Iniquity Exception'

Material is not privileged under either head of legal professional privilege if it falls within the 'iniquity exception'.[157] LAP and litigation privilege have always been subject to the exception that the advice is not privileged if it involves the commission of a crime, and more recent years have seen an extension of the exception. Stephen J noted that it would be 'monstrous'[158] not to have an exception, but, it not having at that point been set out before, went on to define it.

[I]n each particular case the court must determine on the facts … whether it seems probable that the accused person may have consulted his legal adviser, not after the commission of the crime for the legitimate purpose of being defended, but before the commission of the crime for the purpose of being guided or helped in committing it. We are far from saying that the question whether the advice was taken before or after[159] *the offence will always be decisive as to the admissibility of such evidence … Of course the power in question ought to be used with the greatest care not to hamper prisoners in making their defence, and not to enable unscrupulous persons to acquire knowledge to which they have no right, and every precaution should be taken against compelling unnecessary disclosures.*[160]

The exception is said to apply equally to litigation privilege as to LAP.[161] In relation to documents held by a solicitor acting for a defendant in pending criminal proceedings, a claim to legal professional privilege can be defeated where there is evidence of a specific agreement to pervert the course of justice, which is freestanding and independent, in the sense that it does not require any judgment to be reached in relation to the issues to be tried in the pending proceedings.[162] A litigant's strategy of concealment and deceit in relation to his assets justified an order for disclosure of documents currently held by his solicitors or former solicitors which would otherwise have attracted legal professional privilege.[163]

[157] The expression seems to have started life as by describing an exception to a duty of confidence: *Attorney General v Observer Ltd* [1990] 1 AC 109, only later being transferred to legal professional privilege. Before then, in the line of cases from *O'Rourke v Derbyshire* [1920] AC 581 at 604 to *Chicago Holdings Ltd v Cooper* [2005] EWHC 3466 (Ch), the privilege is limited to the case of 'a definite charge of fraud or illegality' (*Chicago* at para 9). Widespread use of the expression 'iniquity exception' rather than 'crime/fraud exception' in the context of LPP dates from *C's Application for Judicial Review, Re* [2009] UKHL 15; [2009] 1 AC 908.

[158] *R v Cox & Railton* (1884) 14 QBD 153, 165–6.

[159] See this chapter, section entitled 'Legal Advice Privilege—Lawyers and Other Tax Advisers'.

[160] At 175.

[161] *Kuwait Airways Corp v Iraqi Airways Co (No 6)* [2005] EWCA Civ 286; [2005] 1 WLR 2734.

[162] *R (on the application of Hallinan Blackburn-Gittings & Nott (A Firm)) v Middlesex Guildhall Crown Court* [2004] EWHC 2726 (Admin); [2005] 1 WLR 766.

[163] *SC BTA Bank v Ablyazov* [2014] EWHC 2788; [2014] Lloyd's Rep FC Plus 56.

The earlier cases going back to *Cox & Railton*[164] speak of the 'crime/fraud' exception. The important question now is whether the iniquity exception requires criminality or other unlawful behaviour and, if it does, whether the criminality or other unlawful behaviour must be that of the lawyer or the client, or both?[165] In *Eustice v Barclays Bank*,[166] Barclays sought declarations setting aside certain transactions in relation to farmland which was already charged as security for loans made to Mr Eustice. Those transactions were entered into on terms so favourable to Mr Eustice as to amount to undervalues within the meaning of the relevant insolvency provisions (which is directed against 'transactions defrauding creditors').[167] Further, because those transactions occurred with family members at a time when action by the bank to protect its interests was clearly anticipated by the family, and its result was that what remained in his hands barely if at all covered his indebtedness, the court held that there was a strong prima facie case that the purpose of the transactions was to prejudice the interests of the bank. It followed that the preconditions for the making of an order were satisfied. The issue was whether those findings entitled the bank, on an interlocutory application for discovery, to an order for disclosure of the defendant's communications with his legal advisers in relation to those transactions.

The Court of Appeal accepted that the case was about advice sought on how to structure a transaction lawfully, albeit in circumstances where it must have been obvious to the defendant that the bank would challenge it once it knew what he had attempted to do. For the defendant it was argued that neither he nor his solicitors were engaged in a crime or fraudulent purpose: rather, they had openly and jointly engaged in a purpose which was both overt and lawful, namely, seeking and giving advice as to how to remove the defendant's assets out of the temporary reach of the bank *without* falling foul of the Act. In the language of tax law, they were avoiders, not evaders. To this the court responded that the defendant's conduct was 'sufficiently iniquitous for public policy to require that communications between him and his solicitor in relation to the setting up of these transactions be discoverable'.[168] This is exactly the sort of case to which discussions about tax avoidance might give rise. Tax avoiders might ask their legal advisers where to put money, or

[164] *R v Cox & Railton* (1884) 14 QBD 153.

[165] PACE s 10(2) states: 'Items held with the intention of furthering a criminal purpose are not items subject to legal privilege.' *R v Central Criminal Court, ex p Francis & Francis (A Firm)* [1989] AC 346; (1989) 88 Cr App R 213 held that the intention to which the statute refers is that of the client, not the lawyer.

[166] *Eustice v Barclays Bank* [1995] 1 WLR 1156 (CA). See Boon, Andrew, *The Ethics and Conduct of Lawyers in England and Wales* (Oxford: Bloomsbury Publishing, 3rd edn, 2014) 246.

[167] Under Insolvency Act 1986 s 423.

[168] Schiemann LJ at 1249D.

how to dispose of it, so as for it to be outside the reach of HMRC. There is no suggestion that the defendant in *Eustice*, or the lawyer, acted criminally or even *unlawfully*, but it seems that the iniquity exception was held to run more widely, so that it applies not just where communications are made in furtherance of a criminal purpose but also where there is a purpose which breaches a duty of good faith, is contrary to public policy, or is contrary to the interests of justice.[169]

If *Eustice* is correct, for the iniquity principle now to apply, the evidence must disclose a strong prima facie case of iniquity, which has been held in the lower courts not to be limited to crimes but to mean 'fraud in its wider sense'.[170] In *Re McE*, however, Lord Neuberger expressly left open the question whether *Eustice* was correctly decided.[171] It is suggested that it ought not to be followed. People who set out to comply with their legal obligations ought to be differentiated from those who do not. Someone trying to behave lawfully ought to have the benefit of LAP. This is not an area which talk of thin ice, closeness to the wind, or anything of that nature should determine. A lawyer can quite legitimately be asked how minimally to comply to the law, and that advice should be privileged.[172]

The *Eustice* issue arises baldly in money laundering cases. Section 330(6) of POCA provides that a person who is a professional legal adviser or 'relevant professional adviser' does not commit a criminal offence if he fails to make a financial disclosure of information which has been communicated to him in legally privileged circumstances. A provision was inserted into s 330(14) of POCA by a statutory instrument in 2006 which defined 'relevant professional adviser' to include accountants and members of the Chartered Institute of Taxation.[173] For this purpose, legal professional privilege also captures the

[169] See *JSC BTA Bank v Ablyazov* [2014] EWHC 2788 (Comm), para 68 (Popplewell J).

[170] *BBGP Managing General Partner Limited & Ors v Babcock & Brown Global Partners* [2010] EWHC 2176 (Ch); [2011] Ch 296. In *London Borough of Brent v Estate of Kane* [2014] EWHC 4564 (Ch) Simon Monty QC, sitting as a Deputy Judge of the Chancery Division, said at para 32, 'Although the case law refers to crime or fraud or dishonesty, such as fraudulent breach of trust, fraudulent trickery or sham contrivances, it is plain that the term "fraud" is used in a relatively wide sense, see *Eustice* at 1249D. So a scheme to effect transactions at an undervalue was sufficient (*Eustice*), as was deliberate misrepresentation for the purpose of securing a mortgage advance (*Nationwide Building Society v Various Solicitors (No 1)* [1999] PNLR 52 at 72), or making a disposition with the intention of defeating a spouse's claim for financial relief (*C v C* [2008] 1 FLR 115), or the establishment by employees in breach of a duty of fidelity to their employer over a rival business (*Gammon v Roach* [1983] RPC 1 and *Walsh Automation (Europe) Ltd v Bridgeman* [2002] EWHC 1344 (QB)'.

[171] *McE, Re* [2009] UKHL 15; [2009] 1 AC 908 at para 109.

[172] And see also Ives and Pitel, n 126.

[173] Proceeds of Crime Act 2002 and Money Laundering Regulations 2003 (Amendment) Order 2006 SI 308 art 2(5).

situation where information is communicated directly not to a professionally qualified person but to a person employed by, or in partnership with, a relevant professional adviser.[174]

In contrast to the position in s 330(6) of POCA, which deals with the regulated sector reporting obligation, there is no reference to the legal privilege exemption in ss 327 to 329, and until the decision of the Court of Appeal (Civil Division) in *Bowman v Fels*,[175] there was considerable uncertainty as to the position. It made little sense to exempt a lawyer from liability under s 330 for failing to report suspicion of laundering if s/he would in any event be liable under s 328 for being concerned in an arrangement whereby laundering took place. The Court in *Bowman* re-affirmed the fundamental principle that information passed to a solicitor or barrister for the purposes of obtaining legal advice or during the course of litigation was protected by legal privilege and therefore immune from disclosure under the anti-money laundering (AML) disclosure regime. Applying traditional canons of statutory construction, the Court ruled that ss 327 to 329 of POCA did not operate to override, either expressly or by implication, the fundamental principle of legal privilege at common law. In this way, the Court of Appeal ensured that the AML disclosure regime had no application to information communicated to a solicitor or a barrister in legally privileged circumstances, whether the financial disclosure obligation arose under ss 327 to 329 or s 330 of POCA.

The Mechanics of LPP: (i) Resolution of Disputes

In civil or criminal litigation, the judge is the ultimate arbiter as to whether, in any case before him/her, material is privileged. S/he must look at the documents whose production was in issue, to determine whether they carry privilege or came into existence in furtherance of a criminal purpose and should thus be produced. In a civil tax enquiry, where there is a dispute as to whether or not material is privileged, a mechanism for its resolution is set out in the LPP Regulations.[176] The documents go to the tax tribunal for determination. Nowhere in Schedule 36 or the LPP regulations is it stated in terms that the effect of failing to invoke the dispute resolution mechanism offered by the LPP regulations is to waive a claim to LPP. The procedure is expressed to be one for the resolution of disputes, not the determination of the law. This

[174] POCA s 330(7).

[175] *Bowman v Fels* [2005] EWCA Civ 226; [2005] 2 Cr App R 19 disapproving *P v P (Ancillary Relief: Proceeds of Crime)* [2003] EWHC Fam 2260; [2004] Fam 1.

[176] Information Notice: Resolution of Disputes as to Privileged Communications Regulations 2009 SI 1916 ('the LPP regulations') regs 5(5) and 6(5).

leaves open the possibility of involving the courts. The remedy in the criminal case is an action for judicial review or trespass. A procedure is needed by which to allow the matter to be resolved by a judge of equal rank to the one who granted the warrant.

The Mechanics of LPP: (ii) The Execution of Tax Fraud Searches

One major difficulty in conducting searches with a view to identifying and seizing evidence of tax evasion is that some of the evidence may be subject to LPP.[177] Searches are required to be authorized under the conditions set out in PACE.[178] When material which might or might not be subject to privilege is the subject matter of a search with a warrant, there is obviously a need to provide a mechanism for distinguishing between privileged and non-privileged material. PACE does not itself sanction any procedure whereby disputed material can be taken and scrutinized away from the premises or segregated and scrutinized later on the premises.[179] The application of search powers in a digital world has proved especially difficult. Files on a computer hard disk containing relevant and irrelevant material have been held all to be one entity.[180]

[177] For the history and some recommendations on the law pre-PACE see Keith of Kinkel, Lord (Chair), n 15, Vols 1 and 2, 9.16.

[178] PACE ss 8–13 and Sched 1, as modified by Police and Criminal Evidence Act 1984 (Application to Revenue and Customs) Order 2015/1783 art 6.

[179] *R v Chesterfield Justices ex p Bramley* [2000] QB 576, distinguishing *Reynolds v MPC* [1985] 1 QB 881 where the relevant legislation (Forgery Act 1913), unlike PACE, required disputed material to be brought before a magistrate as soon as practicable. *Bramley* was distinguished in the TMA s 20C case of *R (on the application of H) v IRC* [2002] EWHC 2164 (Admin); [2002] STC 1354, but that case must be taken to have gone with s 20C.

[180] *R (on the application of H) v IRC* [2002] EWHC 2164 (Admin); [2002] STC 1354 (under TMA s 20CC but would be the same under PACE). Doubt is expressed by Andrew Roberts in his casenote on *Faisaltex*, [2009] *Criminal Law Review* 353, arguing that 'The problem with this approach is that it does not constitute the least intrusive means of obtaining the evidence sought. Nor does it seem consistent with the powers provided by the Criminal Justice and Police Act 2001. If electronic documents stored on the computer, rather than the machine itself, are relevant to the offences being investigated, the documents (generally described) ought to be specified in the warrant. Further, PACE s 22(4) provides that nothing may be retained as evidence if a copy would be sufficient for that purpose. If electronic documents were to be specified in the warrant, the police would have the power to seize the computer under s 51 of the 2001 Act, it being "something on the premises in respect of there are reasonable grounds for believing it may contain something for which they are authorised to search". Copies could be made of any relevant documents. However, attached to the powers of seizure provided by the 2001 Act are duties to examine the material seized and return any which falls outside the scope of the warrant as soon as reasonably practicable. There is no corresponding duty under PACE s 8, and a lack of specificity in the terms of a warrant may place the person from whom the computer is seized at a considerable disadvantage.'

The ECtHR has held that, where a search warrant is executed at a lawyer's office, 'special procedural safeguards, such as the presence of an independent observer' should be put in place to avoid an unwarranted breach of professional confidence.[181] In *Tamosius v United Kingdom*,[182] the ECtHR held that the interference with the taxpayer's rights was a necessary and proportionate means within a democratic society of preventing crime and protecting the economic well-being of the country. The search had been carried out under a warrant, issued by a judge who had to be satisfied that there were reasonable grounds for suspecting that a tax fraud had been committed, of which there might be evidence at the premises to be searched. Scrutiny by a judge was an important safeguard against abuse. Further, the warrant had included a schedule of companies and individuals under investigation which should have given the applicant an indication of the purpose of the search sufficient to enable him to assess whether the investigation team had acted unlawfully or exceeded their powers. In *R (Tchenguiz) v Director of the Serious Fraud Office*[183] it was said that an independent lawyer should be present at a search where there is a potential issue as to legal professional privilege, and that a lawyer employed by those carrying out the search (such as the SFO) is not independent in this context. A barrister in the same chambers as others instructed in the case is, on the other hand, suitably independent.[184]

While investigating authorities cannot in general seize any material that is subject to LPP, ss 50 and 51 of the Criminal Justice and Police Act 2001 permit the authorities to seize devices that they suspect contain LPP material. Where an investigator finds a device and has reasonable grounds for believing it may contain material they are searching for, they are allowed to seize the device to allow them to determine if such material exists. Investigators can therefore seize devices where it is not reasonably practicable to separate the

[181] *Niemietz v Germany* (1992) 16 EHRR 97.

[182] *Tamosius v United Kingdom (Admissibility)* [2002] STC 1307; [2003] BTC 169, on appeal from *R v IRC, ex p Tamosius & Partners (a firm)* [2000] 1 WLR 453; [1999] STC 1077, highlighting differences, now gone, between the PACE and TMA regimes—where, in the first place, there was no statutory obligation under the TMA to specify in the warrant the items sought. By comparison, with PACE (section 15) there are clearly fewer safeguards designed to ensure privacy for the suspect. The court's rejection of the need for greater specificity in the warrant was founded on the statutory formula in s 20C (coupled with the fact that no fewer than four amending statutes to the TMA since PACE have failed to incorporate a provision requiring such specificity) and the 'insuperable authority of the House of Lords in *R v CIR, ex p Rossminster*' ([2000] 1 WLR 453 at 460 (Moses J)).

[183] *R (Rawlinson & Hunter Trustees) v Central Criminal Court; R (Tchenguiz) v Director of the Serious Fraud Office* [2012] EWHC 2254 (Admin); [2013] 1 WLR 1634; [2013] Lloyd's Rep FC 132.

[184] *R (Faisaltex Ltd) v Preston Crown Court* [2008] EWHC 2832 (Admin); [2009] 1 Cr App R 37.

LPP from the non-LPP material contained on the device. The provisions of the 2001 Act apply not only to electronically stored material but also to material stored in hard copy.[185]

In *R (on the application of Colin McKenzie) v Director of the Serious Fraud Office*,[186] the procedure set out in the SFO's Handbook for isolating material potentially subject to LPP, for the purpose of making it available to an independent lawyer for review, was held to be lawful. 'The purpose is to ensure that such material will not be read by members of the investigative team before it has been reviewed by an independent lawyer to establish whether privilege exists'.[187] The court[188] ruled that the SFO may use in-house technical experts to isolate privileged files, rather than external contractors. The use of the SFO's in-house lawyers as 'independent' lawyers to determine whether material was subject to LPP would be unlawful. However, using them to determine whether material may or may not be subject to LPP at the preliminary stage before sending it out independently to be assessed was not.[189]

Obtaining Information Otherwise than From the Taxpayer

What if information about the taxpayer is acquired by the authorities otherwise than from the taxpayer under compulsion? If documents come lawfully into the hands of the authorities they may be used against the taxpayer, and even if obtained unlawfully they need not necessarily be excluded from any subsequent criminal trial.[190] Communications protected by legal professional privilege are still admissible in criminal proceedings if they fall into the hands of the prosecution.[191]

HMRC does receive information from informers, and it has the power to reward them.[192] Where an informer has been paid, the jury should be made

[185] S 63.

[186] *R (on the application of Colin McKenzie) v Director of the Serious Fraud Office* [2016] EWHC 102 (Admin).

[187] Para 34.

[188] Building on the 'Chinese wall' idea in *Bolkiah v KPMG (A Firm)* [1999] 2 AC 222.

[189] *R (on the application of Colin McKenzie) v Director of the Serious Fraud Office* [2016] EWHC 102 (Admin), paras 31–4, 37, and 40–1.

[190] *Attorney General's Reference (No 3 of 1999)* [2001] 2 AC 91; [2001] 1 Cr App R 34.

[191] For example, *R v Tompkins* (1978) 67 Cr App R 181.

[192] CRCA s 26 replaced a similar power in relation to Customs and Excise matters—CEMA s 165—and a more limited power to pay rewards to informers in relation to Inland Revenue (Inland Revenue Regulation Act 1890 s 32). See *R (Churchhouse) v IRC* [2003] EWHC 681 Admin; [2003] STC 629 and 'UK Tax Authorities Pay Record £605,000 to Informants', *The Guardian*, 15 June 2015.

aware of this. A person might pass on documents to HMRC. If that person is an employee s/he may be able to claim whistle-blower protection.[193] There is also the possibility of information being gleaned by targeted surveillance. The investigation might include test purchases and observations in shops and restaurants so as to estimate their turnover. These are usually consistent with the *Loosely*[194] criteria.

The investigative functions usually undertaken by HMRC are governed by PACE and the legislation on investigatory powers.[195] *C's Application for Judicial Review*[196] decided that the provisions of the Regulation of Investigatory Powers Act 2000 overrode LPP, so that if bugging had been lawfully ordered under the Act, information thereby obtained and admissible[197] could be used, subject to applicable exclusionary discretions.[198]

Sometimes HMRC will acquire information via a mandatory or a protected disclosure under the AML regime. Under the decision in *Bowman v Fels*,[199] LPP is not excluded by the main laundering provisions of Part VII of POCA. Where the 'iniquity exception'[200] does apply, however, LPP will not be available, the reporting obligations upon the regulated sector will apply, and the lawyer will have a duty under POCA to report suspicions to the National Crime Agency (NCA) and will commit a crime by not doing so.[201] This makes the ambit of the 'iniquity exception'[202] crucial. If the exception is restricted to crime, then it will not cover tax *avoidance*. If it is wider—that is, if *Barclays v Eustice*[203] remains good law and applies here—then the law is significantly less clear. Suppose the lawyer acted for one of the UBS employees.[204] If *Eustice* governs, LPP would be lost because of the nature of the scheme. If the lawyer has a suspicion[205] that the client is engaged in activity that might amount to tax evasion and if the decision in *R v William*[206] is correct (that wherever there is tax evasion there will also be money laundering), then the communications will not be privileged, even if the client's proposed further behaviour is lawful.

193 Under the Public Interest Disclosure Act 1998.

194 *R v Loosely* [2001] UKHL 53; [2001] 1 WLR 2060.

195 Regulation of Investigatory Powers Act 2000, and now Investigatory Powers Act 2016.

196 *C's Application for Judicial Review, Re* [2009] UKHL 15; [2009] 1 AC 908.

197 That is, not excluded in virtue of RIPA s 17.

198 Under the Investigatory Powers Act 2016 s 55 *et seq*.

199 *Bowman v Fels* [2005] EWCA Civ 226; [2005] 2 Cr App R 19.

200 See this chapter, section entitled 'The "Iniquity Exception"'.

201 S 330.

202 See this chapter, section entitled 'The "Iniquity Exception"'.

203 n 167.

204 That is, the taxpayers in *HMRC v UBS* [2016] UKSC 13; see Chapter 3, section entitled 'Avoidance—Remedies'.

205 The 'inkling' referred to in *R v Da Silva* [2006] EWCA Crim 1654; [2007] 1 WLR 303.

206 See Chapter 9, section entitled 'The Substantive Laundering Offences'.

Taxpayer Confidentiality

The system of income tax was developed against the background of a view that requests by the State to know about the wealth and income of a gentleman were serious intrusions, the effects of which should be minimized.[207] Although there is some evidence of taxpayers' returns being disposed of and used by tradespeople to wrap their produce in the nineteenth century,[208] the theory of taxpayer confidentiality is firmly ingrained. This gave rise to a very strict policy on the disclosure of tax returns, that apart from investigations of murder and treason, the Revenue would only make disclosures to the police in consequence of court orders, which themselves were not granted routinely.

Beyond those dealing with State intrusion,[209] the sorts of arguments that are usually advanced for confidentiality[210] are to free the taxpayer from approaches by fraudsters or kidnappers or from pursuit of grudges, and to facilitate management (by keeping employees' salaries confidential one from another).[211] The argument for secrecy to protect management is really an argument for protecting poor, non-transparent management, and often for concealing unlawful discrimination. The argument for protecting property from states that might appropriate it without due cause or due process is a more powerful one, and does need to be addressed. A connected issue is that these are frequently the same states in which such currency controls operate. A large number of the clients of Mossack Fonseca named in the *Panama Papers* were Chinese or Russian. China and Russia both operate currency controls. The Financial Action Task Force (FATF) has yet to recognize breach of currency controls as compulsory predicates to money laundering, but the inexorable thrust of its position is that in due course they will be included.

Information from disclosures to the NCA may be passed on to HMRC.[212] The legislation merging the Inland Revenue and Customs and Excise to form HMRC[213] made express provision as to the uses to which they might put information, and the requirements of confidentiality. HMRC is permitted

[207] And see Chapter 2, section entitled 'Income Tax', and Keith Report, para 9.16 *et seq*.

[208] Tax returns were used to wrap cheese, meat, butter, and fish. Colley, Robert, 'The Shoreditch Tax Frauds: A Study of the Relationship between the State and Civil Society in 1860' (2005) 78 *Historical Research* 540–62.

[209] On which see Sharman, Jason, 'Privacy as Roguery: Personal Financial Information in an Age of Transparency' (2009) 87 *Public Administration* 717–31.

[210] And see Mba, Osita, 'Transparency and Accountability of Tax Administration in the UK: The Nature and Scope of Taxpayer Confidentiality' [2012] *British Tax Review* 187–225.

[211] And see Blank, Joshua, 'In Defense of Individual Tax Privacy' (2011) 61 *Emory Law Journal* 265.

[212] Crime and Courts Act 2013 s 7(7)(a).

[213] Commissioners for Revenue and Customs Act 2005.

to use information it acquires in connection with one function in connection with any other function.[214] Disclosure of information held by HMRC in connection with a function of HMRC is prohibited,[215] saving for certain excepted cases involving compulsion or disclosure to prosecuting authorities,[216] either to consider whether or not to bring proceedings or to advise on a criminal investigation[217] or consent.[218]

Offences of disclosure of information were created in 1989.[219] Wrongful disclosure is a criminal offence.[220] In *R (on the application of Ingenious Media Holdings Plc & Anr) v HMRC*[221] the Supreme Court held[222] that the Revenue and Customs Commissioners had breached s 18(1) or 18(2) of the Act in disclosing information about the claimants to journalists in an off-the-record briefing which led to the publication of articles about tax-avoiding film investment schemes which named the claimants. So far as concerns disclosure of information to third parties, including other government agencies, there is a protocol governing disclosures between agencies.[223] Greater use of publicity as a mechanism to combat both avoidance and evasion would probably be welcome, but legal bases upon which it is done must be secure.

Conclusions

The period since *Rossminster* has seen a move towards adopting criminal law mechanisms for the gathering of evidence of tax evasion. It has been recognized that these powers will be necessary in some cases, but that their use needs to be closely circumscribed. This is consistent with the alignment of tax evasion to other crimes and its installation within the main criminal justice agenda, involving the rhetoric of security. The relationship between HMRC and the taxpayer provides a test for the underlying rationale of the privilege against self-incrimination. We need a better account of the privilege than one which simply describes the position of the taxpayer relative to the State as an exception. It is possible to overstate the significance of

[214] S 17. [215] S 18. [216] S 21. [217] S 35(5)(b). [218] S 18(2)(h).

[219] FA 1989 s 182. [220] Commissioners for Revenue and Customs Act 2005 s 19.

[221] *R (on the application of Ingenious Media Holdings Plc & Anr) v HMRC* [2016] UKSC 54.

[222] Reversing *R (on the application of Ingenious Media Holdings Plc & Anr) v HMRC* [2015] EWCA Civ 173 and *R (on the application of Ingenious Media Holdings Plc & Anr) v HMRC* [2013] EWHC 3258 (Admin); [2014] STC 673. An appeal to the Supreme Court was heard in July 2016.

[223] Third party disclosure protocol (CPS, Revenue and Customs Prosecutions Office, SFO, ACPO, and Her Majesty's Revenue and Customs). <http://www.cps.gov.uk/legal/p_to_r/prosecutors__convention/>.

legal professional privilege. Communications which will not be privileged may well be made orally, and in the context of taxation, anecdotal evidence is that access to the lawyer's client file is in any event of limited value to HMRC. So far as concerns acquisition of evidence otherwise than from the taxpayer, tax evasion does not give rise to different legal issues from any other investigations.

7

Prosecution and Its Alternatives

By no means all tax evaders will be prosecuted. This chapter will deal with the decision whether or not to prosecute, and the alternative options at Her Majesty's Revenue and Customs' (HMRC's) disposal.

The Prosecution Decision

The standard procedure for deciding whether or not to prosecute in an individual case is the 'two-stage' test, asking first whether there is a 50 per cent chance of success[1] and then whether or not the bringing of the prosecution is in the public interest.[2] This is an operable test in individual cases. It does not answer broader questions of selection. If there are a thousand suspected tax evaders against whom there is strong evidence of guilt (so that the 50% test will be satisfied in them all), the general view seems to be that some, but not all, of them should be prosecuted. A public interest test may identify a proportion of them that should be prosecuted, but the actual selections still need to be made. As with the factors influencing sentence,[3] there does appear to be a residual effect of the history of distinction between Inland Revenue and Customs and Excise. A five-figure smuggling offence will tend to generate a criminal charge. A five-figure income tax fraud, on the other hand, might well not.[4] Beyond that, it is difficult to see on what basis the choices are made.

[1] This test is applied flexibly.

[2] Ashworth, Andrew, 'Developments in the Public Prosecutor's Office in England and Wales' (2000) 8 *European Journal of Crime, Criminal Law and Criminal Justice* 257, 269.

[3] See Chapter 4, section entitled 'Sentencing'.

[4] 'The Revenue defends its strategy by arguing that bringing high-profile cases such as the Redknapp trial—and in the past, its pursuit of Ken Dodd and Lester Piggott—helps persuade ordinary people to fill in their tax returns properly.' 'Redknapp Acquittal Raises Queries over

Criminal Justice and Taxation. First Edition. Peter Alldridge. © Peter Alldridge 2017. First published 2017 by Oxford University Press.

Given the large number of cases upon which to draw, the 75 per cent conviction rate[5] is surprisingly low.

The HMRC Criminal Investigation Policy[6] states:

Examples of the kind of circumstances in which HMRC will generally consider commencing a criminal, rather than civil investigation are:

in cases of organised criminal gangs attacking the tax system or systematic frauds where losses represent a serious threat to the tax base, including conspiracy

where an individual holds a position of trust or responsibility

where materially false statements are made or materially false documents are provided in the course of a civil investigation

where, pursuing an avoidance scheme, reliance is placed on a false or altered document or such reliance or material facts are misrepresented to enhance the credibility of a scheme

where deliberate concealment, deception, conspiracy or corruption is suspected

in cases involving the use of false or forged documents

in cases involving importation or exportation breaching prohibitions and restrictions

in cases involving money laundering with particular focus on advisors, accountants, solicitors and others acting in a 'professional' capacity who provide the means to put tainted money out of reach of law enforcement

where the perpetrator has committed previous offences/there is a repeated course of unlawful conduct or previous civil action

in cases involving theft, or the misuse or unlawful destruction of HMRC documents

where there is evidence of assault on, threats to, or the impersonation of HMRC officials

where there is a link to suspected wider criminality, whether domestic or international, involving offences not under the administration of HMRC

When considering whether a case should be investigated using the civil fraud investigation or is the subject of a criminal investigation, one factor will be whether the taxpayer(s) has made a complete and unprompted disclosure of the offences committed.

However, there are certain fiscal offences where HMRC will not usually adopt the civil fraud investigation procedures … Examples of these are:

VAT 'Bogus' registration repayment fraud

Organised Tax Credit fraud.

These criteria sit in the place of what used to be called the 'badges of heinousness'.[7] They leave prosecutors a wide discretion in individual cases.

HMRC', *Financial Times*, 8 February 2012. <https://www.ft.com/content/b2cc6d5e-527f-11e1-ae2c-00144feabdc0>; see also 'HMRC: The Taxman Cometh', *Financial Times*, 20 August 2015. <https://www.ft.com/content/3fa2fd16-42bd-11e5-b98b-87c7270955cf>.

[5] 'HMRC Steps Up Tax Evasion Drive after 58% Rise in Convictions', *Financial Times*, 14 December 2015.

[6] *HMRC, Criminal Investigation Policy*, 2015, <https://www.gov.uk/government/publications/criminal-investigation/hmrc-criminal-investigation-policy>.

[7] *R v IRC, ex p Mead and another* [1993] 1 All ER 772; [1992] STC 482, citing Keith of Kinkel, Lord (Chair), *The Enforcement Powers of the Revenue Departments*. Vols 1 and 2 (Cmnd 8822, March 1983) Committee paras 22.1.7 and 8.

Beyond these guidelines, there are various ways, for various reasons, in which prosecutions might be targeted, or consciously not targeted.

First, it is sometimes argued that tax prosecutions should be brought disproportionately frequently against high-profile individuals: the idea is that the prosecution of celebrities will generate more publicity, and thus have a greater effect in terms of general deterrence.[8] The record of prosecution of high-profile defendants, however, is not very encouraging. Lester Piggott, the most significant high-profile conviction in the latter part of the twentieth century, was only prosecuted when, during Hansard procedure interviews, he gave incorrect information.[9] Other prosecutions have failed. It may be that juries sympathize disproportionately with the famous. In 1989 the prosecution of Ken Dodd failed and in 2012 football manager Harry Redknapp was acquitted of evasion, at a time when he was a serious contender to become England manager.[10] Neither the search of his house preceding the charges[11] nor the prosecution were handled well. The allegations were that he and his former club chairman Peter Mandaric had evaded tax on payments totalling £189,000 that were made by Mandaric into Redknapp's offshore bank account while the two men were at Portsmouth football club. Both Redknapp and Mandaric argued that the money was given as a gesture of friendship and had nothing to do with Redknapp's job. The total amount of tax at stake was estimated to be below £80,000. A prosecution policy which, on deterrence grounds, favours the prosecution of high-profile defendants could only be defended if convictions could be assured in at least as high a proportion as those for the whole of the population.

Other possible bases upon which defendants may be selected are geographical area and sector of the economy. There was at one stage a deliberate Inland Revenue policy of spreading prosecutions geographically as well as into different economic sectors. Thus, if the taxpayer happened to be in a particular economic sector in a particular geographical area, then a prosecution would be more likely to be brought if there had not been a recent prosecution either in the sector or the area. The aim of this policy was to get reports into the local and specialist press. Even if this had been a good policy in earlier times,

[8] Braithwaite, John, and Peter Drahos, 'Zero Tolerance, Naming and Shaming: Is There a Case for It with Crimes of the Powerful?' (2002) 35 *Australian & New Zealand Journal of Criminology* 269–88.

[9] 'Lester Piggott Jailed for Three Years', <http://news.bbc.co.uk/onthisday/hi/dates/stories/october/23/newsid_3755000/3755282.stm>.

[10] 'Harry Redknapp and Milan Mandaric Cleared of Tax Evasion', *The Guardian*, 8 February 2012.

[11] Which was unlawful and gave the impression of heavy-handedness: *R (on the application of Redknapp) v Commissioner of the City of London Police* [2008] EWHC 1177 (Admin); [2009] 1 WLR 2091.

it would be less easy to operate in an era of a greater diversity of news outlets and social media, and seems to have been abrogated.

Publicity Without Prosecution?

Could the benefits of publicity be secured without the expense and risk of prosecution? For some years HMRC has been engaged in a conscious programme of 'naming and shaming' for non-compliance, and also publishing lists of fugitives.[12] Since 2009, it has been allowed to publish the names of deliberate tax defaulters.[13] Lists are published periodically.[14] In a small number of serious cases it published the names of people who deliberately defaulted with at least £25,000 of tax owing and had not told HMRC about it.[15] HMRC has also launched an offshore media publicity campaign and published two interactive maps to show the results of its criminal investigations and its taskforces.[16] Much more could be done in this area.

Judicial Review of Prosecution Decisions

The making of prosecution decisions is, in theory, subject to judicial review, but the discretion afforded to prosecutors is wide. The Inland Revenue's then prosecution policy was considered in *R v IRC, ex p Mead and another*,[17] *R v IRC, ex p Allen*,[18] and *R v Werner*.[19] In *Mead*, the Court of Appeal dealt with a challenge to the Inland Revenue's selective prosecution policy in the following manner:

[the Inland Revenue does] so for three main reasons: first their primary objective is the collection of revenue and not the punishment of offenders; second they have inadequate resources to prosecute everyone who dishonestly evades payment of taxes; and third and perhaps more importantly they consider it necessary to prosecute in some cases because of the deterrent effect that this has on the general body of taxpayers, since they know that if they behave dishonestly they may be prosecuted.[20]

[12] <https://www.flickr.com/photos/hmrcgovuk/sets/72157631087785530/>.

[13] FA 2009 s 94. Most of the defaults are in four or five figures. <https://www.gov.uk/government/publications/publishing-details-of-deliberate-tax-defaulters-pddd/current-list-of-deliberate-tax-defaulters>.

[14] <https://www.gov.uk/government/uploads/system/uploads/attachment_data/file/425639/150501_deliberate_defaulters.pdf>.

[15] HM Treasury, *Tackling Tax Evasion and Avoidance* (Cm 9047, 2015) para 2.13.

[16] <http://hmrcdigitalpilots.com/>.

[17] *R v IRC, ex p Mead and another* [1993] 1 All ER 772; [1992] STC 482.

[18] *R v IRC, ex p Allen* [1997] STC 1141.

[19] *R v Werner* [1998] STC 550.

[20] *Mead* at 783C.

In *ex p Allen*, the court held that an application to review was out of time, but (unsurprisingly in the light of the litigation that followed)[21] the bringing of a prosecution was in line with the Revenue's own practice. In *R v Werner*, the Court of Appeal described the Inland Revenue's common law power to prosecute[22] as being 'ancillary to, supportive of and limited by their duty to collect taxes'.[23] Rose LJ said:

The revenue on behalf of the Crown have no express statutory power to prosecute but have such a power at common law in aid of their own overall functions.[24] *The revenue have a policy of selective prosecution, considering each case on its merits ...*[25] *In selecting, the revenue have the power to decide whether to prosecute for fraudulent evasion or to accept a monetary settlement: prosecution on the one hand and acceptance of a monetary settlement on the other have always been regarded by the revenue as alternatives and their 1990 Code of Practice dealing with their approach in cases of suspected serious fraud (published as part of the Citizens' Charter*[26]*) says in terms: 'It is the board's policy to prosecute the most serious cases covering all types of fraud, but they may accept a monetary settlement instead of starting criminal proceedings.' Ministerial statements to Parliament have recognised these alternatives for many years (see most recently the Chancellor of the Exchequer's statement*[27] *which echoed the Code of Practice of that year which we have cited).*[28]

While decisions by prosecutors *not* to prosecute may in theory be reviewed,[29] they can be successfully challenged in the courts only in the most exceptional

[21] *R v Allen* [2001] UKHL 45; [2002] 1 AC 509. See Chapter 6, section entitled 'The Privilege against Self-incrimination in Tax Law'.

[22] That is to say, arising because of the right of any individual legal person to bring a private prosecution, as affirmed in *R v Rollins* [2010] UKSC 39; [2010] 1 WLR 1922.

[23] *R v Werner* [1998] STC 550, citing *Mead* at 778B per Stuart Smith LJ, Inland Revenue Circular ST2/88 para 2, Keith of Kinkel, Lord (Chair), n 7, para 176.1, and the reference in s 4(2) of the Criminal Justice Act 1987 to the Commissioners of Inland Revenue as a designated authority for the purpose of transferring proceedings to the Crown Court.

[24] Citing *ex p Mead*, the Inland Revenue Statement of Practice, *Civil Tax Penalties and Criminal Prosecution Cases* SP 2/88 (10 May 1988) para 2, the Keith Report (Committee on Enforcement Powers of the Revenue Departments (1983) (Cmnd 8822, para 176.1), and the inclusion in s 4(2) of the Criminal Justice Act 1987 of the IRC as a designated authority for the purpose of transferring proceedings to the Crown Court.

[25] Citing *ex p Mead* at 492 per Stuart-Smith LJ (footnote added).

[26] The Citizens' Charter was a government initiative in the early days of the Major government. See Barron, Ann, and Colin Scott, 'The Citizens' Charter Programme' (1992) 55 *Modern Law Review* 526.

[27] That is, the Hansard statement by John Major, Chancellor of the Exchequer: HC Debates, 18 October 1990 Col 882W (footnote added).

[28] *R v Werner* [1998] STC 550 at 555.

[29] *R v DPP, ex p Chaudhary* [1995] 1 Cr App R 136; *R v DPP, ex p Manning* [2001] QB 330; *Webster v Crown Prosecution Service* [2014] EWHC 2516 (Admin); Burton, Mandy, 'Reviewing Crown Prosecution Service Decisions Not to Prosecute' [2001] *Criminal Law Review* 374.

circumstances.[30] It is very unlikely that a decision not to prosecute a case of tax evasion could be subject to successful challenge, because if aggrieved, people with the relevant information (former partners, bookkeepers, and so on) will use other avenues.

While HMRC is in principle amenable to judicial review,[31] if the taxpayer could show that it had failed to discharge their statutory duty towards him/her or that it had abused its powers or acted *ultra vires*, unfairness in the purported exercise of power could amount to an abuse or excess of power if HMRC were guilty of conduct equivalent to a breach of contract or breach of representation. No other individual taxpayer has a sufficient interest in the matter to compel HMRC to act upon one taxpayer's complaint that another taxpayer has been under-assessed.[32]

Deal-making

The decision whether or not to prosecute is one between prosecuting, on the one hand, and a range of other responses, on the other. Some of that range involve agreements with the taxpayer. One reason not to prosecute a tax evader is that an accommodation has been reached with the taxpayer. The face of English criminal law has historically been turned against any kind of overt or court-approved bargaining between prosecution and defence as to the liability of the defendant or as to disposition.[33] The relationship between, on the one hand, financial inducements and, on the other, agreements not to prosecute, or agreements not to press for the imposition of the fullest rigour of the law, is central both to tax and to criminal law. The starting point is that if a person is able to pay money to avoid criminal liability, then he or she is not really subject to the criminal law at all. Allowing people to pay to avoid criminal proceedings very clearly undermines the rule of law, which requires impartial application of clear rules to everybody. This fundamental principle is clear and does not admit of shades of grey. A rule whose effects can be avoided by paying the appropriate person is a rule whose generality is compromised.

[30] *R (on the application of Bermingham) v Director of the SFO* [2006] EWHC 200 (Admin); [2007] QB 727 at paras 63–4. See also *R (on the application of Corner House Research) v Director of the Serious Fraud Office* [2008] UKHL 60; [2009] 1 AC 756.

[31] *Preston v IRC* [1985] AC 835; [1985] STC 282.

[32] *R v IRC, ex p National Federation of Self Employed and Small Businesses Ltd* [1982] AC 617.

[33] See, eg, *R v Innospec plc* [2010] EW Misc 7 (EWCC). What actually happens has been known since Baldwin, John, and Michael McConville, *Negotiated Justice: Pressures on Defendants to Plead Guilty* (London: Martin Robertson, 1977), to be rather different.

And yet we live in the real world. Financial crime is precisely the area that has attracted the greatest pressure for the establishment of some sort of system of agreements. The costs of investigations and the cumbersome nature of adversarial jury trial make it very difficult to operate criminal prosecution as an everyday mode of adjudication enforcement for financial crime.[34] It is better that some adverse consequence be visited upon someone who evades tax than none. All systems of criminal justice have arrangements for dealing with cases in which some kind of agreement has been made between the prosecutor and the accused. Plea-bargaining has long been a feature of criminal justice in the Anglo-American systems.[35] The agreements may be informal or even covert, or may be public and require endorsement by courts. Typically, the less these agreements are approved formally, the more they will happen informally or covertly. One such arrangement that has always been publicized by courts in England and Wales, to the point that there is no need for it to be mentioned in individual cases, is the sentencing discount following a guilty plea.[36] Additional statutory mechanisms are in place under which agreements can be reached.[37]

In the area of financial crimes *other than tax evasion*, the pressure for deals is generated partly because of the exceptional difficulties that the Serious Fraud Office (SFO) has encountered in securing convictions. Its chequered history (in the 1980s and 1990s, County Natwest, Guinness, Blue Arrow, Barlow Clowes, Brent Walker, and the Maxwell brothers;[38] in this century the Tchenguiz brothers[39] and the Libor

[34] Alschuler, AW, 'Mediation with a Mugger: The Shortage of Adjudicative Services and the Need for a Two-Tier System in Civil Cases' (1986) 99 *Harvard Law Review* 1808–59.

[35] Pace Alschuler, AW, 'Plea Bargaining and Its History' (1979) 79 *Columbia Law Review* 1–43; Baldwin and McConville, n 33; Brants, Chrisje, 'Consensual Criminal Procedures: Plea and Confession Bargaining and Abbreviated Procedures to Simplify Criminal Procedure' (2007) 11 *Electronic Journal of Comparative Law*, <http://www.ejcl.org/111/art111-6.pdf>; Boll, M, *Plea Bargaining and Agreement in the Criminal Process* (Hamburg: Diplomica Verlag, 2009).

[36] This remains a matter of judicial discretion, not of law, but an offender who pleads guilty may expect some credit in the form of a discount in sentence. Criminal Justice Act 2003 s 144 does not confer a statutory right to a discount, but the court must take into account '(a) the stage in the proceedings for the offence at which the offender indicated his intention to plead guilty, and (b) the circumstances in which this indication was given' (s 144(1)). In early 2016 the Sentencing Council launched a consultation on the discount: press release, 16 February 2016, <http://www.sentencingcouncil.org.uk/news/item/reduction-in-sentence-for-a-guilty-plea-consultation-launched-on-sentencing-guideline>.

[37] The Serious Organised Crime and Police Act 2005 puts in place a statutory regime enabling prosecutors to grant immunity to offenders or to give them an undertaking that what they say will never be used to incriminate them. See Corker, David, Gemma Tombs, and Tamara Chisholm, 'Sections 71 and 72 of Serious Organised Crime and Police Act 2005: Whither the Common Law?' [2009] *Criminal Law Review* 261.

[38] Cases summarized in Appendix B of Levi, Michael, *The Investigation, Prosecution, and Trial of Serious Fraud* (Royal Commission on Criminal Justice Research Study No 14, 1993).

[39] 'SFO Humbled after Latest Trial Collapse', *The Times*, 13 February 2015.

prosecutions[40]) has been costly and embarrassing for the SFO and underpins the periodic calls for its abolition. In the field of tax evasion there have been high-profile acquittals, and the costs and benefits of prosecution as against other ways of proceeding tend to indicate that, if the money can be obtained, prosecutions should be confined to a small range of cases.

Customs and Excise had power to end (compound) a prosecution at any point.[41] This need not necessarily have affected the outcome of the discussions that took place between defendant and tax authority, but at least affected the timing of those discussions, because Customs and Excise retained some control of a case far later than did the Inland Revenue.

In the area of direct taxation, the history is one of efforts by HMRC and its predecessor organizations to conduct civil enquiries and to make offers in order to secure information without giving a caution and the other PACE rights, and without the evidence thereby obtained being excluded from subsequent criminal proceedings by PACE or falling foul of Article 6. Meanwhile, before co-operating, the taxpayer wants to be able to secure a guarantee that there will be no criminal prosecution. There have been various attempts to reconcile these competing claims.

The Hansard Procedure

HMRC and its predecessors have saved resources by extending to known wrongdoers the opportunity to avoid prosecution by making a full confession and paying penalties.[42] The issue that has arisen from time to time, particularly in the period since the Human Rights Act 1998, is whether confessions obtained by promises not to prosecute could be admitted in evidence in subsequent criminal proceedings against the taxpayer.

[40] Following the scandal about the manipulation of the LIBOR rate, there was one conviction (*R v Hayes* [2015] EWCA Crim 1944) but a series of acquittals in January 2016: 'Cleared Brokers "Were Scapegoats" for Scandal', <http://www.bbc.co.uk/news/business-35428279>, 28 January 2016. The third trial (R v Mathew, Contogoulas, Merchant, Pabon, Reich (2016)) did yield convictions.

[41] The power is in CEMA s 152, deriving from Customs and Excise Act 1952, s 288. Subsections 152(c) (mitigation and remission of penalties, etc) and (d) (early discharge from prison), were repealed by Commissioners for Revenue and Customs Act 2005 s 52(1)(a). And see Mowbray, Alastair, 'The Compounding of Proceedings by the Custom and Excise: Calculating the Legal Implications' [1988] *British Tax Review* 290 and HC Debates, 26 April 1989: vol 151 cc 560–61W (Peter Lilley, Financial Secretary to the Treasury).

[42] Ormerod, David, 'Hansard Invitations and Confessions in the Criminal Trial' (2000) 4 *International Journal of Evidence and Proof* 147.

The first statement in Parliament referring to the former Board of Inland Revenue's practice concerning tax fraud was in 1923.[43] In *R v Barker*[44] the information was secured under this procedure, which involved the statement that where the taxpayer was compliant 'the board will not institute criminal proceedings, but will accept the pecuniary settlement'. After the statement had been read, the defendant produced two ledgers which had been fraudulently prepared to induce the Revenue authorities to believe that the sum involved was smaller than in fact it was. At a later interview, two further ledgers and working papers were produced which showed that the earlier ledgers were incomplete and had been brought into existence to deceive the Revenue. Subsequently a letter was written which made it clear that the full amount of the irregularities was higher than had been represented.

The Court of Criminal Appeal held that the inducement held out by the Hansard statement meant that the evidence thereby gained fell foul of what were then the rules on induced confessions,[45] and that the ledgers should not have been admitted.[46] The fallacy in this decision was that the judge treated the information in the books as statements made by the defendant. *Barker* was overturned on its facts by statute,[47] has long been disapproved of in the literature,[48] and was mentioned very unfavourably in *Allen*.[49]

The version of the Hansard policy under consideration in *Allen* dated from 1990. It provided:

The Board may accept a money settlement instead of instituting criminal proceedings in respect of fraud alleged to have been committed by a taxpayer. They can give no undertaking that they will accept a money settlement and refrain from instituting criminal proceedings even if the case is one in which the taxpayer has made a full confession and has given full facilities for investigation of the facts. They reserve to themselves full discretion in all cases as to the course they pursue. But in considering whether to accept a money settlement

[43] HC Debates, 19 July 1923: Vol 166 cc 2514–16W, Sir William Joynson-Hicks, Financial Secretary to the Treasury (at that time the new Prime Minister, Baldwin, had himself remained Chancellor for a time and Financial Secretary was a cabinet post).

[44] *R v Barker* [1941] 2 KB 381; [1941] 3 All ER 33, CCA, which quoted, at 381, the original statement.

[45] In *Ibrahim v R* [1914] UKPC 1; [1914] AC 599.

[46] At 384–5 (Tucker J).

[47] FA 1942 s 34 (see now TMA s 105).

[48] '... [E]xtremely unsatisfactory': Cross, Rupert, and Colin Tapper, *Cross and Tapper on Evidence* (London: Butterworths, 8th edn, 1995) 535 n 4.

[49] *R v Allen* [2001] UKHL 45; [2002] 1 AC 509 para 32 *et seq*. It also appears to be inconsistent with s 76(4)(a) of PACE: '(4) The fact that a confession is wholly or partly excluded in pursuance of this section shall not affect the admissibility in evidence—(a) of any facts discovered as a result of the confession.' This provision was intended to restate the common law.

or to institute criminal proceedings, it is their practice to be influenced by the fact that the taxpayer has made a full confession and has given full facilities for investigation into his affairs and for examination of such books, papers, documents or information as the Board may consider necessary.[50]

Allen considered the argument that the statement left open the possibility that a tax recalcitrant might make a confession and still then be prosecuted, the confession being part of the evidence against him/her, and that such a procedure might not violate Article 6 of the European Convention on Human Rights (ECHR). The House of Lords held that the Human Rights Act 1998 was not retrospectively effective, and therefore that the appellant could not rely on Article 6, but it did onsider the arguments based on Article 6. On the facts, the House rejected the argument that the use of material gained under the Hansard statement breached Article 6. Lord Hutton said: 'To the extent that there was an inducement contained in the Hansard statement, the inducement was to give true and accurate information to the Revenue, but the accused in both cases did not respond to that inducement and instead of giving true and accurate information gave false information.'[51]

The House held that the Crown had the right to require citizens to declare their income and could enforce sanctions for failure to do so for the purpose of tax collection.[52] *Allen* turned, however, on its own facts.[53] Lord Hutton said that the defendant had given true and accurate information, which disclosed that he had earlier cheated the Revenue, and had he then been prosecuted for that earlier dishonesty, he would have had a strong argument that the criminal proceedings were unfair and an even stronger argument that the Crown should not rely on evidence of his admission; however, that is the reverse of what actually occurred.[54]

As a consequence of *Allen,* the Hansard procedure was again revised, this time to state:

[50] John Major, Chancellor of the Exchequer: HC Debates, 18 October 1990 Col 882W.

[51] At paras 34–5.

[52] Thus rejecting the argument that the requirement of the TMA s 20(1) infringed the privilege against self-incrimination, as recognized under Article 6. See Chapter 6, section entitled 'The Privilege against Self-incrimination in Tax Law'.

[53] In the context of the inducement procedure used by the UK Customs and Excise Commissioners, Potter LJ in *Han & Yau v HMRC* [2001] EWCA Civ 1048; [2001] 1 WLR 2253 at 2279F–G stated it was unlikely that the argument that the offending paragraph of the Hansard statement violated Article 6(1) would be upheld, as the requirements of Article 6(1) 'are of a general nature and are not prescriptive of the precise means or procedural rules by which domestic law recognizes and protects such rights'.

[54] At paras 34–5.

The Board will accept a money settlement and will not pursue a criminal prosecution, if the taxpayer, in response to being given a copy of this Statement by an authorised officer, makes a full and complete confession of all tax irregularities.[55]

The possibility that the Hansard procedure might not have survived the exigencies of Article 6 fell again into issue in *R v Gill*,[56] in which Special Compliance Officers held an interview with the defendants at which it was made clear to them that although the Revenue was not carrying out a criminal investigation, it reserved the right to do so in future. The interview was not conducted in accordance with the provisions of PACE Code of Practice C. The defendants were later charged with various counts of cheating the Revenue. The defendants sought to have excluded from that trial, under s 78 of PACE, a number of statements which they had made in the course of the Hansard interview and on which the prosecution sought to rely as lies which supported the conclusion that the defendants acted dishonestly. The trial judge held that the Special Compliance Officers were not 'charged with the duty of investigating offences' within the meaning of the relevant provisions of PACE,[57] consequently that the provisions of Code C did not apply, and accordingly that the statements were admissible. On appeal, the Court of Appeal held that the role of the Special Compliance Officers *did* involve the investigation of a criminal offence and that they were charged with the duty of investigating offences within the meaning of the provisions, and that consequently Code C did apply to the interview conducted with the defendants. Nonetheless, it did not follow from the breach of the Code that the evidence had to be excluded.[58] The court went on to hold that the Revenue were entitled to rely on the statements as lies told by the defendants, to prove the defendants' dishonest state of mind. It also held that the Revenue's actions did not involve a flagrant disregard for the Code's provisions[59] and that the defendants were made aware that criminal proceedings were in prospect and were advised, but chose not, to have professional representation at the interview. It followed that the admission of the statements did not have such an adverse effect on the fairness of the proceedings that the judge should have excluded them under s 78. In effect, therefore, the court determined that, once HMRC had started a civil investigation, it could not subsequently

[55] HC Debates, 7 November 2002: Vol 392 c 784W (Gordon Brown, Chancellor of the Exchequer).

[56] *R v Gill (Sewa Singh)* [2003] EWCA Crim 2256; [2004] 1 WLR 469.

[57] S 67(9).

[58] Not every breach of Code C leads to the exclusion of evidence thereby obtained: *R v Absolam* (1989) 88 Cr App R 332; *R v Walsh* (1990) 91 Cr App R 161; *R v Keenan* [1990] 2 QB 54; (1990) 90 Cr App R 1.

[59] Which would have triggered exclusion under PACE s 78.

switch to a criminal investigation on the same facts *and* deploy the evidence gained in the civil investigation in the criminal proceedings.

Gill was later distinguished on the PACE issue, and PACE Code C was held not to apply, in a value added tax (VAT) case.[60] In another case, where Customs and Excise officers had assured an interviewee that they were not investigating his conduct with a view to criminal prosecution, although he might be made subject to a civil penalty, they were not 'charged with the duty of investigating offences' within the terms of s 67(9) of PACE, and therefore were not required to comply with Code of Practice C.[61] This was not a satisfactory state of affairs.

Code of Practice 9

As a consequence of the uncertainties arising from *Allen* and more particularly from *Gill*,[62] and also the curious constitutional status of a series of statements made in the House of Commons (not having the status of law, but frequently cited as though they did), the possibility arose that, in any given case, the use of the Hansard procedure to obtain evidence might fall foul of Article 6, or evidence it had yielded might be excluded under s 78, or both. Instead the Hansard procedure was replaced by Code of Practice 9,[63] which attempted to 'de-police' the procedure by dispensing with cautions and taped interviews.

A National Audit Office report in December 2010 criticized aspects of HMRC's Civil Investigation of Fraud procedure.[64] The report identified a significant proportion of the cases where Code of Practice 9 had been used but failed to result in a disclosure. There are various reasons why a disclosure might not be submitted, including poor case selection and uncooperative taxpayers. Where a taxpayer failed to co-operate fully under Code of Practice 9, HMRC was not able to conduct a criminal prosecution, even where it had sufficient evidence, because Code of Practice 9 as introduced provided the taxpayer with automatic immunity from prosecution.

[60] *Khan (t/a Greyhound Dry Cleaners) v Customs and Excise Commissioners* [2005] EWHC 653 (Ch); [2005] STC 1271.

[61] *R v Doncaster* [2008] EWCA Crim 5.

[62] And see Oates, Chris, and Ed Dwan, 'Hansard R.I.P.', *Taxation*, 22 September 2005, 686.

[63] <https://www.gov.uk/government/uploads/system/uploads/attachment_data/file/494808/COP9_06_14.pdf>.

[64] Comptroller and Auditor General, *HM Revenue & Customs Managing Civil Tax Investigations* (HC 677: 2010–11).

Contractual Disclosure Facilities

The Contractual Disclosure Facility (CDF) replaced Code of Practice 9 from 31 January 2012.[65] Under this procedure, HMRC writes to the taxpayer to inform him/her that s/he is suspected of tax fraud. The taxpayer has an opportunity to enter into a contract to disclose the fraud within sixty days. During that period, or, where earlier, until such time as the taxpayer confirms his acceptance of the CDF and makes an outline disclosure, HMRC will not engage in dialogue with either the taxpayer or his/her adviser (so as not to prejudice HMRC's ability to instigate a criminal investigation). Co-operating taxpayers no longer get automatic immunity from prosecution. Taxpayers who decide not to sign up to the CDF face an intrusive investigation by HMRC—in some instances, this is a criminal investigation with a view to prosecution. If HMRC decides not to pursue a criminal investigation in these circumstances, and investigates using civil powers, the resulting penalties will be substantially higher than where the taxpayer has adopted the CDF. Taxpayers who sign the contract but do not admit and disclose fraud will also face the prospect of a criminal investigation.

The question that still arises is whether the CDF/Code of Practice 9 procedure necessarily involves a criminal charge for the purposes of Articles 6.2 and 6.3. In *Gold Nuts Ltd and Others v Commissioners for HMRC*[66] the First-tier Tribunal said[67] that if HMRC sought to rely on the information obtained through compulsory powers for the purpose of prosecuting the taxpayer, the judge should consider PACE s 78 and the fairness of including that evidence, in the light of the guidance given in *ex parte Green*,[68] *Beghal v Director of Public Prosecutions*,[69] and similar cases. In *Beghal* the Supreme Court used the s 78 discretion, but would have preferred a blanket exclusionary rule dealing with statements made under compulsion by the Terrorism Act 2000. In *Gold Nuts*, the tribunal also took the view that an offer under the CDF procedure did constitute a criminal charge for the purposes of Articles 6.2 and 6.3. This could have important consequences where a taxpayer may require legal advice instead of, or in addition to, the assistance that his/her accountant would ordinarily provide.

[65] Lee, Natalie, *Revenue Law: Principles and Practice* (Haywards Heath: Bloomsbury, 2015) 102.

[66] *Gold Nuts Ltd and Others v Commissioners For Her Majesty's Revenue & Customs* [2016] UKFTT 82 (TC); [2016] Lloyd's Rep FC Plus 24.

[67] Para 288.

[68] *R v Hertfordshire CC, ex p Green Environmental Industries Ltd* [2000] 2 AC 412; [2000] 1 All ER 773; see Chapter 6, section entitled 'The Privilege against Self-incrimination in Tax Law'.

[69] *Beghal v Director of Public Prosecutions* [2015] UKSC 49; [2016] AC 88 at para 65 *et seq* (Lord Hughes).

This leaves the *Gill* issue outstanding—that is, whether there is a breach of Code C, and the requirement therein to issue a caution, where the taxpayer is interviewed under the CDF procedure. If the answer to this is that there is a breach, then it seems that the attempt to use variants upon the successive Hansard statements has arrived at the end of the line, and that the decision to take the civil rather than the criminal route should be treated as irrevocable. The consequence of that might well be an increase in the proportion of cases in which the criminal option is retained.

Offshore Disclosure Facilities

So far as concerns the criminal law aspects of these facilities, there is no reason in principle why there should be different rules and different inducements according to the location of the repository of the money. Nonetheless, specific, more lenient, facilities have been available in respect of particular jurisdictions. The Liechtenstein Disclosure Facility (LDF) was governed by a Tax Information Exchange Agreement and a Memorandum of Understanding signed in 2009. A Joint Declaration was made in 2010. The LDF was targeted at persons with UK tax liabilities that have connections with Liechtenstein, except those under an investigation that fell within HMRC's Code of Practice 9 (that is, suspected of serious fraud or under arrest for a criminal tax offence), who are not permitted to participate. The LDF allowed UK taxpayers to make a voluntary disclosure to HM Revenue and Customs in return for immunity from prosecution and a reduced penalty in most years. Disclosures only needed to go back to April 1999, rather than the normal twenty-year period. The accompanying document stated:

> *What is the assurance against criminal tax investigation? We have agreed that an eligible person who makes a full, accurate and unprompted disclosure to us under the LDF will not be subject to criminal investigation by us for a tax-related offence. This assurance will not apply where the source of the funds from which the relevant person has benefited or may benefit constitutes 'criminal property' as defined by the Proceeds of Crime Act 2002.*[70]

Similarly, the Crown Dependencies Disclosure Facilities (CDDF) were a side-effect of the US' introduction of the Foreign Account Tax Compliance Act (FATCA).[71] FATCA forced banks in the Crown Dependencies (and

[70] The LDF stated that 'Criminal activity, in this respect, does not include tax evasion' (and so property obtained by tax evasion is not excluded from the LDF). Under the wide interpretation of POCA s 340 (as to which see Chapter 9, section entitled 'Laundering the Proceeds of Tax Evasion'), it would have been difficult to commit evasion without also committing a laundering offence.

[71] See Chapter 8, section entitled 'The International Response to Scandals'.

elsewhere) to report their American customers' accounts to the US Internal Revenue Service (IRS), and the UK's tax authorities insisted on receiving the corresponding data on UK residents. At the same time HMRC opened an amnesty for UK clients of Crown Dependency banks, which was to be open until September 2016.

The LDF and CDDF closed in December 2015. HM Treasury considered that both schemes would be made obsolete by the OECD plan for automatic international exchange of bank account data, due to begin in 2016–17, and so ended them early.[72] A new time-limited facility, with tougher penalties and no guarantee that criminal investigations will not be pursued 'in appropriate cases', was introduced in 2016.[73]

Switzerland

Whatever the origins of Swiss banking-secrecy laws,[74] Switzerland has long been thought to be the great intractable issue in international taxation.[75] As the *HSBC Suisse* leaks showed, it was still, at the time in question (2006–8), a popular place to attempt to hide money. The agreement between the UK and Switzerland on co-operation in the area of taxation was given statutory effect.[76] In effect, the agreement provided for an amnesty for those who had evaded tax and had funds in an undisclosed Swiss bank account at the end of 2010, plus the option of maintaining anonymity for the owner of that account in the future. This was far more generous than the treatment of domestic evasion.

The UK government claimed in 2015 that, since 2010, HMRC has brought in about £1.9 billion in previously unpaid tax as a result of the UK's agreement with Switzerland on a withholding tax on Swiss bank accounts and the Liechtenstein disclosure facility.[77] The more general view was that the offshore disclosure facilities had not been successful. In 2012 the expected yield

[72] HMRC, *Implementation of the UK–US Agreement to Improve International Tax Compliance and to Implement FATCA: Data Protection FAQs*, 2012, <www.hmrc.gov.uk/budget-updates/march2012/draft-dpa-fatca-faqs.pdf>.

[73] HM Treasury, *Tackling Tax Evasion and Avoidance* (Cm 9047, 2015) para 3.15.

[74] And see Guex, Sébastien, 'The Origins of the Swiss Banking Secrecy Law and Its Repercussions for Swiss Federal Policy' (2000) 74 *Business History Review* 237–66.

[75] And see Emmenegger, Patrick, 'Swiss Banking Secrecy and the Problem of International Cooperation in Tax Matters: A Nut Too Hard to Crack?' (2015) *Regulation & Governance*, published online before print.

[76] FA 2012 s 218 and Sched 36 give effect to the Agreement. And see Baker, Philip, 'Finance Act Notes: Section 218 and Schedule 36: The UK–Switzerland Rubik Agreement' [2012] *British Tax Review* 489.

[77] HC Debates, 14 January 2014 Col 492W (David Gauke).

from Isle of Man, Guernsey, and Jersey Disclosure Facilities was said to be £1 billion.[78] The actual yield only turned out to be £25 million.[79]

Deferred Prosecution Agreements

The adoption by English law of Deferred Prosecution Agreements (DPAs) is further indicative of its ambivalence about making deals with criminals. DPAs were put on the statute book[80] in imitation of their use in the US.[81] The essence of the agreement is that in exchange for the provision of evidence against itself by the defendant company, the prosecutor agrees to defer prosecution. DPAs may only be entered into with bodies corporate, partnerships, or unincorporated associations, not with individuals.[82] The procedure for DPAs[83] lists a number of relevant tax offences among those for which DPAs may be agreed.[84]

In spite of the much-trumpeted DPA approved by Sir Brian Leveson P in the *Standard Bank* case,[85] it is unlikely that DPAs will figure significantly in the next few years, and the provision of DPAs as a possibility for tax offences does not indicate that they will ever be a preferred response. In order for DPAs to operate, there would need to be a plausible threat that selection for investigation and a successful and damaging prosecution would follow failure to self-report and there must be a prosecutor disposed to make this sort of deal. To achieve this, something significant would have had to be done about the law of corporate criminal liability in England and Wales. The government's failure hitherto to broaden corporate criminal liability, either by the modification of the 'identification' doctrine in corporate criminal liability[86] or the introduction of a 'failure to prevent' offence, meant that it remained very difficult for prosecutors to generate a sufficiently strong threat of criminal conviction to make entering into a DPA a worthwhile option for the defendant. The only types of cases in which it might have been be worthwhile for a company to enter into a DPA are the 'clean breast' ones—those where new management has been put in place and it wishes to draw a line under its past,

[78] 'HMRC Move to Prise Open Secret Accounts Falls Flat', *Financial Times*, 24 July 2015.

[79] <https://www.gov.uk/government/publications/offshore-disclosure-facilities-guernsey/crown-dependency-disclosure-facility-figures-guernsey>.

[80] Crime and Courts Act 2013 s 45.

[81] A classic case of mistaken borrowing.

[82] Crime and Courts Act 2013 Schedule 17 Part 2 para 4(1).

[83] Crime and Courts Act 2013 Schedule 17 Part 2 para 15 *et seq*.

[84] Part 2 para 15 *et seq*. The list includes conspiracy to defraud, cheating the Revenue, and most major statutory offences of tax evasion and laundering offences, as well as offences ancillary to them.

[85] *Serious Fraud Office v Standard Bank* [2016] 1 Lloyd's Law Reports: Financial Crime Plus 121.

[86] *Tesco Supermarkets Ltd v Nattrass* [1971] UKHL 1; [1972] AC 153.

as in *Standard Bank*. The proposal for the 'failure to prevent' offence was restored after the *Panama Papers* and is in the Criminal Finance Bill 2017, but even if DPAs are used more widely, and even if the basis of corporate criminal liability were broadened, it is unlikely that they will be used in tax cases.

The Civil Penalties Regime

The overwhelming preponderance of the book has dealt with criminal liability. From the inception of the income tax, however, the principal response of the Revenue to fraud by the taxpayer has been to avoid the use of criminal prosecutions.[87] At the moment, and for the foreseeable future, HMRC relies and will rely on other means than the criminal law to deal with all but a small group of tax evaders. Most cases of evasion are dealt with informally. HMRC has at its disposal methods such as assessment and debt recovery, liquidators, cross-agency investigation, requirements for guarantees and securities, policy and regulatory change, and campaigns targeted at identified areas of risk. When these mechanisms are used, an evader has to pay the tax or duty evaded, interest,[88] and (frequently) a fee to his/her adviser. In contrast to criminal fines, poverty is not a defence to penalty provisions.[89]

HMRC's main formal sanction even against serious tax fraud is the imposition of civil penalties, involving payment of the tax due and any financial penalty and interest. 'Civil' in this sense means 'imposed by the Revenue itself, not by a court', with reduced procedural rights to the taxpayer.[90] In these cases, the evader has to pay the tax or duty evaded, a penalty, interest, and (frequently) a large fee to his/her adviser. About eight times fewer units of employee time per case are said to be used by HMRC on a civil penalty case than on a prosecution.[91]

From the introduction of the income tax, civil penalties have been available for evasion.[92] The original provisions, in force until 1960, imposed penalties

[87] Income Tax Act 1842 s 55.

[88] TMA Part IX: since the interest compounds, delays can increase the expense and create financial incentives for compliance.

[89] FA 2008 Schedule 41 para 20(2)(a).

[90] In *Attorney-General v Casey* [1930] IR 163 the Supreme Court of the Irish Free State held that under the Income Tax Act 1918, the defendant did not have a right to jury trial even when fraud was alleged.

[91] And see Mike Eland, 'The Case for the Use of Civil Penalties by HMRC', <http://static1.1.sqspcdn.com/static/f/421792/8468920/1283985016957/Eland+tax+fraud+May+2009.pdf?token=tZwuIvbiARYG7Ja3T8mApw3CZZ8%3D>.

[92] Income Tax Act 1842 s 103, Income Tax Act 1918 s 132, Income Tax Act 1952 s 25.

of multiples of the total tax payable, irrespective of the amount evaded. They were applied in the Victorian and Edwardian eras,[93] notwithstanding Lord Loreburn's statement that the penalties were 'unreasonable or oppressive'.[94] Some reasons for the survival of the penalty provisions were set out by Lord Reid:

The incongruities and anomalies in these penalty provisions have a very long history. Some had their origins in the Income Tax Acts of 1799, 1803 and 1806, and even in the Act of 1842 there were already serious anomalies. But in those days the rate of tax was low and penalties based on the total amount of tax payable were probably not oppressive. And this is not the only chapter of the law in which ill-conceived provisions introduced by temporary Acts with limited application have long survived without any radical revision and have to be applied in circumstances very different from those which existed at their origin.[95]

This regime was affirmed, but roundly criticized, by the House of Lords[96]—departing from Diplock J and a strong Court of Appeal[97]—in *Hinchy*, in which the House held that 'treble the tax which he ought to be charged under this Act' meant 'treble the entire tax liability for the relevant year'.[98] The Revenue argued that although the powers granted to it under the statute were draconian, it could be relied upon not to abuse them. The practice in *Hinchy* was used, and defended by the Revenue, because it afforded the Revenue power to recover back-tax which otherwise would be statute-barred. The limitation period in tax matters was normally six years and if there had been an underpayment, it had been going on for more years than that. In consequence, a practice had developed in the Revenue of suing in the High Court, at that time for more money than it actually expected to recover.[99] The obvious and unanswerable objection to the multiple penalties rule was that it punished slips harshly but fraud leniently.[100] After *Hinchy*, a reformed system of civil penalties was quickly enacted, which operated until the reforms in the 2007 Act.[101]

[93] *Attorney-General v Till* [1910] AC 50, on appeal from *Attorney-General v Till* [1909] 1 KB 694.

[94] *Attorney-General v Till* [1910] AC 50 at 51–2.

[95] At 764.

[96] *IRC v Hinchy* [1960] AC 748; [1960] 1 All ER 505.

[97] *IRC v Hinchy* [1959] 2 QB 357; [1959] 2 All ER 512.

[98] Following *Till*, Rowlatt J in *Attorney-General v Johnstone* (1926) 136 LT 31, 32, and the Court of Session in *Lord Advocate v McLaren* (1905) 7 F 984; 5 TC 110. And see GSAW[heatcroft], 'The Hinchy Case' (1960) 23 *Modern Law Review* 425–8.

[99] A practice criticized in the House of Lords: see GSAW, ibid at 426.

[100] Williams, David, 'Surveying Taxes, 1900–14' [2005] *British Tax Review* 222.

[101] FA 1960 Part III, later consolidated as TMA part X.

The Modern Penalty Provisions

The revised penalty provisions, introduced in the Finance Acts 2007, 2008, and 2009, are aimed to change taxpayers' behaviour by applying more severe penalties to those who provide incorrect information,[102] do not notify chargeability to tax,[103] do not submit returns,[104] or do not pay the tax on time.[105] There are analogous provisions for VAT.[106] One of the responses available to HMRC in cases of suspected frauds relying on obtaining refunds from HMRC, as in many VAT frauds, is not to give the (fraudulently claimed) refund.[107]

Penalties for errors may only be imposed if the inaccuracy was careless[108] or deliberate[109] on the taxpayer's part, and they are greater if the latter. If a taxpayer reasonably relies on a reputable accountant for advice in relation to the content of his tax return then there is no liability.[110] A penalty imposed on a taxpayer for a careless inaccuracy in his self-assessment tax return was justified where the taxpayer had no reasonable grounds to believe that a compensation payment received in connection with the termination of his employment was not subject to income tax.[111] The Revenue's policy of refusing to suspend a penalty for a careless inaccuracy in the completion of a tax return where the inaccuracy was a 'one-off' was unlawful. The request of the appellant, who had omitted to mention a severance payment in his tax return, that the relevant penalty should be suspended on condition that he retained tax advisers should have been considered by the Revenue.[112] The taxpayer does have a duty to correct errors should s/he subsequently become aware of them.[113]

The gradations of penalty are fixed as percentages of the lost revenue, by category, as shown in Table 7.1.[114]

[102] FA 2007 Schedule 24. [103] FA 2008 Schedule 41.

[104] FA 2009 Schedule 55. [105] FA 2009 Schedule 56. [106] VATA s 60 *et seq.*

[107] *Kittel v Belgium* (C-439/04) [2008] STC 1537; [2006] ECR I-6161.

[108] Within the meaning of para 3(1)(a): 'if the inaccuracy is due to failure by P to take reasonable care.'

[109] Para 3(1)(b): 'if the inaccuracy is deliberate [on P's part]'—so bona fide reliance upon a dishonest professional adviser will not incur penalties. A person with an agent still had a residual obligation to exercise reasonable care within their ability and competence: *Channa v Revenue and Customs Commissioners* [2013] UKFTT 499 (TC) (FTT (Tax)). Any attempt to conceal deliberate submission of incorrect information is an aggravating factor: 3(1)(c).

[110] FA 2007 Schedule 24 para 18(3), the burden being on the taxpayer: *Hanson v Revenue and Customs Commissioners* [2012] UKFTT 314 (TC); [2012] WTLR 1769 (FTT (Tax)).

[111] *Harding v Revenue and Customs Commissioners* [2013] UKUT 575 (TCC); [2014] STC 891.

[112] *Testa v Revenue and Customs Commissioners* [2013] UKFTT 151 (TC); [2013] SFTD 723.

[113] Para 2.

[114] Schedule 24 Part 2 para 4: category 1 if it is a domestic matter, or an offshore matter where (i) the territory in question is a category 1 territory, or (ii) the tax at stake is a tax other than income tax or capital gains tax. Category 2 if (a) it involves an offshore matter, (b) the territory in question is a category 2 territory, and (c) the tax at stake is income tax or capital gains tax. Category 3 if it

Table 7.1 Gradations of penalty

	Careless	Deliberate but not concealed	Deliberate and concealed
Category 1	30%	70%	100%
Category 2	45%	105%	150%
Category 3	60%	140%	200%

The normal range of penalties was raised to 200 per cent penalty for marketed schemes in the case of offshore evasion.[115]

Procedure, and Burden and Standard of Proof

The procedures under which civil penalties are imposed are laid down in Part 3 of Schedule 24 to the Finance Act 2007. HMRC serves a notice on the taxpayer,[116] and this notice is treated as an assessment to tax. The taxpayer may appeal to the First-tier Tribunal and that appeal is treated as any other appeal against an assessment.[117] Company officers may be made personally liable for deliberate errors in the company accounts,[118] and penalties may be imposed across a partnership.[119] Civil penalties may not be imposed for an inaccuracy or failure in respect of which the person has been convicted of an offence.[120] One further advantage to the Revenue of proceedings for civil penalties is that, because this is the procedure, the burden of proof is on the taxpayer to show that the assessment is incorrect. The applicable standard of proof is the civil one, namely the balance of probabilities.[121]

involves an offshore matter, the territory in question is a category 3 territory, and the tax at stake is income tax or capital gains tax. An inaccuracy 'involves an offshore matter' if it results in a potential loss of revenue that is charged on or by reference to: (a) income arising from a source in a territory outside the UK, (b) assets situated or held in a territory outside the UK, (c) activities carried on wholly or mainly in a territory outside the UK, or (d) anything having effect as if it were income, assets, or activities of a kind just described. Para 21A of Schedule 24 gives power to the Treasury to designate into which category territories fall. The latest list is in Penalties, Offshore Income etc. (Designation of Territories) Order 2011 SI 976, as amended by the Penalties, Offshore Income etc. (Designation of Territories) (Amendment) Order 2013 SI 1618.

[115] FA 2015 s 120 and Sched 20. HMRC, *Tackling Offshore Tax Evasion: Strengthening Civil Deterrents for Offshore Evaders* (2015); HMRC, *Tackling Offshore Tax Evasion: Civil Sanctions for Enablers of Offshore Evasion* (2015).

[116] Para 13. [117] Paras 15–16. [118] Para 19. [119] Para 20.

[120] Para 21. And compare the approach to double jeopardy under the confiscation and forfeiture provisions and the tax jurisdiction of POCA: see Chapter 9, section entitled 'Do Confiscation Orders Affect Tax Liability (and *vice versa*)?'

[121] *Khawaja v Revenue and Customs Commissioners* [2013] UKUT 353 (TCC); [2014] STC 150.

The Human Rights Aspects of Civil Penalties

Articles 6.2 and 6.3 of the European Convention confer upon the defendant a set of rights when s/he is 'charged with a criminal offence'. The question that has arisen recurrently is whether someone upon whom civil penalties are imposed is so charged, and consequently acquires those rights. The significance of these human rights considerations is that if Article 6 is triggered, the advantages to the Revenue (burden and standard of proof, no expense for legal advice for the taxpayer) are lost.

The starting point is *Engel v Netherlands (No 1)*,[122] in which the European Court of Human Rights (ECtHR) set out three criteria, usually referred to as the '*Engel* criteria', which must be satisfied before an action is classified as 'criminal' for Convention purposes. These are: (a) the classification of the proceedings in domestic law, that is whether civil or criminal; (b) the nature of the offence; and (c) the nature and degree of severity of the penalty that the person concerned risked incurring. The third is usually critical. The applicant in *Öztürk v Germany*[123] had committed a breach of traffic regulations. Although he accepted that the resulting penalty was civil under German law, he objected to having to pay a fee for the use of an interpreter, saying that this was incompatible with Article 6.3 of the Convention. The ECtHR first repeated the *Engel* criteria, before holding that the penalty:

> *retained a punitive character, which is the customary distinguishing feature of criminal penalties ... It is a rule that is directed ... towards all citizens in their capacity as road-users; it prescribes conduct of a certain kind and makes the resultant requirement subject to a sanction that is punitive. Indeed, the sanction ... seeks to punish as well as to deter ... Above all, the general character of the rule and the purpose of the penalty, being both deterrent and punitive, suffice to show that the offence in question was, in terms of Article 6 of the Convention, criminal in nature.*[124]

In *Bendenoun v France*[125] the taxpayer was prosecuted and fined by the French customs and tax authorities for various customs, exchange control, and tax offences. He appealed to the *Conseil d'État* on the basis that the authorities had failed to take into account the whole of his customs file, but had chosen particular parts, on which they then relied. He claimed that his right to a fair trial had been contravened in the administrative proceedings on the basis that he had not had access to the facts on which the case against him was based. The ECtHR held that Article 6(1) was applicable as the proceedings were

[122] *Engel v Netherlands (No 1)* (1976) 1 EHRR 647.

[123] *Öztürk v Germany* [1984] ECHR 8544/79.

[124] Para 53.

[125] *Bendenoun v France* (1994) 18 EHRR 54.

criminal in nature, despite their being designated as administrative proceedings by French law, because the penalties were intended not as compensation for damages to the revenue, but as punishment to deter re-offending. They were severe penalties and failure to pay exposed the offender to imprisonment. The Court went on to hold that Article 6(1) had not been contravened by the non-production of the documentation.

In *EL v Switzerland*,[126] a tax penalty fine imposed upon the estate of a deceased person was held to be punitive and to generate Article 6.2 rights. In contrast, in *HM v Germany*[127] a decision to reassess the taxpayer's income tax over ten years rather than the usual four, in the light of her intentional evasion, was held not to engage Article 6, since it lacked the punitive element. In *AP v Switzerland*,[128] the size of the fines made the difference. In *Jussila v Finland*[129] the ECtHR considered whether ten surcharges imposed for book-keeping errors, totalling €300, were criminal for the purposes of the Convention. The Court held that:

> *The second and third [Engel] criteria are alternative and not necessarily cumulative. It is enough that the offence in question is by its nature to be regarded as criminal or that the offence renders the person liable to a penalty which by its nature and degree of severity belongs in the general criminal sphere ... The relative lack of seriousness of the penalty cannot divest an offence of its inherently criminal character.*[130]

The approach in *Öztürk* and *Jussila* has been followed in a significant number of other ECtHR judgments, up to and including *Glantz v Finland*.[131] The ECtHR has thus consistently held that the minor nature of a penalty does not prevent it from being 'criminal' under the Convention. In *Georgiou (t/a Marios Chippery) v United Kingdom*[132] it was decided that Article 6.2 was applicable to VAT penalties, since the imposition of a penalty constituted proceedings of a criminal character having regard to the potential size of the penalty, the punitive and deterrent nature of the proceedings, and the consideration given to mitigation.

Civil tax penalties under the pre-2007 regime[133] did not involve a criminal charge without more so far as the domestic court was concerned, and so

[126] *EL v Switzerland* (1997) 3 BHRC 348; [2000] WTLR 873.
[127] *HM v Germany (Admissibility)* (62512/00) 8 ITL Rep. 206; (2005) 41 EHRR SE15.
[128] *AP v Switzerland* (1998) 26 EHRR 541.
[129] *Jussila v Finland* [2006] A/73053/01; [2009] STC 29.
[130] At [31].
[131] *Glantz v Finland* [2014] STC 2263.
[132] *Georgiou (t/a Mario's Chippery) v United Kingdom* (40042/98) [2001] STC 80.
[133] TMA s 97AA(1)(a).

Articles 6.2 and 6.3 were not engaged.[134] In *C&E Comrs v City of London Magistrates Court*,[135] Lord Bingham of Cornhill said:

> *It is in my judgment the general understanding that criminal proceedings involve a formal accusation made on behalf of the state or by a private prosecutor that a defendant has committed a breach of the criminal law, and the state or the private prosecutor has instituted proceedings which may culminate in the conviction and condemnation of the defendant.*[136]

Tax penalties are thus not criminal under UK law, even when they might be criminal under the Convention.[137] Penalty proceedings are not prosecuted as criminal offences through the criminal courts by a 'formal accusation made on behalf of the state ... that a defendant has committed a breach of the criminal law'. Instead, they are appealed to the First-tier Tribunal.[138]

In *King v Walden*[139] Jacob LJ applied the *Benendoun* criteria,[140] and held that the system then in force for the imposition of penalties for fraudulent or negligent delivery of incorrect tax returns or statements was covered by Article 6.2. His reasons were as follows:

> *(a) Plainly the system is intended to punish the defaulting taxpayer and to operate as a deterrent.*
> *(b) The amount of fine is potentially very substantial.*
> *(c) The amount of fine is not related to any administrative matter. In particular the fine is not limited to the administrative and other extra cost of dealing with the taxpayer concerned.*
> *(d) The amount of fine imposed depends upon the degree of culpability of the taxpayer, the less culpable the more mitigation there is. Mitigation is an essentially criminal rather than civil consideration.*
> *(e) It is accepted that generally it is not for the taxpayer to show that the determination of penalties was wrong. On appeal the burden of proof lies on the Crown. In this regard there is a clear distinction between a penalty determination and an appeal against ordinary assessment where the burden of showing it was wrong lies on the taxpayer.*[141]

[134] *Sharkey v Revenue and Customs* [2005] STC (SCD) 336; [2005] STI 223, affirmed *Sharkey v Revenue and Customs* [2006] EWHC 300 (Ch); [2006] STC 2026.

[135] *C&E Comrs v City of London Magistrates* [2000] 1 WLR 2020; [2000] 4 All ER 763.

[136] At para 17. Endorsed by the House of Lords in *R (on the application of McCann) v Kensington & Chelsea LBC* [2002] UKHL 39; [2003] 1 AC 787 at 20.

[137] *Han & Yau v HMRC* [2001] EWCA Civ 1048; [2001] 1 WLR 2253, per Mance LJ at [88]; *Pendle v HMRC* [2015] UKFTT 27 (TC).

[138] Schedule 55, para 20.

[139] *King v Walden (Inspector of Taxes)* [2001] STC 822; [2001] BPIR 1012.

[140] *Bendenoun v France* (1994) 18 EHRR 54.

[141] Para 71.

Jacob LJ went on to hold that the fact that Article 6 applies is not itself conclusive, however, of the allocation of the burden of proof. Although Article 6.2 is not expressed to have exceptions, the presumption of innocence, which it embodies, can be displaced. In determining whether or not a shift in the burden of proof is warranted, the court must have regard to whether the shift would militate towards a legitimate goal and whether the 'downside' of the shift is proportionate to the ends sought. The burden is on the state to show that the legislative means adopted were not greater than necessary. The considerations that would bear upon that issue would be the effectiveness (as deterrent) of the means used, and fairness in terms of public defensibility and accountability. If the penalties are themselves criminal in nature, the position is that Article 6 applies to the penalty proceedings, so that, for instance, the burden of proof is on HMRC.[142]

The Public Accounts Committee looked into civil tax investigations in 2010–11.[143] Of civil investigations of fraud completed in 2009–10, the average penalty was 21 per cent of the tax due; over a quarter of penalties were for less than 10 per cent and most were for less than 30 per cent; and 14 per cent of cases attracted no penalty at all.[144] While the Committee concluded that there were some problems in rates of collection, it did not criticize the principle of favouring the use of civil penalties.

Civil Actions

In addition to the deployment of the civil penalty regime, criminal prosecutions with or without confiscation orders,[145] and the Proceeds of Crime Act (POCA) tax jurisdiction,[146] there is also the possibility that HMRC could recover funds by a civil action for an economic tort. This rare procedure was adopted in *Customs and Excise Commissioners v Total Network SL*.[147] The VAT legislation contains procedures for recovery of overpaid credits,[148] but the Commissioners were unable to use them against the defendant as it was not VAT-registered in the UK and so relied on the tort of unlawful means conspiracy instead, claiming £1.95 million in damages. The Supreme Court held that the VAT legislation was not exclusive of other action by the commissioners, and that the common law action was available.

142 See *King v Walden* at para 71.

143 Hodge, Margaret (Chair), Public Accounts Committee, *HM Revenue & Customs: Managing Civil Tax Investigations,* Twenty-seventh Report of Session 2010–11.

144 Para 12.

145 See Chapter 9, section entitled 'Confiscating the Proceeds of Tax Evasion'.

146 See Chapter 9, section entitled 'The Proceeds of Crime Act Tax Jurisdiction'.

147 *Customs and Excise Commissioners v Total Network SL* [2008] UKHL 19; [2008] 1 AC 1174.

148 VATA s 78 *et seq.*

8

The International Element

This chapter will deal with the international aspects of crime and tax. Among the last areas of domestic law to be affected by globalization, criminal law and tax are now both at the forefront of change. The 'Revenue Rule' was that one country would not assist another in the enforcement of its tax law,[1] so tax offences tended not to be covered by extradition treaties and arrangements for mutual legal assistance. Double taxation treaties were developed to deal with this, and in a fairly clumsy, bilateral, way, they do. Traditionally, the legal regime governing cross-border tax enforcement was based on information exchange upon request. While the operations of the relevant bodies still fall significantly short of the establishment of a transnational legal order, much has developed in recent years.

International Aspects of Tax Evasion

If it were possible to place money beyond the reach of Her Majesty's Revenue and Customs (HMRC) by using overseas banks or financial institutions, the job of HMRC would be rendered impossible. So far as concerns corporations operating globally, the legal framework for international taxation is old and messy.[2] The system for allocating the profits of transnational companies between the jurisdictions they touch for the purposes of

[1] Lord Keith of Avonholm in *Government of India v Taylor* [1955] AC 491 at 511. And see Albrecht, AR, 'The Enforcement of Taxation under International Law' (1953) 30 *British Yearbook of International Law* 454 and Harris, Peter, and David Oliver, *International Commercial Tax* (Cambridge: Cambridge University Press, 2010) at 466.

[2] And see Picciotto, Sol, *Is the International Tax System Fit for Purpose, Especially for Developing Countries?* ICTD Working Paper 13 (Brighton: Institute of Development Studies, 2013); Miller, Angharad, and Lynne Oats, *Principles of International Taxation* (London: Bloomsbury, 5th edn, 2016).

taxation arose during the 1920s, primarily under the auspices of the League of Nations.[3] Since its inception in 1961, the Organisation for Economic Co-operation and Development (OECD) has taken the lead. A range of avoidance mechanisms exist which take advantage of the differences in rates between jurisdictions. The major one,[4] deriving from the rules on international taxation, is transfer pricing,[5] that is, arranging corporate structures and accounts so as to ensure that profits accrue, for the purposes of the relevant legislation and double taxation treaties,[6] in the jurisdictions that attract the smallest liability to tax, and losses so as to negative as much of the taxable profits as possible. This sort of behaviour is frequently presented as being that of a parasite driven only by its own advantage. The basis of the critique is that these organizations take the benefits of national infrastructure (a comparatively wealthy customer base, roads, and other infrastructure), while not making any, or only making a small, contribution towards paying for them. The general claim of the 'tax justice' movement is that it is bad that corporations and/or individuals avail themselves of favourable rates of taxation, deductions, and so on by exercising a flexibility that they have as a result of choices made as to their structures, those choices not being available to the normal human taxpayer.

The move to identify the beneficial owners of all trusts and companies came from the 2013 Lough Erne declaration of the G8. The UK legislated on the beneficial ownership of companies (but not trusts) in 2015.[7] President Obama took an interest in tax-haven issues, declaring in 2009 that Ugland House, a building in the Cayman Islands that then housed some 19,000 companies, was either 'the largest building in the world or the largest tax scam in the world. It's the kind of tax scam that we need to end'.[8] The acts of the US in this arena, as those of the UK, are ambivalent. If and when it does put its full weight behind the movement to end havens and enhance transparency, then change will follow.

[3] Graetz, Michael, and Michael O'Hear, 'The "Original Intent" of US International Taxation' (1997) 51 *Duke Law Journal* 1021; Taxation (International and Other Provisions) Act 2010 (UK).

[4] For others see Gravelle, Jane G, *Tax Havens: International Tax Avoidance and Evasion* (Philadelphia, PA: Diane Publishing, 2013) 8 *et seq*.

[5] Sikka, Prem, and Hugh Willmott, 'The Dark Side of Transfer Pricing: Its Role in Tax Avoidance and Wealth Retentiveness' (2010) 21 *Critical Perspectives on Accounting* 342–56.

[6] OECD, 2003. The United Nations has issued a model DTA for use by developing countries. It aims to keep profits generated in a country within that country. <http://www.un.org/esa/ffd/documents/UN_Model_2011_Update.pdf>.

[7] Small Business, Enterprise and Employment Act 2015 Part 7 and Schedule 3, inserting Part 21A of the Companies Act 2006.

[8] Remarks by the President on International Tax Policy Reform, 4 May 2009.

Capital flight[9] from developing nations to rich nations, frequently via 'offshore' secrecy jurisdictions, is bad for developing nations, because it erodes the tax base for the countries from which the money moves, and taxation is the best and most sustainable way in which to fund government.[10] It also conduces towards a 'race to the bottom'[11] in which the jurisdiction that is regulated least, and least effectively, attracts the most business. It has a number of causes, including tax avoidance, tax evasion, corruption, fraud, plunder, money laundering, caprice, and rational and irrational investment. Money migrates to offshore jurisdictions, both as a semi-permanent haven and en route, for example, to London or New York.[12]

While capital flight is frequently presented as being a problem arising from the 'illicit' nature of the money involved, it occurs for a number of reasons, legal and illegal, and insofar as the harmful economic consequence is the erosion of the tax base of developing nations, it is unrelated to the lawfulness or otherwise of the money's provenance. If capital flight is bad and it is possible to inhibit capital flight,[13] then the inhibition ought not to be dependent upon allegations of criminality. In an early and highly influential piece on the economics of money laundering, Tanzi argued that laundering was harmful because the movements of money involved would be for reasons other than the optimal and efficient operation of markets.[14] The same kind of attitude underpins the later fuller account of the International Monetary Fund (IMF).[15]

[9] Heggstad, Kari, and Odd-Helge Fjeldstad, *How Banks Assist Capital Flight from Africa: A Literature Review*, CMI Report 2010, no. 6.

[10] OECD, 2013, <http://www.oecd.org/ctp/BEPSActionPlan.pdf>. For the Tax Justice Network response see <http://www.taxjustice.net/cms/upload/pdf/OECD_Beps_130327_No_more_shifty_business.pdf>.

[11] OECD, *Harmful Tax Competition: An Emerging Global Issue* (Paris: OECD, 1998); Reuter, Peter (ed), *Draining Development? Controlling Flows of Illicit Funds from Developing Countries* (Washington DC: World Bank, 2012). Note the word 'illicit'. Cf Morriss, Andrew P, and Lotta Moberg, 'Cartelizing Taxes: Understanding the OECD's Campaign Against "Harmful Tax Competition"' (2012) 4 *Columbia Journal of Tax Law* 1.

[12] Karzon, Allaire Urban, 'International Tax Evasion: Spawned in the United States and Nurtured by Secrecy Havens' (1983) 16 *Vanderbilt Journal of Transnational Law* 757–832.

[13] Reuter, Peter (ed), *Draining Development? Controlling Flows of Illicit Funds from Developing Countries* (Washington DC: World Bank, 2012).

[14] Tanzi, Vito, *Money Laundering and the International Financial System*, IMF Working Paper 96/55 (Washington DC: International Monetary Fund, 1996).

[15] International Monetary Fund, *Anti-Money Laundering and Combating the Financing of Terrorism (AML/CFT)—Report on the Review of the Effectiveness of the Program Prepared by the Legal Department* (2011).

Offshore

Offshore tax havens are not new,[16] but attention to them has grown, and there have been many strong attacks upon their use.[17] The Tax Justice Network argued in its widely cited report *The Price of Offshore Revisited* that in 2010, $21 to $32 trillion in 'financial' wealth was 'hidden' in offshore financial centres (OFCs) and so 'virtually tax free'.[18] While OFCs have some defenders,[19] the general idea of many of the complaints is that offshore contributes to many of the world's evils.[20] Sol Picciotto, for example, argued that, '[b]y providing a haven for routing global flows through the use of artificial persons and transactions, "offshore" has helped to dislocate the international state system and induce its substantial reconstruction'.[21] Rhetorical and other links have been made between corruption, tax avoidance, tax evasion, and money laundering. The UK government has acquired a reputation for being at the heart of a 'spider's web' of offshore jurisdictions which enable avoidance, evasion, corruption, and laundering.[22] Overseas territories and Crown dependencies did not just appear. So far as concerns the UK, they are usually the result of one or another eighteenth-century military adventure.[23]

To people disposed to paying less tax, there are three main attractions to offshore. First, there is secrecy, in the senses both of having legal protections upon access to information and of a culture of not asking questions. Some forms of financial secrecy have given rise to concern since the 1980s,[24] and the era of unchallenged bank secrecy has now been declared

[16] Workman, Douglas J, 'The Use of Offshore Tax Havens for the Purpose of Criminally Evading Income Taxes' (1973) 73 *Journal of Criminal Law and Criminology* 675–706.

[17] Vlcek, William, *Offshore Finance and Small States: Sovereignty, Size and Money* (London: Palgrave Macmillan, 2008).

[18] Henry, James, *The Price of Offshore Revisited* (Tax Justice Network, 2012); Gould, James Jackson, *OECD Initiative on Tax Havens* (London: DIANE Publishing, 2010).

[19] Gordon, Richard, and Andrew P Morriss, 'Moving Money: International Financial Flows, Taxes, and Money Laundering' (2014) 37 *Hastings International and Comparative Law Review* 1–120. See the critique of Wiesbach, David A, 'Ten Truths about Tax Shelters' (2002) 52 *Tax Law Review* 215 and Green, Stuart P, 'What Is Wrong with Tax Evasion?' (2008) 9 *Houston Business and Tax Law Journal* 221 by Katz, Leo, 'In Defense of Tax Shelters' (2007) 26 *Virginia Tax Review* 799.

[20] Shaxson, Nicholas, *Treasure Islands* (London: Vintage Books, 2012); Palan, Ronen, Richard Murphy, and Christian Chavagneux, *Tax Havens: How Globalization Really Works* (Ithaca, NY: Cornell University Press, 2013); Murphy, Richard, *Over Here and Undertaxed: Multinationals, Tax Avoidance and You* (London: Random House, 2013).

[21] Picciotto, Sol, 'Offshore: The State as Legal Fiction' in Hampton, Mark P, and Jason P Abbott (eds), *Offshore Finance Centres and Tax Havens: The Rise of Global Capital* (London: Palgrave, 1999) 43.

[22] Shaxson, n 20, at 103 *et seq.*

[23] Palan, Ronen, 'Financial Centers: The British Empire, City-States and Commercially-Oriented Politics' (2010) 11 *Theoretical Inquiries in Law* 142–67.

[24] OECD, *Taxation and the Abuse of Bank Secrecy* (Paris: OECD, 1985).

to be at an end.[25] Tax evasion can be assisted by the anonymity that can be furnished by shell companies (companies whose major function is to serve as a repository of money[26]), secret trusts, hybrid entities, attorney–client privilege, anonymous beneficial ownership (whether achieved by bearer shares and other securities or otherwise), and so on. Bearer instruments (e.g. companies constituted with bearer shares, so that control is exercised by and dividends are payable to the bearer) have also been used in the past, and were one focus in the *Panama Papers*. Second, offshore jurisdictions tend to operate low tax rates on the relevant matters. This is important only if the actor intends to pay any tax.[27] A company might want a low tax regime because it *does* intend to publish accounts and have them audited. An individual tax evader looking for a place to park money outside the reach of his/her domestic authorities might not care either about the rate of interest, management fees, and so on charged by the financial institution or about the local rates of income tax, corporation tax, or capital gains tax (CGT), to which s/he will not be liable so long as s/he does not pay domestic taxes. Third, offshore jurisdictions offer political stability[28] and financial products that provide what Sharman calls 'calculated ambiguity'.[29] A person might want to put his/her money in a more politically stable and economically prosperous jurisdiction than that in which s/he resides because s/he is less likely to lose it.

Many governments and distinguished economists[30] decry the use of offshore. One of the consequences of the existence of tax havens is that they skew markets to the benefit of multinationals at the expense of striving domestic entrepreneurs. How can the local independent coffee shop, which pays domestic income or corporation tax, contend with Starbucks, which pays

[25] OECD, *The Era of Bank Secrecy is Over* (Paris: OECD, 2011). And see Schoueri, Luís Eduardo, and Mateus Calicchio Barbosa, 'Transparency: From Tax Secrecy to the Simplicity and Reliability of the Tax System' [2013] *British Tax Review* 666–81.

[26] Young, Mary Alice, *Banking Secrecy and Offshore Financial Centres: Money Laundering and Offshore Banking* (London: Routledge, 2012); Young, Mary Alice, 'The Exploitation of Global Offshore Financial Centres: Banking Confidentiality and Money Laundering' (2013) 16 *Journal of Money Laundering Control* 198–208. EU legislation dealing with corporate anonymity will revive interest in trusts: <https://twitter.com/GFI_Tweets/status/601154193160859648?s=02>.

[27] The rate of corporation tax is the critical one. Some secrecy jurisdictions have quite high rates of consumption taxes.

[28] And see Shaxson, n 20, at 179–81.

[29] Sharman, JC, 'Offshore and the New international Political Economy' (2010) 17 *Review of International Political Economy* 1–19. Orwell called it 'doublespeak'.

[30] 'Tax Havens Have No Economic Justification, Say Top Economists', *The Guardian*, 8 May 2016.

little or no tax in the jurisdiction? The independent purveyor may well serve a superior *doppio* to Starbucks' but cannot compete on price. The 'Starbucks' argument from unfair competition in tax law is entirely analogous to the 'empty pizzeria' argument against money laundering.[31] We may well want to do something about undesirable cross-subsidies within companies. Whether or not the subsidy comes from a lawful source does not, on this account, affect the harm it does.

What transnational corporations say is that they organize their affairs, locate their headquarters, and account for their profits so as to minimize liability to tax; that they are allowed to do so; and that if the OECD governments, individually or collectively, want to change the basis upon which tax is levied, then they have it in their power to do it. Tax planning is presented by the corporations as a rational response to tax laws. Indeed, it is the only response possible for an individual or firm faced with the need to comply with the conflicting provisions, definitions, and exemptions of multiple jurisdictions' tax laws.[32] Anger at the losses and the damage occasioned by them should be directed at legislators, not corporations.

The International Response to Scandals

If a remedy is needed for offshore, the first two (secrecy and low taxes) of these three identifying criteria need to be challenged.[33] Attempts to anonymize or otherwise obscure the beneficial ownership of property are addressed by transparency and disclosure.[34] In 2013, the G20 affirmed as a principle that the international community should:

1. *Address tax avoidance, particularly, base erosion and profit shifting to ensure profits are taxed in the location where the economic activity takes place.*
2. *Promote international tax transparency and the global sharing of information so that taxpayers with offshore investments comply with their domestic tax obligations.*
3. *Ensure that developing countries benefit from the G20's tax agenda, particularly in relation to information sharing.*[35]

[31] That is, the argument that failure to criminalize laundering gives rise to unfair competition between the restaurant subsidized from income from crime and that which is not. This is best treated as a competition law issue.

[32] Ordower, Henry, 'Utopian Visions toward a Grand Unified Global Income Tax' (2013) 14 *Florida Tax Review* 361.

[33] Christensen, John, 'The Hidden Trillions: Secrecy, Corruption, and the Offshore Interface' (2012) 57 *Crime, Law and Social Change* 325–43.

[34] The details of which are as important as the principle.

[35] <http://www.g20.utoronto.ca/2013/2013-0906-declaration.html#aml>.

The OECD's base erosion and profit shifting (BEPS) initiative[36] and the Foreign Account Tax Compliance Act (FATCA),[37] which compels banks all over the world to disclose accounts the beneficial owners of which are US citizens, are both examples of compelled exposure.[38] The EU, as part of the revision of its money laundering regime, put in place regulations under which the ultimate owners of companies and trusts would have to be listed in public registers in EU countries, under updated anti-money laundering (AML) rules.[39] The OECD started an initiative on tax and crime in 2011 that has involved fora, action plans,[40] and Council recommendations,[41] and these seem to have been the reason for the adoption, in the 2012 revised recommendations, of FATF.[42]

The BEPS package[43] was launched in October 2015.[44] The principal mechanism for change is the introduction of exchange of information between jurisdictions, together with better mutual assistance.[45] The OECD has an Action Plan on BEPS[46] and has revised the wording of Article 26 of the OECD model tax convention to let tax authorities ask other countries for any financial information that is 'foreseeably relevant' about taxpayers.[47] The Global Forum on Transparency and Exchange of Information for Tax Purposes monitors the standards on tax transparency, tax information exchange 'on request' (EOIR), and automatic exchange of information.[48] Setion 113 of the Companies Act 2006 creates an obligation on the part of companies to maintain a register of shareholders which is available to the

[36] <http://www.oecd.org/ctp/beps.htm>.

[37] Foreign Account Tax Compliance Act 2010.

[38] Morse, Susan, 'Ask for Help, Uncle Sam: The Future of Global Tax Reporting' (2012) 57 *Villanova Law Review* 529–50; Grinberg, Itai, 'The Battle Over Taxing Offshore Accounts' (2012) 60 *UCLA Law Review* 304–506. FATCA is not universally popular: see eg Behrens, Frederic, 'Using a Sledgehammer to Crack a Nut: Why FATCA Will Not Stand' (2013) *Wisconsin Law Review* 205–36; Denealt, Sean, 'Foreign Account Tax Compliance Act: A Step in the Wrong Direction' (2014) 24 *Indiana International & Comparative Law Review* 729.

[39] Fourth Money Laundering Directive (EU) 2015/849 Article 3.

[40] OECD BEPS Action Plan 2013.

[41] 2010 Council Recommendation to facilitate co-operation between tax and other law enforcement authorities to combat serious crimes.

[42] Interpretive Note to FATF Recommendation 3 para 4. See definition of 'categories of offences'.

[43] And see Panayi, Christiana HJI, *Advanced Issues in International and European Tax Law* (Oxford: Hart, 2015) chs 2–4.

[44] <http://www.oecd.org/tax/aggressive/>.

[45] OECD Convention on Mutual Administrative Assistance in Tax Matters.

[46] OECD, *Action Plan on Base Erosion and Profit Shifting* (Paris: OECD Publishing, 2013).

[47] <http://www.oecd.org/ctp/exchange-of-tax-information/120718_Article%2026-ENG_no%20cover%20(2).pdf>.

[48] Baker, Philip, 'The BEPS Project: Disclosure of Aggressive Tax Planning Schemes' (2015) 43 *Intertax* 85–90.

public. Public entitlement to examine this information can be seen as a price in the reduction of privacy that attaches to the use of a company structure. EU Directive 2014/107/EU implements the July 2014 OECD Global Standard on automatic exchange of financial account information within the EU, with a scope covering not only interest income but also dividends and other types of capital income, and the annual balance of the accounts producing such items of income. It entered into force on 1 January 2016. The introduction in the UK of the diverted profits tax,[49] dubbed the 'Google tax', is intended to raise more than £1 billion over five years and took effect on 1 April 2015. By making it 5 per cent higher than the UK's corporation tax rate of 20 per cent, the Treasury hopes to encourage companies to dismantle tax avoidance structures. The March 2015 budget introduced further measures.[50]

In the field of anti-avoidance, so far as concerns the international system for the taxation of multi-national corporations, there is much pressure for change—the 'reform agenda' which has been brought to the political forefront by publicity given to the tax treatment of multinationals.[51] Just as the 'aggressive vs non-aggressive' tax evasion issue is unresolved,[52] it is also contentious whether or not and to what extent tax competition between jurisdictions is a good idea or not. The decision of the European Court of Justice (ECJ) that Irish corporation tax rates represent state aid in violation of EU rules again brings those sorts of issues to the forefront.[53]

Even offshore, tax evasion differs from avoidance: it is criminal.[54] The taxpayer has property as a result of under- or non-declaration of income or capital gains or other taxable events, or the making of untrue representations in order to gain relief from taxation. Either the property is already in, or the taxpayer sends it to, a bank account or other investment vehicle offshore by

[49] FA 2015 Part 3. See Neidle, Dan, 'The Diverted Profits Tax—Flawed by Design' [2015] *British Tax Review* 147–66; Baker, Philip, 'The Diverted Profits Tax—A Partial Response' [2015] *British Tax Review* 167–71.

[50] F (No 2) A 2015 part 3.

[51] Palan, Murphy, and Chavagneux, n 20; *Tax Havens: How Globalization Really Works* (Ithaca, NY: Cornell University Press, 2013); Murphy, n 20; Hodge, Margaret (Chair), Public Accounts Committee, *Tax Avoidance—Google,* Ninth Report of Session 2013–14. And see Hodge, Margaret (Chair), Public Accounts Committee, *Charity Commission: The Cup Trust and Tax Avoidance,* Seventh Report of 2013–14. On the Public Accounts Committee's work between 2010 and 2015, see Sikka, Prem, 'No Accounting for Tax Avoidance' (2015) 86 *Political Quarterly* 427–33.

[52] See Chapter 3, section entitled 'The Jurisprudence of Tax Avoidance and Statutory Interpretation'.

[53] The court on Friday 23 April 2016 agreed with two previous European Commission rulings which stated that tax relief given for the Aughinish Alumina facility in Askeaton, Co Limerick, amounted to illegal state aid. *Ireland v European Commission* (2016) ECLI:EU:T:2016:227.

[54] See Chapter 3.

using which it will be impossible or unlikely to connect the beneficial owner to the property, and hence to levy tax upon the beneficial owner. If it is possible to operate, in any jurisdiction in the world, untraceable bearer securities, shares, and other instruments, or legal mechanisms (trusts, shell companies) which disguise or anonymize the beneficial ownership of property, then a great deal of property will gravitate to these jurisdictions, and a great deal of tax revenue will be lost. The difficulty that is caused to the tax authorities by secrecy jurisdictions goes further than simply concealing crime. If it is possible to hide money in a bank account in a secrecy jurisdiction, then the usual mechanism used by the Revenue to check income and wealth (expenditure plus savings) will not work because some savings are unknown. The anti-avoidance agenda based upon exchange of information between jurisdictions should also militate against evasion. All these measures form part of the continuing dialectic of attempts to make avoidance and evasion more difficult, and the responses of those not disposed to pay. None will provide an instant solution.

Specific Offences of Offshore Evasion

A UK tax return requires the taxpayer to declare income or capital gains worldwide. That is, so long as the behaviour in question falls with the jurisdiction of the English criminal courts,[55] it is an offence deliberately not to declare. There were, however, only eleven prosecutions for offshore tax evasion in the five years to 2015.[56] Either side of the 2015 general election, HMRC, as part of its 'No Safe Havens' project, consulted on specific offences dealing with offshore tax evasion. There were to have been two distinct new offences: one of offshore evasion,[57] and the other of failure by a corporation to prevent offshore evasion by an employee.[58] The offshore evasion offence was put in place pretty much as proposed.[59] It extends the boundaries of criminal liability to cover negligent behaviour by the taxpayer.

55 Cheat is a Group A offence under Criminal Justice Act 1993. Knowingly submitting an incorrect UK tax return from anywhere would clearly attract jurisdiction.

56 Hillyer, Meg (Chair), Public Accounts Committee, *HM Revenue & Customs Performance in 2014–15,* Sixth Report of Session 2015–16, conclusion 9.

57 HMRC, *Tackling Offshore Tax Evasion: A New Criminal Offence for Offshore Evaders: Summary of Responses* (London: HMRC, 2015), responding to responses to HMRC, *Tackling Offshore Tax Evasion: A New Criminal Offence* (London: HMRC, 2014).

58 HMRC, *Tackling Offshore Tax Evasion: A New Corporate Criminal Offence of Failure to Prevent the Facilitation of Evasion* (London: HMRC, 2015).

59 FA 2016 s 166, inserting TMA s 106B.

The offence[60] only applies to income tax and CGT. It extends the criminal law to cover three possible cases (in each case where this leads to an understatement or underpayment of tax relating to relevant offshore income, assets, or activities). They are: failing to notify HMRC of chargeability to tax; failing to file a return; and filing an inaccurate return. The offence applies to all offshore income and gains and not just to under-declared investment returns. The threshold applies to each tax year separately. There is an option for a prison sentence of up to six months.[61]

One aspect of the new offence that seems particularly unusual is a defence of *de minimis*. The crime is restricted to evasion over a given sum.[62] The possibility of introducing a general *de minimis* defence in criminal law is considered from time to time, and usually rejected.[63] Such a defence, were it to exist, might cover theft of small amounts, possession of very small amounts of drugs, exceeding the speed limit by a very small amount, and very small violations of proscriptions related, for example, to the age of one of the participants. While the matters involved may influence the exercise of a prosecutorial discretion, the orthodox position suggested elsewhere in criminal law theory is that none of them may provide a substantial criminal defence of *de minimis*. It was particularly surprising to see the proposal for a *de minimis* defence coming from HMRC. It has never been suggested that *de minimis* should provide a defence in the case of small failures to discharge a liability to pay tax, so it is peculiar to institute such a defence for the new offence, for which the main test of criminal liability will be that of liability to pay the tax.

As to the basis of liability, the offence is not a strict liability offence properly so called. There is an affirmative defence for a person who demonstrates that s/he had taken reasonable care in conducting her/his tax affairs,[64] but this, unlike the domestic offences, no longer requires dishonesty or any more active culpability. As to sentence, courts are to take account of the corresponding civil penalty to

[60] TMA s 106B.

[61] TMA 1970 s 106G. There is much literature on whether it can even be justifiable to imprison for an offence of negligence.

[62] The original proposal was for a limit of £5,000, subsequently raised to £25,000: TMA s 106F(2).

[63] Robinson, Paul, 'Criminal Law Defenses: A Systematic Analysis' (1982) 82 *Columbia Law Review* 199–291, deals, at 258, with the Model Penal Code *de minimis* infraction defence. See also Husak, Douglas, 'The De Minimis "Defence" to Criminal Liability' in Duff, RA, and Stuart Green (eds), *Philosophical Foundations of Criminal Law* (Oxford: Oxford University Press, 2011) ch 13.

[64] 'It is a defence for a person accused of an offence under this section to prove that the person took reasonable care to ensure that the return was accurate.' FA 2016 s 166 inserting TMA s 106D(2).

ensure that individuals subject to civil sanctions are not at risk of being treated more severely than corresponding individuals who are guilty of the crime.[65]

The introduction of this new basis for liability could be presented in one of two ways. In the first, it is a recognition that the taxpayer who uses offshore accounts is in a special position, on notice that s/he is behaving in a way that may suggest evasion is likely and which attracts particular scrutiny. The duty on the taxpayer—even its expression in criminal law—may properly be enhanced. On this account, the arrangement is almost contractual. The law says: 'If you do not bank offshore, the threshold for criminal liability will be that you lie to HMRC. If you do, it is legitimately lowered and now you will be criminally liable for any negligent mistake.'

Alternatively, the introduction of this offence may be seen as the thin end of a wedge, a step on a slippery slope towards the reduction of the level of fault throughout the criminal law of evasion. The history of the expansion of English criminal law is of the creation of exceptional liability, for cases presented as particularly dangerous, and then subsequently the extension being applied throughout, for reasons of consistency. There are many episodes in which a specific, harsh rule is brought in to deal with a specific perceived threat, and then subsequently, for reasons of consistency, for ease of administration, or because of a continued perceived threat, extended—only subsequently to be extended to cover a much wider field. It may be, therefore, that this presages the abolition of the dishonesty threshold for liability and its replacement with a negligence threshold. If that is to happen, then it should not happen incrementally. In either case, we should not expect the introduction of the new offence to generate significant numbers of prosecutions.

In any event, to have any effect independently of the macro-level measures for greater transparency in beneficial ownership, the level of prosecutions will have to be more than a couple a year to justify the change in the law. If the legislation proves (in the pejorative sense) 'symbolic', it would probably have been better not to enact it.

Failure to Prevent Offences

The other offence which was considered was one of failure by a corporation to prevent either participation by an employee in offshore evasion,[66] or economic crime more broadly.[67] The model is the offence under of the Bribery Act 2010,

65 FA 2016 s 166, inserting TMA s 106B *et seq*.

66 HMRC, n 58.

67 Attorney-General's [Jeremy Wright's] keynote address to the 32nd Cambridge International Symposium on Economic Crime, 2 Sept 2014.

and was an extension of the idea of holding professional advisers liable. Under s 7 of the Bribery Act 2010 it is an affirmative defence to show that the company had put in place 'adequate procedures' to ensure that its employees do not commit the offences. Guidance is published as to what might amount to 'adequate procedures'.[68]

So far as concerns tax evasion, the idea is that where, for example, a large accountancy firm markets a product or technique which amounts to tax evasion, the firm would be liable for failure to prevent its employees using it unless it had in place 'adequate procedures' for the prevention of such behaviour by its employees. The response to consultation[69] and to the return of a majority Conservative government in the 2015 election was that the proposal was not pursued. The same view was taken as to financial crimes more generally.[70] This was a reflection of the more relaxed approach to corporate misconduct and the 'end of banker-bashing'[71] since the election.

The *Panama Papers* and the 2016 London Anti-corruption Summit precipitated a further *volte-face* and the reinstatement and alteration of the proposal,[72] which is in Part 3 of the Criminal Finances Bill 2017 and s 162 of the Finance Act 2016 provides for civil penalties for enabling.[73]

Extradition for Tax Evasion

Under the old law, the 'Revenue Rule' applied to extradition.[74] Since extradition would be a means by which the tax obligations of one jurisdiction were enforced by the courts of another, tax offences were excluded from the lists of extraditable offences. Thus Article 5 of the European Convention on Extradition[75] excluded fiscal offences unless there was express agreement

[68] The Ministry of Justice published guidance about procedures which relevant commercial organizations can put into place to prevent persons associated with them from bribing (s 9 of the Bribery Act 2010), in particular as to how corporations might satisfy the 'adequate procedures' defence under Bribery Act 2010 s 7: Ministry of Justice, *Guidance about Procedures which Relevant Commercial Organisations can Put into Place to Prevent Persons Associated with Them from Bribing (section 9 of the Bribery Act 2010)* (2011).

[69] HMRC, n 57.

[70] 'MoJ Drops "Failure to Prevent Economic Crime" Offence Plans', *Law Gazette*, 29 September 2015.

[71] 'George Osborne to Signal End to "Banker Bashing"', *Financial Times*, 5 June 2015.

[72] 'Companies Face Criminal Liability for Corporate Fraud', *Financial Times*, 12 May 2016.

[73] FA 2016 Part 10.

[74] The authorities are explored in *Schemmer v Property Resources Ltd* [1975] Ch 273; [1974] 3 All ER 451; *R v Governor of Pentonville Prison, ex p Khubchandani* (1980) 71 Cr App R 241; and *R v Chief Metropolitan Stipendiary Magistrate, ex parte Secretary of State for the Home Department* [1989] 1 All ER 151.

[75] European Convention on Extradition ETS 24 1957.

between the parties. This rule was changed in the early 1990s.[76] The UK–US Extradition Treaty 2003 incorporated, for the first time,[77] tax evasion. Extradition from Switzerland for tax evasion may now happen.[78] Under the Extradition Act 2003, no differentiation is made that might make extradition for tax offences more difficult.[79] Extradition under the European Arrest Warrant (EAW) is now established and treats tax evasion as unexceptional.[80] So far as concerns extradition from the UK, the uncertainty in the offence of cheating the Revenue has generated some case law on the dual criminality provisions.[81] There do not appear to have been any particular difficulties in the operation of the mutual legal assistance provisions for tax evasion.

Evidence-gathering

As for extradition, so to for assisting other countries in the prosecution of evaders and in securing information from other countries for use in prosecutions for evasion, the 'Revenue Rule' has disappeared. The shift began in *State of Norway's Application*,[82] in which an application for evidence by a fiscal authority was allowed as it was not enforcing foreign fiscal law but was evidence-gathering. Now the arrangements for mutual legal assistance to which the UK is party apply equally to tax evasion and to other crimes.

Conclusion

The enormity of the sums involved, and their importance both to avoidance and evasion, mean that international aspects of the relationship between tax and criminal justice will continue to grow in importance. If there is a leaky

[76] European Convention on Extradition (Fiscal Offences) Order 1993 SI 2663. And see European Convention on Extradition (Fiscal Offences) Order 2001 SI 1453, which gave effect to the second additional protocol to the Convention, under which the rule was abrogated.

[77] And see Zagaris, Bruce, 'US Efforts to Extradite Persons for Tax Offenses' (2002) 25 *Loyola of Los Angeles International and Comparative Law Review* 653.

[78] Zagaris, Bruce, 'Swiss Highest Court Affirms Extradition to Germany for Tax Evasion International Enforcement', *Law Reporter* July 2010. Raymond Woolley, who escaped while serving a sentence for VAT fraud, was extradited from Switzerland to the UK in 2009: *RCPO, Annual Report* 2008–9, 18.

[79] And see, as to charges, Extradition Act 2003 s 64(8).

[80] *R v Leaf (Ian)* (Unreported, December 1, 2005) (Crown Ct). And see *R (on the application of Commissioners of HMRC) v Crown Court at Kingston* [2001] EWHC Admin 581.

[81] *Mauro v United States* [2009] EWHC 150 (Admin); *Hertel v Canada* [2010] EWHC 2305 (Admin); *Davis v Germany* [2013] EWHC 710.

[82] *State of Norway's Application, Re* [1990] 1 AC 723.

bathtub with several holes and one hole is plugged, the water will go through the others, and if there is no restriction on the amount of water that may pass through any of the holes the water will continue to leak at pretty much the same rate. Only when the last hole is plugged will any effect register. So it is with the international cash flows, except that it is less obvious when the last hole is plugged. The changes in the past ten years have brought greater State access to information about bank accounts, introduction of exchange of information, and other attempts to identify beneficial owners of property. Those things may prevent some avoidance. The question that remains is whether there should be greater involvement of the criminal justice system in tax collection. To date there have been too few prosecutions for overseas evasion to enable a view to be taken as to whether they are achieving anything at the micro-level beyond the results of the macro-level OECD policies, which are directed principally against avoidance.

9

Problems at the Intersections of Tax and Criminal Law

This chapter will deal with a number of issues which have arisen because of the increased interrelationship of tax and criminal justice. Their significance has been amplified by the increased attention that has been given to the international aspects both of tax and of criminal justice.

Taxing the Proceeds of Crime

Under what circumstances are the proceeds of crime taxable?[1] Some other jurisdictions have a rule that the proceeds of crime are not taxable—either being subject to confiscation or not in the context of the criminal justice process, but having no effect on the criminal's liability to tax. The United Kingdom has never taken that view. There are some crimes whose proceeds are subject to income tax, usually as trading income, and others where value added tax (VAT) is payable.

Income Tax

The pursuit of tax on illegal activities has never been a priority for the Revenue: where a conviction is obtained and money is available it might be relatively straightforward to recover the tax, but usually the entire sum will be subject to confiscation. In the absence of a conviction, Her Majesty's Revenue and Customs (HMRC) does not usually regard itself as having a significant role in the collection of evidence of criminality.

[1] And see Cory, Richard, 'Taxing the Proceeds of Crime' [2007] *British Tax Review* 356.

Criminal Justice and Taxation. First Edition. Peter Alldridge. © Peter Alldridge 2017. First published 2017 by Oxford University Press.

The same is not true elsewhere. Famously, in the US, Al Capone was convicted of tax evasion.[2] He was suspected of being a large-scale racketeer.[3] Legally, Capone's profits from criminal activity did not have to be entered on a tax return until 1927, when the United States Supreme Court ruled that requiring a person to declare income on a federal income tax return does not violate an individual's right to remain silent,[4] although the privilege against self-incrimination may apply to allow the person to refrain from revealing the source of the income.[5] Successive prosecutors and other law enforcement officials had difficulty in gaining convictions for the 'real' offences of which he was suspected. This was partly because of the distance between Capone and the street-level crimes from which he benefited, and partly because of the level of corruption in the state (Illinois) criminal justice system. The success of the tax evasion prosecution led some to think that the tax system could be a powerful weapon against crime.[6] The 'pretextual prosecution'[7] relied upon the claim that Capone should have paid tax on his (illegal) income.

There are further examples of the 'pretextual' use of tax prosecutions. The Department of Justice (DoJ) investigation into FIFA that led to the arrest of senior officials in Zurich in May 2015[8] gained its most significant information from an Internal Revenue Service (IRS) investigation into the question of how it was that one of the recipients of bribes, the American Chuck Blazer, had not paid tax on them. In 2016, Thomas 'Slab' Murphy was convicted in

[2] *Capone v United States* 56 F 2d 927 (1931), cert denied, 286 US 553 (1932); *United States v Capone* 93 F2d 840 (1937), cert denied, 303 US 651, 82 LEd 1112, 58 SCt 750 (1938).

[3] Kobler, John, *Capone: The Life and World of Al Capone* (Boston, MA: Da Capo Press; reprint edn 1992).

[4] *US v Sullivan* 274 US 259 (1927).

[5] *Garner v US* 424 US 648 (1976).

[6] Baker, Russell, 'Taxation: Potential Destroyer of Crime' (1951) 29 *Chicago-Kent LR* 197; Gallant, Michelle, 'Tax and the Proceeds of Crime: A New Approach to Tainted Finance?' (2013) 16 *Journal of Money Laundering Control* 119–25; Bucci, Amy, 'Taxation of Illegal Narcotics: A Violation of the Fifth Amendment Rights or an Innovative Tool in the War Against Drugs?' (2012) 11 *Journal of Civil Rights and Economic Development* 22; Bucy, Pamela H, 'Criminal Tax Fraud: The Downfall of Murderers, Madams and Thieves' (1997) 29 *Arizona State Law Journal* 639.

[7] A 'pretextual prosecution' is one undertaken where the prosecutor suspects another, usually more serious crime, but lacks the admissible evidence to prove it. And see Litman, Harry, 'Pretextual Prosecution' (2003) 92 *Georgetown Law Journal* 1137; Richman, Daniel C, and William J Stuntz, 'Al Capone's Revenge: An Essay on the Political Economy of Pretextual Prosecution' (2005) 105 *Columbia Law Review* 583–640; Shimick, Scott, 'Heisenberg's Uncertainty: An Analysis of Criminal Tax Pretextual Prosecutions in the Context of *Breaking Bad*'s Notorious Anti-hero' (2014) 50 *Tulsa Law Review* 43.

[8] 'FIFA Arrests: How a Well-placed Insider and Stashed Cash Helped US Build Case', *The Guardian*, 27 May 2015.

Ireland of tax evasion.[9] He was suspected of involvement in terrorism and racketeering.

Despite the absence of clear authority on the point, the UK law of income tax on the profits of illegal trade is, apparently, that unlawfully or illegally obtained income remains subject to income tax.[10] Thus, for example, the export of whisky to the United States during Prohibition was held to be taxable,[11] as was the income of a prostitute.[12] This does coincide with US law.[13] The law on VAT is slightly more nuanced, because of the exigencies of EU law in the case where the supply of the goods and services in question is not criminal in every EU member state.[14]

Deductions for Illegal Expenses?

Where profits of unlawful activity are taxed, deductions may be made for lawful[15] business expenses.[16] If the operative model is that the criminal is

[9] 'Thomas "Slab" Murphy Jailed over Tax Like Chicago Gangster', *Irish Times*, 26 February 2016.

[10] Cockfield, Roger, and Mary Mulholland, 'The Implications of Illegal Trading' [1995] *British Tax Review* 572. *Southern (Inspector of Taxes) v AB* [1933] 1 KB 713: taxpayer carried on street betting and ready-money betting businesses which were wholly illegal. Following *Mann v Nash* [1932] 1 KB 752, the court held there was a 'trade' carried on by the respondents within Case I of Schedule D of the Income Tax Act 1918, and, that being so, the fact that that trade was illegal did not prevent the profits arising therefrom being assessable to income tax.

[11] *Woodward and Hiscox v IRC* (1932) 18 TC 43.

[12] See *IRC v Aken* [1990] 1 WLR 1374; [1990] STC 497, reserving the point explicitly by pointing out that prostitution is not *ipso facto* illegal, but doubting the decision of the Supreme Court in Ireland in *Hayes v Duggan* [1929] 1 IR 406. The POCA taxation jurisdiction (see this chapter, section entitled 'The Proceeds of Crime Act Tax Jurisdiction') would be of very limited value if income tax did not apply to illegal profits. Although commercial sex workers are rarely prosecuted for evasion alone, in *R v Asutaits, Daily Telegraph*, 10 July 2012 a prison sentence followed conviction.

[13] Cf *James v United States*: the Supreme Court held that an embezzler was required to include his ill-gotten gains in his 'gross income' for federal income tax purposes. *James v United States* 366 US 213 (1961), overruling *Commissioner v Wilcox* 327 US 404 (1946). Income, for the purposes of the US federal income tax, is not taxed according to source, but as a (non-capital) accretion to wealth.

[14] The Court of Justice has held that VAT does not arise on the unlawful importation of drugs: *Einberger v Hauptzollamt Freiburg* [1984] ECR 1177, and see *R v Goodwin (John Charles)* [1997] STC 22; [1997] BTC 5226; *R v Citrone and another* [1998] STC 29; [1999] *Criminal Law Review* 327. But where lawful services compete with unlawful ones, the unlawful ones are not given a competitive advantage: *Polok v Customs and Excise Commissioners* [2002] EWHC 156; [2002] STC 361 (prostitution), as to which see Mumford, Ann, 'VAT, Taxation and Prostitution: Feminist Perspectives on Polok' (2005) 13 *Feminist Legal Studies* 163.

[15] The issue became a live one because bribes of public officials overseas were deducted until the insertion of Income and Corporation Taxes Act 1988 s 577A by the FA 1992 and FA 1993. The international move against permitting such bribes can be traced back to the Paris Convention of the OECD: OECD Convention on Combating Bribery of Foreign Public Officials in International Business Transactions, Paris, 17 December 1997 (Cm 3994).

[16] The taxing provision (Income Tax (Trading and Other Income) Act 2005 s 5) applies to the 'profits' of a trade, profession, or vocation. This is clearly differentiable from proceeds.

conducting a business for profit, then, for the purposes at least of taxation,[17] deductions should be permitted as if the trade or profession is a lawful one.[18] Thus, while there is enormous resistance to allowing deductions in confiscation cases regarding the expenditure involved in running the unlawful business (purchase of drugs, protection, and so on), they should be allowed for income tax purposes. There may be arguments about the evidence required to give rise to the deduction, and it may be difficult for the taxpayer to overturn an assessment, in which enterprise the burden of proof and the lack of credibility of the taxpayer will both assist the Revenue, but in principle the deduction should be allowed.

Until 1992 at the earliest, and most probably 2000, companies were able to deduct from their profits for the purposes of taxation bribes paid overseas, and the mechanisms for proving the purposes of the relevant deduction were reasonably robust.[19] Now the relevant provisions[20] disallow deductions for expenses incurred in making a payment if the making of the payment constitutes a criminal offence; or in making a payment outside the United Kingdom if the making of a corresponding payment in any part of the United Kingdom would constitute a criminal offence in that part; and for expenses incurred in making a payment induced by a demand which constitutes blackmail or the equivalent Scottish or Northern Irish offences.[21] They[22] are not so clear as they should be, but should be read with the principle that statutes should be interpreted so as to ensure compliance by the UK with its treaty obligations.[23] '[T]he making of the payment constitutes a criminal offence' is an important limitation. A payment

[17] See this chapter, section entitled 'Deductions for Illegal Expenses?'.

[18] Cockfield and Mulholland, n 10.

[19] It was unclear whether or not this had been achieved by the insertion, by the FAs 1992 and 1993, of Income and Corporation Taxes Act 1988 s 577A. It was put beyond argument, under the pre-2006 law, from 1 April 2002, by s 68(2) of the FA 2002.

[20] Income Tax (Trading and Other Income) Act 2005 s 55. The drafting is rather peculiar, and seems more straightforwardly to apply to the expenses involved in making a payment than the payment itself, but taken with the extended definition of 'expenses' provided by Income Tax (Trading and Other Income) Act 2005 s 27 ('In the Income Tax Acts … references to receipts and expenses are to any items brought into account as debits or credits in calculating the profit'), the unlawful expenditure would not be an allowable expense.

[21] S 55(2).

[22] Income Tax (Trading and Other Income) Act 2005 s 55, read with s 27 ITTOIA: 'references to receipts and expenses are to any items brought into account as debits or credits in calculating the profit'. The cash in the case then would be an 'expense' and caught by s 55 ITTOIA.

[23] OECD, Recommendation on the Tax Deductibility of Bribes of Foreign Public Officials, adopted on 11 April 1996, C(96)27/FINAL; OECD, Recommendation of the Council on Tax Measures for Further Combating Bribery of Foreign Public Officials in International Business Transactions, adopted on 25 May 2009; United Nations Convention against Corruption (UNCAC) (2005) Article 12.4.

for a getaway car, or for (lawful)[24] security, would not, without more, constitute a criminal offence, and would therefore be deductible.

The practical difficulty faced by the taxpayer is of disproving any assessment, however fanciful, when there is an admission of criminality. As soon as the taxpayer admits to having profited from illegal activity, s/he faces the difficulty that any evidence s/he produces will be treated as part of the fraud.

A final question is whether expenditure on the defence of criminal charges, confiscation proceedings, or civil recovery proceedings is deductible from profits for the purpose of computing trading income. For the purposes of taxation of profits, the costs of defending legal actions[25] or paying fines[26] are not deductible.

Confiscating the Proceeds of Tax Evasion

Confiscation is the procedure, following conviction, in which the court enquires into the defendant's benefit from the crime and his/her means, and orders the payment of a sum representing the proceeds of the crime to be paid.[27] At their inception, it was not thought that the confiscation orders could or need be used to deal with unpaid taxes.[28] Someone who did not declare liability to tax put off the payment of a debt. The debt remained due. The tax authorities have extensive powers to obtain the money and impose penalties and interest.[29] The tax authorities were preferred creditors on insolvency.[30] It would have been possible simply to take the view that the Revenue had ample powers already, whether by civil penalties, interest, or attachment of earnings, or simply by bringing an action to recover the unpaid tax plus interest. There would have been much to be said for this.

So far as concerns confiscation, tax evasion might be different from other types of acquisitive crime. The typical case of evasion is one of deferral of the debt to the State. Only if the deferral of a debt is regarded as giving rise to

[24] Ie not extending to carrying firearms or other unlawful weapons.

[25] *Smiths Potato Estates v Bolland* [1948] AC 508; 30 TC 267.

[26] *McKnight (Inspector of Taxes) v Sheppard* [1999] 1 WLR 1333; 71 TC 419; *McLaren Racing Ltd v Revenue and Customs Commissioners* [2014] UKUT 269 (TCC); [2014] STC 2417.

[27] Alldridge, Peter, 'The Limits of Confiscation' [2011] *Criminal Law Review* 827–43.

[28] Alldridge, Peter, 'Are Tax Evasion Offences Predicate Offences for Money laundering Offences?' (2001) 4 *Journal of Money Laundering Control* 350–59; Alldridge, Peter, and Ann Mumford, 'Tax Evasion and the Proceeds of Crime Act 2002' (2005) 25 *Legal Studies* 353–73.

[29] TMA Parts VI, IX, X and for civil penalties Chapter 7.

[30] Enterprise Act 2002 s 251.

something that can be treated as the proceeds of crime can the claim be made that profits of tax evasion could be confiscated or laundered. Ambivalence towards tax evasion, seen at various points in this book, is evident once again. At one and the same time, tax is treated as special (so that we need a deeming provision written into the relevant statutes to generate liability at all) and not special (so it is right that tax evasion be a predicate offence 'just like any other serious offence').

Pressure for increased amounts to be secured under the laundering regime has led to a move towards the use of confiscation orders in tax prosecutions.[31] The drive to incorporate tax within the confiscation regime was driven not by the Revenue but by the anti-money laundering (AML) industry. The size of the orders that may be made in tax evasion cases is so large, compared even to drug crime, that anyone whose job it is to confiscate money will be drawn to this area. The two original orders in *R v Ahmed*[32] were of more than £92 million on each of two defendants—a sum which, had the order been upheld and realized, would have exceeded the total of all other confiscations, civil recovery, and forfeiture in that year.

The move to using confiscation orders against tax evaders has raised a series of complex questions on the interpretation both of the statute and of the application of the First Article of the First Protocol to the ECHR (A1P1).[33] Some tax evaders[34] will obtain 'property'.[35] Others, in the standard case of evasion by non- or undeclaration, will not—hence the relevant provisions, as follows.

76 Conduct and benefit ...

(4) A person benefits from conduct if he obtains property as a result of or in connection with the conduct.

(5) If a person obtains a pecuniary advantage as a result of or in connection with conduct, he is to be taken to obtain as a result of or in connection with the conduct a sum of money equal to the value of the pecuniary advantage.

(6) References to property or a pecuniary advantage obtained in connection with conduct include references to property or a pecuniary advantage obtained both in that connection and some other.

(7) If a person benefits from conduct his benefit is the value of the property obtained.

[31] The operative international influences are explored in relation to the expansion of criminal laundering in this chapter, section entitled 'Laundering the Proceeds of Tax Evasion'.

[32] *R v Ahmad* (CA) [2012] EWCA Crim 391; [2012] 1 WLR 2335.

[33] See Alldridge, Peter, 'Two Key Areas in Proceeds of Crime Law' [2014] *Criminal Law Review* 170–88.

[34] Those claiming rebates or VAT input tax.

[35] Which includes money: s 84(1)(a). In addition, under s 84(2), (a) property is held by a person if he holds an interest in it; (b) property is obtained by a person if he obtains an interest in it.

The expression 'pecuniary advantage' has a chequered history, which seemed to be airbrushed when it was chosen in this context.[36] It was to cover the case where an advantage was gained which could not easily be identified or quantified. The problem encountered by the draftspeople responsible for the confiscation provisions was that there were some cases in which it seemed that the defendant had benefited from crime, but where the causal links and the property were both quite difficult to identify. This issue went back to pre-Theft Act 1968 cases on obtaining property by false pretences. A person who obtained the right to earn money in a job by misrepresenting his/her qualifications was held not to have obtained property by deception (because of the remoteness of the causation),[37] and a separate offence[38] was created to cover the person who obtained the deferral of a debt by deception (gaining insurance and other rights and the being treated as having staked money are others). This led to 'a judicial nightmare',[39] difficult litigation,[40] referrals to law reform bodies,[41] more legislation,[42] and in consequence, a wider criminal law.[43] The alternative would have been not to criminalize the cases of the extended debts. At the time of the enactment of the Theft Act 1968, it was thought that dishonest borrowing, without more, should not attract a criminal sanction. The widening of the law of fraud by the Fraud Act 2006 may evidence a change.

The fundamental wrong turn was in the early case of *R v Smith (David Cadman)*,[44] which was decided under the pre-2003 legislation, but the relevant provisions were in the same terms as s 76 and the case is followed. Smith sailed a boat laden with tobacco cigarettes into the Humber estuary, past the customs houses at Immingham and Hull (which was the point at which duty became payable),[45] and on to Goole, where there was

[36] See Alldridge, Peter, 'Smuggling, Confiscation and Forfeiture' (2002) 65 *Modern Law Review* 781–91.

[37] *R v Lewis* (Somerset Assizes, 1922) (Rowlatt J).

[38] Theft Act 1968 s 16.

[39] Edmund Davies LJ in *R v Royle* [1971] 1 WLR 1764.

[40] *DPP v Turner* [1974] AC 357; [1973] 3 All ER 124; *DPP v Ray* [1974] AC 370; [1973] 3 All ER 131; *MPC v Charles* [1977] AC 177; [1976] 3 All ER 112.

[41] Criminal Law Revision Committee, Thirteenth Report, *Section 16 of the Theft Act 1968* (Cmnd 6733, 1977).

[42] Theft Act 1978; Fraud Act 2006.

[43] In particular, hesitance about the imposition of criminal liability for dishonest borrowings, evidenced by the specific offences under Theft Act 1968 ss 11 and 12, and for lying more generally seems to have gone.

[44] *R v Smith (David Cadman)* [2001] UKHL 68; [2002] 1 Cr App R 35. For a contemporaneous reaction see Alldridge, n 37.

[45] And see, on the difficulties of administering this ('nightmare') area of law, *R v Bajwa* [2011] EWCA Crim 1093; [2012] 1 WLR 601.

no customs house. On conviction for fraudulent evasion of excise duty[46] he was sentenced to prison, and the boat and the tobacco were seized. Confiscation proceedings were then brought in respect of the duty on the tobacco, which were appealed to the House of Lords. There were two issues on *quantum*. The first was whether the fact that the defendant had not in fact acquired anything prevented it from being treated as a benefit for the purposes of confiscation law. On this, the House held that he benefited by evading the duty from the time at which he passed the tax point until he was apprehended. That is, the debt was deferred for the period during which he sailed upstream. So far, so good. This is clearly the intention of the legislator. Had the offence existed at the time, he would have been guilty of evading liability by deception.[47] The second issue, as to the *value* of the 'pecuniary advantage', is a matter that has consistently been ducked. On a simple, and principled, reading of the statute, the relevant value should be that of the deferral, not that of the debt; yet the House held that the 'value of the advantage' to which the statute refers was the value of the debt to the Revenue.[48] This has been followed ever since.[49] There has been extensive case law, and the relevant provisions have been considered by the highest courts several times. The law expressed in *Smith (David Cadman)* is now sufficiently settled that in *R v Fields, R v Ahmed/Ahmad*[50] the Supreme Court did not even consider the matter to be open to argument. This decision has the effect that confiscation orders in respect of evaded tax are greatly inflated. The consequence is that where prosecution and confiscation is incentivized, it will operate to produce reasons to prosecute offences of tax evasion that would not otherwise have been prosecuted.[51]

[46] Contrary to CEMA s 170(2).

[47] The offence under s 16(2)(a) of the Theft Act 1968. S 16(2)(a) was repealed by the Theft Act 1978. 'Pecuniary advantage' had a definition set out in Theft Act 1968 s 16(2), but for the purposes of the natural meaning of 'pecuniary advantage' which applied to the proceeds of crime legislation, the meaning is the natural one. Per Lord Rodger in *Smith* [2001] UKHL 68; [2002] 1 Cr App R 35 at para 20.

[48] And see the failed attempt to amend the Proceeds of Crime Bill, HC Debates, 26 Feb 2002 Col 639, HL Debates, 22 Apr 2002 Col 57 *et seq.*

[49] Eg *R v Kakkad (Freshkumar)* [2015] EWCA Crim 385; [2015] 1 WLR 4162; *R v Tatham* [2014] EWCA Crim 226; [2014] Lloyd's Rep FC 354; and (although dissenting) Lord Hughes in *R v Harvey* [2015] UKSC 73; [2016] 1 Cr App R (S) 60.

[50] *R v Fields, R v Ahmad* [2014] UKSC 36; [2015] AC 299.

[51] As they are under the Asset Recovery Incentivization Scheme (ARIS): see this chapter, section entitled 'Who Gets the Money? Incentivised Criminal Law Enforcement'.

Deductions from Confiscation Orders

The Supreme Court has on a number of occasions dismissed the idea that expenses of committing crimes should be allowable deductions from confiscation orders:

To attempt to enquire into the financial dealings of criminals as between themselves would usually be equally impracticable and would lay the process of confiscation wide open to simple avoidance. Although these propositions involve the possibility of removing from the defendant by way of confiscation order a sum larger than may in fact represent his net proceeds of crime, they are consistent with the statute's objective and represent proportionate means of achieving it.[52]

In *Department for Work and Pensions v Richards*,[53] a benefit fraud case, no reduction was allowed to the assessed (Proceeds of Crime Act 2002; POCA) benefit to take account of the notional benefits to which he would have been entitled had he behaved honestly and made a truthful claim. The analogous approach to tax fraud would be to treat the tax return as being a full statement of the facts giving rise to his/her liabilities, and, at the least, to disregard any aspects of the tax return stating facts to the advantage of the defendant (claiming allowances, deducting allowable expenses in the computation of income or profits, and so on).[54]

In *R v Louca*,[55] a case of being knowingly concerned in the fraudulent evasion of excise duty, the appellant paid £10,000 for a consignment of smuggled cigarettes. The Court of Appeal held that the value of the cigarettes formed part of the benefit which he had obtained: 'By section 76(7) his benefit is the value of the property obtained. He is not entitled to deduct what he paid for them. Benefit is not to be equated with profit. We do not consider that this ground has any validity.'[56]

An ad hoc exception to the general antipathy for deductions was created in *Harvey*.[57] The defendant owned a plant hire and contracting company, which had regularly acquired and sold stolen plant. The judge assessed the revenue from rentals of the stolen plant, and made a confiscation order of around £2.3 million. Harvey argued that the VAT on the sums gained by using the plant, which had been passed on to HMRC, should have been deducted from this sum. The Court of Appeal refused to permit such a deduction.[58] The

[52] Para 26.
[53] *Department for Work and Pensions v Richards* [2005] EWCA Crim 491.
[54] Hence *R v Fields*, *R v Ahmad* [2014] UKSC 36; [2015] AC 299 and *R v Harvey* [2015] UKSC 73; [2016] 1 Cr App R (S) 60 deal only with the creation of exceptions, not the more general issue.
[55] *R v Louca* [2013] EWCA Crim 2090; [2014] 2 Cr App R (S) 9.
[56] Royce J at para 13.
[57] *R v Harvey* [2015] UKSC 73; [2016] 1 Cr App R (S) 60.
[58] *R v Harvey* [2013] EWCA Crim 1104.

amount of the confiscation order was thus well above the amount the criminal had gained. The Supreme Court crafted a narrow exception to the general non-allowability of deductions for the purposes of confiscation orders, using the A1P1 cases[59] to hold that it would be disproportionate, where VAT output tax had been accounted for to HMRC, to make a confiscation order calculated on the basis that the VAT had been 'obtained by the offender' for the purposes of the Act. Lords Hughes and Toulson dissented, arguing that it was not disproportionate to the proper object of the scheme to treat the entirety of the company's receipts from its criminal conduct as having been obtained by the defendant.

In *R v Eddishaw*[60] the appellant operated a factory producing counterfeit vodka. The liquid was bottled and sold to retailers. In this way, payment of duty otherwise due under the Alcoholic Liquor Duties Act 1979 was avoided. The defendant pleaded guilty to conspiring[61] to cheat the Revenue. In the subsequent confiscation proceedings, in the first instance the prosecution asked for the amount of duty which would have been payable had the vodka been genuine and properly sold. The problem was that no duty had ever fallen due, as none had been demanded by HMRC. In light of this, the prosecution changed its approach and calculated the applicant's benefit as the money received for selling bottles of counterfeit vodka, or the value of those bottles unsold. The court held that the appellant's argument took too narrow a view of s 76(4). The appellant was operating an enterprise bottling and selling a dutiable liquid without paying the duty. The vodka produced, held, or sold was obtained as a result of or in connection with the conspiracy to cheat HMRC, to which he had pleaded guilty. The court held that the ambit of s 76(4) is a relatively wide one, and it will be read so as to catch tangible items produced in the commission of an offence. This is a decision that is difficult to justify on the words of the statute, but which illustrates a judicial mood. So far as concerns legal expenses, the policy of the POCA statute is that the money that is the subject matter of the litigation ought not to be used to pay for them. In this case a more appropriate charge would have related to counterfeiting the goods.

The Serious Crime Act 2015 introduced a new provision after POCA s 6(5), to state: 'Paragraph (b) applies[62] only if, or to the extent that, it would not be

[59] Especially *R v Waya* [2012] UKSC 51; [2013] 1 AC 294 and *R v Ahmad, R v Fields* [2014] UKSC 36; [2015] AC 29.

[60] *R v Eddishaw* [2014] EWCA Crim 2783; [2015] Lloyd's Rep FC 212.

[61] A general issue exists in ascribing benefits to conspiracies. The courts seem to ignore the distinction between inchoate and complete offences for this purpose.

[62] S 6 is the provision imposing the duty to impose a confiscation order.

disproportionate to require the defendant to pay the recoverable amount'.[63] The explanatory notes[64] say that this provision is intended to give statutory effect to *Waya*.[65] It will not make any difference to the inflated values given to the proceeds of tax evasion unless *Smith* is overruled or the basis of the computation of proceeds altered to permit a more realistic quantification directed towards placing the criminal in the position in which s/he would have been had it not been for the crime.

Do Confiscation Orders Affect Tax Liability (and *Vice Versa*)?

Does the fact that a confiscation order has been made and satisfied extinguish the liability to tax, and does the fact that the tax has been paid stand as a bar to the making of a confiscation order? The logical implication of the view that confiscation orders are assessed on gross receipts and that tax liability is not extinguished otherwise than by being paid would be that the imposition—and the payment—of a confiscation order in respect of evaded tax would not discharge the liability to tax, and that, conversely, the payment of the tax would not affect the liability under the confiscation order. Various mechanisms have been suggested by which this harsh outcome could be avoided. In *R v Edwards*,[66] the Court of Appeal received an undertaking that there would be no attempt to claim the tax, and the Supreme Court subsequently recognized that under the current state of the law this was the preferred outcome.[67]

Conversely, does the fact that the defendant has been made subject to a confiscation order relieve him/her of the tax? In *Martin v Commissioners for HMRC*[68] the defendant was convicted in relation to trademark offences and a confiscation order was made. Tax assessments were raised against the defendant, who asserted that his confiscation order had included consideration of the criminal lifestyle provisions and his tax liability had therefore been dealt with. The tribunal approved HMRC's policy of not undertaking court proceedings to recover the unpaid duty—to ensure that there is no 'double recovery'—where the amount of the confiscation order matches the amount of the unpaid duty, but went on to say that the confiscation order did not prevent HMRC from conducting its own investigation into tax affairs for the period concerned. The court held that the provisions of POCA in relation to

[63] Serious Crime Act 2015 Schedule 4, para 19.
[64] Para 352.
[65] *R v Waya* [2012] UKSC 51; [2013] 1 AC 294.
[66] *R v Edwards* [2004] EWCA 2923; [2005] 2 Cr App R (S) 160, paras 24–5.
[67] *Harvey*, para 29.
[68] *Martin v Commissioners for HMRC* [2015] UKUT 0161 (TCC).

confiscation orders should not be construed in a way which would result in preventing the collection of the proper amount of tax.[69]

This is a contrast to the House of Lords' attitude to the Inland Revenue policy in *Hinchy*,[70] and the cases in this area are hardly satisfactory. Where the tax and the confiscation order for evaded tax relate to the same transactions, each should provide a complete legal bar to proceedings in respect of the other, rather than being a matter to be dealt with by concessions and discretions.

Confiscation or Compensation Orders?

Compensation orders predate confiscation orders.[71] The idea is that where there is an identifiable victim, s/he should be compensated first and thus spared the difficulty of having to bring further proceedings. There was a standing instruction to prosecuting counsel at least until 1990 not to seek the use of court powers for compensation in Revenue prosecutions, on the ground that the Revenue's powers were so much more extensive.[72] HMRC may now be granted compensation orders in respect of lost revenue,[73] which makes the move to using confiscation in these cases all the more peculiar.

Who Gets the Money? Incentivized Criminal Law Enforcement

There has been much debate about the use of financial incentives to law enforcement by giving the bodies responsible for investigation and prosecution a share in whatever proceeds were obtained by the State,[74] rather than deploying them for the general purposes for which taxation is paid. When the

[69] And see *Revenue and Customs Commissioners v Crossman* [2007] EWHC 1585 (Ch); [2008] 1 All ER 483.

[70] See this chapter, section entitled 'Taxing the Proceeds of Crime'. The House was not impressed by the argument that the Inland Revenue claimed only to enforce unjustifiable penalty provisions in what it thought to be appropriate cases.

[71] Powers of Criminal Courts Act 1973 and Drug Trafficking Offences Act 1986 respectively.

[72] I am grateful to Richard Walters for this fact.

[73] *Revenue and Customs Prosecution Office v Duffy* [2008] EWHC 848 (Admin); [2008] 2 Cr App R (S) 103; [2008] *Criminal Law Review* 734. In the Court of Appeal in *R v Dimsey; R v Allen* [2000] 1 Cr App R (S) 497 the distinction was noted but not explored (at 500).

[74] Fan, Mary D, 'Disciplining Criminal Justice: The Peril amid the Promise of Numbers' (2007) 26 *Yale Law & Policy Review* 1–74; Holcomba, Jefferson E, Tomislav V Kovandzicb, and Marian R Williams, 'Civil Asset Forfeiture, Equitable Sharing, and Policing for Profit in the United States' (2011) 39 *Journal of Criminal Justice* 273–85.

Assets Recovery Agency (ARA) was abolished, the rule that the sums received by it be paid into the Consolidated Fund[75] was repealed. The Home Secretary then put in place the Asset Recovery Incentivization Scheme (ARIS).[76]

English law has always been suspicious of incentivized law enforcement (that is, systems under which the agency responsible for the enforcement receives a proportion of monies recovered), and there is one possible constitutional objection to any incentivized criminal law enforcement. In the recitals in the Bill of Rights 1689, King James is said to have imposed 'severall Grants and Promises made of Fines and Forfeitures before any Conviction or Judgment against the Persons upon whome the same were to be levied'. In response, Article 12 of the Bill provides 'That all Grants and Promises of Fines and Forfeitures of particular persons before Conviction are illegall and void'. The grievance seems to have been that the King made promises to persons involved in prosecutions that they would benefit.[77] Litigants from time to time[78] argue that this provision prohibits fines without conviction. In fact, the perceived vice is the *grant* prior to the conviction, not the forfeiture itself, so the Bill of Rights does not prohibit fines without conviction.

There is, however, a remaining technical problem. While any statute could, if expressed in appropriate terms, amend the Bill of Rights,[79] it is doubtful whether the apportionment of proceeds of *forfeitures* under ARIS,[80] which does not have a statutory basis but is apparently an exercise of the 'Ram Doctrine',[81] could be taken as a deliberate amendment. It is suggested that

[75] POCA Schedule 1 para 5.

[76] Put in place upon the abolition of the ARA in 2007. Under the most recent version of the scheme, agencies get back 50 per cent of assets they recover by civil recovery, split between the investigation, prosecuting, and enforcing agencies (currently) in the ratio 18.7 per cent: 18.7 per cent: 12.5 per cent. See HC Debates, 11 June 2012: c86W (James Brokenshire).

[77] Article 12 was 'only declaratory of the old constitutional law: and accordingly we find it expressly holden, long before, that all such previous grants are void; since thereby many times undue means, and more violent prosecution, would be used for private lucre, than the quiet and just proceeding of law would permit': 4 Blackstone, *Commentaries* 379 (citing 2 *Inst* 48).

[78] *R (on the application of Herron) v The Parking Adjudicator* [2009] EWHC 1702 (Admin), citing Collins J in *R (on the application of Crittenden) v National Parking Adjudication Service* [2006] EWHC 2170 (Admin) and on appeal by Scott Baker LJ, *R (on the application of Crittenden) v National Parking Adjudication Service* [2006] EWCA 1786 (Civ); *Pendle v Revenue and Customs Commissioners* [2015] UKFTT 27 (TC).

[79] *Thoburn v Sunderland City Council* [2003] QB 151.

[80] Under the ARIS, half of all assets recovered are returned to law enforcement and prosecution agencies involved in the asset recovery process. The Home Office calculates quarterly the amounts to be allocated. For cash forfeitures, civil recovery, and taxation, agencies receive a 50 per cent share of the money remitted to the Home Office: HC Debates, 11 June 2012, c86W (James Brokenshire). The Bill of Rights only bears upon forfeitures.

[81] Weait, Matthew J, and Anthony Lester, 'The Use of Ministerial Powers without Parliamentary Authority: The Ram Doctrine' [2003] *Public Law* 415–28.

the ARIS arrangements still might not fall foul because it does not relate to proceedings against 'particular persons'.

This leaves the issue of principle. Is it a good policy for the State to operate a system of incentivized law enforcement, and how does this operate in tax cases? If no prosecution is brought, funds raised by HMRC, whether by raising assessments or by the imposition of civil penalties, go to the Consolidated Fund. If, on the other hand, a prosecution is brought and a confiscation order obtained, then under the ARIS scheme, 50 per cent of whatever is recovered under the confiscation order is divided between the Crown Prosecution Service (CPS) and HMRC in the ordained ratio. This creates a financial incentive that did not exist previously for prosecutions to be brought. Because the other criminal sectors in which substantial amounts had been targeted for confiscation failed to yield the sums that had been spoken of, increased attention was given to tax evasion, and increased use was made of confiscation orders in tax cases. It may or may not be a good idea to increase the level of prosecutions in tax cases,[82] but it would be to be regretted if the reason for the increase were the division of monies.

Laundering the Proceeds of Tax Evasion

In order to deal with the anxiety that had arisen by the mid-1980s about the profits that criminals obtained from crime, it would have been sufficient to put in place a system for the confiscation of the proceeds of crime. However, for reasons not relevant to this book,[83] the decision was taken to introduce a crime of money laundering and to make it a serious offence. The crime required a category of offences ('predicate offences') the profits from which can give rise to laundering offences.

Proceeds-of-crime law is strongly expansionist in three important respects: geographically; by area of the economy; and in respect of its treatment of legal and administrative impediments to the AML industry.[84] The global assault upon laundering grew from concern about drugs[85] and then moved into 'organized crime',[86] typically involving other 'victimless crimes', and

[82] See Chapter 10.

[83] And see Alldridge, Peter, *What Went Wrong with Money Laundering Law?* (London: Palgrave, 2016).

[84] Alldridge, Peter, 'Money Laundering and Globalization' (2008) 35 *Journal of Law and Society* 437–63.

[85] UN Convention Against Illicit Traffic in Narcotic Drugs and Psychotropic Substances (Vienna Convention) 1998.

[86] And see Campbell, Liz, *Organised Crime and the Law* (Oxford: Hart, 2013).

rackets.[87] When terrorism became an issue, rightly or wrongly,[88] AML measures were adapted and the same legal structures put to work as countering the financing of terrorism (CFT).[89] AML now has as particular concerns corruption and tax evasion.

As the range of offences acceptable as predicates has increased, the nature of the predicate offence has become increasingly irrelevant. Laundering offences have come to be regarded as harmful, for reasons unconnected either to the nature of the predicate or to the mental state of the perpetrator (which, in classic liberal criminal law theory, usually provides a restriction on liability for consequences). There has been a shift in the core of the offence from the predicate to the laundering. Money laundering as complicity in property offences is becoming property offences as a form of complicity in money laundering.

When, following the first EU Money Laundering Directive,[90] the Money Laundering Regulations 1993[91] were put in place, little concern was expressed about tax evasion. In the earlier attempts to deal at an international level with laundering, explicit exceptions were made for tax offences.[92] The National Criminal Intelligence Service (NCIS)[93] had indicated that it only wished to receive reports of suspicious financial transactions derived from the profits of serious crimes including drug trafficking, terrorist activity, major thefts and fraud, robbery, forgery and counterfeiting, blackmail, and extortion.

[87] Convention for the Suppression of the Financing of Terrorism (1999); United Nations Convention against Transnational Organized Crime (Palermo Convention 2004).

[88] Roberge, Ian, 'Misguided Policies in the War on Terror? The Case for Disentangling Terrorist Financing from Money Laundering' (2007) 27 *Politics* 196–203; King, Colin, and Clive Walker, 'Counter Terrorism Financing: A Redundant Fragmentation?' (2015) 6 *New Journal of European Criminal Law* 372–95; Léonard, Sarah, and Christian Kaunert, '"Between a Rock and a Hard Place?": The European Union's Financial Sanctions against Suspected Terrorists, Multilateralism and Human Rights' (2012) 47 *Cooperation and Conflict* 473–94.

[89] The Financial Action Task Force (then) Special Recommendations on Counter-Terrorist Finance, endorsed by UN Security Council Resolution 1617. Passas, Nikos, 'Terrorism Finance: Financial Controls and Counter-proliferation of Weapons of Mass Destruction' (2012) 44 *Case Western Reserve Journal of International Law* 747–955. In *Bank Mellat v HM Treasury; Bank Mellat v HM Treasury (No 2)* [2013] UKSC 38 & 39, the UK Supreme Court decided that directions made by the Treasury under Schedule 7 of the Counter-terrorism Act 2008, to implement United Nations Security Council Resolutions 1737 (2006) and 1747 (2007), were in breach of the rules of natural justice, and/or Article 6 ECHR, and/or the procedural obligation in A1P1: *Council of the European Union v Bank Mellat* ECJ (Fifth Chamber), 18 February 2016, Case C-176/13 P.

[90] Directive 91/308/EEC (First Money Laundering Directive).

[91] Money Laundering Regulations 1993 SI 1933.

[92] UN Convention against Illicit Traffic in Narcotic Drugs and Psychotropic Substances (Vienna Convention) 1998, Art 3(10); Council of Europe Convention on Instrumentalities, Art 18.

[93] The National Criminal Intelligence Service (NCIS) was the predecessor of SOCA.

In the mid-1990s the Financial Action Task Force (FATF) and a number of other international bodies began to broaden the category of offences capable of amounting to predicate offences. Schemes to avoid tax frequently depend upon complex routings of deals without apparent commercial rationale. Money movements under a tax avoidance scheme make other money movements that do launder the profits of crime less easy to detect.[94]

An FATF directive, issued on 2 July 1999 in the form of an interpretative note to Recommendation 15 on money laundering, proclaimed:

> *In implementing Recommendation 15, suspicious transactions should be reported by financial institutions regardless of whether they are also[95] thought to involve tax matters. Countries should take into account that, in order to deter financial institutions from reporting a suspicious transaction, money launderers may seek to state inter alia that their transactions relate to tax matters.*[96]

Late in 1999, the Tampere European Council meeting[97] placed enormous emphasis upon money laundering, calling, in particular, for an increase in consistency in the definition of predicate offences, the adoption of the Amending Directive, and the greater availability of all relevant information for the purposes of exchange, irrespective of arguments regarding banking secrecy. At the International Monetary Fund (IMF) meeting in Washington DC in April 2000 the Chancellor of the Exchequer, Gordon Brown, told world economic leaders that he wanted Britain to spearhead a major international crackdown on offshore tax havens, money laundering, and financial crime.[98]

It has been argued cogently that the introduction to the AML scheme of tax evasion reporting was to encourage the financial sector into making disclosures in revenue cases where no underlying criminal activity is involved, by taking advantage of the ambiguity which hovers over the line between lawful tax avoidance and dishonest tax evasion.[99] This development can be traced to a G7 meeting in 1998.[100]

[94] Blum, Jack et al, *Financial Havens, Banking Secrecy and Money laundering*, UNDCP Technical Series Issue 8 (New York: UN, 1998) 51.

[95] Note the use of 'also', not 'only'. FATF did not then itself require a report in the case where the only offence is tax evasion.

[96] Interpretive Note to Recommendation 15 (July 1999). Under the revised recommendations (2012) this is now paragraph 2 of the Interpretative Note to Recommendation 13, but the text is unchanged.

[97] Schutte, Julian, 'Tampere European Council Presidency Decisions' (1999) 70 *Revue Internationale de Droit Pénal* 1023 at 1034–5.

[98] *Daily Telegraph*, 17 April 2000.

[99] Fisher, Jonathan, 'The Anti-Money Laundering Disclosure Regime and the Collection of Revenue in the United Kingdom' [2010] *British Tax Review* 235.

[100] Ibid at 246.

In the period from around 2005 and culminating in the revised FATF recommendations in 2012, pressure rose to bring tax evasion under the general umbrella of the FATF. Until 2012, the FATF did not require individual countries to have in place criminal liability for tax fraud. From a position in which tax evasion was not a required predicate offence for the crime of money laundering, it has now become a focus. The FATF now insists upon tax offences forming part of the irreducible core of offences that all compliant nations must treat as predicates to laundering.[101] The Fourth EU Money Laundering Directive expressly (for the first time) includes tax offences as mandatory predicates.[102]

In the same way that, when the eyes of the world were upon terrorism, we were told of the links between terrorism, drug-dealing, and money laundering, when they fell upon tax avoidance by large corporations, or tax evasion by individuals, again these phenomena were associated with laundering. What once might have been considered tax evasion followed by hiding unaccounted wealth on a tropical island is now characterized as 'tax evasion *and* money laundering', as though some fresh evil had been added. This has an important set of consequences. The security agenda in criminal justice follows from the idea that some crimes are so serious that their commission involves a security threat and that they can be combatted with extraordinary means. Laundering is one of the offences within the security agenda,[103] so the shift from 'tax evasion' *simpliciter* to 'tax evasion and money-laundering' implies a move up the table of seriousness for these offences. Not all offences can be the highest priority. The AML regime is now in play, carrying with it greater investigatory powers, greater potential sentences reporting requirements, attenuated professional privileges, and so on. This change should be made as part of a conscious policy directed to evasion, rather than by the laundering connection.[104]

The real significance of the laundering offences is not that the conduct involved is a distinct and threatening form of evil, but that the offences trigger the regulatory regime, including the reporting procedures, which is set out partly by the existence of the failure-to-report offence in s 330 *et seq* of

[101] Interpretative Note to Recommendation 3 of FATF 40 recommendations, 2012; Fourth Money Laundering Directive (EU) 2015/849.

[102] Fourth Money Laundering Directive (EU) 2015/849 Article 57.

[103] Zedner, Lucia, 'Security, the State, and the Citizen: The Changing Architecture of Crime Control' (2010) *13 New Criminal Law Review* 379–403; Vlcek, William, 'The Global Pursuit of Tax Revenue: Would Tax Haven Reform Equal Increased Tax Revenues in Developing States?' (2013) 27 *Global Society* 201–16.

[104] And see Vlcek, William, 'Power and the Practice of Security to Govern Global Finance' (2012) 19 *Review of International Political Economy* 639–62.

POCA and partly in the Money Laundering Regulations 2007.[105] What triggers the duty to inform the authorities is a set of conditions, the first of which is that:

he:

(a) knows or suspects, or
(b) has reasonable grounds for knowing or suspecting, that another person is engaged in money laundering.[106]

Before tax offences were incorporated as predicates by the FATF, the empirical basis of the interrelationship between two claims:

Capital flight is bad because it involves money laundering; and
Money laundering is bad because it involves capital flight

was tenuous, since it depended upon an overlap between the two which was unsupported by the data. Not much laundering fell within the 'transnational' category, and not much capital flight was laundering. That may remain the case, but the incorporation of tax evasion as a predicate offence will raise estimates of the global sums laundered, the proportion of international capital movement that amounts to laundering, and the amount of laundering that is included in international capital movement. This will in turn add impetus to the AML industry. There will be more reports, more people employed in the industry,[107] more suspicion, and so on. The decision to include tax evasion among recognized predicates was not a small step: it was a very large one, which should have been subject to far more rigorous scrutiny.

Tax Offences and the Identification of their Proceeds

If a person has more property as a result of tax evasion, the possibility arises of activity in regard of that additional property being treated as money laundering. This broadens considerably the scope of money-laundering, and will do so even more with the offshore evasion offence in place.[108] Quantification of the sums in respect of which confiscation orders are to be made is difficult, but in the case of criminal laundering it is also necessary to identify the property that is the subject matter of the offence. There is an infinite number

[105] Money Laundering Regulations 2007 SI 2157.

[106] POCA ss 330(2), 331(2). The use of a negligence test for criminal liability for an omission is very unusual. Even manslaughter requires more than simple negligence.

[107] Verhage, Antoinette, *The Anti Money Laundering Complex and the Compliance Industry* (Abingdon: Taylor & Francis, 2011), is one of a number of commentators to develop a functionalist account of the industry.

[108] See Chapter 8, section entitled 'Specific Offences of Offshore Evasion'.

of ways in which people might try to defraud the Revenue, but for present purposes they fall into two broad categories. In some of them (falsely claiming rebates or, perhaps, loss relief) the property acquired is identifiable, and the consequences are the same as in any other case of obtaining property by deception. The second type is of non-declaration of earnings, profits, or gains. One form of income that typically[109] goes undeclared is income from criminal activity, where without fictions, no identifiable property can be linked to the crime.

It is important to the tax justice movement that evasion be among the predicates to laundering, and, on the face of it, it seems natural that it should. If the category of predicate offences is to be extended to make it very wide, why not include tax evasion? On the other hand, there are some considerations at play in tax cases which might militate against using the criminal law. They focus on the relationship between tax and criminal justice. On a number of issues there has been significant integration in the UK, not so much driven by the FATF Recommendations, but being the product of the same forces that gave rise to the revisions of the Recommendations.[110] Because it provides the trigger for the reporting requirement, the question whether tax evasion can provide the predicate offence to criminal laundering is of enormous practical significance. The FATF required that there be criminal liability for laundering when the alleged launderer *knew* that the property was of criminal provenance.[111] English law, in important relevant areas, throws the net much wider, being satisfied by suspicion.[112] The effect of this is to broaden the scope both of the substantive offences and of the reporting requirements, giving rise to more reporting, more investigation, and further growth of the AML industry.

The Substantive Laundering Offences

In English law the crime of money laundering is doing 'something' in respect of 'criminal property'.[113] The list of potential 'somethings' is written very widely. The laundering offences have been put in place on the model of the

[109] Though not invariably: income from corruptly obtained contracts is often declared.

[110] International Standards on Combating Money Laundering and the Financing of Terrorism & Proliferation—the FATF Recommendations (Paris: February 2012).

[111] UN Convention against Illicit Traffic in Narcotic Drugs and Psychotropic Substances (Vienna Convention) 1998, Article 3(10), Article 3(1)(b); United Nations Convention against Transnational Organized Crime (Palermo Convention 2004), Article 6.

[112] POCA s 340(6).

[113] POCA s 340: '(3) Property is criminal property if—(a) it constitutes a person's benefit from criminal conduct [defined in s 340(2)] or it represents such a benefit (in whole or part and whether directly or indirectly), and (b) the alleged offender knows or suspects that it constitutes or represents such a benefit.'

Vienna Convention.[114] It is an offence to conceal, disguise, convert, or transfer criminal property, or remove it from the jurisdiction.[115] It is an offence to enter into or become concerned in an arrangement which the defendant knows or suspects facilitates (by whatever means) the acquisition, retention, use, or control of criminal property by or on behalf of another person.[116] It is an offence to acquire, use, or have possession of criminal property.[117] It is also an offence to be complicit in any of these things.[118]

As soon as the category of predicate offences was made sufficiently broad to encompass tax evasion,[119] the question became open: when could there be laundering of the proceeds of evasion? The conceptual problems raised as to the quantity and identity of the criminal property have consistently been ducked in the laundering case law in England and Wales. In the case of tax fraud by under- or non-declaration,[120] it is clear that the taxpayer will have more property, but there will not necessarily be any identifiable property arising from the evasion to which a laundering charge can be attached. Even if there is identifiable property, the defendant will not necessarily hold the required mental state (knowledge that or suspicion as to whether the property in question 'represented or constituted'[121] the proceeds of the offence) for conviction.[122]

The first thing to notice is that s 340(6) is a deeming provision. Deeming provisions occasionally work satisfactorily in tax statutes, but almost invariably cause problems when the criminal law is involved. Section 340(6) deems the defendant to have a sum of money that s/he does not actually have. Here, in the transfer of the text from s 76(5) (dealing with confiscation) to s 340(6) (imposing criminal liability for laundering), the consequence of the use of the deeming provision does not seem to have been properly worked through. The sum of money does not actually exist. It might therefore be thought that it is simply impossible to conceal, disguise, convert, or transfer property[123] whose existence is only hypothetical. It is no more possible to conceal (and the rest) property that does not exist than it is to conceal a unicorn. The same goes for the third set of laundering offences, under s 329, which involve acquisition, use, or possession of criminal property. As with s 327, it may be thought that

[114] UN Convention against Illicit Traffic in Narcotic Drugs and Psychotropic Substances (Vienna Convention) 1998, Article 3(10).

[115] POCA s 327. [116] S 328. [117] S 329. [118] S 340(11).

[119] Alldridge, n 85. [120] But not falsely claiming rebates or refunds.

[121] A legal judgment is implied in 'constituted', and consequently mistake or ignorance in that regard should, in principle, provide a defence.

[122] The technicalities of the arguments were made out in Alldridge and Mumford, n 25, 353.

[123] S 327.

the notional money cannot be acquired, used, or possessed because it does not actually exist.

The *actus reus* of the offence under s 328 is entering or being concerned in an arrangement which in fact facilitates the acquisition, etc., of criminal property, and the *mens rea* required is knowledge or suspicion.[124] Under s 328(1):

> *A person commits an offence if he enters into or becomes concerned in an arrangement which he knows or suspects facilitates (by whatever means) the acquisition, retention, use or control of criminal property by or on behalf of another person.*

Here the drafting is less specific about the criminal property.[125] No article is used before 'criminal property'. The provision seems to contemplate that the criminal property is property that might come into existence (or become criminal property) at some point after the arrangement is entered into. So, it might be argued, the property could not be identified *at the time of the arrangement*, and the fact that it could not be identified does not prevent there being criminal property for the purposes of the reporting obligation. The contrary argument is that s 328 still contemplates that there be at some time identifiable property when the arrangement comes to fruition, and that unless that property is criminal property there will be no offence. It is suggested that this is the better interpretation. In *R v GH*[126] the Supreme Court held that it was a prerequisite of the offences under ss 327, 328, and 329 that the property should be criminal property at the time of the alleged offence.

Suppose a person within the regulated sector is helping a person deal with his/her money. They suspect that the person is not declaring their full liability to tax. Section 340(6) deems the evader of tax to possess a sum of money. Even if the specific property need not be identified as a matter of law, the mental state implied in 'criminal property' (that the alleged offender knows or suspects that it constitutes or represents such a benefit)[127] still provides further possible defences to one charged either with laundering or failing to report. First, the arranger may well not 'know or suspect' the property represented the benefit of criminal conduct, since s/he might well be ignorant of s 340(6). If this is the case, because of s 340(3), it is not criminal property. The arranger can say that s/he did not know or suspect the property represented the benefit of criminal conduct because s/he did not understand the relevant law. A claim of mistake of

[124] See *R v Montila* [2004] UKHL 50; [2004] 1 WLR 3141, a decision of the House of Lords regarding different but analogous wording in earlier legislation.

[125] It is wider than the offence generated by Criminal Law Act 1977 s 1 of conspiring to commit the offence under s 327.

[126] *R v GH* [2015] UKSC 24; [2015] 2 Cr App R 12.

[127] POCA s 340(3).

law, where it negatives the relevant *mens rea*, can provide a defence.[128] Second, the person upon whom the reporting requirement is placed may well not know or suspect that the property was criminal property because, even if s/he knew the relevant law, s/he might not ascribe to the arranger the knowledge or suspicion required by s 340(3).

It is therefore suggested that a perfectly plausible interpretation of POCA would have been that in the case of tax evasion by non-declaration or under-declaration, there was no supplementary laundering crime to charge. Notwithstanding the force of the arguments in English law, defendants have been held to launder the proceeds of the crime of evasion. In *R v William, William & William*[129] the Court of Appeal held that where a taxpayer cheated the Revenue by falsely representing the turnover of a business, he obtained a pecuniary advantage and was taken to have obtained a benefit equal to tax due on the undeclared turnover. Moreover, the 'criminal property' was held to be the entirety of the undeclared turnover, not merely the tax due. Once the law commits to the fiction that the tax evader actually has in his/her possession property that s/he does not have and uses that as a basis for conviction, there is no obvious point to stop. If tax evasion is a predicate offence to criminal laundering, then, since almost all income from unlawful sources is taxable, there is a danger that the chosen enforcement mechanism—against, for example, drug dealers—will be to treat their money as the proceeds of tax evasion. If the prosecution need only establish that money was undeclared income then, unless the sentences for laundering vary according to the predicate offence, there is no point in proving any other, more serious 'criminal conduct' as a predicate. This trend is exemplified and extended by *R v Kuchhadia*,[130] in which the defendant's lifestyle was taken as evidence of a number of possible predicates, of which evasion was one, and the most easily proven.

Beyond the technical detail, what does it imply that the FATF requires that tax offences be now treated as predicates? Except in those jurisdictions (Germany is one[131]) which do not allow liability for 'self-laundering' (laundering the proceeds of one's own crime),[132] it is difficult to imagine any

[128] *R v Smith (DR)* [1974] QB 354; [1974] 1 All ER 632.

[129] *R v William, William & William* [2013] EWCA Crim 1262, approving and expanding upon *R v Gabriel* [2006] All ER (D) 26 (Feb); *R v K (appeal under s 58 of the Criminal Justice Act 2003)* [2007] All ER (D) 138 (Mar); *SOCA v Bosworth* [2010] All ER (D) 273 (Mar).

[130] *R v Kuchhadia* [2015] EWCA Crim 1252; [2015] Lloyd's Rep FC 526.

[131] German Criminal Code § 261(9).

[132] Where convictions for self-laundering are permitted, self-launderers will make up a significant proportion, and the argument that penalizing laundering somehow breaks down a criminal network will be weakened.

case of tax evasion that will not also necessarily amount to money laundering. What previously was charged (if at all) as evasion now amounts to evasion *and* money laundering. Significant shifts will follow in the reporting of laundering and capital movements. The inevitable consequence of the incorporation of tax offences as predicates has been to raise estimates of money laundered,[133] and also to raise the amount of both laundering as a proportion of capital flight and capital flight as a proportion of laundering. The Organisation for Economic Co-operation and Development (OECD) identified tax crime as one of the top three sources of money laundering.[134] If it was not before, it will be soon, because this claim will become self-authenticating. The effect is more firmly to embed the AML narrative.[135] There seems to be little doubt now, however, that laundering offences and the AML narrative have occupied and altered the treatment of tax evasion, and not necessarily for the better.

The Proceeds of Crime Act Tax Jurisdiction

Part VI of POCA created a tax jurisdiction associated to the proceeds of crime and put it in the hands of the Director of the ARA. It is now held by the National Crime Agency (NCA).[136] The Cabinet Office review preceding POCA considered as a problem people with a high standard of living but no visible lawful means of financing it. The Irish Criminal Assets Bureau, in many respects the progenitor of the ARA, uses its tax jurisdiction very actively.[137]

Assessing tax based on lifestyle carries with it the potential attraction, for politicians, of boosting taxpayer morale:

> *Taxation must be applied consistently and fairly. The ordinary taxpayer is disadvantaged if others do not pay their share according to their income, not least because it increases the tax burden on the rest of society's taxpayers whose activities are lawful. The application of Inland Revenue powers to individuals who have acquired assets derived from criminal conduct will send out a strong message that the UK taxation system is indeed fairly applied across all sections of society.*[138]

[133] Unger, Birgitte, 'Can Money Laundering Decrease?' (2013) 41 *Public Finance Review* 658–76.

[134] OECD, *Money Laundering Awareness Handbook for Tax Examiners and Tax Auditors* (Paris: OECD, 2009).

[135] Naylor, RT, *Counterfeit Crime* (Montreal: McGill-Queen's University Press, 2015) at 110 *et seq* for a critique.

[136] Crime and Courts Act 2013 Schedule 8(2) para 122(2).

[137] Campbell, n 87, ch 8, esp p 238; Criminal Assets Bureau, *Annual Report 2014* (Dublin: Criminal Assets Bureau, 2016).

[138] Draft Proceeds of Crime Bill (Cm 5066, March 2001), para 6.2.

Described within the literature as the 'net worth' weapon against tax evasion ever since the US Supreme Court approved assessments on this basis in the 1954 case of *Holland v US*,[139] this approach carries with it several dangers in terms of procedural fairness, outlined by Duke.[140] POCA conferred power on the ARA to deal with the tax affairs of those people in receipt of any income, gains, or profits which the Director had reasonable grounds to suspect to have resulted from the proceeds of crime.[141] The text that accompanied the draft Bill was as follows.

The intention here is to counter the efforts of persons to protect their criminal assets by arguing they were accumulated from legitimate sources. In many such cases the income, gain or profits are in fact unknown to the Revenue. Since they have not been declared the subject will be exposed not only to the collection of tax, but also to interest and penalties on it. This means that much, and in some cases all, of a subject's illegally gained wealth can be recovered by taxation.[142]

The Cabinet Office review[143] had identified as an obstacle to the taxation of suspicious income the rules, apparently stemming from the early history of the schedular system of assessment, first that in order for an assessment to be made to income tax (but not those to capital gains tax or corporation tax), there must be an identifiable source of income to which it is to be attributed, such as a particular trade; and second, that the income had to be attributable to a specified year. The NCA is able to raise a tax assessment where neither a source of income nor a year of assessment has been identified. In the case of a person who is in receipt of suspected criminal proceeds and has no tax history, there may be no obvious taxable source to which income represented by unexplained assets can be attributed. This may be the case, for example, where there are grounds for suspecting that income has accrued from one or more of a number of possible criminal activities but it is impossible to identify which. This rule does not change substantive tax law, in particular the boundary between taxable and non-taxable activity, but prevents suspected recipients of criminals' assets from avoiding tax by refusing to identify the source of their income, and places the onus on the taxpayer to displace the tax assessment by providing evidence on appeal that assets came from a non-taxable source.

[139] *Holland v United States* (1954) 348 US 121; Avakian, Spurgeon, 'Net Worth Computations as Proof of Tax Evasion' (1954) 10 *Tax Law Review* 431.

[140] Duke, Steven, 'Prosecutions for Attempts to Evade Income Tax: A Discordant View of a Procedural Hybrid' (1966) 76 *Yale Law Journal* 1.

[141] POCA s 317.

[142] Draft Proceeds of Crime Bill (Cm 5066, March 2001), para 6.1.

[143] Ibid, para 10.6 *et seq.*

There are two major policy questions about the role of the tax jurisdiction in law enforcement. The first is whether obtaining tax from criminals is best achieved by a separate body established specifically for that purpose and for no other, with performance indicators set overwhelmingly by reference to sums of money brought in, or whether it is better used as one of a range of legal responses available when acting against someone's assets suspected to be the proceeds of crime. This is not an issue of principle. It is a question of whatever works better. The 'dedicated agency' approach, which does have the advantage that it is easier to isolate the expenditure involved, was tried with the Proceeds of Crime Act 2002's introduction of the ARA. Although the Agency is regarded[144] as having succeeded in Northern Ireland, where there was a history of racketeering linked to terrorism, it was judged an unequivocal failure in England and Wales. It operated until 2007 and was then abruptly abolished. A report by Grant Shapps MP established that in the first four years of its existence, the Agency had not been able to acquire enough money to cover its own costs.[145] A critical Public Accounts Committee report followed shortly afterwards.[146] Chapter 11 of Anthony King and Ivor Crewe's *The Blunders of Government*[147] is devoted to the ARA, and seems to hold that the problem was a lack of clear focus.

With the end of the ARA, the Serious Crime Act 2007 placed the duties and powers of the Director in the hands of various Directors responsible for prosecutions.[148] The civil recovery and taxation powers of the Agency were given to the Serious Organised Crime Agency (SOCA) and thence to the NCA. The CPS does not emphasize the use of its civil recovery powers,[149] but the Serious Fraud Office (SFO) has a team specifically dedicated to the active pursuit of proceeds of crime and clearly sees civil recovery as a significant element in its shift away from the use of criminal prosecutions.

In 2015, the NCA, the successor agency to the ARA, announced that its policy on civil recovery and taxation of the proceeds of crime was that its objective was disruption, not the raising of revenue.[150] This institutional *volte-face* was announced at the same time as the NCA was criticized by the House

[144] HL Debates, 27 March 2007 Cols 1591–94 (Baroness Scotland).

[145] Shapps, Grant, *Report into the Underperformance of the Assets Recovery Agency* (London: Shapps, June 2006).

[146] Leigh, Edward (Chair), Public Accounts Committee, *The Assets Recovery Agency*, Fiftieth Report of Session 2006–07.

[147] King, Anthony, and Ivor Crewe, *The Blunders of Our Governments* (London: Oneworld Publications, 2013) ch 11.

[148] Serious Crime Act 2007 s 74 and Scheds 8 and 9.

[149] HC 10 Feb 2009 Col 1861W (Vera Baird QC, Solicitor-General).

[150] <http://www.nationalcrimeagency.gov.uk/news/88-nca-website/about-us/what-we-do/549-nca-approach-to-criminal-assets>.

of Commons Home Affairs Committee[151] for its record in respect of civil recovery. If the ARA had been able to make the same response when attacked in 2007, it might still be with us.

The second policy question is as to the relationship between the use of criminal justice (prosecution, conviction, and sentence) and other approaches to acquisitive crime. To what extent is the use of alternatives to prosecution and conviction in this area appropriate? As first introduced, interventions directed against criminal assets were not intended to be an alternative to criminal proceedings where conviction and a subsequent confiscation order were available. During the parliamentary stages of POCA, a clear hierarchy seems to have been contemplated in the approach the ARA was to take to someone suspected of being in possession of the proceeds of crime. The first preference was for criminal prosecution, followed by civil recovery, and only then, if appropriate, the invocation of the tax jurisdiction.[152]

After the end of the ARA, the hierarchy of enforcement mechanisms was also abolished. The POCA revenue jurisdiction is now in the hands of the NCA, and the exercise of the tax jurisdiction no longer requires as a precondition the consideration and rejection of prosecution and civil recovery.[153] The NCA acquires the tax jurisdiction if it has reasonable grounds[154] to suspect that:

(a) *income arising or a gain accruing to a person in respect of a chargeable period is chargeable to income tax or is a chargeable gain (as the case may be) and arises or accrues as a result of the person's or another's criminal conduct (whether wholly or partly and whether directly or indirectly), or*
(b) *a company is chargeable to corporation tax on its profits arising in respect of a chargeable period and the profits arise as a result of the company's or another person's criminal conduct (whether wholly or partly and whether directly or indirectly).*[155]

151 Vaz, Keith (Chair), Home Affairs Committee, *Evaluating the New Architecture of Policing: The College of Policing and the NCA*, Tenth Report of 2014–15, at 9, para 21.

152 Alldridge, Peter, *Money Laundering Law* (Oxford: Hart, 2003) 246 *et seq.*

153 POCA s 2(5) and (6) and guidance.

154 *Fenech v SOCA* [2013] UKFTT 555. S 317(1) only requires that the NCA has reasonable grounds to suspect criminal conduct, and that there was income, however indirect and however little, flowing from it. SOCA did not have to prove that any of the income assessed on F arose from criminal conduct; it merely had to have a reasonable suspicion that he had received some income directly or indirectly from criminal conduct for the relevant year.

155 S 317(1). And for a challenge to jurisdiction under this provision see *Khan v Director of the Assets Recovery Agency* [2006] STC (SCD) 154; [2006] STI 593.

Once the tax affairs are taken over by the NCA, it has all the powers that would be exercisable by HMRC.[156] The principal mechanism by which the POCA tax jurisdiction operates is the raising of an assessment. The effect is to place the burden on the taxpayer to show, on the balance of probabilities, that the assessment is incorrect. The assessments must not be fanciful,[157] but if they are based on solid evidence and could be sustained they will be upheld.[158] Using saving and spending ('net worth') as the method of quantifying the taxpayer's income has been held to be entirely reasonable.[159] Where a source of income is identified incorrectly, then the NCA does not get the benefit of s 319(1).[160] This is all the more reason why the source should not be identified, as the statute allows. The tax jurisdiction has not been used a great deal. It remains to be seen whether the introduction of unexplained wealth orders will make it easier to apply the tax jurisdiction, or less necessary, because of the effect of UWOs upon rates of civil recovery.

Double Counting

In *Higgins v National Crime Agency*[161] the defendant was successfully prosecuted for disposing of waste illegally over a number of years. The Crown Court made a confiscation order for £400,000 pursuant to POCA. SOCA then assessed H's tax liability (income tax and national insurance contributions) and imposed a penalty of 75 per cent, which was reduced on review to 60 per cent. Interest was also sought on these sums. He appealed on the basis of double recovery, arguing that the original confiscation order had already accounted for these sums. H also argued that the imposition of the penalty was disproportionate for the purposes of A1P1. The tribunal held that as he had not paid the appropriate amount of tax, it was proportionate for the NCA to raise a penalty, which was specifically designed to ensure that he observed his responsibilities with regard to his tax affairs in the future. The penalty was a fine and was different in concept to the payment under the confiscation order, and it was not either disproportionate or a double payment. This harsh decision may need to be reconsidered in the light of *Harvey*.[162]

156 *Fenech v SOCA* [2013] UKFTT 555.
157 *Forbes v Director of the Assets Recovery Agency* [2007] STC (SCD) 1; [2006] STI 2510.
158 *Harper v Director of the Assets Recovery Agency* [2005] STC (SCD) 874; [2005] STI 1906.
159 *Lynch v National Crime Agency* [2014] UKFTT 1088 (TC) (FTT (Tax)).
160 *Rose v Director of the Assets Recovery Agency* [2006] STC (SCD) 472; [2006] STI 1631.
161 *Higgins v National Crime Agency* [2015] UKFTT 46 (TC).
162 *R v Harvey* [2015] UKSC 73; [2016] 1 Cr App R (S) 60; and see this chapter, section entitled 'Confiscating the Proceeds of Tax Evasion'.

Forfeitures and Other *In Rem* Seizures

Forfeitures

Under Part 5 of POCA there is a civil recovery jurisdiction. Since civil recovery operates *in rem*, it may have some application in the case of cash or other property that is held as a consequence of tax evasion, but the more normal course in respect of domestic evasion is to prosecute and ask for the imposition of a confiscation order, or to impose civil penalties. One of the principal powers available to the authorities in respect of smuggling has always been forfeiture of the contraband items, the vessels carrying them, and other instrumentalities. Customs forfeitures usually operate without a conviction,[163] and do not engage Article 6. The sums involved can be very large.[164] The ECtHR has declined to interfere.[165] Once the items have been seized there is a procedure under which the owner may apply for the restoration of the goods. In order for restoration to be granted, exceptional circumstances need to be shown.[166]

Cash Forfeiture

As a way of holding property, there is something different about cash, the ultimate bearer instrument. The dangers of loss or theft make it at best a peculiar choice for someone with large amounts of money. It has always been favoured by tax evaders, because it is far less easy to trace cash than transactions involving bank accounts. Until they were lifted in 1979,[167] post-war exchange controls in the UK, under the Exchange Control Act 1947, made it illegal to take cash or gold out of the country without Treasury consent. Any such cash could be forfeit either after or without criminal proceedings. Just when increased capital mobility seemed to have swept away controls on

[163] *Customs and Excise Commissioners v Newbury* [2003] EWHC 702 (Admin); [2003] 1 WLR 2131; *Lindsay v Customs and Excise Commissioners* [2002] EWCA Civ 267; [2002] 1 WLR 1766; *Darren Hope v Director of Border Revenue* [2015] UKFTT 18 (TC).

[164] Famously an aeroplane in *Customs and Excise Commissioners v Air Canada* [1989] QB 234; [1989] 2 All ER 22; *Customs and Excise Commissioners v Air Canada* (CA) [1991] 2 QB 446; [1991] 2 WLR 344; [1991] 1 All ER 570.

[165] *Allgemeine Gold- und Silberscheideanstalt AG (AGOSI) v United Kingdom* (1987) 9 EHRR 1; *Air Canada v United Kingdom* (1995) 20 EHRR 150.

[166] CEMA Schedule 3: *Amps v Director of Border Revenue* [2013] UKFTT 570 (TC).

[167] Exchange Control (General Exemption) Order 1979 SI 1660. The 1947 Act was finally repealed by FA 1987, ss 68(1), (2), (4), 72, Schedule 16, Pt XI.

the movement of capital between jurisdictions, along came another set of concerns about the movement of cash. No longer was the concern that huge international movements of money would destabilize sterling within the Bretton Woods structures.[168] From 1979, the cause for concern about cash being moved between jurisdictions has been that it might be the proceeds of crime and that its movement might enable the profits of crime to be enjoyed or reinvested elsewhere.

From 1990 onwards, if a person was found leaving the country carrying a suitcase full of money, it could be seized if there were reasonable grounds to suspect, and then forfeit if the state was able to show on the balance of probabilities, that it was obtained from drugs.[169] Since 2002, the power has extended beyond customs officials at ports to all constables anywhere, and the suspicion no longer need be entertained only in respect of drugs, but may be of any crime.[170] There is power to search for such cash[171] with the prior approval of a magistrate or, where that is not practicable, a senior police officer. There is a Code of Practice governing such searches and seizures.[172] POCA confers power upon either a customs officer or a constable to seize cash amounts of or above a minimum amount[173] if he has reasonable grounds for suspecting that it is recoverable property or intended by any person for use in unlawful conduct.[174] A magistrates' court may then order the forfeiture of the cash. The court must be 'satisfied' as to its provenance, but the proceedings are civil and the standard of proof is the civil one.[175]

POCA cash forfeiture has two limbs, therefore—one directed against 'recoverable property' and the other against property intended by any person

[168] Articles of Agreement of the International Monetary Fund (Cmd 6546, 1945), to which effect was given by the Bretton Woods Agreements Act 1945.

[169] Criminal Justice (International Co-operation) Act 1990 s 25; Drug Trafficking Act 1994 s 42.

[170] POCA s 298. And see *Fletcher v Chief Constable of Leicestershire* [2013] EWHC 3357 (Admin); [2014] Lloyd's Rep FC 60.

[171] POCA s 289. Cash is defined (s 289(6) and (7)) widely, to include notes and coins in any currency, postal orders, cheques, bankers' drafts, and bearer bonds.

[172] The Proceeds of Crime Act 2002 (Cash Searches: Code of Practice) Order 2016 SI 947, replacing the Proceeds of Crime Act 2002 (Cash Searches: Code of Practice) Order 2008 SI 208, to satisfy POCA s 292. The exercise of such powers by members of the executive without such a code would not satisfy the Convention: *Camezind v Switzerland* (1999) 28 EHRR 458.

[173] The minimum amount is to be fixed from time to time by order of the Home Secretary: POCA s 303. The amount at the time of writing (July 2016) is £1,000: Proceeds of Crime Act 2002 (Recovery of Cash in Summary Proceedings: Minimum Amount) Order 2006 SI 1699.

[174] POCA s 294.

[175] Note that use of forfeiture provisions in respect of cash is a move away from the historical root of forfeiture in identifying the harm with the thing.

for use in unlawful conduct.[176] This makes cash forfeiture a hybrid: it is a *civil recovery* procedure so far as it relates to recoverable property and a *forfeiture* procedure so far as it relates to property intended for use in crime.[177] The justification, so far as it operates as a civil recovery procedure, is clear and will not be considered further. The property has its provenance in crime and is covered by the principle against permitting people to benefit from crime. To the extent that civil recovery is justified at all, it is justified so far as it deals with cash.[178] It is not sufficient for the officer to point to criminal conduct of an unspecified kind.[179] This is where the tax element enters. Suppose a large amount of cash is found in the premises of the defendant.[180] In order that it be forfeit, the authorities would normally have to specify the type of offence which they suspect generated it. It is easier to describe it as the proceeds of tax evasion than of drug-dealing, person-trafficking, or any other more specific crime.

The 'intended for use' limb is more difficult to justify. The assumption that property may legitimately be forfeit if *intended* for criminal use, without more, is problematic. Moreover, while possession of a large amount of cash is, in the absence of an explanation, good evidence that the cash has unlawful provenance, it is by no means so compelling as evidence that the cash is intended for illegal use *unless that use is the evasion of tax*. The fact that the property in question is cash makes the argument for forfeiture a stronger one, because cash is fungible.[181]

As a means of acquiring cash for the State from suspected criminals, cash forfeiture is relatively efficient, because the money frequently comes to light during a search for something else, usually drugs, and the proceedings are frequently uncontested. The Policing and Crime Act 2009 replaced previous, unnecessarily complex law, by putting in place forfeiture without a court

[176] The definition in POCA s 304 applies.

[177] Hence the use of forfeiture of part of the cash involved in *Ahmed v Revenue and Customs Commissioners* [2013] EWHC 2241 (Admin) may have been less easy to justify had the proceedings been under the forfeiture than the recovery head.

[178] In the case of cash seizure, mere possession of a large quantity of cash may be regarded as evidence that the cash *was* obtained through crime. *R (on the application of the Director of the Assets Recovery Agency) v Green* [2005] EWHC 3168 at paras 32–3 (Sullivan J).

[179] *Angus v United Kingdom Border Agency* [2011] EWHC 461 (Admin); [2011] Lloyd's Rep FC 329; *Secretary of State for the Home Department v Tuncel* [2012] EWHC 402; [2012] Lloyd's Rep FC 475; *Wiese v UK Border Agency* [2012] EWHC 2549.

[180] Sums *are* sometimes very large: '£30m "Biggest Ever" Seizure from Organised Crime Network': BBC News, 21 April 2016.

[181] Amounts seized at borders, which form about two-thirds of cash seizures, are falling. HMIC, *Proceeds of Crime: An Inspection of HMRC's Performance in Addressing the Recovery of the Proceeds of Crime from Tax and Duty Evasion and Benefit Fraud* (London: TSO, 2011) para 5.49 *et seq*.

order in uncontested cases.[182] As at 2011, cash forfeiture represented 32 per cent of all proceeds of crime seizures.[183] These statistics do not differentiate forfeitures of recoverable property from forfeitures of property intended for illegal use, but it can reasonably be assumed that the former are far more significant, and they are easily justified.

Human rights challenges to cash forfeiture have not been successful. In *Butt v HM Customs and Excise*,[184] the court held that proceedings under the preceding legislation did not fall foul of Article 6.2 and 6.3. Hallett J (as she then was) dismissed the argument:

> *It would, in my view, defeat Parliament's clearly expressed and enacted intention if the courts were to find that every case of forfeiture under s 43 [of the Drug Trafficking Act 1994, the preceding legislation] involves a finding of criminal activity and, therefore, the standard to be applied is the criminal standard of proof.* [185]

With respect, this is hardly persuasive. It will always defeat Parliament's clearly expressed and enacted intention to hold that Article 6 applies where it was thought not to. Nonetheless, it is typical of the judicial response to challenges to the exercise of the various powers conferred by the Act.

How does this relate to taxation? A large amount of cash raises suspicions as to its provenance, at least sufficient that an explanation might be called for. If a person cannot or will not even defend an action for cash forfeiture of recoverable property, it is right that they lose the cash. If the authorities have insufficient evidence to show its provenance in crime, they will be unlikely to be able to show that the cash was intended for criminal use (so as to give cash forfeiture properly so called). If, however, they can, then it is legitimate for the State to freeze the money until such time as the defendant no longer intends its use in crime. To allow the State to take it altogether is to go too far.

Unexplained Wealth Orders

There is increased pressure to change the basis upon which people account to the State for their wealth. As part of the revisions to the UK government's action plan for anti-money laundering and counter-terrorist finance,[186] a mechanism called an unexplained wealth order (UWO) is contemplated.[187]

[182] Inserting a new POCA s 297A.

[183] <www.justice.gov.uk/downloads/statistics/mojstats/cjs-stats/cjs-stats-bulletin-sept2010.pdf>.

[184] *Butt v HM Customs* and *Excise* [2001] EWHC Admin 1066.

[185] Para 25.

[186] Home Office and HM Treasury, *Action Plan for Anti-Money Laundering and Counter-terrorist Finance* (April 2016).

[187] And see HL Debates, 18 Jun 2015 Col GC2 (Lord Rooker) Criminal Finances Act 2017.

The idea is that orders will be made when the individual appears to have wealth for which there is no apparent source. It would require the individual to declare the source of his/her wealth. Where the subject of a UWO fails to respond or responds unsatisfactorily, that fact is to provide evidence in support of a civil recovery order. UWOs allow the seizure of bank accounts even outside the jurisdiction. One of the problems that the owner of such accounts will encounter in the face of these proceedings is to establish that s/he came by the property that is the subject of the UWO without committing tax evasion.

The shift in attitudes to taxpayer confidentiality has thus taken a predictable turn with the proposal for UWOs. The relationship between the State and the owner of property has changed. We have moved from a position where the State needed to put in place constraints to protect financial privacy, to one where it wants to know everything about the financial affairs of everyone, and wants to exchange that information with other States. The proceeds of crime industry has now expanded, via the confiscation of the proceeds of drug trafficking into confiscation of the proceeds of tax evasion, to a state of affairs where the citizen may now be called upon, under circumstances that are not very clearly defined, to explain how s/he comes to hold property, on peril of it being forfeit if no explanation or an insufficient explanation is given. This radical change has been made incrementally, without ever there having been a full debate.

Conclusions

In the days when there was no confiscation or civil recovery and very few prosecutions, the links between tax law and proceeds-of-crime law were limited. They have now grown substantially, and have had imposed upon them 'follow the money' as a crime-control axiom. These things, coupled with the failure of the AML industry as a means of generating significant amounts of revenue in other fields, have caused a turn towards tax evasion and made the relationship a hugely important one to the future both of criminal justice and of tax law. This may not be a bad thing, but ought not to have been achieved by the knee-jerks and incrementalism this chapter has described.

10

Should More Alleged Tax Evaders Be Prosecuted?

We know what the tax system is for. It is to raise the money to govern—pay for education, health, social services, defence, and so on. There is less clarity as to the purpose of tax prosecutions. It might be characterized as merely an adjunct to the collection system or as a central part of the law of financial crime, and upon which of these accounts is selected will depend conclusions on the level of enforcement.

As part of the 2010 Spending Review, Her Majesty's Revenue and Customs (HMRC) was provided with additional funds to prosecute, and with the funds came raised targets. Keir Starmer QC, as Director of Public Prosecutions (DPP), announced in 2013 that there would be more prosecutions of tax evaders and increased targets.[1] The reasons given in the speech were disappointingly unconvincing. Starmer started by setting up and knocking down an Aunt Sally—the idea that tax evasion is a victimless crime. He claimed—a recurrent theme—that tax evasion is particularly bad in times of recession.[2] He then enumerated a few successful prosecutions of culpable defendants and praised tough sentences.[3] He repeated HMRC's claim that '[i]n 2011 ... criminal cases prevented the loss to the Revenue of around £1 billion'. That is, Starmer did not make the case for additional prosecutions in terms of any deterrent effect the prosecutions might have, but rather in moral terms, perhaps tapping into public sentiments of outrage. The prosecution targets moved up to 1,165 for 2014–15. A total of 1,258 individuals were convicted

[1] 'Prosecuting Tax Evasion', Speech by Keir Starmer QC, Director of Public Prosecutions, 23 January 2013, <http://www.cps.gov.uk/news/articles/prosecuting_tax_evasion>.

[2] The same type of claim is commonly made in wartime.

[3] Especially the remarks of Rafferty LJ in the *Operation Reciprocal* case, *R v Perrin & Faichney* [2012] EWCA Crim 1729; [2012] EWCA Crim 1730; see Chapter 4, section entitled 'Sentencing'.

of evasion or fraud in the year to 2015, up from 795 a year earlier.[4] HMRC recruited an additional 200 criminal investigators to increase the number of people prosecuted for tax evasion from 165 in 2010–11, to 565 in 2012–13, and to 1,165 in 2014–15.[5]

Is this likely to have any effect on compliance? The social psychology of compliance is equivocal. An early experiment[6] found that both appealing to taxpayers' consciences and reminding them of the risk of sanctions increased compliance, with the former working better than the latter. A later field experiment seemed to find the opposite,[7] and others have found little or no effect in appealing to people's morality at all.[8] Levi[9] reviewed the literature and concluded that there was little in the way of clear evidence that more or fewer prosecutions have that much effect, but that increased prosecution might be justified for purposes of moral retribution as well as perceived social fairness. Levi[10] argues for the greater deployment of the criminal law against (serious) tax frauds.[11] It may well be that the overall rate of prosecutions for evasion in general, and offshore evasion in particular, makes little difference to the rate of compliance. The worst possible outcome of the current attention to evasion would be more prosecutions of tax credit frauds and small-scale tax evasion, but no impact upon rates of large-scale evasion by using 'offshore'.

Should the substantive or procedural criminal law of tax evasion be more extensive? So far as concerns the taxpayer's own criminal liability, the law does not need to be more extensive. Criminal tax evasion should be restricted to the case where the taxpayer lies to HMRC to reduce his/her liability. The offences ancillary to evasion are probably unnecessarily wide as things stand. The introduction of the new offshore offence dealing with offshore evasion and having as its basis the negligence of the taxpayer throws the net too far as a matter of criminal law doctrine. The liability of professionals is already

[4] 'HMRC Steps Up Tax Evasion Drive after 58% Rise in Convictions', *Financial Times*, 14 December 2015.

[5] <https://www.govuk/government/policies/reducing-tax-evasion-and-avoidance>.

[6] Schwartz, Richard D, and Sonya Orleans, 'On Legal Sanctions' (1967) 34 *University of Chicago Law Review* 274.

[7] Hallsworth, Michael, John A List, Robert Metcalfe, and Ivo Vlaev (2014), *The Behavioralist Tax Collector: Using Natural Field Experiments to Enhance Tax Compliance*. Available at <http://www.nber.org/papers/w20007>.

[8] Blumenthal, Marsha, Charles Christian, Joel Slemrod, and Matthew G Smith, 'Do Normative Appeals Affect Tax Compliance? Evidence from a Controlled Experiment in Minnesota' (2001) 54 *National Tax Journal* 125.

[9] Levi, Michael, 'Serious Tax Fraud and Noncompliance: A Review of Evidence on the Differential Impact of Criminal and Noncriminal Proceedings' (2010) 9 *Criminology and Public Policy* 493–514.

[10] Ibid.

[11] Cf Braithwaite, Valerie, 'Criminal Prosecution within Responsive Regulatory Practice' (2010) 9 *Criminology & Public Policy* 515–23.

sufficiently expressed in the criminal law, and the 'enabling' offence in the Criminal Finance Bill does not seem to make criminal any activity that is not already criminal. There is, however, much to be said for more active enforcement against professionals. The new provisions[12] directed at professionals, imposing civil penalties on those who enable another person to carry out offshore tax evasion or non-compliance, although difficult to justify in principle, will give HMRC another useful tool, and publicity for proceedings, civil or criminal, against professionals would be worthwhile.

Administration of the substantive criminal offences might benefit from their being organized more rationally, but rationalization cannot be thought a priority. Prosecutions can fail in areas of law that are untidy because prosecutors charge the wrong crime, or charge under the wrong statute.[13] The haphazard, disorganized range of offences does not appear to have presented too great a problem to prosecutors in tax evasion cases.

Moves towards confiscation rather than taxation as a means of recouping the profits of crime, or towards charges of laundering the proceeds of tax evasion rather than those of any substantive offence as a means of punishing people involved in acquisitive crime, are radical ones, which endanger the traditionally accepted distinctions between the systems of taxation and criminal justice. Similarly, the use of the Revenue's investigative powers to generate evidence of crime, and the deployment of its power to raise assessments against alleged offenders, are not steps to be undertaken lightly, because of the dangers of discriminatory treatment arising from enhanced State powers. The security agenda emphasizes terrorism, 'organized crime', and 'security'. Increasingly, tax evasion has found its way onto lists of the most serious crimes, as laid out in this agenda.

When in February 2015 the extent of HSBC's involvement in providing shelter for clients' money in Switzerland became clear, amid much sound and fury,[14] a statement made by the relevant minister (David Gauke) referred to a 'long-standing approach' expressing civil penalties to be the preferred HMRC option.[15] There was, in the *HSBC Suisse* affair, considerable evidence of avoidance and some of evasion, but Mr Gauke emphasized the provision of disclosure facilities to encourage tax evaders to sort out their affairs, backed by civil penalties to fine them for the offence, and added that '[w]hen these cases have been taken to the Crown Prosecution Service, it has taken the view that a

[12] FA 2016 s 162 Sched 20.
[13] *R v Natji* [2002] EWCA Crim 271; [2002] 1 WLR 2337.
[14] HC Debates, 11 February 2015 Col 851.
[15] HC Debates, 9 February 2015 Col 556 *et seq*.

successful prosecution would be unlikely without corroborating or additional evidence and just on the basis of the data from the leaks'.[16]

He said that this has been the consistent approach under governments of all parties,[17] and that the government of which he formed part had supported HMRC's approach by increasing investment in its enforcement capacity and strengthening its powers, including increasing the maximum fines for hiding money in tax havens to 200 per cent of the tax evaded.[18] Only one prosecution had been brought in respect of *HSBC Suisse*,[19] and only eleven prosecutions for offshore tax evasion in the preceding five years.[20] Of a list of 130,000 potential tax evaders using the Geneva branch of HSBC, HMRC identified 3,600 potentially non-compliant UK taxpayers, from whom it has recovered £135 million.[21] The *Panama Papers* first elicited statements as to how difficult it would be to bring prosecutions.[22] There may have been elements of expectation-management in Mr Gauke's statement, and also of bargaining within government for funding. A further tranche of funding did follow.[23] In the 2015 Budget around £60 million was earmarked for serious and complex tax-crime investigations,[24] but prosecution can never become the principal weapon against offshore evasion, which must be dealt with predominantly by situational crime prevention.

[16] HC Debates, 9 February 2015 Col 561 (David Gauke). This is doubtless true, but not compelling: the existence of the evidence of the *HSBC Suisse* file could, in many cases, have led to other evidence.

[17] HC Debates, 9 February 2015 Col 556. A further statement was issued by HMRC: <https://www.gov.uk/government/news/statement-by-hmrc-on-tax-evasion-and-the-hsbc-suisse-data-leak>. In another debate the Chancellor, George Osborne, referred to the statement (HC Debates, 7th November 2002 Col 704) by his predecessor, Gordon Brown (HC Debates, 23 February 2015 Col 23).

[18] And see Chapter 8.

[19] Michael Shanly: see Chapter 4, section entitled 'Sentencing'.

[20] Hillyer, Meg (Chair), Public Accounts Committee, *HM Revenue & Customs Performance in 2014–15,* Sixth Report of Session 2015–16, conclusion 9.

[21] This is around the amount gathered in a year from all confiscation orders.

[22] 'Panama Papers: HMRC "Starved" by Austerity Could Not Pursue Tax Evaders Even If It Wanted To', *The Independent*, 6 April 2016; 'Financial Watchdog Says Panama Papers Charges "Will Be Difficult" ', *Financial Times*, 6 April 2016.

[23] This way of funding the SFO ('blockbuster funding') has its critics: Crown Prosecution Service Inspectorate, *Inspection of the Serious Fraud Office Governance Arrangements* (London: May 2016) para 4.35 *et seq.*

[24] 'Budget Boost for HMRC in New Push on Tax Evasion', *The Guardian*, 8 July 2015.

Bibliography

DOCUMENTS AND REPORTS

Auld LJ, *A Review of the Criminal Courts of England and Wales* (Lord Chancellor's Department, September 2001)

Beith, Sir Alan (Chair), Justice Committee, *The Crown Prosecution Service: Gatekeeper of the Criminal Justice System,* Ninth Report of Session 2008–09, Ev 61

Bingham, T (Chair), *Inquiry into the Collapse of BCCI* (HC 198, 1992)

Board of Inland Revenue, *The Inland Revenue and the Taxpayer: Proposals in Response to the Recommendations of the Keith Committee on Income Tax, Capital Gains Tax and Corporation Tax* (London: HMSO, 1986)

Butterfield, Hon Mr Justice, *Review of Criminal Investigations and Prosecutions Conducted by HM Customs and Excise by the Hon Mr Justice Butterfield* (HM Treasury, 2003)

Comptroller and Auditor General, *HM Revenue & Customs: Managing Civil Tax Investigations* (HC 677, 2010–11)

Consultation Paper CP6/2012, *Public Bodies Act 2011: Consultation on an Order to Give Legal Effect to the Administrative Merger of the Crown Prosecution Service and Revenue and Customs Prosecutions Office* (Cm 8250, 2012)

Criminal Law Revision Committee, Eighth Report, *Theft and Related Offences* (Cmnd 2977, 1966)

Criminal Law Revision Committee, Thirteenth Report, *Section 16 of the Theft Act 1968* (Cmnd 6733, 1977)

Draft Proceeds of Crime Bill (Cm 5066, March 2001)

Fisher, Sir Henry (Chair), *Report of an Inquiry into the Circumstances Leading to the Trial of Three Persons on Charges Arising out of the Death of Maxwell Confait and the Fire at 27 Doggett Road, London SE6* (London: HMSO, 1977)

Glidewell, Sir Iain (Chair), *The Review of the Crown Prosecution Service: A Report* (London: HMSO, 1998) Cm 3960

Gower, J, and A, Hammond, *Review of Prosecutions Conducted by the Solicitor's Office of HM Customs and Excise* (2000)

Hillyer, Meg (Chair), Public Accounts Committee, *HM Revenue & Customs Performance in 2014–15,* Sixth Report of Session 2015–16, HC 393

HMIC, *Proceeds of Crime: An Inspection of HMRC's Performance in Addressing the Recovery of the Proceeds of Crime from Tax and Duty Evasion and Benefit Fraud* (London: TSO, 2011)

HM Treasury, *The Informal Economy: The Grabiner Report* (2000)

HM Treasury, *Reform of the Taxation of Non-domiciled Individuals: A Consultation* (HM Treasury, 2011)

HM Treasury, *Reform of the Taxation of Non-domiciled Individuals: Responses to Consultation* (HM Treasury, 2011)

HM Treasury, *Tackling Tax Evasion and Avoidance* (Cm 9047, 2015)

HMRC, *A General Anti-Abuse Rule* (GAAR) consultation document, June 2012

HMRC, *Strengthening the Code of Practice on Taxation for Banks* (HMRC, May 2013)

HMRC, *Report on Our Powers of Entry* (London: HMRC, 2014)

HMRC, *Tackling Offshore Tax Evasion: A New Criminal Offence* (London: HMRC, 2014)

HMRC, *Measuring Tax Gaps* (London: HMRC, 2015)

HMRC, *Strengthening Sanctions for Tax Avoidance—A Consultation on Detailed Proposals* (London: HMRC, 2015)

HMRC, *Tackling Offshore Tax Evasion: A New Corporate Criminal Offence of Failure to Prevent the Facilitation of Evasion* (London: HMRC, 2015)

HMRC, *Tackling Offshore Tax Evasion: Civil Sanctions for Enablers of Offshore Evasion* (London: HMRC, 2015)

HMRC, *Tackling Offshore Tax Evasion: Strengthening Civil Deterrents for Offshore Evaders* (London: HMRC, 2015)

Hodge, Margaret (Chair), Public Accounts Committee, *HM Revenue & Customs: Managing Civil Tax Investigations*, Twenty-seventh Report of Session 2010–11

Hodge, Margaret (Chair), Public Accounts Committee, *Tax Avoidance: The Role of Large Accountancy Firms*, Forty-fourth Report of Session 2012–13, HC 870 (2013)

Hodge, Margaret (Chair), Public Accounts Committee, *Charity Commission: The Cup Trust and Tax Avoidance*, Seventh Report of Session 2013–14

Hodge, Margaret (Chair), Public Accounts Committee, *Tax Avoidance—Google*, Ninth Report of Session 2013–14

Hodge, Margaret (Chair), Public Accounts Committee, *Tax Avoidance: The Role of Large Accountancy Firms (Follow-up)*, Thirty-eighth Report of 2014–15

Hodge, Margaret (Chair), Public Accounts Committee, *Improving Tax Collection*, Fiftieth Report of Session 2014–15

Home Office, *An Independent Prosecution Service for England and Wales* (Cmnd 9074, 1983)

Home Office Consultation Paper CP6/2012, *Public Bodies Act 2011: Consultation on an Order to Give Legal Effect to the Administrative Merger of the Crown Prosecution Service and Revenue and Customs Prosecutions Office* (Cm 8250, 2012)

Home Office and HM Treasury, *Action Plan for Anti-Money Laundering and Counter-Terrorist Finance* (April 2016)

Inland Revenue Statement of Practice, *Civil Tax Penalties and Criminal Prosecution Cases* SP 2/88 (10 May 1988)

Joint Committee on Human Rights (Ninth Report), *Counter-terrorism Policy and Human Rights* (2008)

Joint Committee on Human Rights, *(Eighth Report): Counter-Terrorism Bill* (2008)

Keith of Kinkel, Lord (Chair), *The Enforcement Powers of the Revenue Departments.* Vols 1 and 2 (Cmnd 8822, March 1983)

Keith of Kinkel, Lord (Chair), *The Enforcement Powers of the Revenue Departments.* Vol 3 (Cmnd 9120, Jan 1984)

Keith of Kinkel, Lord (Chair), *The Enforcement Powers of the Revenue Departments*. Vol 4 (Cmnd 9440, Feb 1985)

Law Commission Working Paper No 56, *Conspiracy to Defraud* (1974)

Law Commission Report No 177, *A Criminal Code for England and Wales* (1989)

Law Commission Report No 228, *Conspiracy to Defraud* (1994)

Law Commission Consultation Paper No 145, *Legislating the Criminal Code: Corruption* (1997)

Law Commission Consultation Paper No 155, *Legislating the Criminal Code: Fraud and Deception* (1999)

Law Commission Report No 276, *Fraud* (Cm 5560, 2002)

Law Commission Consultation Paper No 183, *Conspiracy and Attempts* (HMSO, 2007)

Law Commission Report No 311, *Tenth Programme of Law Reform* (2008)

Law Commission, *Misconduct in Public Office Issues Paper 1: The Current Law* (2016)

Leigh, Edward (Chair), Public Accounts Committee, *Tackling VAT Fraud*, Thirty-sixth Report (HC 512, 2004)

Leigh, Edward (Chair), Public Accounts Committee, *The Assets Recovery Agency*, Fiftieth Report of Session 2006–07

McFall, John (Chair), Treasury Committee, *The Merger of Customs & Excise and the Inland Revenue*, Ninth Report of Session 2003–04, HC 556

Ministry of Justice, *Guidance about Procedures which Relevant Commercial Organisations Can Put into Place to Prevent Persons Associated With Them from Bribing (section 9 of the Bribery Act 2010)* (London: Ministry of Justice, 2011)

National Audit Office, *Confiscation Orders* (HC 738, 2013–14)

National Audit Office, *Tackling Tax Fraud: How HMRC Responds to Tax Evasion, the Hidden Economy and Criminal Attacks* (HC 610, 2015–16)

O'Donnell, Gus, *Financing Britain's Future: A Review of the Revenue Departments* (HM Treasury, March 2004, Cm 6163)

Philips, Sir Cyril (Chair), *Royal Commission on Criminal Procedure* (Cmnd 8092, 1981)

Post-Legislative Assessment of the Fraud Act 2006 carried out by the Ministry of Justice, Memorandum to the Justice Select Committee (Cm 8372, 2012)

Radcliffe, Lord (Chair), *Royal Commission on the Taxation of Profits and Income*, Final Report (London: Cmd 9474, 1956)

RCPO, *Annual Report* 2008–09 (London: Stationery Office, HC 658)

Roskill, Lord (Chair), *Fraud Trials Committee Report* (1986)

Seely, Antony, *Tax Avoidance: A General Anti-abuse Rule* (HC Library Standard Note: SN6265 2015)

Sentencing Council, *Fraud, Bribery and Money Laundering Offences: Definitive Guidelines* (2014)

Taylor, Martin, *Report on Tobacco Smuggling* (1999), <https://www.gov.uk/government/uploads/system/uploads/attachment_data/file/220997/foi_240712.pdf>

Vaz, Keith (Chair), Home Affairs Committee, *Evaluating the New Architecture of Policing: The College of Policing and the NCA*, Tenth Report of 2014–15

Vaz, Keith (Chair), Home Affairs Committee, *The Work of the UK Border Agency*, Fourteenth Report of 2012–13

Vaz, Keith (Chair), Home Affairs Committee, *Tobacco Smuggling*, First Report of Session 2014–15

GENERAL BIBLIOGRAPHY

Albrecht, AR, 'The Enforcement of Taxation under International Law' (1953) 30 *British Yearbook of International Law* 454

Alldridge, Peter, 'Are Tax Evasion Offences Predicate Offences for Money laundering Offences?' (2001) 4 *Journal of Money Laundering Control* 350–9

Alldridge, Peter, 'Smuggling, Confiscation and Forfeiture' (2002) 65 *Modern Law Review* 781–91

Alldridge, Peter, *Money Laundering Law* (Oxford: Hart, 2003)

Alldridge, Peter, 'Money Laundering and Globalization' (2008) 35 *Journal of Law and Society* 437–63

Alldridge, Peter, and Ann Mumford, 'Tax Evasion and the Proceeds of Crime Act 2002' (2005) 25 *Legal Studies* 353–73

Alldridge, Peter, 'The Limits of Confiscation' [2011] *Criminal Law Review* 827–43

Alldridge, Peter, 'The Bribery Act 2010—Guidance to Corporations' (2012) 6 *Law and Financial Markets Review* 140–4

Alldridge, Peter, 'Two Key Areas in Proceeds of Crime Law' [2014] *Criminal Law Review* 170–88

Alldridge, Peter, 'Some Uses of Legal Fictions in Criminal Law' in Twining, William, and Maksymilian Del Mar (eds), *Legal Fictions in Theory and Practice* (Springer, 2015) 367–84

Alldridge, Peter, *What Went Wrong with Money Laundering Law?* (London: Palgrave, 2016)

Alschuler, AW, 'Plea Bargaining and Its History' (1979) 79 *Columbia Law Review* 1–43

Alschuler, AW, 'Mediation with a Mugger: The Shortage of Adjudicative Services and the Need for a Two-tier System in Civil Cases' (1986) 99 *Harvard Law Review* 1808–59

Anderson, Gary M, William F Shughart, and Robert D Tollison, 'Adam Smith in the Customhouse' (1985) 93 *Journal of Political Economy* 740–59

Andreas, Peter, 'Smuggling Wars: Law Enforcement and Law Evasion in a Changing World' (1998) 4 *Transnational Organized Crime* 75–90

Ashworth, Andrew, 'Developments in the Public Prosecutor's Office in England and Wales' (2000) 8 *European Journal of Crime, Criminal Law and Criminal Justice* 257

Ashworth, Andrew, 'Testing Fidelity to Legal Values: Official Involvement and Criminal Justice' (2000) 63 *Modern Law Review* 633

Ashworth, Andrew, 'Self-incrimination in European Human Rights Law—A Pregnant Pragmatism' (2008) 30 *Cardozo Law Review* 751

Ashworth, William J, *Customs and Excise Trade, Production, and Consumption in England 1640–1845* (Oxford: Oxford Univeristy Press, 2003)

Atton, H, and H Holland, *The King's Customs* (London: Frank Cass & Co Ltd, 1967)

Avakian, Spurgeon, 'Net Worth Computations as Proof of Tax Evasion' (1954) 10 *Tax Law Review* 431

Avery Jones, John, 'The Sources of Addington's Income Tax' in Tiley, John (ed), *Studies in the History of Tax Law* Vol 1 (Oxford: Hart, 2004) 1

Baker, Philip, 'Finance Act Notes: Section 218 and Schedule 36: The UK–Switzerland Rubik Agreement' [2012] *British Tax Review* 489

Baker, Philip, 'The BEPS Project: Disclosure of Aggressive Tax Planning Schemes' (2015) 43 *Intertax* 85–90

Baker, Philip, 'The Diverted Profits Tax—A Partial Response' [2015] *British Tax Review* 167–71

Baker, Russell, 'Taxation: Potential Destroyer of Crime' (1951) 29 *Chicago-Kent Law Review* 197

Baldwin, John, and Michael McConville, *Negotiated Justice: Pressures on Defendants to Plead Guilty* (London: Martin Robertson, 1977)

Barron, Ann, and Colin Scott, 'The Citizens Charter Programme' (1992) 55 *Modern Law Review* 526

Bastin, Lucas, 'Should "Independence" of In-house Counsel Be a Condition Precedent to a Claim of Legal Professional Privilege in Respect of Communications between Them and Their Employer Clients?' [2011] *Civil Justice Quarterly* 33

Behrens, Frederic, 'Using a Sledgehammer to Crack a Nut: Why FATCA Will Not Stand' (2013) *Wisconsin Law Review* 205–36

Berger, Mark, 'Self-incrimination and the European Court of Human Rights: Procedural Issues in the Enforcement of the Right to Silence' (2007) 5 *European Human Rights Law Review* 514–33

Blank, Joshua, 'In Defense of Individual Tax Privacy' (2011) 61 *Emory Law Journal* 265

Blum, Jack et al, *Financial Havens, Banking Secrecy and Money laundering*, UNDCP Technical Series Issue 8 (New York City: UN, 1998)

Blumenthal, Marsha, Charles Christian, Joel Slemrod, and Matthew G Smith, 'Do Normative Appeals Affect Tax Compliance? Evidence from a Controlled Experiment in Minnesota' (2001) 54 *National Tax Journal* 125

Boll, M, *Plea Bargaining and Agreement in the Criminal Process* (Hamburg: Diplomica Verlag, 2009)

Boon, Andrew, *The Ethics and Conduct of Lawyers in England and Wales* (Oxford: Bloomsbury Publishing, 3rd edn, 2014)

Braithwaite, John, *Markets in Vice, Markets in Virtue* (Oxford: Oxford University Press, 2005)

Braithwaite, John, and Peter Drahos, 'Zero Tolerance, Naming and Shaming: Is There a Case for It with Crimes of the Powerful?' (2002) 35 *Australian & New Zealand Journal of Criminology* 269–88

Braithwaite, Valerie, 'Criminal Prosecution within Responsive Regulatory Practice' (2010) 9 *Criminology & Public Policy* 515–23

Braithwaite, Valerie, 'Resistant and Dismissive Defiance towards Tax Authorities' in Crawford, Adam, and Anthea Hucklesby (eds), *Legitimacy and Compliance in Criminal Justice* (London: Routledge, 2012) 91

Braithwaite, Valerie A, *Defiance in Taxation and Governance: Resisting and Dismissing Authority in a Democracy* (Cheltenham: Edward Elgar Publishing, 2009)

Brants, Chrisje, 'Consensual Criminal Procedures: Plea and Confession Bargaining and Abbreviated Procedures to Simplify Criminal Procedure' (2007) 11 *Electronic Journal of Comparative Law*, <www.ejcl.org/111/article111-6.pdf>

Brants, Chrisje, and Allard Ringnalda, *Issues of Convergence: Inquisitorial Prosecution in England and Wales?* (Nijmegen: Wolf Legal Publishers, 2011)

Bridges, Martyn, Paul Atkinson, Robert Rhodes, and Rowan Bosworth-Davies, '*Regina v Charlton, Cunningham, Kitchen and Wheeler* [1995]' (1999) 2 *Journal of Money Laundering Control* 197–208

Brown, B, 'Inland Revenue Powers of Search' [1999] *British Tax Review* 16

Brown, Logan, and Aurash Jamali, 'Tax Violations' (2014) 51 *American Criminal Law Review* 1751

Brownlee, Ian, 'The Statutory Charging Scheme in England and Wales: Towards a Unified Prosecution System?' [2004] *Criminal Law Review* 896

Bucci, Amy, 'Taxation of Illegal Narcotics: A Violation of the Fifth Amendment Rights or an Innovative Tool in the War Against Drugs?' (2012) 11 *Journal of Civil Rights and Economic Development* 22

Bucy, Pamela H, 'Criminal Tax Fraud: The Downfall of Murderers, Madams and Thieves' (1997) 29 *Arizona State Law Journal* 639

Burton, Mandy, 'Reviewing Crown Prosecution Service Decisions Not to Prosecute' [2001] *Criminal Law Review* 374

Button, Mark, 'Fraud Investigation and the "Flawed Architecture" of Counter Fraud Entities in the United Kingdom' (2011) 39 *International Journal of Law, Crime and Justice* 249–65

Cabinet Office, *Security in a Global Hub—Establishing the UK's New Border Arrangements* (London: Cabinet Office, 2009)

Calderón Carrero, José Manuel, and Alberto Quintas Seara, 'The Concept of "Aggressive Tax Planning" Launched by the OECD and the EU Commission in the BEPS Era: Redefining the Border between Legitimate and Illegitimate Tax Planning' (2016) 44 *Intertax* 206–26

Campbell, Liz, *Organised Crime and the Law* (Oxford: Hart, 2013)

Campbell, RH, AS Skinner, and WB Todd (eds), *Adam Smith, The Wealth of Nations* (Oxford: Oxford University Press, 3rd edn, 1976)

Carson, Edward, *The Ancient and Rightful Customs: A History of the English Customs Service* (London: Faber and Faber, 1972)

Cebula, Richard J, and Edgar L Feige, 'America's Unreported Economy: Measuring the Size, Growth and Determinants of Income Tax Evasion in the US' (2012) 57 *Crime, Law and Social Change* 265–85

Chitty, Joseph, *Wyndham Beawes's Lex Mercatoria* (London: Rivington, 6th edn, 1813)

Choo, Andrew L-T, *Abuse of Process and Judicial Stays of Criminal Proceedings* (Oxford: Oxford University Press, 2008)

Choo, Andrew L-T, *The Privilege against Self-incrimination and Criminal Justice* (Oxford: Hart Publishing, 2013)

Christensen, John, 'The Hidden Trillions: Secrecy, Corruption, and the Offshore Interface' (2012) 57 *Crime, Law and Social Change* 325–43

Clarkson, Christopher, 'Attempt: The Conduct Requirement' (2009) 29 *Oxford Journal of Legal Studies* 25–41

Clarkson, Christopher MV, and Sally Cunningham (eds), *Criminal Liability for Non-aggressive Death* (Farnham: Ashgate, 2013)

Cockfield, Roger, and Mary Mulholland, 'The Implications of Illegal Trading' [1995] *British Tax Review* 572

Colley, Robert, 'Mid Victorian Employees and the Taxman: A Study in Information Gathering by the State in 1860' (2001) 21 *Oxford Journal of Legal Studies* 593–608

Colley, Robert, 'The Arabian Bird: A Study of Income Tax Evasion in Mid-Victorian Britain' [2001] *British Tax Review* 207–21

Colley, Robert, 'Railways and the Mid-Victorian Income Tax' (2003) 24 *Journal of Transport History* 78–102

Colley, Robert, 'The Shoreditch Tax Frauds: A Study of the Relationship between the State and Civil Society in 1860' (2005) 78 *Historical Research* 540–62

Collier, Richard, 'Intentions, Banks, Politics and the Law: The UK Code of Practice on Taxation for Banks' [2014] *British Tax Review* 478

Corker, David, Gemma Tombs, and Tamara Chisholm, 'Sections 71 and 72 of Serious Organised Crime and Police Act 2005: Whither the Common Law?' [2009] *Criminal Law Review* 261

Cory, Richard, 'Taxing the Proceeds of Crime' [2007] *British Tax Review* 356

Cramton, Roger C, 'The Lawyer as Whistleblower: Confidentiality and the Government Lawyer' (1991) 5 *Georgetown Journal of Legal Ethics* 291–315

Criminal Assets Bureau, *Annual Report 2014* (Dublin: Criminal Assets Bureau, 2016)

Cross, Rupert, and Colin Tapper, *Cross and Tapper on Evidence* (London: Butterworths, 8th edn, 1995)

Crown Prosecution Service Inspectorate, *Inspection of the Serious Fraud Office Governance Arrangements* (London: HM Crown Prosecution Service Inspectorate, May 2016)

Daly, Stephen, 'Recent Developments in Tax Law: *Vires* Revisited' (2016) 2 *Public Law* 190–8

Damaska, Mirjan, *The Faces of Justice and State Authority* (New Haven, CT: Yale University Press, 1986)

Daunton, Martin, *Just Taxes* (Cambridge: Cambridge University Press, 2002)

Davis, Ralph, 'The Rise of Protection in England, 1689–1786' (1966) 19 *Economic History Review* 306–17

de la Feria, Rita, and Stefan Vogenauer (eds), *Prohibition of Abuse of Law: A New General Principle of EU Law?* (Oxford: Hart, 2011)

Delalande, Nicolas, and Romain Huret, 'Tax Resistance: A Global History?' (2013) 25 *Journal of Policy History* 301–7

Denealt, Sean, 'Foreign Account Tax Compliance Act: A Step in the Wrong Direction' (2014) 24 *Indiana International & Comparative Law Review* 729

Devereux, Michael, Judith Freedman, and John Vella, *Review of DOTAS and the Tax Avoidance Landscape* (Oxford: Oxford University Press, 2012)

Dillon, Patrick, *The Much-lamented Death of Madam Geneva: The Eighteenth-century Gin Craze* (London: Review, 2002)

Dixon, Dennis, 'Legal Professional Privilege and Advice from Non-lawyers' [2010] *British Tax Review* 83–101

Duff, RA, Lindsay Farmer, SE Marshall, Massimo Renzo, and Victor Tadros, 'Introduction' in Duff et al (eds), *Criminalization: The Political Morality of the Criminal Law* (Oxford: Oxford University Press, 2014) 1–53

Duke, Steven, 'Prosecutions for Attempts to Evade Income Tax: A Discordant View of a Procedural Hybrid' (1966) 76 *Yale Law Journal* 1

Elliffe, Craig, 'The Thickness of a Prison Wall—When Does Tax Avoidance Become a Criminal Offence?' (2011) 17 *New Zealand Business Law Quarterly* 441–66

Emmenegger, Patrick, 'Swiss Banking Secrecy and the Problem of International Cooperation in Tax Matters: A Nut too Hard to Crack?' (2015) *Regulation & Governance*, published online before print

Emsley, Clive, *Crime and Society in England, 1750–1900* (London: Routledge, 3rd edn, 2010)

Fan, Mary D, 'Disciplining Criminal Justice: The Peril amid the Promise of Numbers' (2007) 26 *Yale Law & Policy Review* 1–74

Farmer, Lindsay, 'Reconstructing the English Codification Debate: The Criminal Law Commissioners, 1833–45' (2000) 18 *Law and History Review* 397–426

Farnsworth, A, 'The Income Tax Act, 1842—A Century of Judicial Interpretation' (1942) 58 *Law Quarterly Review* 314–33

Farnsworth, A, 'Addington, Author of the Modern Income Tax' (1950) 66 *Law Quarterly Review* 358

Fisher, Jonathan, 'The Anti-Money Laundering Disclosure Regime and the Collection of Revenue in the United Kingdom' [2010] *British Tax Review* 235

Fisher, Jonathan, 'Unwarranted Conduct' (2012) 8 *Tax Journal* 1145

Fisher, Jonathan, 'HSBC, Tax Evasion and Criminal Prosecution' (March 2015) *Tax Journal* 2

Freedman, Judith, 'Interpreting Tax Statutes: Tax Avoidance and the Intention of Parliament' (2007) 123 *Law Quarterly Review* 53

Freedman, Judith, 'Improving (Not Perfecting) Tax Legislation: Rules and Principles Revisited' [2010] *British Tax Review* 717

Freedman, Judith, 'Lord Hoffmann, Tax Law and Principles', in Davies, Paul, and Justine Pila (eds), *The Jurisprudence of Lord Hoffmann* (Oxford: Hart, 2015) 269

Gallant, Michelle, 'Tax and the Proceeds of Crime: A New Approach to Tainted Finance?' (2013) 16 *Journal of Money Laundering Control* 119–25

Gammie, Malcolm, 'Moral Taxation, Immoral Avoidance—What Role for the Law?' [2013] *British Tax Review* 577

Gammie, Malcolm, and John Kay, 'Taxation, Authority and Discretion' (1983) 4 *Fiscal Studies* 46–61

Gardner, John, 'Wrongs and Faults', in AP Simester (ed), *Appraising Strict Liability* (Oxford: Oxford University Press, 2005) 51–80

Garoupa, Nuno, Anthony Ogus, and Andrew Sanders, 'The Investigation and Prosecution of Regulatory Offences: Is There an Economic Case for Integration?' (2011) 70 *Cambridge Law Journal* 229–59

Genschel, Philipp, and Peter Schwarz, 'Tax Competition: A Literature Review' (2011) 9 *Socio-economic Review* 339–70

Gillard, Michael, *In The Name of Charity: The Rossminster Affair* (London: Chatto & Windus, 1987)

Glantz, Andrew E, 'A Tax on Light and Air: Impact of the Window Duty on Tax Administration and Architecture, 1696–1851' (2008) 15 *Penn History Review* 1–23

Glazebrook, Peter, 'Revising the Theft Acts' (1993) 52 *Cambridge Law Journal* 191

Gololobov, Dmitry, 'The Yukos Tax Case or Ramsay['s] Adventures in Russia' (2008) 7 *Business Law Review* 165

Gordon, Richard, and Andrew P Morriss, 'Moving Money: International Financial Flows, Taxes, and Money Laundering' (2014) 37 *Hastings International and Comparative Law Review* 1–120

Graetz, Michael, and Michael O'Hear, 'The "Original Intent" of US International Taxation' (1997) 51 *Duke Law Journal* 1021

Gras, NSB, 'The Tudor "Books of Rates": A Chapter in the History of the English Customs' (1912) 26 *Quarterly Journal of Economics* 766–75

Gravelle, Jane G, *Tax Havens: International Tax Avoidance and Evasion* (Philadelphia, PA: Diane Publishing, 2013)

Gravelle, Jane G, *Tax Havens: International Tax Avoidance and Evasion*, Congressional Research Service 7-5700 (Washington, DC: Congressional Research Service, 2014)

Gray, Charles M, RH Helmholz, John H Langbein, and Eben Moglen, *The Privilege against Self-incrimination: Its Origins and Development* (Chicago, IL: University of Chicgo Press, 1997)

Green, Stuart, 'Moral Ambiguity in White Collar Criminal Law' (2004) 18 *Notre Dame Journal of Law, Ethics and Public Policy* 501

Green, Stuart, *Lying, Cheating and Stealing* (Oxford: Oxford University Press, 2005)

Green, Stuart P, 'Thieving and Receiving: Overcriminalizing the Possession of Stolen Property' (2011) 14 *New Criminal Law Review* 35–54

Griew, Edward, 'Dishonesty: The Objections to Feely and Ghosh' [1985] *Criminal Law Review* 341

Griffiths, Hugh, 'Smoking Guns: European Cigarette Smuggling in the 1990s' (2004) 6 *Global Crime* 185–200

Grinberg, Itai, 'The Battle Over Taxing Offshore Accounts' (2012) 60 *UCLA Law Review* 304–506

GSAW[heatcroft], 'The Hinchy Case' (1960) 23 *Modern Law Review* 425–8

Guex, Sébastien, 'The Origins of the Swiss Banking Secrecy Law and Its Repercussions for Swiss Federal Policy' (2000) 74 *Business History Review* 237–66

Hall, Jerome, 'Nulla Poena Sine Lege' (1937) 47 *Yale Law Journal* 165

Hall, Jerome, *Theft, Law and Society* (Bloomington, IN: Bobbs Merrill, 2nd edn, 1952)

Hallsworth, Michael, John A List, Robert Metcalfe, and Ivo Vlaev (2014), 'The Behavioralist Tax Collector: Using Natural Field Experiments to Enhance Tax Compliance', <www.nber.org/papers/w20007>

Halpin, Andrew, 'The Test for Dishonesty' [1996] *Criminal Law Review* 283

Harris, Peter, and David Oliver, *International Commercial Tax* (Cambridge: Cambridge University Press, 2010)

Hatfield, Michael, 'Tax Lawyers, Tax Defiance, and the Ethics of Casual Conversation' (2011) 10 *Florida Tax Review* 2010–26

Hazard, GC, 'An Historical Perspective on the Attorney–Client Privilege' (1978) 66 *California Law Review* 1061

Heggstad, Kari, and Odd-Helge Fjeldstad, 'How Banks Assist Capital Flight from Africa: A Literature Review' *CMI Report* 2010, no. 6

Henry, James, *The Price of Offshore Revisited* (Tax Justice Network, 2012), <http://www.taxjustice.net/cms/upload/pdf/Price_of_Offshore_Revisited_120722.pdf>

Higgins, Andrew, 'Corporate Abuse of Legal Professional Privilege' (2008) 27 *Civil Justice Quarterly* 377–406

Higgins, Andrew, 'Legal Advice Privilege and its Relevance to Corporations' (2010) 73 *Modern Law Review* 371–98

Higgins, Andrew, *Legal Professional Privilege for Corporations: A Guide to Four Major Common Law Jurisdictions* (Oxford: Oxford University Press, 2014)

Higgins, Andrew, and Adrian Zuckerman, 'Re *Prudential plc* [2013] UKSC 1: The Supreme Court Leaves to Parliament the Issue of Privilege for Tax Advice by Accountants, What Parliament Should Do Is Restrict Privilege for Tax Advice Given by Lawyers' (2013) 32 *Civil Justice Quarterly* 313

Hill, Christopher, *Reformation to Industrial Revolution* (Harmondsworth: Penguin Books, 1969)

HMRC Criminal Investigation Policy, 2015, <www.hmrc.gov.uk/prosecutions/crim-inv-policy.htm>

Hodgson, Jacqueline, and Victor Tadros, 'How to Make a Terrorist Out of Nothing' (2009) 72 *Modern Law Review* 984–98

Hoffmann, Lord, 'Tax Avoidance' [2005] *British Tax Review* 197

Holcomb, Jefferson E, Tomislav V Kovandzic, and Marian R Williams, 'Civil Asset Forfeiture, Equitable Sharing, and Policing for Profit in the United States' (2011) 39 *Journal of Criminal Justice* 273–85

Holdsworth, Sir William, *History of English Law* (London: Methuen, 2nd edn, 1937)

Hope-Jones, Arthur, *Income Tax in the Napoleonic Wars* (Cambridge: Cambridge University Press, 1939)

Horder, Jeremy, '*Rex v Bembridge* (1783)' in Mares, Henry, Phil Handler, and Ian Williams (eds), *Landmark Cases in Criminal Law* (Oxford: Bloomsbury, 2017) 81–101

Hornsby, Rob, and Dick Hobbs, 'A Zone of Ambiguity: The Political Economy of Cigarette Bootlegging' (2007) 47 *British Journal of Criminology* 551–71

Humphry, William Woolrych, *The History and Results of the Present Capital Punishments in England* (London: Saunders and Benning, 1832)

Huret, Romain D, *American Tax Resisters* (Cambridge, MA: Harvard University Press, 2014)

Husak, Douglas, 'The De Minimis "Defence" to Criminal Liability' in Duff, RA, and Stuart Green (eds), *Philosophical Foundations of Criminal Law* (Oxford: Oxford University Press, 2011) 328–51

International Monetary Fund, *Anti-Money Laundering and Combating the Financing of Terrorism (AML/CFT)—Report on the Review of the Effectiveness of the Program Prepared by the Legal Department* (Washington, DC: International Monetary Fund, 2011)

Ives, Dale E, and Stephen GA Pitel, 'Filling In the Blanks for Litigation Privilege: *Blank v Canada (Minister for Justice)*' (2007) *International Journal of Evidence and Proof* 49

Jenkins, Rhys, and Peter Newell, 'CSR, Tax and Development' (2013) 34 *Third World Quarterly* 378

Kadish, Sanford H, 'Codifiers of the Criminal Law: Wechsler's Predecessors' (1978) 78 *Columbia Law Review* 1098–144

Karlinsky, Stewart, Hughlene Burton, and Cindy Blanthorne, 'Perceptions of Tax Evasion as a Crime' (2004) 2 *E-Journal of Tax Research* 226–40

Karzon, Allaire Urban, 'International Tax Evasion: Spawned in the United States and Nurtured by Secrecy Havens' (1983) 16 *Vanderbilt Journal of Transnational Law* 757–832

Katz, Leo, 'In Defense of Tax Shelters' (2007) 26 *Virginia Tax Review* 799

King, Anthony, and Ivor Crewe, *The Blunders of Our Governments* (London: Oneworld Publications, 2013)

King, Colin, and Clive Walker, 'Counter Terrorism Financing: A Redundant Fragmentation?' (2015) 6 *New Journal of European Criminal Law* 372–95

Kobler, John, *Capone: The Life and World of Al Capone* (Boston, MA: Da Capo Press, reprint edn, 1992)

Kornhauser, Marjorie E, 'For God and Country: Taxing Conscience' [1999] *Wisconsin Law Review* 939–1016

Kwon, Michelle M, 'The Criminality of Tax Planning' (2015) 18 *Florida Tax Review* 153

Lazar, Leonard, 'Finance Act 1965: The Capital Gains Tax' (1966) 29 *Modern Law Review* 181

Lee, Natalie, *Revenue Law: Principles and Practice* (Haywards Heath: Bloomsbury, 2015)

Leftwich, BR, 'The Later History and Administration of the Customs Revenue in England (1671–1814)' (1930) 13 *Transactions of the Royal Historical Society (Fourth Series)* 187–203

Léonard, Sarah, and Christian Kaunert, '"Between a Rock and a Hard Place?" The European Union's Financial Sanctions against Suspected Terrorists, Multilateralism and Human Rights' (2012) 47 *Cooperation and Conflict* 473–94

Lethaby, H, 'Reflections on Tax and the City' (2014) 1220 *Tax Journal* 10

Levi, Michael, 'Serious Tax Fraud and Noncompliance: A Review of Evidence on the Differential Impact of Criminal and Noncriminal Proceedings' (2010) 9 *Criminology and Public Policy* 493–514

Levi, Michael, *Regulating Fraud* (London: Routledge Revivals, 2014)

Levi, Michael, *The Investigation, Prosecution, and Trial of Serious Fraud* (Royal Commission on Criminal Justice Research Study No 14, 1993)

Likhovski, Assaf, 'Tax Law and Public Opinion: Explaining IRC v Duke of Westminster' in Tiley, John (ed), *Studies in the History of Tax Law* Vol 2 (Oxford: Hart, 2007) 183

Litman, Harry, 'Pretextual Prosecution' (2003) 92 *Georgia Law Journal* 1137

Loughrey, Joan, 'Legal Advice Privilege and the Corporate Client' (2005) 9 *International Journal of Evidence and Proof* 183–203

Loughrey, Joan, *Corporate Lawyers and Corporate Governance* (Cambridge: Cambridge University Press, 2011)

Loughrey, JM, 'An Unsatisfactory Stalemate: *R (on the application of Prudential plc) v Special Commissioner of Income Tax*' (2014) 18 *International Journal of Evidence and Proof* 65–77

Marriott, Lisa, 'Justice and the Justice System: A Comparison of Tax Evasion and Welfare Fraud in Australia and New Zealand' (2013) 22 *Griffith Law Review* 403

Marriott, Lisa, 'An Investigation of Attitudes towards Tax Evasion and Welfare Fraud in New Zealand' (2015) *Australian & New Zealand Journal of Criminology*, published online before print

Mba, Osita, 'Transparency and Accountability of Tax Administration in the UK: The Nature and Scope of Taxpayer Confidentiality' [2012] *British Tax Review* 187–225

McBarnet, Doreen, 'The Royal Commission and the Judges' Rules' (1981) 8 *British Journal of Law and Society* 109–17

McBarnet, Doreen, 'Law, Policy, and Legal Avoidance: Can Law Effectively Implement Egalitarian Policies' (1988) 15 *Journal of Law and Society* 113

McBarnet, Doreen, 'It's Not What You Do But the Way That You Do It: Tax Evasion, Tax Avoidance and the Boundaries of Deviance', in Downes, D (ed), *Unravelling Criminal Justice* (London: Macmillan, 1992) 247–68

McBarnet, Doreen, 'Legitimate Rackets: Tax Evasion, Tax Avoidance, and the Boundaries of Legality' (1992) 3 *Journal of Human Justice* 56–74

McKeever, Grainne, 'Social Citizenship and Social Security Fraud in the UK and Australia, (2012) 46 *Social Policy & Administration* 465–82

McLaughlin, Mark (ed), *HMRC Investigations Handbook 2015–16* (London: Bloomsbury, 2015)

McLynn, Frank, *Crime and Punishment in Eighteenth Century England* (London: Routledge, 3rd edn, 2013)

Middleton, David, and Michael Levi, 'Let Sleeping Lawyers Lie: Organized Crime, Lawyers and the Regulation of Legal Services' (2015) 55 *British Journal of Criminology* 647–68

Mill, John Stuart, Principles of Political Economy (1848) <http://eet.pixel-online.org/files/etranslation/original/Mill,%20Principles%20of%20Political%20Economy.pdf>

Miller, Angharad, and Lynne Oats, *Principles of International Taxation* (London: Bloomsbury, 5th edn, 2016)

Mirfield, Peter, 'A Challenge to the Declaratory Theory of Law' (2008) 124 *Law Quarterly Review* 190–95

Monod, Paul, 'Dangerous Merchandise: Smuggling, Jacobitism, and Commercial Culture in Southeast England, 1690–1760' (1991) 30 *Journal of British Studies* 150–82

Monroe, HH, *Intolerable Inquisition? Reflections on the Law of Tax* (London: Stevens, 1981)

Moohr, Geraldine Szott, 'Prosecutorial Power in an Adversarial System: Lessons from Current White Collar Cases and the Inquisitorial Model' (2004) 8 *Buffalo Criminal Law Review* 165–220

Moohr, Geraldine Szott, 'Tax Evasion as White Collar Fraud' (2009) 9 *Houston Business and Tax Law Journal* 207–445

Morris, Donald, *Tax Cheating: Illegal—But Is It Immoral?* (Albany, NY: SUNY Press, 2012)

Morriss, Andrew P, and Lotta Moberg, 'Cartelizing Taxes: Understanding the OECD's Campaign Against "Harmful Tax Competition"' (2012) 4 *Columbia Journal of Tax Law* 1

Morse, Susan, 'Ask for Help, Uncle Sam: The Future of Global Tax Reporting' (2012) 57 *Villanova Law Review* 529–50

Mowbray, Alastair, 'The Compounding of Proceedings by the Custom and Excise: Calculating the Legal Implications' [1988] *British Tax Review* 290

Mumford, Ann, 'VAT, Taxation and Prostitution: Feminist Perspectives on Polok' (2005) 13 *Feminist Legal Studies* 163

Murphy, Richard, *The Joy of Tax* (London: Bantam, 2015) 7

Naylor, RT, *Counterfeit Crime* (Montreal: McGill-Queen's University Press, 2015)

Neidle, Dan, 'The Diverted Profits Tax—Flawed by Design' [2015] *British Tax Review* 147–66

O'Brien, Patrick K, and Philip Hunt, 'The Emergence and Consolidation of Excises in the English Fiscal System before the Glorious Revolution' [1997] *British Tax Review* 35–58

Oates, Chris, and Ed Dwan, 'Hansard R.I.P' *Taxation* (22 September 2005) 686

Oats, Lynne, and Pauline Sadler, '"This Great Crisis in the Republick of Letters"—The Introduction in 1712 of Stamp Duties on Newspapers and Pamphlets' [2002] *British Tax Review* 353

OECD, *Taxation and the Abuse of Bank Secrecy* (Paris: OECD, 1985)

OECD, *Harmful Tax Competition: An Emerging Global Issue* (Paris: OECD, 1998)

OECD, *Money Laundering Awareness Handbook for Tax Examiners and Tax Auditors* (Paris: OECD, 2009)

OECD, *The Era of Bank Secrecy Is Over* (Paris: OECD, 2011)

OECD, *Action Plan on Base Erosion and Profit Shifting* (Paris: OECD, 2013)

Office of Fair Trading, *Competition in Professions: A Report by the Director General of Fair Trading* (London: The Stationery Office, 2001)

Ordower, Henry, 'Utopian Visions toward a Grand Unified Global Income Tax' (2013) 14 *Florida Tax Review* 361

Ormerod, David, 'Cheating the Public Revenue' [1998] *Criminal Law Review* 627–45

Ormerod, David, 'Hansard Invitations and Confessions in the Criminal Trial' (2000) 4 *International Journal of Evidence and Proof* 147

Ormerod, David, 'Summary Evasion of Income Tax' [2002] *Criminal Law Review* 3–24

Ormerod, David, 'The Fraud Act 2006—Criminalizing Lying?' [2007] *Criminal Law Review* 193

Ormerod, David, and David Williams, *Smith's Law of Theft* (Oxford: Oxford University Press, 9th edn, 2007)

Ormerod, David, and Karl Laird, *Smith & Hogan's Criminal Law* (Oxford: Oxford University Press, 14th edn, 2015)

Palan, Ronen, 'Financial Centers: The British Empire, City-States and Commercially-Oriented Politics' (2010) 11 *Theoretical Inquiries in Law* 142–67

Palan, Ronen, Richard Murphy, and Christian Chavagneux, *Tax Havens: How Globalization Really Works* (Ithaca, NY: Cornell University Press, 2013)

Parker, Leanna T, 'Southampton's Sixteenth-century Illicit Trade: An Examination of the 1565 Port Survey' (2015) 27 *International Journal of Maritime History* 268–84

Parrot, David, and John F Avery Jones, 'Seven Appeals and an Acquittal: The Singer Family and their Tax Cases' [2008] *British Tax Review* 56

Passas, Nikos, 'Terrorism Finance: Financial Controls and Counter-proliferation of Weapons of Mass Destruction' (2012) 44 *Case Western Reserve Journal of International Law* 747–955

Passmore, C, 'The Future of Legal Professional Privilege' (1993) 3 *International Journal of Evidence and Proof* 71–86

Pattenden, Rosemary, 'Legal Professional Privilege' (2011) *International Journal of Evidence and Proof* 79

Perkins, Rachelle Holmes, 'The Tax Lawyer as Gatekeeper' (2010) 49 *University of Louisville Law Review* 185–230

Picciotto, Sol, 'Offshore: The State as Legal Fiction' in Hampton, Mark P, and Jason P Abbott (eds), *Offshore Finance Centres and Tax Havens: The Rise of Global Capital* (London: Palgrave, 1999) 43

Picciotto, Sol, *Is the International Tax System Fit for Purpose, Especially for Developing Countries?* ICTD Working Paper 13 (Brighton: Institute of Development Studies, 2013)

Preuss, Lawrence, 'Punishment by Analogy in National Socialist Penal Law' (1936) 26 *Journal of Criminal Law and Criminology* 847

Redmayne, Mike, 'Rethinking the Privilege against Self-incrimination' (2007) 27 *Oxford Journal of Legal Studies* 209–32

Reeves, John, *A History of the Law of Shipping and Navigation* (London: Brooke, 1792)

Reuter, Peter (ed), *Draining Development? Controlling Flows of Illicit Funds from Developing Countries* (Washington, DC: World Bank, 2012)

Rice, Ralph S, 'Judicial Techniques in Combating Tax Avoidance' (1953) 51 *Michigan Law Review* 1021–52

Richman, Daniel C, and William J Stuntz, 'Al Capone's Revenge: An Essay on the Political Economy of Pretextual Prosecution' (2005) 105 *Columbia Law Review* 583–640

Roberge, Ian, 'Misguided Policies in the War on Terror? The Case for Disentangling Terrorist Financing from Money Laundering' (2007) 27 *Politics* 196–203

Robinson, Paul, 'Criminal Law Defenses: A Systematic Analysis' (1982) 82 *Columbia Law Review* 199–291

Sabine, Basil, 'Life and Taxes 1932–1992. Part 3: 1965–1992: Reform, Rossminster and Reductions' [1993] *British Tax Review* 504

Sabine, BEV, *History of Income Tax* (London: George Allen & Unwin, 1966)

Salter, David, 'Some Thoughts on Fraudulent Evasion of Income Tax' [2002] *British Tax Review* 489

Sanders, Andrew, 'An Independent Crown Prosecution Service?' [1986] *Criminal Law Review* 16

Schoueri, Eduardo Luís, and Mateus Calicchio Barbosa, 'Transparency: From Tax Secrecy to the Simplicity and Reliability of the Tax System' [2013] *British Tax Review* 666–81

Schumacher, Scott A, 'Magnifying Deterrence by Prosecuting Professionals' (2014) 89 *Indiana Law Journal* 511

Schutte, Julian, 'Tampere European Council Presidency Decisions' (1999) 70 *Revue Internationale de Droit Pénal* 1023

Schwartz, Richard D, and Sonya Orleans, 'On Legal Sanctions' (1967) 34 *University of Chicago Law Review* 274

Seligman, ERA, *The Income Tax: A Study of the History, Theory, and Practice of Income Taxation at Home and Abroad* (New York: Macmillan, 1911)

Shapps, Grant, *Report into the Underperformance of the Assets Recovery Agency* (London: Shapps, June 2006)

Sharman, Jason, 'Privacy as Roguery: Personal Financial Information in an Age of Transparency' (2009) 87 *Public Administration* 717–31

Sharman, JC, 'Offshore and the New international Political Economy' (2010) 17 *Review of International Political Economy* 1–19

Shaxson, Nicholas, *Treasure Islands* (London: Vintage Books, 2012)

Shimick, Scott, 'Heisenberg's Uncertainty: An Analysis of Criminal Tax Pretextual Prosecutions in the Context of *Breaking Bad*'s Notorious Anti-hero' (2014) 50 *Tulsa Law Review* 43

Sigala, Maria, *Social Norms, Occupational Groups and Income Tax Evasion: A Survey in the UK Construction Industry* (Maidenhead: Open University, 2000)

Sikka, Prem, 'No Accounting for Tax Avoidance' (2015) 86 *Political Quarterly* 427–33

Sikka, Prem, and Hugh Willmott, 'The Dark Side of Transfer Pricing: Its Role in Tax Avoidance and Wealth Retentiveness' (2010) 21 *Critical Perspectives on Accounting* 342–56

Simester, AP, 'The Mental Element in Complicity' (2006) 122 *Law Quarterly Review* 578

Smith, Graham, *Something to Declare: 1000 Years of Customs and Excise* (London: Chambers Harrap, 1980)

Smith, KJM, *Lawyers, Legislators, and Theorists: Developments in English Criminal Jurisprudence 1800–1957* (Oxford: Oxford University Press, 1998)

Stebbings, Chantal, 'Public Health Imperatives and Taxation Policy: The Window Tax as an Early Paradigm in English Law', in Tiley, John (ed), *Studies in the History of Tax Law* Vol 5 (Oxford: Hart Publishing, 2011)

Stefanelli, Justine N, 'Expanding Azko Nobel' (2013) 62 *International & Comparative Law Quarterly* 485

Stockdale, Michael, and Rebecca Mitchell, 'Who Is the Client? An Exploration of Legal Professional Privilege in the Corporate Context' (2006) 27 *Company Lawyer* 110–18

Stopforth, David, 'Settlements and the Avoidance of Tax on Income—The Period to 1920' [1990] *British Tax Review* 225

Stopforth, David, '1922–36: Halcyon Days for the Tax Avoider' [1992] *British Tax Review* 88–105

Sunstein, Cass R, 'Nudges, Agency, and Abstraction: A Reply to Critics' (2015) 6 *Review of Philosophy and Psychology* 511–29

Sutherland, Edwin, *White Collar Crime* (New York: Dryden Press, 1949)

Sutherland, EH, 'White-collar Criminality' (1940) 5 *American Sociological Review* 1–12

Sutherland, EH, *White Collar Crime: The Uncut Version* (New Haven: Yale University Press, 1983)

Tanzi, Vito, *Money Laundering and the International Financial System,* IMF Working Paper 96/55 (Washington, DC: International Monetary Fund, 1996)

Tarvin, Tim, 'The Privilege Against Self-incrimination in Bankruptcy and the Plight of the Debtor' (2014) 44 *Seton Hall Law Review* 47

Templeman, Lord, 'Tax and the Taxpayer' (2001) 117 *Law Quarterly Review* 575

Thaler, Richard H, and Cass R Sunstein, *Nudge: Improving Decisions about Health, Wealth, and Happiness* (New Haven, CT: Yale University Press, 2008)

Troup, Edward, 'Unacceptable Discretion: Countering Tax Avoidance and Preserving the Rights of the Individual' (1992) 13 *Fiscal Studies* 128–38

Tutt, Nigel, *The Tax Raiders: The Rossminster Affair* (London: Financial Training, 1985)

Unger, Birgitte, 'Can Money Laundering Decrease?' (2013) 41 *Public Finance Review* 658–76

van Duyne, Petrus, 'Organizing Cigarette Smuggling and Policy Making, Ending Up in Smoke' (2003) 39 *Crime, Law and Social Change* 285–317

Verhage, Antoinette, *The Anti Money Laundering Complex and the Compliance Industry* (Abingdon: Taylor & Francis, 2011)

Virgo, Graham, 'Cheating the Public Revenue: Fictions and Human Rights' (2002) 61 *Cambridge Law Journal* 47

Vlcek, William, *Offshore Finance and Small States: Sovereignty, Size and Money* (London: Palgrave Macmillan International Political Economy, 2008)

Vlcek, William, 'Power and the Practice of Security to Govern Global Finance' (2012) 19 *Review of International Political Economy* 639–62

Vlcek, William, 'The Global Pursuit of Tax Revenue: Would Tax Haven Reform Equal Increased Tax Revenues in Developing States?' (2013) 27 *Global Society* 201–16

Walker, Clive, 'Post-charge Questioning of Suspects' [2008] *Criminal Law Review* 509–24

Walters, John, 'Revenue Raids' [1998] *British Tax Review* 213

Ward, WR, 'The Administration of the Window and Assessed Taxes, 1696–1798' (1952) 67 *English Historical Review* 522–42

'Watchful', 'Common Law Revenue Offences' [1956] *British Tax Review* 119

Weait, Matthew J, and Anthony Lester, 'The Use of Ministerial Powers without Parliamentary Authority: The Ram Doctrine' [2003] *Public Law* 415–28

Webb, Simon, *Execution: A History of Capital Punishment in Britain* (Stroud: The History Press, 2011)

Wheatcroft, GSA, 'The Attitude of the Legislature and the Courts to Tax Avoidance' (1955) 18 *Modern Law Review* 20

Whiting, RC, 'Ideology and Reform in Labour's Tax Strategy, 1964–1970' (1998) 41 *Historical Journal* 1121–40

Wiesbach, David A, 'Ten Truths about Tax Shelters' (2002) 52 *Tax Law Review* 215

Wilkie, J Scott, and Peter W Hogg, 'Tax Law within the Larger Legal System' (2015) 52 *Osgoode Hall Law Journal* 460–90

Williams, David, 'Surveying Taxes, 1900–14' [2005] *British Tax Review* 222

Winslow, Cal, 'Sussex Smugglers' in Hay, Douglas et al (eds), *Albion's Fatal Tree* (London: Penguin, 1975) 119–66

Woolrych, Humphry William, *The History and Results of the Present Capital Punishments in England* (London: Saunders and Benning, 1832)

Workman, Douglas J, 'The Use of Offshore Tax Havens for the Purpose of Criminally Evading Income Taxes' (1973) 73 *Journal of Criminal Law and Criminology* 675–706

Young, Mary Alice, *Banking Secrecy and Offshore Financial Centres: Money Laundering and Offshore Banking* (London: Routledge, 2012)

Young, Mary Alice, 'The Exploitation of Global Offshore Financial Centres: Banking Confidentiality and Money Laundering' (2013) 16 *Journal of Money Laundering Control* 198–208

Zagaris, Bruce, 'US Efforts to Extradite Persons for Tax Offenses' (2002) 25 *Loyola of Los Angeles International & Comparative Law Review* 653

Zagaris, Bruce, 'Swiss Highest Court Affirms Extradition to Germany for Tax Evasion International Enforcement' *Law Reporter* (July 2010)

Zedner, Lucia, 'Security, the State, and the Citizen: The Changing Architecture of Crime Control' (2010) *13 New Crim Law Review* 379–403

Zuckerman, Adrian, 'A Colossal Wreck—The BCCI–Three Rivers Litigation' (2006) 25 *Civil Justice Quarterly* 287–311

Index

A1P1 (ECHR First Protocol, Article 1), 46, 162, 166, 171
alcohol, 13, 166
Alexander, Danny, 30
American Revolution, 13
Anti-Money Laundering (AML), 114, 149, 162, 170–4, 188
Asset Recovery Incentivization Scheme (ARIS), 4, 169–70
Assets Recovery Agency (ARA), 169, 181, 182, 183
Attorney-General, 75, 76

Baird, Vera, 42, 79, 181
Base Erosion and Profit Shifting (BEPS), 149
Beccaria, Cesare, 12
Bloody Code, 12
Board of Customs and Excise, 11, 76
Board of Inland Revenue, 10, 127
Book of Rates, 9
Brougham, Lord, 98
Brown, Gordon, 78, 129, 172, 192

Cabinet Office, 80, 179
Camden, Lord, 84
Cameron, David, 30, 35, 39
capital flight, 145, 174, 179
Capital Gains Tax (CGT), 27, 61, 147, 152
cash, 183, 184
caveat emptor, 19
Central Fraud Group (CFG), 81
Charles II, King, 10
cheat, 18, 22, 34, 35, 42, 43, 45, 46, 47, 53, 54, 55, 56, 60, 61, 64, 67, 69, 96, 97, 128, 129, 151, 155, 178
Citizens' Charter, 123
Civil War, 10
Code for Crown Prosecutors, 76
Code of Practice 9, 130, 131
codification, 41
commercial sex worker, 97
compounding, 77, 126
Consolidated Fund, 10, 169
conspiracy to defraud, 42, 43, 44, 45, 48, 52, 54, 64, 66, 73, 134
constructive compliance, 25
Contractual Disclosure Facility (CDF), 131, 132
corporation tax, 27, 147, 150
council tax benefit fraud, 64
council tax fraud, 64
Criminal Law Revision Committee, 42
Crown Dependencies Disclosure Facilities (CDDF), 132, 133
Crown Prosecution Service (CPS), 45, 47, 64, 73, 74, 75, 78, 79, 80, 81, 170
Customs and Excise Prosecutions Group, 76
Customs and Excise Prosecutions Office (CEPO), 76, 79
Customs and Excise, Board of, 11, 76
Customs, Board of, 10

Deferred Prosecution Agreements (DPAs), 134
Department of Work and Pensions (DWP), 64, 81
Director of Border Revenue, 90
Director of Public Prosecutions (DPP), 80, 90, 190
Dodd, Ken, 51, 119, 121
Double Taxation, 38, 141, 144

European Arrest Warrant (EAW), 155
Excise, Board of, 10
export licences, 14

Falciani, Hervé, 37
Faulks, Lord, 79, 80
FIFA, 158
Financial Action Task Force (FATF), 115, 149, 172, 173, 174, 175
Financial Conduct Authority (FCA), 4, 81
Fink, Lord, 30
Foreign Account Tax Compliance Act 2010 (FATCA), 132, 149
freetrader, 12

Gauke, David, 133, 191, 192
General Anti Abuse Rule (GAAR), 33, 36
Gerald Butler, Judge, 75
gin craze, 26
Glorious Revolution, 15

go equipped to cheat, 61
Gower–Hammond Report, 75
Grabiner, Tony, 57

Hansard Procedure, 51, 121, 123, 126, 127, 128, 129
Hartnett, Dave, 38
Healey, Denis, 37
Healey, John, 78
hearth tax, 15
HM Customs and Excise (HMC&E), 4, 58, 74, 76, 78, 86, 88, 115, 119, 126
Hoffmann, Lord, 32, 93
Howe, Sir Geoffrey, 85
HSBC Suisse, 19, 22, 30, 37, 38, 58, 191

in-house lawyers, 103, 105
Inland Revenue, 7, 51, 74
Inland Revenue, Board of, 10, 127
Inland Revenue Service (IRS), 133, 158
International Consortium of Investigative Journalists, 38, 39
International Monetary Fund (IMF), 145, 172

John, King, 9
Johnson, Samuel, 9
Joynson-Hicks, Sir William, 127

Keith Committee, 69, 85, 102, 105

Law Commission, 42, 43, 54
Legal advice privilege (LAP), 98, 102
Lehmann Brothers, 34
Liechtenstein Disclosure Facility (LDF), 132
Lilley, Peter, 126
Lloyd of Berwick, Lord, 42
London Gazette, 13
Long Parliament, 9

Major, John, 123, 128
Mandaric, Peter, 121
McKenzie of Luton, Lord, 29
merger of Customs and Excise and Inland Revenue, 4, 8, 78, 79, 81
Mossack Fonseca, 39
MTIC (missing trader intra-community) fraud, 58
Murphy, Thomas ('Slab'), 158

National Audit Office, 130
National Crime Agency (NCA), 5, 80, 114, 115, 179, 180, 181, 182
National Criminal Intelligence Service (NCIS), 5, 171
No Safe Havens, 151
nudges, 26

O'Donnell, Gus, 78
OECD, 39, 133, 144, 149, 150, 179
Osborne, George, 30, 192
outlawry, 13

Panama Papers, 37, 115, 192
'Philips Principle', 72
Piggott, Lester, 51, 119, 121
Plummer, Ron, 83
poll tax, 14
pornography, 14, 49
Prerogative, Royal, 2, 9, 10
profit shifting, 28, 29, 144
prostitution, 159
Protectionism, 11, 14
Public Accounts Committee, 142, 181

Ramsay principle, 32, 33
Redknapp, Harry, 31, 55, 90
regulation, 44
Rehnquist, Justice (William), 98
Restoration, 9, 10, 11
Revenue and Customs Division (RCD), 81
Revenue and Customs Prosecution Office (RCPO), 4, 78
Revenue Rule, 5, 52, 143, 154, 155
revenue rulings, 64
Ricci, Arlette, 19
Richard II, King, 7, 14
Rule of Law, the, 31, 33, 124
Rump Parliament, 11

Scotland, (Patricia) Baroness, 79, 181
Sentencing Council for England and Wales, 66
Serious Fraud Office (SFO), 6, 74, 76, 81, 89, 90, 112, 113, 125, 181
Serious Organised Crime Agency (SOCA), 5, 78, 80, 181
Shanly, Michael, 38, 68, 192
Shapps, Grant, 181
Smith, Adam, 12
Smith, Sir John, 42
Spanish Inquisition, 84
Stamp duty, 60
Stamp Duty Land Tax, 60
Stamps and Taxes, Board of, 10
Starmer, Keir, 18, 189, 190
Switzerland, 133, 155, 191

Tax Credit Fraud, 63, 64
tax justice movement, 5, 29, 144, 146, 175
Taylor of Gosforth, Lord (CJ), 98
Templeman, Lord, 29, 35, 72
tobacco, 13, 26, 49
tradespeople, 115
transfer pricing, 144
Treasury, HM, 13, 78, 133
Tucker, Roy, 83

UK Border Agency (UKBA), 80
unexplained wealth order (UWO), 187, 188
Utilitarians, 42

victimless crime, 17, 18, 170, 189

Williams of Mostyn, Lord, 75
window tax, 15

The manufacturer's authorised representative in the EU for product safety is Oxford University Press España S.A. of el Parque Empresarial San Fernando de Henares, Avenida de Castilla, 2 – 28830 Madrid (www.oup.es/en or product.safety@oup.com). OUP España S.A. also acts as importer into Spain of products made by the manufacturer.

www.ingramcontent.com/pod-product-compliance
Lightning Source LLC
LaVergne TN
LVHW011757200926
848484LV00003B/727
* 9 7 8 0 1 9 8 7 5 5 8 3 8 *